IMAGES OF THE
SPANISH-AMERICAN WAR

APRIL–AUGUST 1898

by Stan Cohen

Camp Cuba Libre, Jacksonville, Florida.

LIBRARY OF CONGRESS
CATALOG CARD NUMBER 97-66760

ISBN 1-57510-031-2

First Printing: September 1997

Cover Art Work: Jack Stewart, a reenactor with the Spanish War 1898,
in a Rough Riders uniform.
Original painting of the *USS Maine*.
Original sheet music.
Postcard of the charge up San Juan Hill.

Typography by Leslie Maricelli
Cover Graphics by Mike Egeler, Egeler Design

PICTORIAL HISTORIES PUBLISHING CO., INC.
713 South Third Street West, Missoula Montana 59801
Phone (406) 549-8488   Fax (406) 728-9280

Introduction

1998 will be the centennial year for what has been called "America's Most Popular War," or the "Splendid Little War." While the actual fighting lasted only a little more than three months, it can be said to be the final unifying force for the North and South. It also thrust the United States onto the world stage and into future global predominance.

The war made heroes and household names of Teddy Roosevelt and George Dewey and a legend of the Rough Riders. Most of the general officers of both the army and navy had gained their first military experience in the Civil War. Four had even been generals in the Confederate Army.

It was a time of transition between the Indian Wars army and the more modern army of the World War One era. Automobiles, airplanes and more modern and destructive implements of war were only a few short years away from that "Summer of '98."

The army was ill-prepared for war and more casualties occurred from the tropical sicknesses than from enemy bullets. Other than the land battles around Santiago, Cuba, most of the sensational headlines came from the great naval victories in Cuba and the Philippines.

The War not only spread the American flag from the Caribbean to the far reaches of the Pacific Ocean, it also helped reorganize the army which had serious weaknesses before 1898. The power of the navy was greatly enhanced which led to the Great White Fleet cruise a few years later. The war demonstrated a need for a canal through Central America and as a result, construction of the Panama Canal started in the early 1900s.

The United States became a world power, politically, economically and militarily in just a few months—few events in American history have had such a dramatic impact on the country.

The sinking of the *Maine*, the most remembered of the incidents of the war is still somewhat of a mystery although most experts now conclude spontaneous combustion probably caused the explosion. It will go down in history as one of those still unsolvable mysteries along with the Hindenburg disaster, Roosevelt's alleged knowledge of the Pearl Harbor attack and who actually assassinated President Kennedy.

While the war was of very short duration, the volume of material for my research was overwhelming. Most of the chapters in this book could be expanded to full-length books on their own.. I have not attempted to make this the definitive narrative or pictorial piece, but rather a very comprehensive overview of the entire sequence of events leading up to the conflict, the military actions and the aftermath of the war. I have tried to seek out not only the most important events, but some of the more unusual and little-known facets in a most-important chapter in American history.

For those readers who want more in-depth details of the events, I urge them to seek out the excellent narratives listed in the bibliography. Freidel's pictorial history still remains one of the most thorough photo treatments of the war published to date.

This book encompasses the four month conflict between Spain and the United States in 1898. The ensuing Philippine Insurrection which lasted from 1899 to 1902 and was a direct result of America's victory over Spain must be reserved for a future project.

I hope this book will serve to rekindle interest in this little-known or remembered part of American history. With the impact it had on this country, the late 1890s deserve more attention.

Stan Cohen
Missoula, Montana
September 1997

Dedicated to all the warriors who have gone off to war and have been lost to history.

Acknowledgments

Many people contributed to the final completion of this book in the past four years. First, I must thank my two hometown friends and military history experts—Kermit Edmonds and Hayes Otoupalik. They provided both information and photos and allowed me to photographs their artifacts. My fellow collecting friend, Larry Sypolt of Morgantown, W.Va., provided both photos and many of the campaign medals. Naval historian, Ernie Arroyo of Stratford, Conn., provided photos for the naval chapter. Blaine Taylor of Towson, Md., provided much help with some of the narrative and photos. John MacDonald of Sunnyvale,Calif., provided the article on The Battle of Santiago. John Bracken provided artifacts from his vast collection at his New Market Battlefield Military Museum in New Market, Va., as did Gil Mangels of the Miracle of America Museum of Polson, Mont.

In addition the following provided information, photos or both: William Weatherwax, Key West, Fla.; Beverly Walker, Frederic Remington Art Museum, Ogdensburg, N.Y.; Max Newhart, New Hope, Pa.; Melinda Chavez, Henry B. Plant Museum, Tampa, Fla.; Shaun Moffitt, Tom Mix Museum, Dewey, Okla.; American Saddlebred Horse Association, Lexington, Ky.; Barbara Walton, Denver Public Library; Michael Jones, Iowa, La.; Merv Bloch, New York City; Mel Brown, Austin, Texas; James Ogden III, historian, Chickamauga & Chattanooga National Military Park; Dennis Copeland, Golden Gate National Recreation Area; Charles Etlinger, Boise, Idaho; Ken Taylor, Sierra Madre, Calif.; C. Edgar Hires, Cruiser *Olympia* Association; Tricia Wood, Montauk Historical Society; Karen Flanzbaum, Turner Network Television; Gene Harrower of the Oregon Maritime Center and Museum, Portland; Jay Hoar, Temple, Maine; Will Mickels, Battleship *Texas*, La Porte, Texas; Helen Devine, Bremerton Naval Museum, Bremerton, Wash.; Charles Bogart, Frankfort, Ky.; Paul Eugen Camp, The Library, Special Collections, University of South Florida, Tampa;

Judith Ann Bowman, U.S. Army Museum Hawaii; Mike Lewis, the Spanish War 1898, Tracy, Calif.; Dennis Wrynn, Fairfax Station, Va.; Dawn Crumpler, U.S. Military Academy Library; Merle Johnston, Tim Gordon and Mrs. Paul Miller of Missoula, Mont.; Richard Andre of Charleston, W.Va.; Kathleen Sheedy, Sagamore Hill National Historic Site; Charles Markis, Theodore Roosevelt Birthplace National Historic Site; Janet Fisher, Ft. Leonard Wood History Office; Montana National Guard, Helena; Samuel Colt Heritage Museum of Fine Firearms, Gettysburg, Pa.; and the staffs of the following: Historical Museum at Fort Missoula; Rutherford B. Hayes Presidential Center; Columbia River Maritime Museum, Astoria, Ore.; New York Historical Society; Academy of Motion Picture Arts and Sciences, Beverly Hills, Calif.; Oregon Historical Society, Portland; VMI Museum, Lexington, Va.; Tampa Library; American Red Cross Archives; Hawaii Archives; U.S. Naval Historical Center; Library of Congress; National Archives; U.S. Army Military History Institute, Carlisle, Pa.; Denver Public Library, Western History Department; Idaho State Historical Society; Montana Historical Society; Washington State Historical Society; Nevada State Museum; Arizona Historical Society Library; Arkansas Historical Commission; California State Library; Minnesota Historical Society; Bettmann Archive; Utah State Historical Society; Kansas State Historical Society; Vermont Historical Society; Museum of New Mexico; Sharlot Hall Museum, Prescott, Ariz.; Institute of Texan Culture, San Antonio; and the Theodore Roosevelt Collection at The Houghton Library, Harvard University.

And, finally a special thanks to Charles Bennett of the Museum of New Mexico in Santa Fe for the use of his extraordinary photos of present-day Havana and Santiago, Cuba.

My staff of Leslie Maricelli, Billy Coyle, Stephanie Badzioch and Gene Stephens were a great help. Mike Egeler designed the cover.

Chronological History of the War

1895

Feb. 24 – Insurgents rise against Spanish Tyranny in Santiago, Santa Clara and Matanzas provinces.

March 4 – Governor-General proclaims Martial Law in Santiago and Matanzas.

June 12 – President Cleveland issues proclamation warning citizens against joining or aiding filibustering expeditions.

July 15 – Provisional Government formally constituted and a Declaration of Independence proclaimed.

1896

Feb. 17 – General Weyler arrives at Havana, Cuba.

July 30 – President Cleveland issues another proclamation against filibustering.

1897

May 17 – President McKinley sends a message to Congress suggesting an appropriation of $50,000 to relieve the distress of American Citizens in Cuba. Passed by Congress and signed May 24.

Dec. 28 – President McKinley issues an appeal to the country to aid starving Cubans.

1898

Jan. 8 – A second appeal issued by President McKinley for contributions to aid suffering Cubans announces the cooperation of the American Red Cross Society.

Jan. 17 – General Fitzhugh Lee, Consul General, suggests a ship be sent to Cuba to protect Americans in the event of another riot.

Jan. 25 – Battleship *Maine* arrives at Havana, Cuba.

Feb. 15 – Battleship *Maine* blows up in Havana Harbor; 264 men and two officers killed. Spanish Minister de Lome sails for Spain.

March 6 – Spain unofficially asks for the recall of Consul General Fitzhugh Lee.

March 8 – $50,000,000 war fund voted unanimously by the House of Representatives.

March 9 – War Fund of $50,000,000 passed unanimously by the Senate.

March 25 – *Maine* report delivered to the President and he officially announces the *Maine* was blown up by a mine.

March 30 – President McKinley, through Minister Woodford, asks Spain for a cessation of hostilities in Cuba, and negotiations for ultimate independence.

April 19 – Both Houses of Congress adopt resolutions declaring Cuba free, and empowering the President to compel Spain to withdraw her army and navy.

April 20 – President McKinley signs the resolutions and sends his ultimatum to Spain, and the Queen Regent sends a warlike message to Cortez.

April 21 – Minister Woodford receives his passport from Spain.

April 22 – The President issues his proclamation to the neutral powers. Commodore Sampson's fleet sails from Key West to begin a blockade of Havana. Gunboat *Nashville* captures the Spanish ship *Buena Ventura*.

April 23 – President McKinley issues a call for 125,000 volunteers.

April 24 – Spain formally declares that war exists with Spain.

April 25 – United States formally declares war with Spain.

May 1 – Commodore Dewey defeats Admiral Montojo in Manila Bay, destroying 11 ships and killing and wounding more than 500 of the enemy.

May 11 – Commodore Dewey promoted to Rear-Admiral. Attacks made on Cienfiegus and Cardenas, when Ensign Worth Bagley and five of the Winslow crew are killed.

May 12 – Bombardment of San Juan, Puerto Rico, by Commodore Sampson.

May 24 – Battleship *Oregon* arrives off Jupiter Inlet, Florida, from her great trip from San Francisco, which she left March 12.

May 25 – President McKinley issues his second call for volunteers for 75,000 men. First Manila Expedition leaves San Francisco.

June 3 – Lieutenant Hobson and seven men sink the *Merrimac* in the channel entrance of Santiago Harbor.

June 12-14 – General Shafter embarks at Tampa, Florida, for Santiago with an army of 16,000 men.

July 1-2 – Terrific fighting in front of Santiago. El Caney and San Juan carried by assaults with great loss in American dead and wounded.

July 3 – Commodore Schley's blockading fleet annihilates Admiral Cervera's squadron of four armored cruisers and two torpedo boat destroyers.

July 17 – General Torral surrenders Santiago and the Eastern Province of Cuba to General Shafter.

July 20 – General Leonard Wood appointed Military Governor of Santiago, entering upon his duties by feeding the hungry, clothing the destitute and cleaning the city.

July 25 – General Miles, with 8,000 men, land at Guanica, Puerto Rico.

Aug. 9 – A large force of Spanish defeated at Coamo, Puerto Rico, by American troops under General Ernst.

Aug. 12 – The peace Protocol is signed, armistice proclaimed and the Cuban blockade raised.

Sept. 20 – First American flag raised in Havana, Cuba.

Oct. 18 – United States takes formal possession of Puerto Rico.

Nov. 2 – Spain agrees to cede the Philippines to the United States.

Dec. 10 – Peace Treaty signed in Paris, France.

Dec. 31 – Last day of Spanish Sovereignty in the Western Hemisphere.

1899

Feb. 6 – Treaty with Spain ratified by the Senate.

Feb. 10 – Capture of Caloocan, Philippine Islands, and capture of Iliolo by General Miller.

March 31 – Capture of Malolos, capital of Philippines.

April 11 – General Lawton defeats the insurgents at Santa Cruz. Proclamation by President McKinley announcing restoration of peace between Spain and the United States.

Written in 1898.

"REMEMBER THE MAINE"

U.S. BATTLESHIP MAINE CENTENNIAL COMMISSION

1898 ★ 1998

U.S. Battleship Maine
Centennial Celebration

The Key West Art & Historical Society, Inc., founded in 1949 as a non-profit institution, is sponsoring the U.S. Battleship *Maine* Centennial Celebration from December 1997 to August 1998. The celebration will honor Key West's critical role in the Spanish American War and the 100th anniversary of the sinking of the *Maine* in Havana harbor on Feb. 15, 1898. Honorary chairmen include President Bill Clinton and ex-presidents George Bush, Jimmy Carter and Gerald Ford. A four-day celebration will take place in February 1998 to include a new exhibit at the historic Key West Custom House.

A patriotic band from York, Nebraska. This appears to be a family affair. The American and Cuban flags are painted on the base drum. USAMHI

Contents

The Spanish American War could be said to be the
final uniting of North and South.

The Cuban Situation

Cuba had been a colony of Spain since Columbus landed on its shores in 1492 except for two years during the Seven Years' War. The Spaniards usually treated their colonies poorly and there were many uprisings against them through the years.

In 1868 a struggle began that lasted 10 years. At the end, Spain promised reform. Between uprisings the rebel leaders sought sanctuary in nearby United States and through the years convinced a majority of the American people that Cuba should be free.

Jose Martí was the leader of the Cuban Revolutionary Party and landed in Cuba in 1894 to take command of the rebel movement. Unfortunately, he was soon killed by Spanish troops.

Maximo Gomez, a native of Santo Domingo, took up the cause and an armed revolt started in 1895. By the spring of 1896 with the collapse of Spanish control imminent, Spain sent Gen. Valeriano Weyler to restore order.

Weyler implemented his famous *reconcentrado* orders which restricted Cubans to live in enclosed towns or villages, thus depriving the rebels of civilian help and a supply of food. Weyler's troops kept constant pressure on the guerrilla bands and by the summer of 1897 was in control of much of Cuba.

The burning of plantations by both the Spanish and the rebels caused a food shortage and pressure from the American government. A change of government in Madrid forced Weyler, who had become known as "The Butcher" to be recalled. Spain offered the island some measure of self-rule but the rebels wanted total independence.

All the American presidents from the 1870s to the '90s wanted to remain neutral and not provoke a war with Spain, but each continued to exert pressure on the Spanish government to liberalize Cuban policies.

American had not only a moral interest in this island, only 90 miles from her shores, but a large financial interest in the sugar industry. The Cuban rebels and American newspapers kept up a steady barrage of stories of Spanish atrocities until finally the *Maine* was destroyed on Feb. 15, 1898, and war was declared on April 25, 1898.

The Throne of Spain

The throne of Spain was in turmoil throughout most of the 1800s. Ferdinand VII died in 1833 and his daughter, Isabella, was proclaimed Queen, with her mother, Maria Christiana of Naples as Regent. Ferdinand's brother, Don Carlos asserted that the choice of Isabella violated the Salic Law, which forbade inheritance by women.

Isabella II became of age 10 years later but for many years there was open rebellion against her rule. Finally in 1870, she was overthrown and Amadeus of Aosta, the second son of Victor Emanuel of Italy, was invited to govern as a constitutional king.

After three years he resigned and several forms of government were tried without a reigning monarch at its head. In 1874 Isabella's son, Alphonse XIII accepted the crown. He died in 1885 and his widow, Christiana of Austria was made regent. Their son was born in 1886 and was known as the "Little King" and was on the throne under the Queen Regent at the time of the Spanish American War.

Gen. Valeriano Weyler y Nocolau, known as "The Butcher" was the Governor General of Cuba from February 1896 until his resignation in October 1897. He issued the reconcentrado orders that herded thousands of Cubans into concentration camps. Weyler died in 1930 at age 92.

La Revolucion.

DE

CUBA

EIGHTH YEAR. New York, October 23, 1875. **NUMBER 1.**

TO THE AMERICAN PEOPLE

AND AMERICAN PRESS.

After this date La Revolucion de Cuba, as a political organ of the patriots and regenerators of Cuba, will be published with one of its pages in English, as the Editor desires to give his paper a a rger circulation among American readers, and afford them a clearer insight into the progress of the struggle for independence now going on, in that Island. We will do our best to make our paper both instructive and interesting to Americans on all the topics that more particularly fall within the purpose to which it is devoted.

Besides our own Editorials we shall insert articles published by other newspapers upon the subject of Cuba, casting and stereotyping our columns so as to have them republished in the press, all over the world, if possible. This we propose to do, through the "International Newspaper Union" which we are establishing.

We give this explanation of our views and call on the free American people and press, as they honor their Centennial, as they prize the liberty which Washington and his compatriots established in the free States of America, to give their earnest aid and hearty sympathy to a cause equally glorious with their own !

R LANZA.
EDITOR.

OUR AMERICAN POLITICAL

ORGANIZATION.

The aim and purpose of this organization is this, that every cuban who is an American citizen shall become a member of a political club, and by this means, promote the cause of Cuban Independence, both with his own vote and the vote of every friend or person employed or conected with him.

Also, that the Cubans, shall assume amongst ourselves, as practical and powerful an organization as we can control, appealing to every friend of liberty in America to enforce upon the American Government the duty of assisting Cuba in asserting her independence This (we are constrained to say) the government has hitherto assisted to crush rather than to benefit.

Cubans, and friends of Cuba ! As citizens of America, proud of her heritage of freedom we claim that the influence and *prestige* of her government should be given to further the cause of liberty, and not to promote the schemes of its adversaries. The cause of liberty is not a selfish interest, but a generous sentiment, in promoting the growth of liberal principles in the country of our birth. In the election polls is the binding tie ! Let us then work at once, and altogether promptly and efficiently, and give our aid to those candidates of either party, that will aid us, for *Cuba must and shall be free and independent.*

OCTOBER 10, 1868.

The republic of Cuba celebrated yesterday the seventh anniversary of its declaration of independence, and we can well imagine how the day was hailed by the gallant, determined, and much suffering patriots in the field, as well as by those in the forests of the island.

Not only the soldiers of the liberating army of Cuba, but the whole native population of the island have for seven years endured trials and hardships in behalf of their cause, not only surpassing by far those experienced by any and all other American colonies in their respective wars of independence, but of such a nature that they have deservedly called down upon the head of their enemy the anathemas of the civilized world.

The opposition which Cuba, for seven years has had to encounter, and has learned effectively to resist by the bravery of her sons is, we fear, but little appreciated. team, electricity, and the multifarious improvements in arms have tended during the last thirty years to make wars short, sharp, and decisive ; and, where all these facilities are, as in the war between Cuba and Spain, at the command of one belligerent and wanting to the other, the disadvantage can only be counterbalanced by greater courage and determination on the part of the weaker party.

oreover, the insular character and physical conformation of Cuba, with coasts of over eighteen hundred miles in length, and with an average breadth of not over fifty miles, have enabled Spain not only to transport with rapidity her forces from one point of the coast to the other but to concentrate them at will at any point of the interior. Since October 10, 1 68, Spain has sent over 150,000 soldiers to Cuba ; and to-day the demand for fresh and powerful reinforcements is as urgent as ever. Spain has spent over two hundred millions of dollars, drawn, of course from the wealth of the island, in her efforts to suppress the revolution : and she will drain the last dollar she can get before she gives up the fight.

But the determination of the patriots to deprive their enemy of the sinews of war by destroying the still standing sugar estates of the Villas and the Western Department will be carried into execution as soon as the effect of the rains which this year have been excessive, shall have passed away. Samson drove the Philistines out of Askelon by firebrands tied to foxes' tails, and we never heard of his being blamed for it. The Cuban fox is the jutia, and the Spanish sugar cane will be destroyed as was the corn of the Philistines. The Cubans will probabl celebrate th ir next anniversary in Havana.—*The Sun, New York, Oct.* 11, 1875.

HIMNO BAYAMÉS.

HIMNO BAYAMÉS. Concluded.

On opposite page: As early as 1875 Cuban patriots were issuing propaganda newspapers to further the cause of Cuban independence.

This letter was written by Ulysses S. Grant in 1883.

NEW YORK CITY, *Apl. 30th*, 1883.

"Dear Badeau:

"I beg your pardon for not answering your letter requesting my views about the capabilities of the defences of the harbor of Havana to resist any navy. I supposed I had answered it, but your last letter reminds me that I have not. On my visit to Havana three years ago I had the opportunity of seeing hte forts and armament. Both are formidable, and with additions that could easily be made before any country could attack them, impregnable from direct attack. But I should not regard Havana as a difficult place to capture with a combined army and navy. It would have to be done however by effecting a landing elsewhere and cutting off land communication with the army while the navy would perform the same service on the water. The hostility of the native population to the Spanish authority would make this a comparatively easy task for any first-class power, and especially easy for the United States in case of a war with Spain. I have no special news to write you. Buck and Jesse have returned from abroad all well.

"Yours truly,

U.S. Grant."

CUBAN COAT OF ARMS.

A Chicago sympathy meeting for Cuban Independence, 1890s.

-4-

THE FIRST BOAT ASHORE—JUST BEFORE SUNRISE.

THE CARGO ON THE SHORE.

LANDING THE CARGO.

THE LAST BOAT LOAD.

Filibustering, from the Spanish word *filibustero,* was a term used for the illegal delivery of arms and supplies to the Cuban revolutionaries. It had gone on for years and had picked up in the 1890s. The most daring American helping the Cubans was John, "Dynamite Johnny," O'Brien, a U.S. Navy Civil War veteran and a confirmed filibuster in the Caribbean area. Some have contended that O'Brien conspired to blow up the *Maine* to force the United States into a war with Spain but this theory holds no credability. In fact, O'Brien had the job of piloting the hulk of the ship to her final resting place beyond Havana's harbor on March 16, 1912.

SPANIARDS HAD TO RETIRE

Severe Engagement with the Forces of Gen. Garcia Near Manzanillo.

LARGE PART OF AN IMPORTANT CONVOY CAPTURED.

Official Reports Contradict the Insurgent Version.—Marquis of Esteban Appointed Mayor of Havana.

New York, Jan. 8.—A Havana special says that a severe engagement was reported from Manzanillo yesterday between the Spanish column of Gen. Fodon and the patriotic forces of Gen. Calixto Garcia. The battle took place on the road between Manzanillo and Guamo, and the official report given to the press here tries to minimize the importance of the affair by saying that the Spaniards had only one killed, and that the insurgents were utterly dispersed.

The column of Gen. Rodon belongs to the forces of Gen. Pando, which were routed by Gen. Garcia two weeks ago. Rodon was left in charge of it to see if he could get convoys from Manzanillo through to the interior. His first effort to do so has resulted in his defeat, because the positions held by the patriots on the road from Manzanillo to Bayamo are very strong.

According to the best reports, and even according to the report actually received from Gen. Rodon by the Governor General, the Spanish, after eight hours of continuous fighting, had to retire to Manzanillo again with a loss of more than 80 officers and men. The most important part of the convoy was seized by the patriots.

Several skirmishes were reported officially yesterday at Cayo Espino and Paso Banao in Sancti Spiritus. The patriots are said to have been entirely routed by the Spanish troops.

The struggle for the office of Mayor of the city of Havana ended yesterday with the appointment by Gen. Blanco of Don Pedro Esteban y Gonzalez de Larrinaga, Marquis of Esteban, and a member of the Autonomist Junta in this city.

Senor Don Ricardo Galesis has been appointed Governor of the Spanish Bank of the Island of Cuba.

The Spanish garrisons on the sugar estates in the province of Matanzas have been heavily reinforced with regular troops.

In Puerto Principe it is almost certain that very few sugar estates will grind. The Cuban Government has sternly refused the permission asked by sugar planters who were disposed to pay heavy taxes to the revolutionists.

Senor Palma in Philadelphia.

Philadelphia, Jan. 7.—Senor Palma was one of the speakers at a largely attended Cuban-American meeting here tonight, called to protest against the scheme of autonomy. When he saw the Havana dispatch stating that he was to accompany Gen. Blanco and Consul General Lee on a mission to Gen. Gomez he read it aloud and for some time it formed a topic of ridicule and merriment in the meeting. Palma himself asserted that it was too absurd for consideration.

An Absurd Rumor.

The report that Gen. Fitzhugh Lee, the United States Consul General, will accompany Capt. Gen. Blanco when the latter takes the field is looked upon by the members of the Cuban society as highly improbable.

This cigar label was copyrighted in 1896 portraying the heroic symbols of the Cuban war for independence. It typifies the kinds of images of Cuba put before the American public during the years before the Spanish American War. USF

Newspaper article prior to the outbreak of war between the United States and Spain.

Many books were published prior to the war describing the atrocities committed by the Spanish in Cuba.

Leaders of the Cuban Revolution. Top left: Gen. Maximo Gomez first served in the Spanish army in Santo Domingo, then settled in Cuba. He joined the Cuban Revolution in 1868 and rose to general later leading Cubans in the 1895 uprising. After the war, he lived quietly until his death in 1917. Top right: Gen. Calixto Garcia, a Cuban leader in the Ten Years War, spent four years imprisoned by the Spanish. He commanded insurgent forces in Eastern Cuba in the 1895-98 war for independence. Bottom right: Gen. Antonio Maceo was a mulatto and was involved with the Cuban independence movement from the Ten Years War until he was killed on the outskirts of Havana on Dec. 7, 1896.

Jose Martí a leader of the Cuban revolution spent considerable time in the United States advocating Cuban independence. He was killed in an ambush by Spanish troops near the town of Dos Riós on May 20, 1895.

JOSE MARTI,
Late President of the Revolutionary Party.

Headquarters of the Cuban patriots in Key West, Florida.

The V.M. Ybor cigar factory in Ybor City, Tampa, Florida. The famous iron steps from which Jose Martí spoke to the Tampa cigar workers are at the right.

Cuban officers in Tampa, Florida.
Notice the Cuban flag on the
middle officer's hat. MNHS #61405

Cuban soldiers and a
recruiting officer in the
insurgent army pose for a
formal photograph. MNHS 61405

Cubans drilling in Tampa, Florida,
in preparation for an invasion of
Cuba, 1895. USF

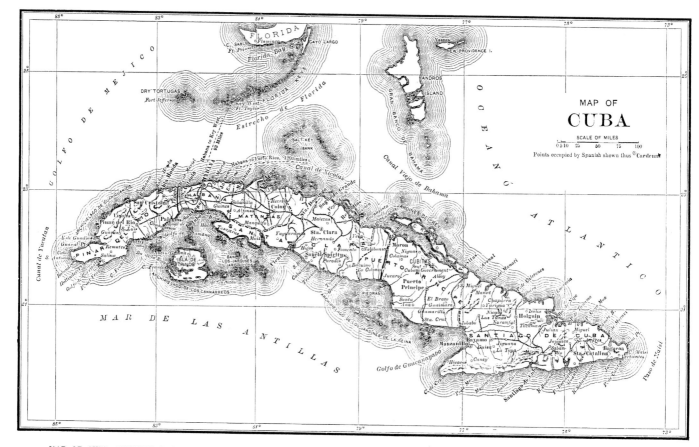

MAP OF CUBA COMPILED FROM LATEST INFORMATION, AND SHOWING THE LOCATION OF PRINCIPAL POINTS NOW HELD BY SPANISH FORCES.

GENERAL JUAN NEPOMUCENO BURRIEL, AUTHOR OF THE "VIRGINIUS" BUTCHERY.

One of the First American Casualties

Months before war was declared with Spain, an American was killed fighting with the insurgents in Cuba. W. Dana Osgood, a well-known football player formerly of the University of Pennsylvania, was an artilleryman under Frederick Funston.

The insurgents attacked the Spanish forces at Guimaro but were under intense fire all day. Funston's troops had a 12-pound Hotchkiss rifle and its fire soon forced the Spaniards from one of their largest forts. But the next day, other Spanish guns trained on the Hotchkiss and when leaning over the gun, Osgood was shot through the head.

Gen. Juan Burriel, governor of Santiago, ordered the execution of 53 members, including Cubans, Americans and British subjects, of the filibuster ship *Virginius* in 1873 which was captured in international waters off of Jamaica. War fever increased over this incident but at this time the United States could muster only a handful of rusted Civil War vessels at Key West to confront the more powerful Spanish fleet, which fortunately never happened.

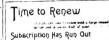
The Weekly Examiner.

VOL. XXXVII.—NO. 9.
SAN FRANCISCO: THURSDAY MORNING, AUGUST 12, 1897.

SPAIN'S PREMIER IS ASSASSINATED.

"Viva el Espana!" the Last Loyal Cry of the Statesman as He Expires.

BY DON FERNANDEZ RODRIQUEZ.

MADRID, August 8—Prime Minister Canovas del Castillo was shot this afternoon by an Italian anarchist. He fell dying at the feet of his wife.

The assassination occurred at the sulphur baths of Santa Agueda, which are situated between San Sebastian and Vittoria. He had taken the prescribed noon bath and was walking along the gallery with his wife, partly reading a paper and partly laughing and chatting, when an unkempt, rough-looking man, whom the attendants had taken to be a servant suddenly drew a revolver and opened fire on him.

Three shots were fired at close quarters in quick succession. The first hit the Premier in the head, the second in the region of the heart and the third fell in the chest. Canovas staggered back and fell with

HIS MAJESTY ALFONSO XIII

THE BOY KING OF SPAIN.

the cry, "Viva l'Espana!" He evidently thought the assassin to be a Cuban, not an anarchist.

Bystanders rushed forward and helped the agonized wife to stanch the flow of blood, but it was evident that all aid was useless, and the Premier, lapsing into unconsciousness, speedily passed away.

The assassin, who proved to be a Neapolitan anarchist named Michael Angelo Groili, was at once seized by bystanders, but not before he fired twice, ineffectually, at them. He was deathly pale, and the crowd was shouting "Death!"

Profound consternation prevails throughout Spain. The Queen Regent, who hurried up her own doctors on a special train, is plunged in grief, since there is now no one save General Martinez Campos on whom she thoroughly relies. All garrisons, particularly in the large towns, are held in readiness in the barracks to repress any trouble, but so far all has been quiet.

All the political leaders have forwarded to the Government expressions of sympathy over the tragic event. Much despondency, however, prevails, and either the Republicans or Carlists may attempt to excite trouble. Every one is full of anxiety about the future of Cuba, since Canovas was the mainstay of the war party. In the Cabinet people generally expect important modifications of policy. General Ascarraga, Minister of War, has been appointed provisional head of the Cabinet. The Government is stopping many telegrams. All churches are filled with mourners.

CANOVAS' CAREER.

FREE EXCURSION FOR EXAMINER SUBSCRIBERS

TO THE GREAT

KLONDYKE GOLD FIELDS

Three First-Class Tickets from San Francisco to Klondyke and Return.

FREE   **FREE**

NEWS OF THE GREAT GOLD DISCOVERIES on the Klondyke river, a branch of the upper Yukon, in the northwestern Canadian Dominion was continued by the arrival of forty-four miners on the steamer Excelsior, July 14, at San Francisco, bringing three-quarters of a million dollars worth of gold in dust and nuggets. Just as the world was becoming excited over the advent of this argosy, the steamer Portland arrived at Seattle, Washington, with sixty-eight miners on board with an additional million dollars worth of gold. Most of the miners who came back rich were wandering prospectors with no capital but their picks and scanty rations when they entered the northwestern territories. In creeks and ravines close to the Arctic circle they picked up gold as a farmer picks up potatoes. No mining knowledge or machinery or capital was needed. Gold in stacks was to be had for the taking. All this has inflamed the desire and imagination of the world. Next spring, when the journey may be made without peril, tens of thousands will depart for the new Golconda. With this exodus the Weekly Examiner has decided to send three (only three) of its subscribers in June, 1898, giving each one a first-class ticket from San Francisco to Dawson and return.

On May 15, 1898, the Weekly Examiner will decide on the three subscribers to be presented with tickets as above, and the names and addresses of such will appear in the first issue of the Weekly Examiner immediately following May 15, 1898.

One of the conditions is that all subscribers who desire to compete must cut out and preserve the coupons which will appear regularly in each week's issue of the Weekly Examiner, commencing with this, until May 15, 1898. Other conditions and methods will be published subsequently.

If any coupons of the series are missing, the lack of such will bar the subscriber from the competition.

This proposition is open to all present subscribers of the Weekly Examiner, without exception. Every one desiring to compete has the privilege of doing so provided he has all of the coupons for the series.

Those whose subscriptions to the Weekly Examiner expire between now and May 15, next year, and who desire to enter into this competition should be extremely careful to see that their renewals are sent to this office in time that they may not miss any of the coupons, all of which will be numbered in consecutive order.

Back numbers of the coupons will not be offered for sale.

Each of the three subscribers to whom the excursion tickets will be given has the privilege of selling his return ticket should he decide to remain in the gold fields, and he should be able to sell such return ticket at a price sufficient to enable him to lay in a year's supply of provisions.

The last steamer during the present season has departed for Klondyke, and from now until June of next year it would be neither wise nor safe for anyone to attempt this perilous journey. In June of next year there will be a tremendous rush for the Klondyke country, and it is to meet such contingencies that we have made our present arrangements.

At Juneau the freight has accumulated in such large quantities for transportation by the Chilcoot Pass, that it will be impossible under existing transportation facilities for the same to be handled within the next twelve months. The only safe route is by the Yukon river, and that is now closed and will remain closed until June of next year.

Renewals can be sent to this office direct or through postmasters or local agent or authorized traveling solicitor.

CANOVAS DEL CASTILLO, THE MURDERED PREMIER OF SPAIN.

CHRISTINA, QUEEN REGENT OF SPAIN.

Alfonso XIII legally ascended the throne of Spain on his 16th birthday in 1902. He reigned until 1931 when he left Spain to an elected republican government. The Spanish government in the 1890s was in constant turmoil. The premier, Canovas Del Castillo was assassinated in August 1897.

To The American People!

As your forefathers fought for independence, so the brave army of my Compatriots is struggling to make Cuba free. Read in these pages the Causes, Progress and certain Triumph of the great Revolution. I have examined the proofs of this work and I find that the account here given is acurate and complete.

The terrible struggle of long-suffering Cuba, the true and heart-thrilling story of which is contained in this comprehensive volume, appeals to all freedom-loving people. Every person in America should know how just and holy is the cause for which so many Cubans are sheding (sic) their blood and giving their lives.

Francisco Bassols
(Late Lieutenant of the "Regiment Prado No. 2" 1st Corps, 1st Division of the Cuban Army)

Frederic Remington's drawing on the *Olivette* search.

The Dupuy de Lome Affair

Enrique Dupuy de Lome was the Spanish minister to the United States. In January 1898, he wrote a letter to a friend in Cuba. The letter was supposed to be confidential but it was intercepted in Cuba and turned over to Cuban nationalists in New York.

The letter, which was highly critical of President McKinley, stated that the Spanish were not really interested in granting reforms in Cuba. It was reprinted in the *New York Journal* including this portion:

"...Besides the natural and inevitable coarseness with which he repeats all that the press and public opinion of Spain have said of Weyler, it shows once more that McKinley is weak and catering to the rabble and, besides, a low politician who desires, to leave a door open to himself and to stand well with the jingos of his party..."

It wasn't so much that the letter was a scathing report on U.S.-Spanish relations as the fact that it was written by a Spanish diplomat posted to the United States. Dupuy de Lome was subsequently fired from his post and the movement toward war increased in both countries.

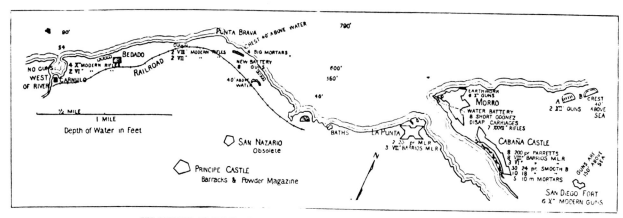

THE DEFENCES OF HAVANA.—From the Official Chart issued to the Vessels of the United States Navy.

Mrs. Bryan's Campaign Experience. See Sunday's Journal.

NEW YORK JOURNAL

Copyright, 1897, by W. R. Hearst.

Mrs. Bryan's Article — IN — The Sunday Journal.

NO. 5,208. NEW YORK, SATURDAY, FEBRUARY 18, 1897.—12 PAGES. PRICE ONE CENT In Greater New York | Elsewhere and Jersey City | Two Cents

MINISTER DE LOME'S RETORT

He Says Spain Has a Perfect Right to Search an American Vessel.

Washington, Feb. 12.---Senor Dupuy de Lome, the Spanish Minister, to-night made the following statement to the Journal regarding Richard Harding Davis's story of the searching of women on the Olivette at Havana:

"I don't care to comment on a newspaper story; for I don't believe a word they say.

"The Spanish authorities have a perfect right to board an American steamer, or any other kind of a vessel, and search persons, be they men or women, whom they suspect. A request to the steamer officials is not necessary.

"The government officers have the authority to make the search without first getting the captain's consent."

Senor Dupuy De Lome, Minister of Spain at Washington.

FEB 16 1897

A FOOT OF SNOW; MANY BLOCKADES.

Yesterday's Big Storm Congested Traffic Everywhere.

WORK FOR THE STARVING

Unemployed to the Number of 6,500 Were Put at Shovelling Snow.

BLOCKADE IN PARK ROW.

Sweeping Machine Broke Down and Delayed Cars Till Its Removal Was Effected.

ELEVATED ROADS, TOO, SUFFERED.

On the Sixth and Third Avenue Lines Men Were Stationed Between Stations to Signal the Condition of the Tracks.

STATISTICS OF THE SNOW STORM.

AROUSED BY SPAIN'S ACT.

Congress Will Hear To-day of the Search Outrage on the Olivette.

LAW · MAKERS INDIGNANT.

Richard Harding Davis's Story of Inhumanity to Cuban Girls Brings Forth Strong Words.

STATE DEPARTMENT HAS NO REPORT YET.

SENATOR WILSON WOULD ANNEX CUBA.

JOHN L. WILSON,
United States Senator from Washington.

ROUGH SEAS INTERFERE.

Fleet at Charleston Prevented from Going Through the Manoeuvres—The Indiana Arrives.

DEPEW MAY NOW PACK HIS TRUNK.

Morton Clears the Way for Him to Be Ambassador to England.

ORGANIZATION FOR HIM.

Platt, Odell, Hackett and Lauterbach Express Their Wishes to McKinley.

STANTONS TO BE ARRESTED.

LONDON PAPERS DISCUSS THE BALL.

Bradley Martin Affair Eulogized in the Cabled Reports.

"PERFECT," SAYS THE TIMES

New York Society Men and Women Seen at Their Best.

PULLMAN COMES TO STOP HIS SON.

Chicago Millionaire Does Not Approve of the Wine Business.

ESCAPADE IN CHICAGO.

It Is Said Young Pullman Was Disinherited as a Matter of Discipline.

HACKENSACK STILL FAST.

Chauncey M. Depew, Our Probable Envoy to England.

War fever was heightened with such incidents as reported in this Feb. 18, 1897, issue of the *New York Journal*, along with the news media's sensationalism of Spanish atrocities in Cuba.

HARPER'S WEEKLY

A JOURNAL OF CIVILIZATION

Vol. XLII.—No. 2158
Copyright, 1898, by Harper & Brothers.
All Rights Reserved.

NEW YORK, SATURDAY, APRIL 30, 1898.

TEN CENTS A COPY.
FOUR DOLLARS A YEAR.

CUBA LIBRE!

The 1890s

America's shortest war came at the end of the decade tabbed "The Gay Nineties." The start of the decade saw the passing of the American frontier. The 1890 census report stated: "Up to and including 1890, the country had a frontier settlement but at present the unsettled area has been so broken into isolated bodies of settlement that there can hardly be said to be a frontier line."

America's foremost historian, Frederick Jackson Turner lamented at the passing of the frontier and with the last big land rush in the country on the Cherokee Strip in Oklahoma, the frontier was definitely a thing of the past.

The great Indian warrior, Chief Sitting Bull was assassinated in 1891 and on Dec. 29, 1890, the Battle of Wounded Knee in South Dakota was the last major Indian battle in the West. One hundred fifty Indians and 25 soldiers were killed.

The economic depression of 1893 was the worst in United States history up to that time and it's effects were felt worldwide. The decade also saw the United States become the dominant world economic leader, surpassing Great Britain.

It was a decade of labor unrest in the country with the 1892 Homestead Strike and the 1894 Pullman Strike. But it was also a time of great industrial growth led by men such as John D. Rockefeller and Andrew Carnegie, and Leland Stanford and Jay Gould, building or consolidating their railroad empires.

Many of America's most famous inventors were at the pinnacle of their fame or just beginning to exercise their potential. Men such as Thomas Edison, the Wright Brothers, Henry Ford, George Westinghouse and Nikola Tesla were, and still are, household names.

It was also a period of social upheaval with terrible poverty in the major metropolitan areas of the country and the so-called Jim Crow laws which essentially segregated the black population. Leaders such as W.E.B. DuBois and Booker T. Washington were leaders in the black community.

The greatest celebration in the country was the 1893 Columbian Exposition in Chicago commemorating the 400th anniversary of Columbus' voyage to the New World. It was a decade of similar but smaller expositions in Omaha, New Orleans, Atlanta and San Francisco.

The last great adventure of the 19th century was taking place a great distance north of the United States' border but was one that would affect the entire country. Gold was discovered on a tributary of the Klondike River in Canada's Yukon Territory in 1896 and by 1898, the mining town of Dawson City and surrounding goldfields, was an enclave of mostly American miners and entrepreneurs. This gold strike would do more than anything else until World War Two to publicize and develop the U.S. Territory of Alaska.

At the dawn of the new century, the United States had emerged as a world economic and political power with possessions from the Atlantic to the Pacific.

Some of the Famous Americans Living in the 1890s

Henry Cabot Lodge — statesman
John Muir — environmentalist
Thomas Edison — inventor
John D. Rockefeller — industrialist
Henry Ford — industrialist
William Jennings Bryan — statesman
Grover Cleveland — ex-President
Samuel Clemens — writer
Andrew Carnegie — industrialist
Susan B. Anthony — suffragette
Jay Cooke — financier
Stephen Crane — writer

Grenville Dodge — railroad construction
Benjamin Harrison — ex-President
Oliver Wendell Holmes Jr. — jurist
Robert Todd Lincoln — President Lincoln's son, statesman, businessman
Thomas Nast — cartoonist
Frederick Law Olmsted — landscape architect
Frederick Remington — artist
Charles Russell — artist
Carl Schurz — statesman
Henry Morton Stanley — journalist, explorer
J. Pierpont Morgan — financier

Troops of the 14th Infantry march down a street in Skagway, Alaska. They were sent north from Vancouver Barracks in Washington State and arrived in Skagway on March 1, 1898. They were sent to the two gold rush towns to keep order at the height of the rush. Soon after they arrived some of the troops were ordered south again for war duty. As they boarded their ship they received a wild send-off party that had been organized by the notorious con man Soapy Smith. Smith earlier had put together his own volunteer company, and offered it for duty but the War Department refused his generosity. (Smith would be killed in a shootout on the Skagway wharf on July 8, 1898). UNIVERSITY OF ALASKA ARCHIVES #72-4-2

At the height of the Klondike gold rush in 1898 Skagway, Alaska, was the gateway for the prospectors to cross the mountains into Canada and float down the Yukon River to Dawson City and the gold fields. This Skagway (modern spelling) paper from April 4, 1898, concerns the avalanche on the Chilkoot Trail but on the back page was an article on the impending war with Spain.

Third Edition---7;30 p. m.

SKAGUAY NEWS.

EXTRA. SKAGUAY, ALASKA, APRIL 4, 1898. EXTRA

ONE HUNDRED DEAD

AT THE SCALES.

An Avalanche of Snow and Ice Swoops Down Upon the Unfortunate Argonauts

Camped There, Killing and Maiming Scores of Them---35 Bodies Already Recovered Up to this Hour.

DEATH LURKS IN THE CHILKOOT TRAIL.

Work of Recovering Bodies Progressing Slowly--Names of Those Already Recovered From the Debris.

That death and destruction is the portion of those who attempt to enter the interior of Alaska by way of Dyea and the Chilkoot trail, was painfully and agonizingly demonstrated at a point above Sheep Camp and between Stone House and The Scales, at midday yesterday, when an avalanche of snow bore down from the treacherous mountain side, sounding in its descent the death knell to from between forty and sixty persons. All of Saturday night snow fell continuously and by yesterday morning twelve inches of the "beautiful" had been added to the several feet already there. The trail from Canyon City to the summit had been crowded all day Saturday by persons intent on pushing through to the lakes. At 2:30 yesterday morning a small avalanche

of snow came down on the trail, covering a large amount of freight which had been cached for the night. At noon yesterday, while many were at work endeavoring to extricate their property from the wreck of the previous night, a slide occurred, carrying with it results which will bring sorrow and desolation to many homes far away, where loved ones are to-day fondly thinking of, and perhaps praying for the success and prosperity of husbands, fathers, sons and brothers, little thinking that the mangled remains of those loved ones are buried beneath an avalanche of debris on the trail of the deadly Chilkoot.

Up to 10 o'clock this forenoon the following bodies had been recovered:

C. P. Harrison, Seattle.
W. L. Riley, "
Gus Zebarth, "
——Stevenson, "
E. D. Wood, New York.
E. Beck, Florida.
Tom Cullin, Portland.
J. Sprague, Ballard.
L. Weidulin, Kansas City.
J. A. Morgan, Emporia, Kansas.
Mrs. A. Maxon, Pennsylvania.
——Grimes, residence unknown.
——Athens, residence unknown.

The work of recovering the bodies is being carried on today, but as additional slides are expected at any time, the work is very slow, as many are afraid to risk their lives by remaining in such a treacherous neighborhood.

The first three on the list had been working the previous night and were asleep in their tent at the time of the disaster. It is not known how many more bodies are in the wreck, but it is feared there are between twenty-five and forty in addition to those already recovered.

It is reported that great consternation prevails at Dyea, and that there are hundreds of men there who will ship their outfits to this place and enter the interior over the White pass, the only safe and accessible route from salt water to the lakes.

Very Latest---6:30 P. M.

At 6:30 o'clock this evening the following telephone message from Sheep Camp to the SKAGUAY NEWS was received:

"Thirteen additional bodies have been recovered, making total number up to 6:30 p. m. thirty-five. The only names of the last thirteen known are:

[Concluded on 2d page.]

WAR PROBABLY RAGING

Latest News Indicated Immediate Hostilities.

SPain Anxious to Try Conclusions With Our Uncle Samuel.

Papers received this morning confirm the prevalent belief that war with Spain is inevitable, and is even now, in all probability, an assured fact. In Washington City last Tuesday, Congress was bringing all its might and power to bear on President McKinley to declare war against Spain without an hour's delay, and it is likely that the president conformed to the demand of public opinion ere this, and war is now being waged between two powerful nations.

Instead of striving to avoid war, Spain rather invites it. Her attitude is sullen and defiant, while her preparations for defence are steadily going on.

On March 29th, the president's private secretary in an interview, said: "There is only one chance in a hundred that war will be averted."

WANTED—Position as cook or dining room work, by young lady. Apply Hotel Wickstrom.

Catastrophe
at Sheep Camp.

(Concluded from First Page.)

Thos. Cullendew, Kirkland, Or.
Ross Hepgard, Baker City, Or.
Con Geppert, Seattle.
E. F. Miller, Vancouver, B. C.

It is confidently believed at Sheep Camp that fully one hundred people were killed in the slide. Not one of the 17 members of the Chilkoot Transportation Co. has yet been heard from."

Gus Zeiborth and Con Geppert were well known Seattle business men, the former a butcher, the latter a dealer in hardware.

The weird work of recovering bodies will be carried on to night in that dark valley of death.

The Trans-Mississippi and International Exposition

One major exposition occurred during the summer of 1898. The Trans-Mississippi and International Exposition took place in Omaha, Nebraska, between June 1 and Nov. 1. Its purpose was to display the art, handiwork and resources of the states and territories west of the Mississippi River. About 2,700,000 people visited the grounds spread over 180 acres on the north side of Omaha. President McKinley received a great ovation when he arrived in Omaha on Oct. 11. From a temporary platform in front of City Hall he and his entourage watched a parade of 40 floats. The following day, before touring the exposition, he lauded the success of the military forces and pointed out the difficulties ahead in managing the newly acquired territories. In 1899 a new organization took over the property and called it the Greater America Exposition. It included a greater display of the culture and products of Cuba, Guam and the Philippines.

William Jennings Bryan, "The Great Populist," rides at the head of his regiment of Nebraska volunteers at the Trans-Mississippi Exposition. Bryan subsequently resigned his commission and refused to participate in what he judged to be an unjust war of imperialism in the Philippines.

President McKinley delivered a patriotic address at the Trans-Mississippi and International Exposition on Columbus Day, Oct. 12, 1898.

July 4, 1898, in Dawson City, Yukon, Canada. The city was populated mainly by Americans and the victories in Cuba and the Philippines were cause for a great celebration. One Cuban and five American flags are flying along with placards of war heroes. Notice the white sombreros worn by the majority of men in town. DAWSON CITY MUSEUM & HISTORICAL SOCIETY

The Yellow Press

The emotional involvement of the American people with the struggle for Cuban independence was intensified by the famous circulation battle between the publishers of the *New York Morning Journal* and the *New York World*.

It became a bitter struggle for journalistic supremacy betwen William Randolph Hearst and Joseph Pulitzer, and Cuba provided the sensational field upon which the two newspapers battled. Correspondents from both papers made trips to the island and often wrote fanciful tales of starvation in concentration camps, and Spanish atrocities.

This type of sensational reporting became known as "Yellow Journalism" (from the use of yellow ink in printing a cartoon strip, "The Yellow Kid" in the *New York Morning Journal*, commencing in 1896).

Such constant, biased presentation of the problems in Cuba had an incendiary effect on the American people, who demanded the government give military aid to the rebels and even intervene with American troops.

The press of the Cuban insurgents in the United States also helped to fuel the flames for American intervention.

First Account of Santiago's Surrender

Over two hundred journalists had been in the Santiago area during the naval and land battles. Due to the severe tropical climate and the threat of yellow fever only nine American newsmen were left at the time of the surrender.

One of the nine was an Associated Press correspondent named Alfred C. Goudie, who spoke both Spanish and French. He decided to get into the town somehow and find out what was happening. He donned native garb, and joined a crowd of refugees. Carrying for a tired mother, a baby on one arm and a parrot cage on the other, Goudie passed into the city. He wrote 3,000 words on the surrender and the plight of the people, which was the first account to reach the outside world.

PORTFOLIO DE LA SEMANA

UNA BROMA PESADA

Frederick Palmer

One of the nation's most prolific war correspondents missed the war in Cuba but managed to get to the Philippines in time to cover the insurrection there. Frederick Palmer was participating in the great Klondike Gold Rush at the time of the Cuban campaign. Palmer covered The Greco-Turkish War (1897), The Philippines (1899), The Boxer Rebellion (1900), The Russo-Japanese War (1904), the San Francisco earthquake (1906), building the Panama Canal, The Balkan War (1912), Mexican Border War (1914), World War I, World War II and the Bikini atom bomb test (1946). He died in 1958 at age 85.

Anti-American cartoon based on the Yankee Pig theme. By Blanco Coris, *Blanco y Negro* (Madrid), Feb. 19, 1898. COURTESY THE MEMORIAL LIBRARY, UNIV. OF WISC., MADISON

THE BIG TYPE WAR OF THE YELLOW KIDS.

The Big Type War of the Yellow Kids. [HEARST AND PULITZER], LITHOGRAPH AFTER LEON BARRITT, IN *VIM*, JUNE 29, 1898. LC-USZ62-34261

The Little King of Spain and the Yankee Pig. DRAWING BY CHARLES BARTHOLOMEW FOR *MINNEAPOLIS JOURNAL*, JULY 12, 1898. LC-USZ62-34355

Joseph Pulitzer

Joseph Pulitzer was born in Hungary in 1847. He left home at 17 for a military career but no army would take him because of his poor health. He finally signed on with the Union Army during the American Civil War and after brief service in the war, he settled in St. Louis, Missouri. He became a U.S. citizen and worked as a laborer.

In 1868, he became a reporter for a German-language newspaper in St. Louis and within four years, had become managing editor and part owner of the paper. He won a seat in the Missouri House of Representatives in 1869. Pulitzer became a powerful leader among the people of German descent in St. Louis, and helped Horace Greeley in his campaign for the presidency in 1872. But three years later, Pulitzer became a Democrat and sold his interest in the paper, which was Republican.

In 1876 and 1877 he served as a correspondent in Washington, D.C., for the *New York Sun*. He bought the *St. Louis Dispatch* and *Evening Post* in 1878, and combined them. Within four years, the newspaper made him a fortune.

In 1883 he bought the *New York World*, a nearly defunct newspaper and he soon transformed it into a vigorous, crusading newspaper with the largest circulation in the nation. The paper was one of the first to use color comics and sensationalism in journalism.

Pulitzer left $2 million to establish a graduate school of journalism at Columbia University and his world-famous Pulitzer prizes were created with part of this money.

After 1887 Pulitzer was almost totally blind and directed his newspaper empire from a yacht until he died in 1911.

William Randolph Hearst Sr.

Hearst founded the Hearst chain of publications. He developed a sensational journalistic style, and spent millions of dollars to attract readers. This style was dubbed "Yellow Journalism."

He was born in San Francisco, California, in 1863, the son of a mining magnate and United States senator. His mother was a philanthropist. He attended Harvard University but was expelled in 1885 because of a practical joke he played on his professors.

His father gave him the *San Francisco Examiner* which Hearst turned into a financial success. In 1895 he bought the *New York Morning Journal* and engaged Pulitzer's *New York World* in a great circulation battle which reached its height just before America declared war on Spain in 1898.

Hearst began buying other papers and magazines and by 1937 owned 25 large dailies. He founded the International News Service (INS) to service his newspapers. He had political ambitions and was in the U.S. House of Representatives from New York State from 1903 to 1907. He sought the 1904 Democratic nomination for president and ran unsuccessfully for governor of New York and mayor of New York City.

His estate at San Simeon in California was one of the most lavish private dwellings in the country. It is now a state park. Hearst died in 1951.

NIGHT SPECIAL.

AN AMERICAN PAPER FOR THE AMERICAN PEOPLE

NEW YORK JOURNAL

NIGHT SPECIAL.

NO. 5,618—P. M.

NEW YORK, MONDAY, APRIL 4, 1898.

PRICE ONE CENT.

BOTH HOUSES,
IN UPROAR, THREATENING REVOLT,
WARN M'KINLEY.

Arraignment of President Cheered in Senate and House.

Washington, April 4.—The Senate is for war. It is for making the Maine the vital issue in the controversy with Spain. If there is not radical action declaring the blowing up of the United States battle ship in itself an act of war, entailing all the consequences of such an act, every indication points to action which will bring matters to a head at once.

The Senate is determined to compel Spain to make reparation for the destruction of the Maine or to lose its hold in Cuba.

Through the speeches to-day of Senator Perkins, of California; Senator Mantle, of Montana, and Senator Clay, of Georgia, warning was given the President that the Senate does not intend he shall minimize the loss of the Maine and the massacre of her crew. Convinced that Spain, is officially responsible, they want to hold her responsible.

Senator Perkins stated the case for the Senate when he said:

"Men do not arbitrate questions of honor; neither do nations. The destruction of the Maine is beyond the pale of arbitration.

"Gold will not atone for blood."

URGED DECLARATION OF WAR AT ONCE.

Senator Rawlins, of Utah, who wants to declare war against Spain, urged Congress to act at once. Congress should not wait upon the President, he argued, but should take the responsibility and act to-day.

He said the Committee on Foreign Relations was satisfied what action ought to be taken, and that he had been informed the Executive had requested the committee not to take that action which it had decided upon.

Forty-eight days had gone by since the destruction of the Maine by Spaniards, he said, and yet no action had been taken. Now the time had come to act.

In the House the same spirit reigned which reigned in the Senate. After

Continued on Fourth Page.

TEXAS SAILS STRIPPED FOR ACTION.

Suddenly Ordered to Leave at Once, with Decks Cleared.

Orders were received late this afternoon by the battle ship Texas, lying in the Brooklyn Navy Yard, to get to sea at once and join the Flying Squadron at Hampton Roads.

The battle ship will sail at the first flood tide.

The orders further divulged that she sail with her decks cleared for action.

Much surprise was caused among the officers of the ship and at the yard at this sudden change of plans. It had been intended to hold the Texas to convoy the new cruisers San Francisco and Albany.

As soon as the sailing orders were received the deck and quarters were stripped of wood. The superfluous articles had all been tagged with pieces of hemp on which the word "overboard" was stamped. Whenever fighting orders are received these articles will be thrown over.

The chests of the marines and man-of-warsmen were stowed away below.

Spain Accepts Pope's Mediation; Says McKinley Planned It.

Washington, April 4.—The one distinct fact that comes out of all the rumors, assertions and denials concerning the alleged intervention of the Pope in the issue between Spain and the United States, is that Spain is clearly trying to create the impression that there is to be such intervention and that it comes at the instigation of the United States.

On this last point an official denial has been issued from the White House. But even that denial is not satisfactory; it reads that the American Government has not "asked" a request to the Pope to use his good offices for peace.

On the other hand the Spanish Minister in London has positively asserted that the United States did ask the Pope to intervene, that the Pope consented, and that Spain saw no reason for objection.

DENIAL BY MARTINELLI.

Here again comes Mgr. Martinelli, the Apostolic Delegate in Washington, with an absolute denial that the Pope has offered to mediate.

"The Holy Father never offers his good offices in disputes," explained Dr. Rooker, Secretary of the Delegate, and speaking for Mgr. Martinelli. "In order for him even to consider such a proposition, it would be necessary for both Governments concerned to make a formal request for such good offices.

"This request would have to come through the recognized channels of diplomacy—that is, the Secretary of State in each nation would write this request to the Papal Secretary of State, and not until the Papal Secretary had formally announced the Pope's willingness to act in such a capacity could it be announced as in the Madrid dispatch this morning. The United States has made no such request."

It was further explained by the Delegate that the presence of Archbishop

Continued on Second Page.

EXTRA
NO 14
LATEST NEWS

BOND SYNDICATE WORKING FOR AN ARMISTICE

WASHINGTON, April 4.—Efforts are being made by the McOn... to arrange an armistice between the Cubans and the... The Cuban insurgent government has stipulated that it will not agree unless the terms provide for the recognition of Cuban independence. Colonel McCook is in Washington to-day.

YOUNG WOMAN NABS A DIAMOND THIEF.

BOSTON, April 4.—Miss Effie M. Burke to-day captured a diamond thief named William Ross, who was running away with a tray of gems from the jewelry store of John L. Graves at No. 42 Bromfield street. The prisoner looks like a minister, and when searched $850 in bills were found in his pockets.

SUICIDE IN WASHINGTON HOTEL.

WASHINGTON, April 4.—William F. Herbert, of Virginia, committed suicide at his hotel by cutting his throat. He left a note saying he was tired of life. Herbert has a son, Edmund, of the Boston Technical Institute, and another named, poverty, studying law at Columbia, D. C.

POWERS TO SAVE SPAIN FROM WAR AT HOME.

Washington, April 4.—Spain, goaded to desperation by a two-hronged menace... knowledge of the hopelessness of conflict with the United States, and of the insurrection that will doubtless follow a surrender to the demands of this country—has, it is stated, found a loophole through which to escape war.

The authority for this statement is a diplomat, high in the service of his country, who, for obvious reasons, has declined to permit the use of his name in connection with the disclosure.

"The plan," he said, "by which Spain hopes, as a last resort, to preserve the semblance of her honor and to ward off war with the United States is, practically, by a surrender to the demands of the American nation.

"While the Spanish Government has been loudly crying that the honor and integrity of its dynasty could not permit a single backward step, Spain has, throughout Europe for a mode of escape. For something which would prove a retreat from her reinsertion stand and save arouse the ire of her people.

GUARANTEE AGAINST REVOLUTION.

"In vain did Spain plead with the European powers—with France, Germany, Austria in turn to reinstate her attitude toward the United States, or to lend their moral support, if not their armed aid.

"But these powers were not to be drawn into no matter in either of it. They had to consider the other millions of Europe as well as Spain, and deterred by matters at their own thresholds.

"Now, however, France, Germany and Austria have come forward in a manner and in a surprising manner. Although they had refused to stand by Spain in the event of insurrection following administration of her people. This offers to Spain the needed loophole. She can now for the first time consider with equanimity the possibility of a subdued clash with the United States of preserving her dynasty, for civil war would not the throw revolt.

"Thus Spain is ready to hoodwink her people and escape from a conflict at once with peace to be so unequal."

Wild Applause in the House Galleries at Representative Bailey's Fierce Thrust at McKinley.

A tremendous storm of applause broke out in the galleries and floor of the House to-day when Representative Bailey, Democratic leader of the House, voiced the disgust of his party and the country at the delay policy of the Administration. Here is the scene sketched by Artist Williams at Washington that caused Speaker Reed to vigorously pound his gavel.

"These galleries are but a miniature of the country. What you hear here can be heard over this country."

Typical front page of the *New York Journal* prior to the outbreak of war.

WE'RE A-COMING, HOBSON.

THE SPANISH BRUTE
ADDS MUTILATION TO MURDER.

"The liveliest spot in Washington at present is the Navy Department. The decks are cleared for action....It remains only to sand down the decks and pipe to quarters for action," or so said the *New York Sun* on Aug. 23, 1897. NEW YORK PUBLIC LIBRARY

Judge Magazine indicted Spain for atrocities as well as the *Maine* deaths. The "mutilated" American dead were actually savaged by land crabs and vultures. LC

Stephen Crane

The war had its share of adventurers, heros and eccentrics. It also had its share of daring correspondents reporting the war to the people back home or for some, giving them a chance to experience war first-hand. Such a correspondent was Stephen Crane, the well-known author of the novel, *The Red Badge of Courage*. He was a writer who lived the adventures he portrayed. He was fascinated by the seamy side of life and lived it most of his short 28-year life span.

Crane was born in Newark in 1871, as his parents 14th child. His father was a Methodist minister who was against everything that a young man wanted to do—tobacco, alcohol, dancing, theater and sports. Crane was a rebel all through his youth and after flunking out of Syracuse University after one term, he tried his hand at reporting and writing.

His first novel, *Maggie: A Girl of the Streets* was completed in 1892. His most famous, *The Red Badge of Courage* marked the beginning of modern fiction in 1894. Now that he had written about war, he wanted to experience it first hand.

He tried to go to Cuba in 1896 when the Cubans revolted against Spanish rule but his ship sank just outside Jacksonville, Florida. He next went to Greece for the short Greco-Turkish War and then moved to England with his mistress, Cora Stewart.

When war broke out in April 1898, Crane got financial assistance from his writer friend, Joseph Conrad to go to Cuba. He tried to enlist as a sailor but flunked the physical (his poor physical condition including tuberculosis would kill him at an early age).He finally made it to Cuba as a highly paid correspondent and was aboard a battleship that was shelling the city of Cardenas. He was soon under fire at Guantanamo, Las Guasimas, Cuzco and San Juan Hill. Cuba was a terrible place to fight a war and one of Crane's article titles was, "Regulars Get No Glory."

While only a correspondent, Crane was in the thick of the action. On one occasion, as bullets whistled by, he calmly sent signal messages by lantern to American ships. He wore a gleaming white raincoat as he charged up San Juan Hill. He stood atop one hill, hands in pockets, puffing a pipe until one bullet knocked off his hat and another chipped the case of his field glasses. He hauled guns and supplies for troops in a battle and carried wounded men to the rear in another.

He seemed to have no fear of dying and he told a friend that his fondest desire was to die in battle. By this time he probably knew that his TB was killing him and when he returned to England in early 1899, his sickness worsened. He died on June 5, 1900, after a mostly torturous life of poverty, bad love affairs and sickness.

His literary legacy will always be his great novel of the Civil War, one of the greatest and best-known war novels of all time.

Crane in Greece.

In Cuba during the war, Hearst said to a wounded *Journal* reporter: "I'm sorry you're hurt, but wasn't it a splendid fight?"

NEW YORK JOURNAL

NO. 3,176.   NEW YORK, SUNDAY, JANUARY 17, 1897.—32 PAGES.   PRICE FIVE CENTS.

RICHARD HARDING DAVIS AND FREDERIC REMINGTON IN CUBA FOR THE JOURNAL.

FREDERIC REMINGTON

RICHARD HARDING DAVIS

Sent to Cuba with writer Richard Harding Davis to provide drawings of the revolution for William Randolph Hearst's *Journal*, artist Frederic Remington became so disgusted with conditions that he vowed to return to Cuba only with the U.S. Army. He kept his pledge in the company of the Rough Riders.

Upon Davis' death, General Wood stated the following: "Throughout the Cuban campaign he was attached to the headquarters of my regiment in Cuba as a military observer. He was with the advanced party at the opening of the fight at Las Guasimas, and was distinguished throughout the fight by coolness and good conduct. He also participated in the Battle of San Juan and the siege of Santiago, and as an observer was always where duty called him. He was a delightful companion, cheerful, resourceful, and thoughtful of the interests and wishes of others. His reports of the game were valuable and among the best and most accurate."

Richard Harding Davis

Richard Harding Davis was a romantic adventurer, war correspondent and writer.

He became the best-known reporter of his time, covering six wars for New York and London newspapers. These included the revolution in Cuba, the Spanish American War, the Greco-Turkish, Boer and Russo-Japanese wars; and the early years of World War One, before he died in 1916.

He toured and wrote for magazines about the American West, the Mediterranean, Central America and the Congo. He was sensational and dramatic, both in his personality and his writing for publication.

Davis was born in 1864 in Philadelphia, the son of novelist Rebecca Harding Davis and L. Clark Davis, editor of the Philadelphia *Public Ledger*. He attended Lehigh and Johns Hopkins universities and began newspaper work in 1886. He wrote 25 plays, seven novels and more than 80 short stories. Davis died in 1916.

NEWSPAPER ROW AT CAMP ALGER—PUTTING UP THE BULLETINS FOR THE INFORMATION OF THE CAMP.

NEWSPAPER BULLETINS AT WASHINGTON—THE WIFE OF SECRETARY LONG READING THE LATEST WAR NEWS.

SECRETARY OF THE NAVY LONG GIVING OUT OFFICIAL INFORMATION TO THE EAGER REPORTERS WHO USED EACH OTHER'S BACKS FOR WRITING-DESKS.

Davis and Roosevelt in Cuba.

SANTIAGO, July 1898.

DEAR FAMILY:

This is just to reassure you that I am all right. I and Marshall were the only correspondents with Roosevelt. We were caught in a clear case of ambush. Every precaution had been taken, but the natives knew the ground and our men did not. It was the hottest, nastiest fight I ever imagined. We never saw the enemy except glimpses. Our men fell all over the place, shouting to the others not to mind them, but to go on. I got excited and took a carbine and charged the sugar house, which was what is called the key to the position. If the men had been regulars I would have sat in the rear as B---- did, but I knew every other one of them, had played football, and all that sort of thing, with them, so I thought as an American I ought to help. The officers were falling all over the shop, and after it was all over Roosevelt made me a long speech before some of the men, and offered me a captaincy in the regiment any time I wanted it. He told the Associated Press man that there was no officer in his regiment who had "been of more help or shown more courage" than your humble servant, so that's all right. After this I keep quiet. I promise I keep quiet. Love to you all.

Richard

Remington's famous painting of the charge up San Juan Hill with Roosevelt, on horseback, in the lead. It is on display at the Frederic Remington Art Museum in Ogdensburg, New York.

Frederic Remington

One of the most prolific artists of the war period, Frederic Remington was born in 1861 in Canton, New York. He studied art at Yale University and in New York City. He moved to the American West at age 19 to seek adventure and fortune. He lived and worked with cowboys and, for a short time, with friendly Indian tribes.

Remington and his contemporary, Charles Russell, are America's best-known western artists. He was sent to Cuba by William Randolph Hearst to record the Cuban revolution but didn't like the conditions there so he returned to the States. When war was declared, he returned and recorded on canvas many of the battles of the short war.

His paintings and bronze statuettes are on display at the Remington Art Museum in Ogdensburg, New York, the Whitney Gallery of West Art in Cody, Wyoming, and other museums throughout the country. Remington died in 1909.

Sculptor, illustrator, painter and writer, Frederic Remington, 1861-1909. FREDERIC REMINGTON ART MUSEUM, OGDENSBURG, NEW YORK

Well-known western artist, Howard Chandler Christy was born in Morgan City, Ohio, in 1873. He was a portrait painter, teacher and writer. Educated in Ohio, Christy moved to New York City in 1893 to study art. He began working for illustrated periodicals and made his reputation as an artist in Cuba, especially with the Rough Riders. He supplied artwork on the Cuban campaign to *Scribner's* and *Leslie's Illustrated*. He went on to paint beautiful girl portrait illustrations including his well-known "the Christy girl" for the top magazines of the day. In the 1920s, he came into favor as a portrait painter for the celebrities of the world and for historical personages such as in the re-creation of *Signing the Constitution* in the U.S. Capitol. He died in 1952.

This was one way that news was brought to the public as it happened. Taken in New York City. BA

A SOLUTION TO THE MAINE EXPLOSION.

Spanish Dons prepare to blow up the *Maine* in a fanciful newspaper "solution" to the tragedy. LC

Andrew Summers Rowan

Andrew Rowan was born in Gap Mills, Monroe County, Virginia in 1857 (later part of the new state of West Virginia). Sometime thereafter his parents moved to the county seat of Union where he received his early education. In 1874, he was appointed to the U.S. Naval Academy but he resigned after three years to become a cadet at the U.S. Military Academy.

After graduating in 1881 he was commissioned a Second Lieutenant of Infantry and assigned to the 15th Infantry. He saw service in the West and was appointed to the Intercontinental Railway Service, surveying a railway route in Central and South America. He was also a military attaché to Chile where he became interested in the developments in Cuba. Although he had never been to the country, he wrote a book entitled, *The Island of Cuba*.

At the time of the outbreak of the Spanish American War, he was attached to the Bureau of Military Intelligence and in this capacity performed his memorable deed.

After the war he served in the Philippines and was awarded the Silver Star for gallantry in action (actually the medal was awarded in 1922). Rowan retired from the army in 1922 due to physical disability with the rank of major. Also in 1922, Congress formally recognized his outstanding contribution in the Spanish American War by awarding him the nation's second highest medal for heroism, the Distinguished Service Cross. Late in his life, he was also awarded Cuba's highest honor, the Order of Carlos Mamelde Caspedes, for his heroic deed in freeing Cuba from the Spaniards.

Rowan died in San Francisco, California, on Jan. 11, 1943. The flag which draped his casket was presented to West Virginia University. In 1931, an honorary cadet organization was formed by the university's ROTC unit and was named Rowan's Rifles. Outstanding military students elected to this organization were presented a fourragére called the "Rowan Rifle Cord." The original fourragére which was presented to Rowan has been returned to the university. The unit was discontinued after 1933 but the "Rowan Rifle Cord" was awarded through 1940.

Andrew Rowan in 1898.

Andrew Rowan late in life. WEST VIRGINIA & REGIONAL HISTORY COLLECTION, MORGANTOWN, WV

Rowan's "Message To Garcia"

In 1922, at the request of the Army Decorations Board, Rowan wrote a full narrative of his trip across Cuba. It was printed in the July 30, 1922 edition of the *San Francisco Chronicle*. He was awarded the Distinguished Service Cross for his gallant action to take a message to Cuban General Calixto Garcia. His narrative is as follows:

San Francisco Chronicle, Sunday, July 30, 1922

Man Who Took Message to Garcia Tells of Exploit

Perilous Trip Through Foe Lines Related

Information Obtained of Great Value to U.S. in War

Winner of Distinguished Service Cross Now San Franciscan

"On April 8, 1898, I was on duty in the office of Military Information, A.G.O., War Department, Washington, D.C., Major Arthur L. Wagner, A.G., was in charge of the office. At noon of that day, Major Wagner informed me that at a conference between President McKinley and Secretary of War Alger, it has been decided to send an officer to Eastern Cuba (Oriente), in case of war, to ascertain the military conditions existing in that region which was likely to become the theater of war, and that I had been selected for the job.

"Major Wagner's instructions to me were delivered orally and were in brief, to proceed to Kingston, Jamaica, by the first available transportation, and there make arrangements to get into Cuba upon receipt of cipher cablegram to that effect. Once in Cuba I was to bring the military data up to date and conduct myself in accordance with my surroundings. I was authorized to attach myself to any body of the Insurgents operating in the field if the Cuban commander might so elect. I was to carry no papers other than such as might serve to identify me with the American consul general at Kingston and through him with the Cuban Junta. In this connection, Major Wagner referred to the case of Nathan Hale in the Revolutionary war and Lieutenant

Richey in the Mexican war, both caught with dispatches on them.

"Leaving Washington, D.C., midnight, April 8-9, 1898, and New York at noon, April 9, I reached Kingston, Jamaica, British West Indies, on the Atlas Line S.S. *Adirondack*, and at once began to prepare to get into Cuba upon receipt of the necessary authority by cablegram. April 23, I received the cipher cable dispatch: 'Join GARCIA as soon as possible.'

"At 10 a.m., dressed as an English hunter, I left Kingston and crossed the island of Jamaica, reaching Saint Ann's bay about 1 a.m. Here I boarded a small sailboat, and by daylight I had passed beyond the neutral waters of Jamaica and had entered the Caribbean. By nightfall (April 23, 1898) our small craft (manned by three Cuban sailors, one orderly, assistants and myself, and carrying some antiquated small arms of various types intended for the Cubans) was approaching the territorial waters of Cuba, habitually guarded at that period, by the enemy (Spanish) lanche patrol. We kept well off until dark, and then, under full sail, made the best of our way to the nearest point of the shore, coming to another about 11 p.m. in a small inlet about fifty yards out. I was thus the first American officer to enter the

enemy's line after the declaration of war, albeit not in our uniform.

"The next morning I proceeded through the forest afoot till mounts could be procured. At one camp I found a number of deserters from the Spanish garrison at Manzanillo. From them I got some statements of doubtful value concerning the conditions in Manzanillo.

"About noon, May 1, 1898, after having crossed the Sierra Maestra range of mountains, I reached Bayamo, the Insurgent headquarters, where I was identified through my escort as delagado Americano, commissioned by the War Department as a man of confidence—a term which suffers in translation, but which, in this instance, served only to show our mutual purpose of acting promptly in an emergency. I was the first to impart the news that the United States had declared war against Spain, and, following this auspicious announcement, I at once delivered, orally, my message to General Garcia, as follows:

"My business in Cuba was not to be considered in any sense as diplomatic in its quality, but military only, although my credentials bore a diplomatic approval as a mark of identification. I was there to learn as much of the military situation in Eastern Cuba (Oriente) as possible; any information, big or little, bearing on the situation, would be gladly received by the U.S. military authorities, who were preparing to carry the war into Cuba. How many Spanish troops were now, 1898, in Cuba? How were they waging war? How were they armed and equipped? How clothed? How fed? The condition and quality of the Spanish forces? The character of their officers, especially the commanding officers; what of the Spanish morale? What were to topographical conditions, local and general? The character and conditions of the roads then, and at all seasons? The sanitary situation of both armies, and throughout the country generally?

"Similar information regarding the Cubans and the Cuban forces was also wanted. How were the Cubans armed, equipped and fed? What was needed in the way of placing the forces in a condition to harass the enemy while the American army was mobilizing? Especially would I be glad to learn something of the topography of the districts where contact was likely to be made. And lastly, I would place myself under his orders in any expedition he might have in view, as it was my desire to get some insight also into the Cuban guerrilla method of fighting in the cuban manigua—jungle.

"After a conference lasting about five hours, General Garcia announced that he had decided to send me back to the United States via the north coast, with three of his ablest and most trusted staff officers, who knew all his plans, were familiar with the status quo, and who would answer all the questions that he, himself, could, respecting existing conditions in Eastern Cuba. Indeed, he proposed to put at the disposal of the American War Department as much information as he himself possessed. What more could I wish? Should I spend days and weeks in that section I could not possibly gather data so intimate and abundant as that in the possession of the envoys whom he had selected to return with me. And

now, since the United States had been prompt to ask him for information, he would be usually prompt in answering. Could I leave at once?—5 p.m., May 1, 1898.

"There was nothing for me to do but 'stand to horse.' What I had come for I had gotten—it was for me to get back to the War Department as soon as possible. I recalled that in a case of this kind, when 'tis done, then 'twere well it were done quickly. Notwithstanding the lack of personal familiarity that haste was engendered, I was in luck, for my work had been anticipated and the men that General Garcia was sending back with me were men of the highest standing, and were the very ones that he himself would have consulted in making a campaign against the now, common enemy. The promptness with which I accepted the general's challenge to start at once seemed to impart an air of confidence and respect which must have had a far reaching influence among the Cubans in the way of stimulating preparation for the coming struggle.

"At 5 p.m., accompanied by General Enrique Collazo, Colonel Carlos Hernandez and Dr. Vieta (an expert in tropical diseases), all of General Garcia's staff, I left the Cuban headquarters in Bayamo for the north coast, taking the Cauto river, by swimming, early May 2, 1898, a few miles above the head of navigation, Cauto-El Embarcadero, where the Spanish troops embarking for the coast of Manzanillo. Up to the time of my reaching Bayamo no member of my escort could speak English, but then to the north coast Colonel Hernandez was familiar with both English and Spanish and was, therefore, of great service as interpreter for his colleague, General Collazo, after reaching the United States.

"My course across the island of Cuba may be roughly described as astride the 77 degree meridian—swinging slightly to the east to reach Bayamo, thence slightly northwest until the said meridian was touched at Victoria-de-las Tunas,

thence to the north coast, approximately along that line to the Gulf of Manati, where our party arrived about sunset May 5, 1898.

"From a mangrove swamp on the west side of the Manati inlet our sailor-guides drew a small ship's boat of about 104 cubic feet capacity, too small to accommodate all our party, who, reduced to six—three officers and three sailors, must sit upright for several days and nights with our supplies under our seats and between our feet. Dr. Vieta was, accordingly, sent back with our abandoned mounts, and at 11 p.m. we boarded our craft and made our way out through the narrow neck of this harbor, passing under the guns of a small Spanish fort on the eastern side of the inlet. Here we again entered the Spanish lancha patrol limits, and at daylight were out of sight of the Cuban littoral and well on our way to Key West via Nassau, New Providence, Bahama islands

"It will be observed that our course from the Cuban coast, over the old Bahama channel (Canal Viejo de Bahama) and in the trough of the Tongue-of-the-Ocean, still followed closely, as, indeed it had from St. Ann's bay in Jamaica, across the Caribbean and over the Cuban terra firma, the seventy-seventh meridian—a note that may be of service in following the route on the map.

"With the aid of the American Consul-General at Nassau, McLean, I was enabled to board the schooner Fearless, bound for Key West, Fla., where our party arrived May 13, 1891. Thence I proceeded to Washington, D.C., where I reported to the Adjutant-General, H.C. Corbin, who congratulated me on my safe return and at once disavowed the wording of a telegram that he had dispatched to me at Tampa, placing the responsibility for the error on some subordinate in his office; he thereupon offered to conduct me 'through the private way' to report to the Secretary of War, Alger. The Secretary, after hearing a narrative of my journey, congratulated me in high terms and then directed me to invite the staff officers of General Garcia, whom I had brought back with me to Washington, and then for all of us to report to the Commanding General of the Army, General Nelson A. Miles.

"On receiving my report the commanding General of the army congratulated me, and on May 23, 1898, wrote to the Secretary of War as follows:

"'I recommend that First Lieutenant Andrew S. Rowan, 19th Infantry, be made a Lieutenant-Colonel of one of the regiments of immunes. Lieutenant Rowan made a journey across Cuba, was with the insurgent army under Lieutenant-General Garcia and brought most important and valuable information to the Government. This was a most perilous undertaking, and in my judgment Lieutenant Rowan performed an act of heroism and cool darying that has rarely been excelled in the annals of warfare. Very respectfully,

"'NELSON A. MILES,'

"'Major-General U.S. Army.'

"General Miles appreciated from the first the vital quality of the information that my penetration of the Spanish lines had placed at his disposal, and from that time things began to move. Expeditions to aid the insurgents and harass the enemy that had failed of their objective by reason of the lack of information and other causes now began to reach their destination with clock-like precision. Among these was the Florida expedition to Banes Bat, piloted by the guides whom I had brought back with me, and carrying back Colonel Hernandez, who, upon rejoining General Garcia, made the arrangements for the concentration of about 5,000 Cuban troops at Aserraderos to act in conjunction with the American army and navy in the pending Santiago campaign.

"At Aserraderos General Garcia met Admiral Sampson and General Shafter and arranged the details for the attack on Santiago de Cuba. This meeting was a direct result of my five hours' conference with General Garcia, May 1, 1898, at Bayamo. The concentration could not have been effected so promptly had I not brought back the means to accomplish it. Other details dependent on the manner in which I fulfilled my mission to General Garcia may be read in the annual report of the commanding General of the army for 1898—pp. 15, 16 et seq. of General Miles' report for that year.

"It will be seen that between April 23, 1898, and May 23, 1898—precisely one month—while the U.S. forces were mobilizing, all the data upon which to formulate the movement of troops were accumulated and digested; and when the order came from the President to send the army forward our military information was up to date, due to the fortuitous circumstances of dispatching a message to Garcia at the psychological moment.

"In speaking of the happy results of my rapid transit across the theater of war and through the enemy's lines, Colonel Wagner, who had transmitted the order that had sent me on my way, said to me that, taking into account the paucity of the information on file at the declaration of war and the celerity with which the hiatus was filled, he could not help quoting Goldwing Smith; 'God has been kind to children, idiots and the United States.'

"In submitting this belated account, in brief official form, of how I penetrated and escaped from the Spanish lines, after having procured the information that I was sent to procure respecting what was expected to be (and what proved to be) the chief theater of war, I have necessarily omitted the details of preparation and methods taken to effect my object; but let it not be thought for a moment that my task was devoid of the usual concomitants of personal advantage, petty envy and low ambition on the part of those who should have sunk out of sight every motive but the common good.

"Of such I may mention a personal quarrel between the United States Consul-General at Kingston, Jamaica, and members of the press, and the miswording of Adjutant General Corbin's telegram, which he was so prompt to disavow. In the case of the consul-general I may say that his conduct, while at first active and helpful, was in the end officious and unworthy, contrasting greatly with the kind and efficient aid given me by McLean, our consul-general at Nassau, New Providence.

"As a sequence of these contretemps, which culminated while I was in the Cuban manigua, beyond the reach of machination, I found on my return to Washington that every officer who had been on duty with me there had been promoted while I, who had been the first to receive and execute a war assignment inside enemy lines, had not been mentioned. If I make but brief reference to these side issues which I was able to sidetrack, I reserve to myself the consolatin for the omission of details in the brevity of this report by recalling that they were Caesar's enemies who assert that 'The Commentaries' would have been longer had the 'mightiest Julius' jotted down a few of his defeats.

"Results count—Gaul was Rome's, Cuba was ours—I had joined Garcia as soon as possible. I had gotten our military data up to date. I had made my journey. It was not possible for the War Department to act upon facts and in conjunction with some 5,000 armed Cubans who were, to say the least, indispensable as guides.

"The result was that the Spanish American war lasted 105 days—from declaration to protocol—and it left the United States in possession of an indispensable strategic stronghold controlling the entrance-exit to the greatest indentation of our coasts: and 'heave it or sink it, leave it or drink it, we are masters of the seas'—our seas, at any rate.

"A report of this kind necessarity involves, in large degree, the personal equation and the ego, to an unusual extent, unavoidable, indeed, since my mission depended on myself alone for its conduct; but, as the Government placed sufficient reliance upon me to trust me to do my work alone, it is but reasonable that it should bear with me in accepting my own account of how I performed my duty throughout a trying period.

"Fortunately, witnesses as to the manner in which I conducted myself from my meeting with General Garcia till I reached United States territory on the return voyage may be still living, as may, also, some at least, of my party that escorted me from Jamaica to Bayamo. And, as to the results, I may refer to the official statements of the General commanding the army in his annual report to the Secretary of War for the year 1898. In this connection, see pages 10, 11, 15, 16, 17, 37 and 38 of said report. (I have at hand only the edition in pamphlet form.)

"At General Miles' request, I wrote a narrative account (omitting the confidential matter) for the press and for the purpose of arousing public feeling and interest in the war. This account was published in McClure's magazine for August 1898. A few months later this was followed by an essay on the subject of the faithful performance of duty, which appeared in the Philistine magazine for March 1899, and which at once achieved an unprecedented popularity and distribution under the title of 'A Message to Garcia,' by Elbert Hubbard.

"In this essay Hubbard used as a text the success of my passage in and out of the Spanish lines and the result of my effort in bringing 'up to date' the data on which the commanding general of the army could confidentially base his plans. This essay, I understand, has appeared in every language that has been reduced to print—and 'he who runs may read'—Aristarchian or Vandal; dilettante or indifferent. As a stimulus to recruiting and training in both army and navy in the World war, the use of Hubbard's essay was extensive.

"After reporting to the com-manding General of the army, by order of the Secretary of War, as already related, I accompanied General Miles, to appear before a Cabinet meeting, and at the close of the session the President McKinley, congratulated me upon the method in which I had performed my task of procuring information of the enemy in the enemy's country, and ended by saying: 'You have done a very brave deed.' With these words the circuit of the President's verbal order to 'send an officer into Eastern Cuba (Oriente) and bring the military information up to date' was closed and complete. I had received the congratulations and the thanks of every officer to whom I was responsible.

"It remains to call to mind the scantiness of the military information at hand regarding the paramount strategic position of the island of Cuba in 1898, and to express the hope that never again may the advent of war find it necessary to dispatch an officer through enemy lines to obtain information that should be at hand, ready to be passed to the commanding General at a moment's notice in order to enable him to act as the occasion demands; for the winds may not always blow from the right direction, as they did in 1898; the marooned insurgent General may not always be able, anxious and complaisant; the return voyage may not always be assured, and the ultimate authority may not always be receptive of information gathered under the circumstances of rush, run and improvisation."

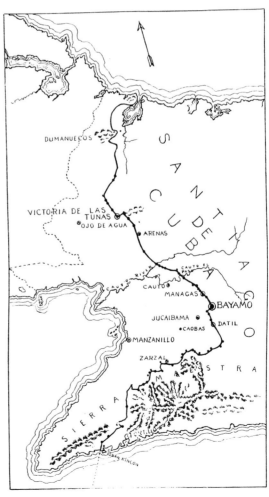

LIEUTENANT ROWAN'S ROUTE ACROSS CUBA.
Dotted Line is the Boundary between Santiago de Cuba and Puerto Principe.

Elbert Hubbard and his "Message to Garcia"

Andrew Rowan received little public recognition for his deed until Elbert Hubbard wrote his "literary trifle" for the March 1898 issue of *Philistine* magazine.

Hubbard was the son of a pioneer country doctor in Bloomington, Illinois. He founded the Society of Philistines at East Aurora, New York, and the Roycroft Press, both in 1895. The Roycroft movement was based on getting back to a simpler lifestyle of arts and crafts and intellectual pursuits.

Hubbard was well-known for his witty, to-the-point messages, such as: "Folks who never do any more than they get paid for, never get paid for any more than they do." His 1899 "Message to Garcia" became world famous. He used the Rowan mission to emphasis his notion of the American work effort.* It is reproduced here in its entirety.

Apologia

This literary trifle, *A Message to Garcia*, was written one evening after supper, in a single hour. It was on the Twenty-second of February, Eighteen Hundred Ninety-nine, Washington's Birthday, and we were just going to press with the March *Philistine*. The thing leaped hot from my heart, written after a trying day, when I had been endeavoring to train some rather delinquent villagers to abjure the comatose state and get radioactive.

The immediate suggestion, though, came from a little argument over the teacups, when my boy Bert suggested that Rowan was the real hero of the Cuban War. Rowan had gone alone and done the thing—carried the message to Garcia.

It came to me like a flash! Yes, the boy is right, the hero is the man who does his work—who carries the message to Garcia.

I got up from the table, and wrote *A Message to Garcia*. I thought so little of it that we ran it in the Magazine without a heading. The edition went out, and soon orders began to come for extra copies of the March *Philistine*, a dozen, fifty, a hundred; and when the American News Company ordered a thousand, I asked one of my helpers which article it was that had stirred up the cosmic dust.

"It's the stuff about Garcia," he said.

The next day a telegram came from George H. Daniels, of the New York Central Railroad, thus: "Give price on one hundred thousand Rowan article in pamphlet form—Empire State Express advertisement on back—also how soon can ship."

I replied giving price, and stated we could supply the pamphlets in two years. Our facilities were small and a hundred thousand booklets looked like an awful undertaking.

The result was that I gave Mr. Daniels permission to reprint the article in his own way. He issued it in booklet form in editions of half a million. Two of three of these half-million lots were sent out by Mr. Daniels, and in addition the article was reprinted in over two hundred magazines and newspapers. It has been translated into all written languages.

At the time Mr. Daniels was distributing the *Message to Garcia*, Prince Hilakoff, Director of Russian Railways, was in this country. He was the guest of the New York Central, and made a tour of the country under the personal direction of Mr. Daniels.

The Prince saw the little book and was interested in it, more because Mr. Daniels was putting it out in such big numbers, probably, than otherwise.

In any event, when he got home he had the matter translated into Russian, and a copy of the booklet given to every railroad employee in Russia.

Other countries then took it up, and from Russia it passed into Germany, France, Spain, Turkey, Hindustan and China.

During the war between Russia and Japan, every Russian soldier who went to the front was given a copy of the *Message to Garcia*.

The Japanese, finding the booklets in possession of the Russian prisoners, concluded that it must be a good thing, and accordingly translated it into Japanese.

And on an order of the Mikado, a copy was given to every man in the employ of the Japanese Government, soldier or civilian.

Over forty million copies of *A Message to Garcia* have been printed. This is said to be a larger circulation than any other literary venture has ever attained during the lifetime of the author, in all history—thanks to a series of lucky accidents!

E.H.
East Aurora,
December 1, 1913

A Message to Garcia

In all this Cuban business there is one man stands out on the horizon of my memory like Mars at perihelion.

When war broke out between Spain and the United States, it was very necessary to communicate quickly with the leader of the Insurgents. Garcia was somewhere in the mountain fastnesses of Cuba—no one knew where. No mail or telegraph message could reach him. The President must secure his co-operation, and quickly.

What to do!

Some one said to the President, "There is a fellow by the name of Rowan will find Garcia for you, if anybody can."

Rowan was sent for and given a letter to be delivered to Garcia. How the "fellow by the name of Rowan," took the letter, sealed it up in an oilskin pouch, strapped it over his heart, in four days landed by night off the coast of Cuba from an open boat, disappeared into the jungle, and in three weeks came out on the other side of the Island, having traversed a hostile country on foot, and delivered his special letter to Garcia—are things I have no special desire now to tell in detail. The point that I wish to make is this: McKinley gave Rowan a letter to be delivered to Garcia; Rowan took the letter and did not ask, "Where is he at?"

By the Eternal! there is a man whose form should be cast in deathless bronze and the statue placed in every college of the land. It is not book-learning young men need, nor instruction about this and that, but a stiffening of the vertebrae which will cause them to be loyal to a trust, to act promptly, concentrate their energies: do the thing—"Carry a message to Garcia."

General Garcia is dead now, but there are other Garcias. No man who has endeavored to carry out an enterprise where many hands are needed, but has been well-nigh appalled at times by the imbecility of the average man—the inability or unwillingness to concentrate on a thing and do it.

Slipshod assistance, foolish inattention, dowdy indifference, and half-hearted work seem the rule; and no man succeeds, unless by hook or crook or threat he forces or bribes other men to assist him; or mayhap, God in his goodness performs a miracle, and sends him an Angel of Light for an assistant.

You, reader, put this matter to a test: You are sitting now in your office—six clerks are within call. Summon any one and make this request: "Please look in the encyclopedia and make a brief memorandum for me concerning the life of Correggio." Will the clerk quietly say, "Yes, sir," and go do the task?

On your life he will not. He will look at you out of a fishy eye and ask one or more of the following questions:

"Who was he?

"Which encyclopedia?

"Was I hired for that?

"Don't you mean *Bismarck*?

"What's the matter with Charlie doing it?

"Is he dead?

"Is there any hurry?

"Sha'n't I bring you the book and let you look it up yourself?

"What do you want to know for?"

And I will lay you ten to one that after you have answered the questions, and explained how to find the information, and why you want it, the clerk will go off and get one of the other clerks to help him try to find Garcia—and then come back and tell you there is no such man. Of course I may lose my bet, but according to the Law of Average I will not. Now, if you are wise, you will not bother to explain to your assistant that Correggio is indexed under the C's, not in the K's, but you will smile very sweetly and say, "Never mind," and go look it up yourself. And this incapacity for independent action, this moral stupidity, this infirmity of the will, this unwillingness to cheerfully catch hold and lift—these are the things that put pure Socialism so far into the future. If men will not act for themselves, what will they do when the benefit of their effort is for all?

A first mate with knotted club seems necessary; and the dread of getting the bounce Saturday night holds many a worker to his place. Advertise for a stenographer, and nine out of ten who apply can neither spell nor punctuate—and do not think it necessary to.

Can such a one write a letter to Garcia?

"You see that bookkeeper," said the foreman to me in a large factory.

"Yes; what about him?"

"Well, he's a fine accountant, but if I'd send him uptown on an errand, he might accomplish the errand all right, and on the other hand, might stop at four saloons on the way, and when he got to Main Street would forget what he had been sent for."

Can such a man be entrusted to carry a message to Garcia?

We have recently been hearing much maudlin sympathy expressed for the downtrodden denizens of the sweatshop and the homeless wanderer searching for honest employment, and with it all often go many hard words for the men in power.

Nothing is said about the employer who grows old before his time in a vain attempt to get frowzy ne'er-do-wells to do intelligent work; and his long, patient striving after help that does nothing but loaf when his back is turned. In every store and factory there is a constant weeding-out process going on. The employer is constantly sending away help that have shown their incapacity to further the interests of the business, and others are being taken on. No matter how good times are, this sorting continues: only, if times are hard and work is scarce, the sorting is done finer—but out and forever out the incompetent and unworthy go. It is the survival of the fittest. Self-interest prompts every employer to keep the best—those who can carry a message to Garcia.

I know one man of really brilliant parts who has not the ability to manage a business of his own, and yet who is absolutely worthless to any one else because he carries with him constantly the insane suspicion that his employer is oppressing, or intending to oppress him. He can not give orders, and he will not receive them. Should a message be given him to take to Garcia, his answer would probably be, "Take it yourself!"

Tonight this man walks the streets looking for work, the wind whistling through his threadbare coat. No one who knows him dare employ him, for he is a regular firebrand of discontent. He is impervious to reason, and the only thing that can impress him is the toe of a thick-soled Number Nine boot.

Of course, I know that one so morally deformed is no less to be pities than a physical cripple; but in our pitying let us drop a tear, too, for the men who are striving to carry on a great enterprise, whose working hours are not limited by the whistle, and whose hair is fast turning white through the struggle to hold in line dowdy indifference, slipshod imbecility, and the heartless ingratitude which, but for their enterprise, would be both hungry and homeless.

Have I put the matter too strongly? Possibly I have; but when all the world has gone a-slumming I wish to speak a word of sympathy for the man who succeeds—the man who, against great odds, has directed the efforts of others, and having succeeded, finds there's nothing in it: nothing but bare board and clothes. I have carried a dinner-pail and worked for day's wages, and I have also been an employer of labor, and I know there is something to be said on both sides. There is no excellence, per se, in poverty; rags are no recommendation; and all employers are not rapacious and high-handed, any more than all poor men are virtuous. My heart goes out to the man who does his work when the boss is away, as well as when he is at home. And the man who, when given a letter for Garcia, quietly takes the missive, without asking any idiotic questions, and with no lurking intention of chucking it into the nearest sewer, or of doing aught else but deliver it, never gets laid off, nor has to go on a strike for higher wages. Civilization is one long, anxious search for just such individuals. Anything such a man asks shall be granted. He is wanted in every city, town and village—in every office, shop, store and factory. The world cries out for such: he is needed and needed badly—the man who can "Carry a Message to Garcia."

Here endeth the preachment, "A Message to Garcia," as written by Fra Elbertus and done into a booklet by the Roycrofters, at their shop, which is in East Aurora, Erie County, New York State, May, MCMXVII

*Elbert Hubbard had the misfortune to be one of the 1,200 passengers lost on the British liner *Lusitania* when it was sunk by a German submarine on May 7, 1915.

Major Rowan was decorated by Jose J. Zarza, Cuban consul, at the Presidio of San Francisco in 1938. Mrs. Rowan is to the left. BA, INP

USS Maine

Capt. Charles Dwight Sigsbee was the captain of the ill-fated battleship *Maine* in Havana harbor. He was born in 1845 and graduated from the Naval Academy in 1863. He participated in several major Civil War naval engagements and then spent much of his career teaching at the Naval Academy and hydrographic work with the Coast Survey. He brought the auxiliary cruiser *St. Paul* into commission in April 1898, captured a collier in the West Indies in May, and defeated the Spanish cruiser *Isabel II* and destroyer *Terror* off Puerto Rico in June. He was promoted to rear admiral in 1903 and had various commands until he retired in 1907.

1st Commanding Officer: Capt. A.S. Crowninshield
Authorized: Aug. 3, 1886
Keel Laid: Oct. 17, 1888
Launched: Nov. 18, 1889
Commissioned: Sept. 17, 1895
Sponsor: Miss Alice Tracy Wilmerding
Displacement Standard Tons: 6,682
Design Crew Complement: 31 officers, 343 enlisted
Main Guns: four, 10-inch .35 caliber, six, six-inch .40 caliber
Secondary Guns: seven, six-pounder, eight, one-pounder
Construction Costs: $2.5 million maximum
Armor: Maximum thickness 12 inches at turret face plates
Length Overall: 319 feet
Mean Draught: 21 feet, six inches
Extreme Beam: 57 feet
Torpedo Tubes: four, 14-inch surface
Catapults: None
Builder: New York Navy Yard, Brooklyn, New York
Original Engines Manufactured: Quintard Iron Works; type: vertical, triple expansion, reciprocating
Original Boilers Manufactured: Quintard Iron Works; type: FT; no. 4
Original Fuel: Coal, 896 tons
Drive: Reciprocating, two screws
Sisters: *Maine* Class Battleship Prototype
Designed Speed: 17 knots
Designed Shaft Horsepower: 9,000
Design Comments:
· No. 1 in battleship prototypes—second class battleship—heavy armored cruiser
Sea-going double-bottomed armored vessel

U.S. second-class battleship *Maine* was sent to Havana on Jan. 25, 1898, to protect American lives and property and to "show the flag." USN NH 74103

U. S. Battle Ship MAINE
Anchored over her Grave
From a Kodak Picture taken 4 o'clock in the afternoon of Feb. 15, 1898,
the date of her destruction.

This photo, taken at 4:00 p.m., Feb. 15, 1898, shows the *Maine* moored to a buoy in Havana harbor. In order to gauge the attitude of the people of Cuba, Captain Sigsbee attended a bullfight with several of his officers that day. They found the people unfriendly but not hostile. At about 9:40 p.m. the captain was writing a letter to his wife and listening to the bugler sound taps. He later recalled: "I laid down my pen to listen to the notes of the bugle, which were singularly beautiful in the oppressive stillness of the night. The echoes floated back to the ship repeating the strains of the bugle fully and exactly. I was enclosing my letter in its envelope when the explosion came. It was a bursting, rending and crashing roar of immense volume. There was a trembling and lurching motion, a list to port, and a movement of subsidence. The electric lights went out. Then there was intense blackness and smoke." LC

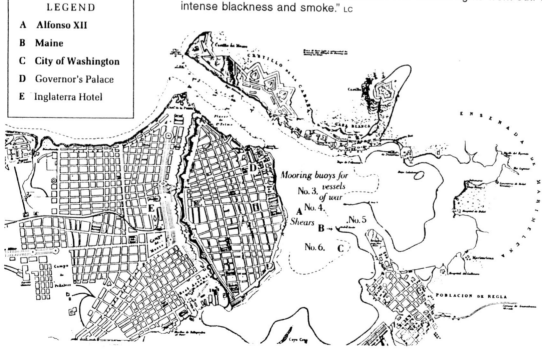

LEGEND	
A	**Alfonso XII**
B	**Maine**
C	**City of Washington**
D	**Governor's Palace**
E	Inglaterra Hotel

Hydrographic office Chart No. 307 of Havana harbor showing position of ships and buildings. The Ward Line steamer *City of Washington* and the Spanish warship *Alfonso XII*, both close to the *Maine*, helped pick up survivors.

863,956
WORLDS CIRCULATED YESTERDAY

The World.

863,916
WORLDS CIRCULATED YESTERDAY

"Circulation Books Open to All."

"Circulation Books Open to All."

VOL. XXXVIII. NO. 13,316

NEW YORK, THURSDAY, FEBRUARY 17, 1898.

PRICE

MAINE EXPLOSION CAUSED BY BOMB OR TORPEDO?

Capt. Sigsbee and Consul-General Lee Are in Doubt---The World Has Sent a Special Tug, With Submarine Divers, to Havana to Find Out---Lee Asks for an Immediate Court of Inquiry---260 Men Dead.

IN A SUPPRESSED DESPATCH TO THE STATE DEPARTMENT, THE CAPTAIN SAYS THE ACCIDENT WAS MADE POSSIBLE BY AN ENEMY.

Dr. E. C. Pendleton, Just Arrived from Havana, Says He Overheard Talk There of a Plot to Blow Up the Ship---
Zalinski, the Dynamite Expert, and Other Experts Report to The World that the Wreck Was Not
Accidental---Washington Officials Ready for Vigorous Action if Spanish Responsibility
Can Be Shown---Divers to Be Sent Down to Make Careful Examinations.

The explosion destroyed a large portion of the *Maine*'s hull from about midships forward. At first it was thought a Spanish mine had blown her up but this has largely been disproven. Some even suggested the Cuban revolutionaries or American sympathizers had blown her up to push America into war with Spain. A court of inquiry convened after the explosion concluded it probably occurred from a mine. Many studies and books have been written since and it is generally agreed that spontaneous combustion probably caused the explosion, but it will continue to be one of the unsolved mysteries of history. In any case the cry "Remember The *Maine*" would push the United States and Spain to war just two months later.

View on deck of the *Maine* taken at Bar Harbor, Maine. USN NH 48622

Photo of the *Maine* the morning after the explosion. USN NH 46772

$50,000 REWARD.—WHO DESTROYED THE MAINE?—$50,000 REWARD

The Journal will give $50,000 for information, furnished to it exclusively, that will convict the person or persons who sank the Maine.

EDITION FOR GREATER NEW YORK

NEW YORK JOURNAL
AND ADVERTISER.

The Journal will give $50,000 for information, furnished to it exclusively, that will convict the person or persons who sank the Maine.

NO. 5,572. Copyright, 1898, by W. R. Hearst.—NEW YORK, THURSDAY, FEBRUARY 17, 1898.—16 PAGES. PRICE ONE CENT In Greater New York and Jersey City. TWO CE...

DESTRUCTION OF THE WAR SHIP MAINE WAS THE WORK OF AN ENEMY

$50,000!

$50,000 REWARD!
For the Detection of the
Perpetrator of
the Maine Outrage!

The New York Journal hereby offers a reward of $50,000 CASH for information FURNISHED TO IT EXCLUSIVELY, which shall lead to the detection and conviction of the person, persons or government criminally responsible for the explosion which resulted in the destruction, at Havana, of the United States war ship Maine and the loss of 258 lives of American sailors.

The $50,000 CASH offered for the above information on deposit with Wells, Fargo & Co.

No one is barred, be he the humble but misguided seaman skulking out a few miserable dollars by acting as a spy, or the attache of a government secret service, plotting, by any devilish means, to revenge fancied insults or cripple menacing countries.

This offer has been cabled to Europe and will be made public in every capital of the Continent and in London this morning.

The Journal believes that any man who can be bought to commit murder can also be bought to betray his comrades. FOR THE PERPETRATOR OF THIS OUTRAGE HAD ACCOMPLICES

W. R. HEARST

Assistant Secretary Roosevelt Convinced the Explosion of the War Ship Was Not an Accident.

The Journal Offers $50,000 Reward for the Conviction of the Criminals Who Sent 258 American Sailors to Their Death. Naval Officers Unanimous That the Ship Was Destroyed on Purpose.

$50,000!

$50,000 REWARD
For the Detection of th
Perpetrator of
the Maine Outrage!

The New York Journal hereby offers a reward of $50,000 CASH for information FURNISHED TO IT EXCLUSIVELY, which shall lead to the detection and conviction of the person, persons or government criminally responsible for the explosion which resulted in the destruction, at Havana, of the United States war ship Maine and the loss of 258 lives of American sailors.

The $50,000 CASH offered for the above information on deposit with Wells, Fargo & Co.

No one is barred, be he the humble but misguided seaman, out a few miserable dollars by acting as a spy or the attache of a government secret service, plotting, by any devilish means, to revenge fancied insults or cripple menacing countries.

This offer has been cabled to Europe and will be made public in every capital of the Continent and in London this morning.

The Journal believes that any man who can be bought to betray his comrades, FOR TH PERPETRATOR OF THIS OUTRAGE HA ACCOMPLICES.

W. R. HEARST.

POWDER MAGAZINE

MAINE

WIRE

NAVAL OFFICERS THINK THE MAINE WAS DESTROYED BY A SPANISH MINE.

George Eugene Bryson, the Journal's special correspondent at Havana, cables that it is the secret opinion of many Spaniards in the Cuban capital that the Maine was destroyed and 258 of her men killed by means of a submarine mine or fixed torpedo. This is the opinion of several American naval authorities. The Spaniards, it is believed, arranged to have the Maine anchored over one of the harbor mines. Wires connected the mine with a powder magazine, and it is thought the explosion was caused by sending an electric current through the wire. If this can be proven, the brutal nature of the Spaniards will be shown by the fact that they waited to spring the mine until after all the men had retired for the night. The Maltese cross in the picture shows where the mine may have been fired.

Hidden Mine or a Sunken Torpedo Believed to Have Been the Weapon Used Against the American Man-of-War---Officers and Men Tell Thrilling Stories of Being Blown Into the Air Amid a Mass of Shattered Steel and Exploding Shells---Survivors Brought to Key West Scout the Idea of Accident---Spanish Officials Protest Too Much---Our Cabinet Orders a Searching Inquiry---Journal Sends Divers to Havana to Report Upon the Condition of the Wreck.
Was the Vessel Anchored Over a Mine?
BY CAPTAIN E. L. ZALINSKI, U. S. A.
(Captain Zalinski is the inventor of the famous dynamite gun, which would be the principal factor in our coast defence in case of war.)

Assistant Secretary of the Navy Theodore Roosevelt says he is convinced that the destruction of the Maine in Havana Harbor was not an acciden

The Journal offers a reward of $50,000 for exclusive evidence that will convict the person, persons or Government criminally responsible for the destruction of the American battle ship and the death of 258 of its crew.

The suspicion that the Maine was deliberately blown up grows stronger every hour. Not a single fact to the contrary has been produced.

Captain Sigsbee, of the Maine, and Consul-General Lee both urge that public opinion be suspended until they have completed their inves They are taking the course of tactful men who are convinced that there has b........treachery.

Washington reports very late that Captain Sigsbee had f......d......as a hidden mine. T......ed all day naval officers in cabling instead of the usual Am...

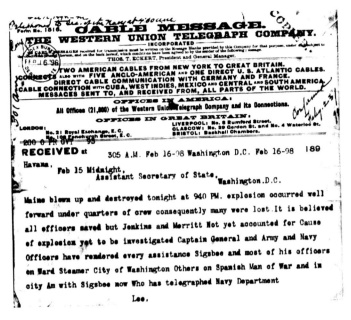

Cable sent to the Assistant Secretary of State by
Counsel Fitzhugh Lee from Havana on Feb. 16,
telling of the *Maine*'s destruction.

Collier's Weekly was one of the most popular news
magazines of the period. This March 11, 1899, issue
was a tribute to the *Maine*, sunk just over a year
earlier.

Outboard profile and forebridge detail drawings from 1893. USN NH 76602

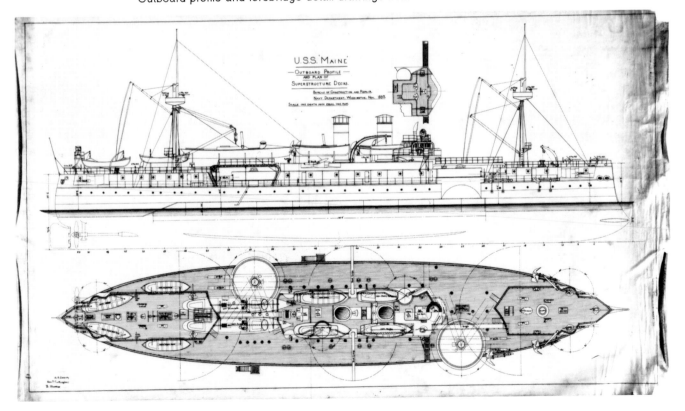

The ex-captain of the *Maine*, Charles Sigsbee brought back the bodies of the ships' victims in December 1899 and they were reinterred at Arlington National Cemetery. One hundred fifty caskets were flag-draped and ornamented with a wreath of green. The President, his Cabinet and ranking army and navy officers, including Admiral Dewey, were in attendance. ARC

Dignitaries at the first burial of the *Maine* victims at the Cristóbal Colón Cemetery outside of Havana on Feb. 17, 1898. Chaplain John Chidwick presided along with Fitzhugh Lee, Captain Sigsbee, Clara Barton, Governor-General Blanco and other Spanish delegates. KE

Funeral of the victims of the *Maine* at Havana shortly after she was sunk. Photo copied from "Uncle Sam's Navy," Vol. IV, No. 3, April 19, 1898. USN NH 46765

Maj. Gen. Fitzhugh Lee, commander of the Seventh Army Corps, on horseback, led a delegation of soldiers and sailors to Colón Cemetery near Havana to honor the dead of the *Maine* on the first anniversary of her sinking, Feb. 15, 1899. USAMHI

Sixty-six victims of the *Maine* were brought back to the United States in February 1912. This is the funeral procession passing along Pennsylvania Avenue in Washington, D.C. USN NH 1801

Views of the *Maine's* wreckage taken from various angles.

Other Battleships *Maine*

BB-10 was authorized on May 4, 1898. The keel was laid on Feb. 15, 1899. She launched on July 17, 1901, and was commissioned on Dec. 29, 1902. This battleship was built by William Cramp & Sons in Philadelphia and displaced 12,846 standard tons with a crew complement of 40 officers and 521 enlisted personnel. She had four 12-inch .45 caliber and 16 six-inch .50 caliber main guns and six three-inch .50 caliber, eight three-pounder, six one-pounder and three .30 caliber secondary guns. Her overall length was 393 feet, 11 inches, and her extreme beam was 72 feet, three inches with a design speed of 18 knots. She was decommissioned in 1920 and scrapped in 1923.

BB-69 was authorized in 1940 as a *Montana*-class battleship. The class was suspended in 1942, and she was never built.

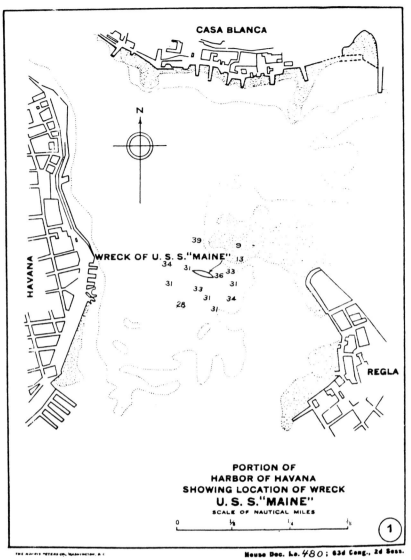

CASA BLANCA

N

WRECK OF U. S. S."MAINE"

39
9
13
34   31
36   33
31   33   31
33
28   31   34
31

HAVANA

REGLA

PORTION OF
HARBOR OF HAVANA
SHOWING LOCATION OF WRECK
U. S. S."MAINE"
SCALE OF NAUTICAL MILES

0   ⅛   ¼   ⅜

1

THE NORRIS PETERS CO., WASHINGTON, D. C.   House Doc. No. 480 ; 63d Cong., 2d Sess.

On Dec. 6, 1897, the *Maine* was assigned to the North Atlantic Squadron stationed at Key West, Florida. As tensions mounted in Cuba in January 1898, American consul general in Havana, Fitzhugh Lee requested an American warship to "show off the flag" in Cuba. He soon rescinded the regiment but the ship had already left Key West. On Jan. 25, the *Maine* entered Havana's harbor. On Feb. 15 at 9:40 p.m., she blew up, taking the lives of two officers, 230 sailors and 28 Marines. Eight survivors would later die.

Interior of the middle of amidship superstructure, looking across ship from port side entrance to the main deck.

Salvage of the guns and small items was carried on until the outbreak of war in April 1898. For the next 13 years the wreck was undisturbed. In 1910 Congress appropriated money to raise the wreck and remove it to deeper water. The only way to do this was to place a cofferdam around the wreck, remove the water, repair the hull to make it float, refloat it and tow it out to sea. The cofferdam was about 350 by 170 feet and would be unwatered to nearly 50 feet. Twenty cylinders of the dam were made of interlocking steel sheet pilings and set nearly tangent to each other interconnected by short arms with a three-way pile in each. On Feb. 13, 1912, water poured into the dam until the *Maine* was afloat, then two cylinders were dismantled and the wreck was floated out and attached to the outside of the dam. A month later she was towed out to sea and sunk.

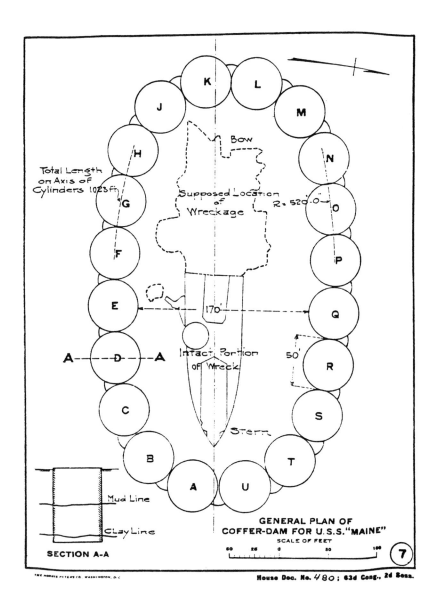

General view from pilot house of *Barnard*, looking aft at water level.

Looking aft from front of bow.

Starboard aft, main deck, showing superstructure containing captain's quarters after cleaning off mud and shell deposits.

Looking forward from top of cofferdam at water level.

Amidship wreckage, starboard side. Top and forward end of A side armor plate is visible under the wreckage at forward end of the standing superstructure, pushed out to starboard at water level.

General view looking aft.

Memorial services for 66 additional victims of the *Maine*, held on the quarterdeck of the *USS North Carolina* (CA-12) on March 16, 1912, at the site of the sinking of the *Maine*, four miles off Havana. USN NH 46795

The Sept. 2, 1911, issue
of *Scientific American* had
a story on the raising of
the *Maine.*

Bottom photo: The *USS Maine*
being scuttled off Havana, March
16, 1912. USN NH 46791

On Feb. 11, 1911, a ceremony was
held at the cofferdam site to honor
the *Maine* victims. EAC

Report of the Court of Inquiry

{
"United States Steamship *Iowa.*
First Rate.
Key West, Florida, Monday, March 21, 1898.

After full and mature consideration of all the testimony before it the court finds as follows:

1. That the United States battleship *Maine* arrived in the harbor of Havana, Cuba, on the 25th day of January, 1898, and was taken to buoy No. 4, in from five and one-half to six fathoms of water, by the regular government pilot. The United States Consul-General at Havana had notified the authorities at that place the previous evening of the intended arrival of the *Maine.*

2. The state of discipline on board the *Maine* was excellent, and all orders and regulations in regard to the care and safety of the ship were strictly carried out. All ammunition was stowed in accordance with prescribed instructions, and proper care was taken whenever ammunition was handled. Nothing was stowed in any one of the magazines or shell-rooms which was not permitted to be stowed there. The magazines and shell-rooms were always locked after having been opened, and after the destruction of the *Maine* the keys were found in their proper place in the Captain's cabin, everything having been reported secure that evening at 8 p.m.

The temperature of the magazines and shell-rooms was taken daily and reported. The only magazine which had an undue amount of heat was the after 10-inch magazine, and that did not explode at the time the *Maine* was destroyed. The dry gun-cotton primers and detonators were stowed in the cabin aft, and remote from the scene of the explosion. Waste was carefully looked after on the *Maine* to obviate danger. Special order in regard to this had been given by the commanding officer. Varnishers, dryers, alcohol and other combustibles of this nature were stowed on or above the main deck, and could not have had anything to do with the destruction of the *Maine.*

The medical stores were stowed aft under the wardroom, and remote from the scene of the explosion. No dangerous stores of any kind were stowed below in any of the other store rooms.

The coal bunkers were inspected daily. Of those bunkers adjacent to the forward magazines and shell-rooms, four were empty, namely: 'B3, B4, B5, B6.'

'A15' had been in use that day, and 'A16' was full of New River coal. This coal had been carefully inspected before receiving it on board. The bunker in which it was stowed was accessible on three sides at all times, and the fourth side at this time on account of bunkers 'B4' and 'B6' being empty. This bunker, 'A16,' had been inspected that day by the engineer officer on duty. The fire-alarms in the bunkers were in working order, and there had never been a case of spontaneous combustion of coal on board the *Maine.* The two after boilers of the ship were in use at the time of the disaster, but for auxiliary purposes only, with a comparatively low pressure of steam, and being tended by a reliable watch. These boilers could not have caused the explosion of the ship. The four forward boilers have since been found by the divers, and are in a fair condition.

On the night of the destruction of the *Maine* everything had been reported secure for the night at 8 p.m. by reliable persons, through the proper authorities, to the commanding officer. At the time the *Maine* was destroyed the ship was quiet, and therefore least liable to accident caused by movements from those on board.

3. The destruction of the *Maine* occurred at 40 minutes past nine in the evening of the 15th day of February 1898, in the harbor of Havana, Cuba, she being at the time moored to the same buoy to which she had been taken upon her arrival. There were two explosions of a distinctly different character, with a very short, but distinct interval between them, and the forward part of the ship was lifted to a marked degree at the time of the first explosion. The first explosion was more in the nature of a report, like that of a gun; while the second explosion was more open, prolonged, and of greater volume. This second explosion was, in the opinion of the court, caused by the partial explosion of two or more of the forward magazines of the *Maine.*

The evidence bearing upon this, being principally obtained from divers, did not enable the court to form a definite conclusion as to the condition of the wreck, although it was established that the after part of the ship was practically intact, and sank in that condition a very few minutes after the destruction of the forward part. The following facts in regard to the forward part of the ship are, however, established by the testimony.

4. That portion of the port side of the protective deck which extends from about frame 30 to frame 41 was blown up aft and over to port. The main deck

from about frame 30 to frame 41 was blown up aft and slightly over the starboard, folding the forward part of the middle superstructure over and on top of the after part. This was, in the opinion of the court, caused by the partial explosion of two or more of the forward magazines of the *Maine*.

5. At frame 17, the outer shell of the ship, from a point 11-1/2 feet from the middle line of the ship, and six feet above the keel when in its normal position, has been forced up so as to be now about four feet above the surface of the water; therefore, about 34 feet above where it would be, had the ship sunk uninjured. The outside bottom-plating is bent into a reversed V-shape, the aft wing of which, about 15 feet broad and 30 feet in length (from frame 17 to frame 25) is doubled back upon itself against the continuation of the same plating extending forward.

At frame 18 the vertical keel is broken in two, and the flat keel bent into an angle similar to the angle formed by the outside bottom-plating. This break is now about six feet above its normal position.

In the opinion of the court this effect could have been produced only by the explosion of a mine situated under the bottom of the ship at about frame 18, and somewhat on the port side of the ship.

6. The court finds that the loss of the *Maine*, on the occasion named, was not in any respect due to fault or negligence on the part of any of the officers or members of the crew of said vessel.

7. In the opinion of the court the *Maine* was destroyed by the explosion of a submarine mine, which caused the partial explosion of two or more of her forward magazines.

8. The court has been unable to obtain evidence fixing the responsibility for the destruction of the *Maine* upon any person or persons.

W.T. Sampson, Captain U.S.N., President.
A. Marix, Lieutenant-Commander U.S.N.,
Judge-Advocate.

The court, having finished the inquiry it was ordered to make, adjourned at 11 a.m. to await the action of the convening authority.

W.T. Sampson, Captain U.S.N., President.
A. Marix, Lieutenant-Commander U.S.N.,
Judge-Advocate.

U.S. Flagship *New York*, off Key West, Fla., March 22, 1898.

The proceedings and findings of the Court of Inquiry in the above case are approved.

M. Sicard, Rear Admiral,
Commander-in-Chief of the United States
Naval Force on the North Atlantic Station."

John Henry "Dick" Turpin (1876-1962) was the U.S. Navy's first black Chief Petty Officer (CPO) and one of the Navy's best-known characters for many years. Turpin enlisted in the Navy in 1896 and survived the explosions of the *USS Maine* (1898) and the *USS Bennington* (1907). He qualified as a master diver and was appointed chief gunners mate on the *USS Marblehead* in 1917. He transferred to the Fleet Reserve in 1919 and retired as a Chief Gunners Mate in October 1925. From 1938 through World War II, he voluntarily made inspirational visits to naval training centers and defense plants. When not on active duty, Turpin worked as a master rigger at the Puget Sound Naval Shipyard. USN NH 89471

Prelude to War

SPEAKER REED TO McKINLEY —"Will, you've got to bank the fire some way or other; I can't hold in this steam much longer."—Minneapolis Tribune.

Following the destruction of the *Maine*, Speaker Reed cooperated with President McKinley in preventing Congress from making a precipitate declaration of war. The picture represents the dome of the capitol with the Speaker and the President vainly trying to keep down the war sentiment.

War Revenues.

Congress proposes to get money to carry on the war from two sources, taxing and borrowing. The taxes, with one exception, are an affair of internal revenue, the duties on foreign goods being considered to be at present as high as it is expedient to make them. The entire sum to be raised by internal revenue taxation will be something over $90,000,000. It is to come from fermented liquors, tobacco and stamp taxes. Beer will be taxed $2 a barrel instead of $1. The tax on beer will bring in, it is expected, $40,000,000. The added taxes on tobacco are expected to produce $20,000,000.

Third, there is the stamp tax. This will mean that deeds, drafts, wills, checks, mortgages and legal documents generally, insurance policies, telegrams, express receipts, patent medicines, perfumery, cosmetics, etc., must have a stamp affixed for which a sum of from 1 cent to $20 has been paid. The stamp tax is expected to bring to the government $30,000,000.

The one exception to the raising of the war tax from domestic sources is the proposed tonnage duty. This would mean that all foreign vessels bringing goods and passengers to the United States should pay a tax of 20 cents per ton of their capacity. Many are of opinion, however, that it would be far wiser to drop this feature of the revenue bill. Foreign vessels arriving in American ports already pay a light tonnage duty. The first effect of the mere proposal to levy such a tax caused an irritation against us in Europe, particularly in Germany, where we are accused of trying by this tax to make European nations pay the expenses of our war with Spain. We want the sympathies of the European powers at present, and it will not be well to alienate them by a petty tonnage tax, especially as it will raise only $2,000,000, a sum not worth irritating even Emperor William for. A tax on tea and coffee may come later.

Army Numbers

On April 1, 1898 the U.S. Army had 2,143 officers and 26,040 enlisted men. They were stationed in 80 posts around the country, but mainly in the West. On April 15, 1898, 10 days before war was declared the bulk of the army was ordered to proceed to camps in Georgia, Louisiana, Alabama and Florida. On April 23, President McKinley called for 125,000 volunteers and on May 25 for an additional 75,000. Congress authorized an increase of the Regular Army to 61,000. By the end of the war in August, the Regular Army numbered 56,365, the Volunteer Army 207,244 — a total of 263,609.

Casualties

During the war 23 officers and 257 enlisted men were killed; 113 officers and 1,464 enlisted men wounded. Between May 1 and September 30, deaths from all causes (battle, sickness, accident) were 207 officers and 2,803 enlisted men — a total of 2,910, a little over one percent of the total in service.

President William McKinley

President William McKinley was born in Niles, Ohio, on Jan. 29, 1843, the seventh child in a family of nine children. His parents William and Nancy were of Scotch-Irish ancestry.

The McKinley's remained in Niles until William was nine when the family moved to Poland, Ohio. In 1860 William entered Allegheny College in Meadville, Pennsylvania, but he left the same year because of poor health. He returned to Poland and taught school and later became an assistant postmaster.

He was working in the post office when the Civil War began and in June 1861 he enlisted in the 23rd Ohio Volunteer Infantry. This was also the regiment of Rutherford B. Hayes, later president of the United States. McKinley saw action at Antietam and in the new state of West Virginia. In March 1865 he was promoted to brevet major and was offered a commission to stay in the army.

At age 22 however, he decided to study law and enrolled in the Albany Law School and was admitted to the Ohio Bar in 1867, He settled in Canton, Ohio, to practice and lived with his sister, Anna. In 1869 he was elected the Stark County prosecuting attorney.

In 1871 he married Ida Saxton, daughter of a local banker. It was a marriage marred by tragedy as both of their daughters died at an early age. Mrs. McKinley became a lifelong invalid but her husband's devotion was ever-lasting.

McKinley ran for Congress in 1876, won the election, and served for 14 years. He was voted out of office in 1890 but won election as Ohio's governor the next year. In 1896 the governor's friends led by industrialist Mark Hanna worked to get him nominated for the Republican presidential race against the Democratic candidate, William Jennings Bryan. Garret A. Hobart of New Jersey was McKinley's running mate.

As President, McKinley proved skillful in dealing with Congress. The economy improved after the panic of 1893. In July 1898 he signed the Congressional resolution approving the annexation of Hawaii and at the end of the Spanish American War presided over a world-wide colonial empire. He promoted "sound money" policies and secured passage of the Gold Standards Act of 1900. He also sent the

Eighteen-year-old Pvt. William McKinley of Co. E, 23rd Ohio Volunteer Infantry. Probably taken at Camp Case, Ohio, prior to leaving for service in western Virginia.

William McKinley
United States President
1897-1901

U.S. Marines to China to put down the Boxer Rebellion.

He was renominated for president in 1900 and took Governor Theodore Roosevelt as his running mate. He again ran against Bryan and was reelected by a wide margin.

On Sept. 6, 1901, the president was at the Pan American Exposition in Buffalo, New York, shaking hands with a long line of people. A man approached whose hand was wrapped with a handkerchief. He fired two shots at the president with a pistol from his concealed hand. The president was taken to a private home where he died eight days later. His assassin, Leon F. Czolgogz, was a neurotic anarchist who said that he wanted "to kill a ruler." It is ironic that the assassin had been working in a nail factory in Charleston, West Virginia, the same city that McKinley was stationed at for a time during the Civil War. William McKinley, the 25th president of the United States is buried in Canton, Ohio.

McKinley Historic Sites:

* The McKinley National Memorial, Canton, Ohio
* The McKinley National Birthplace Memorial, Niles, Ohio
* The Saxton-Barber House, Canton, Ohio

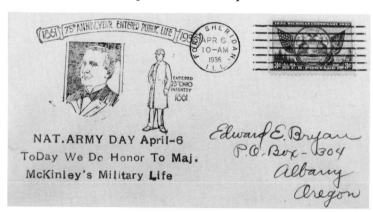

7th Cavalry attending McKinley's memorial service in Havana, 1901. USAMHI

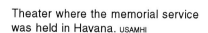

Theater where the memorial service was held in Havana. USAMHI

FEELING IN SPAIN THAT CUBA IS LOST

Right of the United States to Intervene Apparently Recognized

Although Every One Seems to Feel the Country Is Being Forced to War and Is Determined That America's Victory Shall Be Dearly Won.

[SPECIAL CABLE TO THE HERALD.]

The HERALD'S European edition publishes the following from its correspondent:—

MADRID, Monday.—All eyes are directed toward Washington to-day. It is felt that the Cuban question has entered upon its last stage and that the chance for a peaceful solution is a very slender one—namely, whether the House stands firm and keeps to its non-committal attitude or allows itself to be influenced by the example of the Senate.

Change in Public Sentiment.

The extent of progress that has been made in the way this nation regards the question is shown by the fact that now the resolution of Congress is felt still to leave a loophole for a peaceful settlement, whereas only a short time ago such a resolution would have been looked upon as equivalent to a declaration of war. This change in sentiment has been further helped by the speeches of Senators Wellington and White.

One of the Ministers said to me to-day:—"We are particularly gratified by the way Spain is spoken of by several Senators. We regard it as an indication that opinion in the United States is not quite undivided, and we feel that if the counsels of the moderate minded could only prevail peace might be maintained even yet."

This reflection may be fully taken to mean that the essential points of difference between the two governments are capable of a satisfactory adjustment if the counsels of President McKinley are followed, and that all America could justifiably demand would certainly be accorded.

The mere fact that negotiations would not necessarily be broken off after the decision of Congress admits America's right to intervene.

This being conceded clears the ground immensely, and with the chance of peace an inducement this government would spare no efforts to remove the grievances of the United States.

There really is no bellicose feeling here in administration circles. Neither is the feeling a sullen one in bowing to the inevitable. It seems, however, to be felt that war is being forced on the country, and that it could not be avoided no matter what sacrifices were made.

Every one appears to realize that Spain's actual hold on Cuba is lost, but at the same time the people are united in a determination to cling to the sentimental bond that still exists between the mother country and the island. I do not think any one really hopes to keep that bond intact should war break out, but all are determined to make the victory of America a dearly purchased one.

MADRID DESPERATE AND LOSES HOPE.

MADRID, Monday.—The sentiment here is one of resigned desperation and this is so strongly pronounced in the Cabinet that if America only leaves a loophole for a dignified retreat there is no doubt that an agreement would be come to in the briefest possible time.

The fear, however, that such a loophole will be finally denied them has begun to invade every breast.

The Bourse has kept fairly steady to within a week, but the last few days has sagged badly, and to-day witnessed a veritable slump.

A member of the Cabinet, speaking about the rate of exchange, said:—"This means ruin if it continues."

The prices of imported articles in the shops have been increased to-day.

CRUISERS DETAILED TO GUARD COAST

Patrol Squadron Organized with Commodore Howell in Command and the San Francisco as His Flagship.

NEW YORK TO BE ITS HEADQUARTERS.

Fleet Will Include the Auxiliary Cruisers Yosemite, Prairie, Yankee and Dixie.

TO PROTECT THE CITIES.

Will Sail Out to Meet Any Spanish Vessel Which Approaches Ports on the Atlantic.

OTHER SQUADRONS FOR OFFENCE

Naval Militia of Four States Will Man the Auxiliary Cruisers, Which Are Being Hurriedly Fitted.

HERALD BUREAU,
CORNER FIFTEENTH AND G STREETS, N. W.,
WASHINGTON, D. C., Monday.

Seaports of the Atlantic coast of the United States are to be protected by a third squadron formed to-day by orders issued by Secretary Long.

This squadron has been officially designated "The Patrol Squadron," and its commander in chief will be Commodore J. A. Howell, formerly commander in chief of the European station. The cities of the coast which will be provided with protection by this force may thank Captain A. S. Crowninshield, Chief of the Bureau of Navigation, for its formation, for it was he that so strongly urged upon the department the necessity of keeping Commodore Howell afloat with a command which would enable him to prevent any cruisers of the Spanish navy from attempting to destroy property along the coast.

The final decision to organize the fleet was reached at a conference between the Secretary and the Chief of the Bureau of Navigation to-day, although it had been a matter of considerable discussion for several days.

WARRING CONGRESS DECLARES FOR WAR.

Final Action, Making It Mandatory Upon the President to Demand from Spain Her Immediate Withdrawal from Cuba, Seems to Leave No Escape from Hostilities.

MR. M'KINLEY WILL SIGN THE RESOLUTION ADOPTED.

FINAL ACTION OF CONGRESS MEANS WAR.

Resolution Adopted Declares the Cuban People Free, Calls on Spain to Withdraw at Once and Directs Armed Intervention by the President.

NO RECOGNITION OF THE INSURGENTS.

TROOPS ON THEIR WAY TO THE GULF.

Entire Available Military Force of the United States Will Be En Route for Mobilization in the South To-day.

MILES WILL TAKE PERSONAL COMMAND.

Interest of Congress in the Army Reorganization Bill Aroused by Current Agitation.

TO BE INTRODUCED IN HOUSE.

It Will Empower the President to Recruit the Regular Army to Double Its Present Strength.

MAY RETIRE GENERAL CUSHING.

Chief Commissary General of Subsistence Incompetent for Service Because of Illness.

NEW BILL FOR A STANDING ARMY.

Measure To Be Introduced Into Congress Which Would Make the Executive Independent of the Individual States.

PRESIDENT'S POWER OVER NEW TROOPS.

They Would Be Organized on the Model of the Regulars and Could Be Ordered Abroad.

DESIGNATED AS A MILITIA.

But Not To Be Confounded with the National Guards, Whose Prerogatives Will Remain.

SENATE AT LAST YIELDS TO HOUSE.

Gives Up Its Amendment Recognizing the Independence of the Insurgent Government of Cuba.

RADICAL SENATORS CALL FOR ACTION.

Declare Their Willingness to Give Up Convictions for the Sake of Preventing Any Further Delay in the Settlement of the Question.

The President's Message

"For some time prior to the visit of the *Maine* to Havana harbor our Consular representatives pointed out the advantages to flow from the visit of national ships to Cuban waters, in accustoming the people to the presence of our flag as the symbol of good will, and of our ships in the fulfillment of the mission of protection to American interests, even though no immediate need therefore might exist.

"Accordingly on the 24th of January last, after a conference with the Spanish Minister, in which the renewal of visits of our war vessels to Spanish waters was discussed and accepted, the peninsular authorities at Madrid and Havana were advised of the purpose of this government to resume friendly naval visits to Cuban ports, and that, in that view, the *Maine* would forthwith call at the port of Havana. This announcement was received by the Spanish government with appreciation of the friendly character of the visit of the *Maine*, and with notification of an intention to return the courtesy by sending Spanish ships to the principal ports of the United States. Meanwhile the *Maine* entered the port of Havana on the 25th of January, her arrival being marked with no special incident besides the exchange of customary salutes and ceremonial visits.

"The *Maine* continued in the harbor of Havana during the three weeks following her arrival. No appreciable excitement attended her stay; on the contrary, a feeling of relief and confidence followed the resumption of the long-interrupted friendly inter- course. So noticeable was this immediate effect of her visit that the Consul-General strongly urged that the presence of our ships in Cuban waters should be kept up by retaining the *Maine* at Havana, or in the event of her recall, by sending another vessel there to take her place.

"At 40 minutes past nine on the evening of the 15th of February, the *Maine* was destroyed by an explosion, by which the entire forward part of the ship was utterly wrecked. In this catastrophe two officers and 264 of her crew perished; those who were not killed outright by her explosion being penned between decks by the tangle of wreckage and drowned by the immediate sinking of the hull. Prompt assistance was rendered by the neighboring vessels anchored in the harbor, aid being especially given by the boats of the Spanish cruiser, *Alphonse XII*, and the Ward Line steamer, *City of Washington*, which lay not far distant. The wounded were generously cared for by the authorities of Havana, the hospitals being freely opened to them, while the earliest recovered bodies of the dead were interred by the municipality in a public cemetery in the city. Tributes of grief and sympathy were offered from all official headquarters of the island.

"The appalling calamity fell upon the people of our country with crushing force, and for a brief time an intense excitement prevailed, which, in a community less just and self-controlled than ours, might have led to hasty acts of blind resentment."

This stereograph photo of President McKinley was the first one ever taken of a president in the White House. This photo is even more unusual as it was taken on Feb. 15, 1898, only a few hours before word was received that the *Maine* had been destroyed in Havana Harbor. McKinley would be the first president since Lincoln to bear the burden of a major war and he resisted involvement as long as he could. Unfortunately, the country was geared up for war, mainly through the media, and in April McKinley would finally declare war against Spain.

War Declared Between the United States and Spain*

On April 20th the United States government presented its ultimatum to Spain to, before noon on April 23rd, relinquish authority and government in the island of Cuba and withdraw both land and naval forces from Cuba and Cuban waters. Spain protested and refused compliance, and at once our North Atlantic squadron was ordered to Cuban waters to blockade Havana and other port cities.

At noon on April 23rd the President issued his proclamation calling for 125,000 men for service in the military and naval forces of the government in the war with Spain. It is as follows:

"Whereas, by a joint resolution of Congress, approved on the 20th day of April 1898, entitled 'Joint resolution for the recognition of the independence of the people of Cuba, demanding that the government of Spain relinquish its authority and government in the island of Cuba, and withdraw its land and naval forces from Cuba and Cuban waters, and directing the President of the United States to use the land and naval forces of the United States to carry this resolution into effect,' and,

"Whereas, by an Act of Congress entitled 'An Act to provide for temporarily increasing the military establishment of the United States in time of war and for other purposes,' approved April 22, 1898, the President is authorized, in order to raise a volunteer army, to issue this proclamation calling for volunteers to serve in the army of the United States.

"Now therefore, I, William McKinley, President of the United States, by virtue of the power vested in me by the constitution and the laws, and deeming sufficient occasion to exist, have thought it fit to call forth, and hereby do call forth, volunteers to the aggregate number of 125,000, in order to carry into effect the purpose of the said resolution; the same to be apportioned, as far as practicable, among the several states and territories and the District of Columbia, according to population, and to serve for two years, unless sooner discharged. The details for this object will be immediately communicated to the proper authorities through the War Department.

"In witness whereof, I have hereunto set my hand and caused the seal of the United States to be affixed.

"Done at the City of Washington this twenty-third day of April, A.D. 1898, and of the independence of the United States the one hundred and twenty-second.
"By the President: WILLIAM MCKINLEY.
    "JOHN SHERMAN, Secretary of State."

---

*Spain declared war on the United States on April 23. Two days later the United States responded with its formal declaration of war against Spain, stating that she had been at war since April 21.

Secretary of War Russell A. Alger was born in Ohio in 1836. He studied law and was admitted to the bar in 1859. He enlisted as a private in 1861 and by the close of the war was brevetted brigadier general and major general of volunteers. He settled in Michigan after the war and was elected governor in 1885 and commander of the Grand Army of the Republic in 1889. He served as Secretary of War from March 5, 1897, to Aug. 1, 1899. Alger was criticized for the inadequate and inefficient preparation, and inefficient operation of his department during the war and resigned at the request of President McKinley. He served in the Senate from 1903 until his death in 1907.

National Guard Strength in 1898

STATE	OFFICERS	MEN	TOTAL
Alabama	252	2,236	2,488
Arizona	224	1,796	2,020
California	299	3,610	3,909
Colorado	81	975	1,056
Connecticut	187	2,552	2,739
Delaware	47	411	458
Florida	94	1,040	1,134
Georgia	390	3,151	3,541
Idaho	40	468	508
Illinois	421	5,839	6,260
Indiana	205	3,670	3,875
Iowa	234	2,236	2,470
Kansas	110	1,353	1,463
Kentucky	120	1,251	1,371
Louisiana	197	2,496	2,693
Maine	98	1,247	1,345
Maryland	147	1,578	1,725
Massachusetts	339	4,815	5,154
Michigan	177	2,721	2,898
Minnesota	132	1,762	1,894
Mississippi	195	1,600	1,795
Missouri	158	2,191	2,349
Montana	52	580	632
Nebraska	95	1,063	1,158
Nevada	31	337	368
New Hampshire	115	1,190	1,305
New Jersey	343	3,954	4,297
New York	839	13,055	13,894
North Carolina	154	1,383	1,537
North Dakota	55	412	467
Ohio	415	5,589	6,004
Oregon	118	1,310	1,428
Pennsylvania	671	7,850	8,521
Rhode Island	155	1,160	1,315
South Carolina	464	2,663	3,127
South Dakota	63	633	696
Tennessee	104	1,592	1,696
Texas	284	2,739	3,023
Utah	75	505	580
Vermont	86	657	743
Virginia	216	2,523	2,739
Washington	82	655	737
West Virginia	100	865	965
Wisconsin	199	2,512	2,711
Wyoming	33	323	356

In the territories and the District of Columbia likewise there were organized forces:

TERRITORIES	OFFICERS	MEN	TOTAL
Arizona	50	489	539
New Mexico	63	559	622
Oklahoma	53	494	547
District of Columbia	134	1,137	1,271

Making the aggregate of the National Guard and organized militia as follows:

Commissioned officers	9,196
Enlisted men	105,227
Total	114,423

States	Men Available
Alabama	165,000
Arkansas	250,000
California	214,029
Colorado	85,000
Connecticut	108,646
Delaware	28,080
Florida	70,000
Georgia	264,021
Idaho	20,000
Illinois	750,000
Indiana	500,000
Iowa	294,874
Kansas	100,000
Kentucky	361,137
Louisiana	135,000
Maine	106,042
Maryland	150,000
Massachusetts	433,975
Michigan	260,000
Minnesota	175,000
Mississippi	233,480
Missouri	400,000
Montana	31,381
Nebraska	101,926
Nevada	6,200
New Hampshire	34,000
New Jersey	385,273
New York	800,000
North Carolina	245,000
North Dakota	19,937
Ohio	650,000
Oregon	59,522
Pennsylvania	878,394
Rhode Island	85,000
South Carolina	177,000
South Dakota	55,000
Tennessee	180,000
Texas	300,000
Utah	35,000
Vermont	44,164
Virginia	364,227
Washington	89,879
West Virginia	125,000
Wisconsin	372,152
Wyoming	8,000
Territories and Districts—	
Arizona	20,000
New Mexico	25,000
Oklahoma	50,000
District of Columbia	47,000
Total unorganized	10,301,339
Total organized	114,362
Grand Aggregate	10,415,701

TELEGRAPH OPERATOR.   GENERAL MILES.   MR. PORTER, PRESIDENT'S SECRETARY.
                    SECRETARY LONG.   PRESIDENT McKINLEY.
        CAPTAIN CROWNINSHIELD.   MILITARY AIDE.
    SECRETARY ALGER.

THE WAR ROOM IN THE WHITE HOUSE.

Painted by
George Gibbs.

President McKinley and his Cabinet in 1898. Left to right: McKinley; Secretary of the Treasury Lyman Gage; Attorney General John Griggs; Secretary of the Navy John Long; Secretary of Agriculture James Wilson; Secretary of the Interior Cornelius Bliss; Postmaster General Charles Smith; Secretary of War Russell Alger and Secretary of State William Day.

HARPER'S WEEKLY

A JOURNAL OF CIVILIZATION

Vol. XLII.—No. 2159
Copyright, 1898, by Harper & Brothers.
All Rights Reserved.

NEW YORK, SATURDAY, MAY 7, 1898.

TEN CENTS A COPY.
FOUR DOLLARS A YEAR.

RECRUITING FOR THE WAR IN NEW YORK CITY.—DRAWN BY T. DE THULSTRUP.

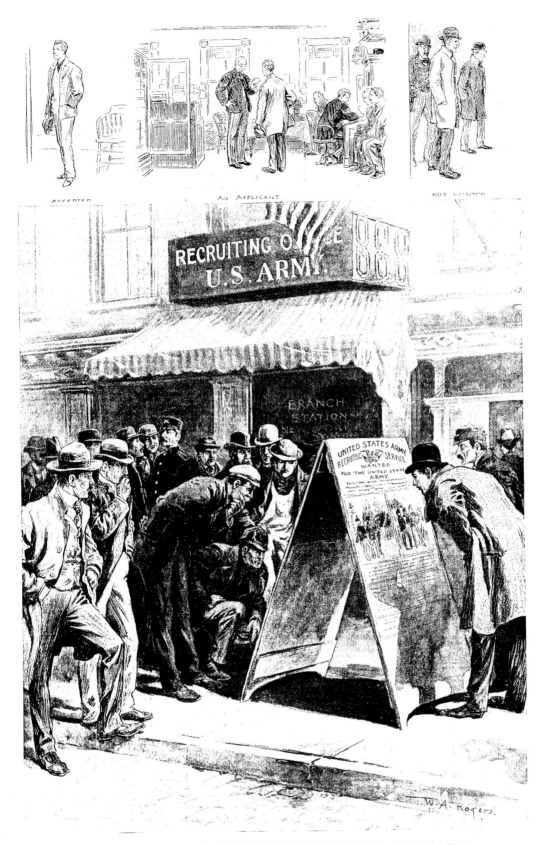

ACCEPTED   AN APPLICANT   NOT WANTED

INCREASING THE ARMY—SCENES AT A RECRUITING-OFFICE IN NEW YORK.—Drawn by W. A. Rogers.

An unusual recruiting effort on the streets of New York using a woman waving flags in front of a military band. BA

The War with Spain was something American's were scrambling to get into. Men were afraid they'd be left behind, or that they'd get to Cuba too late to see action. Some regiments actually fought on the wharf in Tampa Bay; those with the hardest knuckles went up the gangways and claimed the transport/ship. Just before the 1st Montana Infantry went to San Francisco to prepare for action in the Philippines, one chap offered $100,000 to any private who'd give up his place and let him go instead. Then, there was Private McFadden who was a half-inch shorter than the regs allowed. He had a section hand give him a solid whack on the top of his head. The increase in height gained him a headache and a place in the ranks.

Recruiting volunteers on the streets of New York for the New York National Guard. BA

A potential enlistee scans a recruiting poster in New York City. The rush to volunteer was compared to earlier gold rushes and prompted William Allen White of Kansas to write: "In April, everywhere over this good fair land, flags were flying.....at the stations crowds gathered to hurrah for the soldiers, and to throw hats into the air, and to unfurl flags....."

It was reported that eight of the 30 graduating class from the University of Tennessee had enlisted, and 14 of the 44 Seniors at the University of Maine had enlisted.

The destruction of the *Maine* threatened war with Spain and raised a number of problems with the U.S. Navy. As the Navy began to build a modern steel and steam fleet in the 1880s, it ignored all but essential warships despite innovations in both naval technology and warfare that required auxiliary crafts.

Atlantic coastal cities clamored for protection against feared bombardment by Spanish raiders, yet the U.S. Navy had only a dozen Civil War era monitors available to defend the seaboard from Maine to Florida. In addition, operations to blockade or invade Cuba, and perhaps cross the ocean to attack Spain, required many more ships than the Navy could muster.

Congressional appropriation on March 9 of a $50 million emergency fund for the national defense enabled the Navy to purchase the needed ships. In total the Navy purchased or leased over 100 warships and auxiliaries between March 16 and Aug. 12, 1898.

Various yachts, tugs, pilotboats and small steamships were purchased for harbor defense, minelaying and scouting. In addition, naval operations in the Caribbean and Pacific Ocean areas required transports, coal ships and other supply vessels. These ships became known as the "Mosquito Fleet" or the Navy's auxiliary force.

The Spanish Navy, which was feared at the start of the war, proved to be no match for America's front-line warships. The U.S. Navy's two main battles in Manila and Santiago basically set the tone for the war, both in the Caribbean and the Philippines. The Spanish suffered from a lack of will and leadership as well as obsolete equipment.

The Saga of the USS New York

The flagship of Rear Admiral Sampson's fleet blockading Santiago was the 380-foot, 8,200-ton, armored cruiser *New York*. It was commissioned in 1893. Just before 9 a.m. on July 3, 1898, Sampson ordered the ship to leave her station temporarily and head east toward Siboney, where he was to meet with General Shafter. Thirty-five minutes later, just as the *New York* slipped over the horizon, the Spanish fleet attempted to break out of the blockade. The *New York* turned around and steamed back toward Santiago to engage the enemy, but the other ships of the blockading fleet destroyed the enemy fleet quickly, thus depriving Sampson and his flagship of participating in the victory. The *New York* had a distinguished career afterwards, but never had another chance for glory like the one she missed on July 3, 1898. It is ironic that she ended up in the former Spanish possession of Subic Bay, Philippines, where she was scuttled on Dec. 24, 1941, to prevent her being captured intact by the Japanese. The masthead of the ship had been salvaged earlier and is on display at the Intrepid Sea·Air·Space Museum in New York City.

Navies of Spain and the United States

The *Vesuvius* or "dynamite cruiser" was an experimental ship that had on board three forward-firing 15-inch pneumatic guns. These used air pressure to fire shells filled with dynamite. The low speed and unreliability of the new technology finally relegated the ship to service as a harbor defense ram.

THEODORE ROOSEVELT
ASST. SECRETARY

A-11

NAVY DEPARTMENT.

WASHINGTON.

March 25, 1898.

Sir:

Mr. Walcott, Director of the Geological Survey, has just been in to see me, having seen the President. He has shown me some interesting photographs of Professor Langley's flying machine. The machine has worked. It seems to me worth while for this government to try whether it will not work on a large enough scale to be of use in the event of war. For this purpose I recommend that you appoint two officers of scientific attainments and practical ability, who in conjunction with two officers appointed by the Secretary of War, shall meet and examine into this flying machine, to inform us whether or not they think it could be duplicated on a large scale, to make recommendation as to its practicability and prepare estimates as to the cost.

I think this is well worth doing.

This board should have the power to call in outside experts like R. H. Thurston, President Sibley College, Cornell University, and Octave Schanute, President of American Society of Civil Engineers, at Chicago.

Very respectfully,

T. Roosevelt

Assistant Secretary.

The Honorable,

The Secretary

This extraordinary letter was written by then assistant secretary of the Navy, Theodore Roosevelt on March 25, 1898, one month before war was declared and a little over five years before the Wright Brothers made the first successful airplane flight. Professor Samuel P. Langley was a pioneer in American aeronautics.

USS Oregon (BB-03)

Oregon's 13-inch gun that destroyed the *Vizcaya* at Santiago.

USS Oregon (BB-03). USN NH 44467

In February 1898, the *USS Oregon* (BB-03) was on the West Coast guarding San Francisco and San Diego. On March 19, the ship was ordered to steam, as fast as possible, to join the North Atlantic fleet. In a remarkable feat of naval history, the *Oregon* logged 15,000 nautical miles, from San Francisco to Key West around the tip of South America in just 66 days, at an average speed of 12 knots. Fifty-eight days were logged at sea. The ship joined the blockading fleet of Commodore John C. Watson before Havana. She then joined the blockade before Santiago with the rest of the North Atlantic fleet. The *Oregon* saw some service in World War I and became a museum in Oregon in 1925. She was ordered scrapped in 1942 but was turned into an ammunition transport. She was towed to the Central Pacific in 1944 and beached at Guam where she was sold for scrap in 1956.

Ex-*USS Oregon* (1X-22) being scrapped at Kawasaki, Japan, in September 1956. USN NH 3007

Ships of the American and Spanish Navies

AMERICAN NAVY
FIRST RATE

NAME	DISPLACEMENT (TONS)	GUNS IN MAIN BATTERY	HULL
Iowa	11,340	18	Steel
Indiana	10,288	16	Steel
Massachusetts	10,288	16	Steel
Oregon	10,288	16	Steel
Brooklyn	9,215	20	Steel
New York	8,200	18	Steel
Columbia	7,375	11	Steel
Minneapolis	7,375	11	Steel
Texas	6,315	8	Steel
Puritan	6,060	10	Iron
Olympia	5,870	14	Steel

SECOND RATE

Chicago	4,500	18	Steel
Baltimore	4,413	10	Steel
Philadelphia	4,324	12	Steel
Monterey	4,084	4	Steel
Newark	4,098	12	Steel
San Francisco	4,098	12	Steel
Charleston	3,730	8	Steel
Miantonomoh	3,990	4	Iron
Amphitrite	3,990	6	Iron
Monadnock	3,990	6	Iron
Terror	3,990	4	Iron
Lancaster	3,250	12	Wood
Cincinnati	3,213	11	Steel
Raleigh	3,213	11	Steel
Atlanta	3,000	8	Steel
Boston	3,000	8	Steel

THIRD RATE

Hartford	2,790	13	Wood
Katahdin	2,155	4	Steel
Ajax	2,100	2	Iron
Canonicus	2,100	2	Iron
Mahopac	2,100	2	Iron
Manhattan	2,100	2	Iron
Wyandotte	2,100	2	Iron
Detroit	2,089	10	Steel
Montgomery	2,089	10	Steel
Marblehead	2,089	10	Steel
Marion	1,900	8	Wood
Mohican	1,900	10	Wood
Comanche	1,875	8	Iron
Catskill	1,875	2	Iron
Jason	1,875	2	Iron
Lehigh	1,875	2	Iron
Montauk	1,875	2	Iron
Nahant	1,875	2	Iron
Nantucket	1,875	2	Iron
Passaic	1,875	2	Iron
Bennington	1,710	6	Steel
Concord	1,710	6	Steel
Yorktown	1,710	6	Steel
Dolphin	1,486	2	Steel
Wilmington	1,392	8	Steel
Helena	1,392	8	Steel
Adams	1,375	6	Wood
Alliance	1,375	6	Wood
Essex	1,375	6	Wood
Enterprise	1,375	4	Wood
Nashville	1,371	8	Steel
Monocacy	1,370	6	Iron
Thetis	1,250	*	Wood
Castine	1,177	8	Steel
Machias	1,177	8	Steel
Alert	1,020	3	Iron
Ranger	1,020	6	Iron
Annapolis	1,000	6	Comp
Vicksburg	1,000	6	Comp
Wheeling	1,000	6	Comp
Marietta	1,000	6	Comp
Newport	1,000	6	Comp

FOURTH RATE

Vesuvius	929	3	Steel
Yantic	900	4	Wood
Petrel	892	4	Steel
Fern	840	*	Wood
Bancroft	839	4	Steel
Michigan	685	4	Iron
Pinta	550	2	Iron

TORPEDO BOATS

1 – Cushing	105	3	Steel
2 – Ericsson	120	3	Steel
3 – Foote	142	3	Steel
4 – Rodgers	142	3	Steel
5 – Winslow	142	3	Steel
6 – Porter	***	3	Steel
7 – DuPont	***	3	Steel
8 – Rowan	182	3	Steel
9 – Dahlgren	146	2	Steel
10 – T.A.M. Craven	146	2	Steel
11 – Farragut	273	2	Steel
12 – Davis	132	3	Steel
13 – Fox	132	3	Steel
14 – Morris	103	3	Steel
15 – Talbot	46-1/2	2	Steel
16 – Gwin	46-1/2	2	Steel
17 – Mackenzie	65	2	Steel
18 – McKee	65	2	Steel
19 – Stringham	340	2	Steel
20 – Goldsborough	247-1/2	2	Steel
21 – Bailey	235	2	Steel
– Stiletto	31	2	Wood

TUGBOATS

Fortune	450	*	Iron
Iwana	192	*	Iron
Leyden	450	*	Iron
Narkeeta	192	*	Steel
Nina	357	*	Iron
Rocket	187	*	Wood
Standish	450	1	Iron
Traffic	280	*	Wood
Triton	212	*	Steel
Waneta	192	*	Steel
Unadilla	345	*	Steel
Samoset	225	*	Steel

NAME	DISPLACEMENT (TONS)	GUNS IN MAIN BATTERY	HULL
SAILING SHIPS			
Monongahela	2,100	4	Wood
Constellation	1,186	8	Wood
Jamestown	1,150	*	Wood
Portsmouth	1,125	12	Wood
Saratoga	1,025	*	Wood
St. Mary's	1,025	*	Wood
RECEIVING SHIPS			
Franklin	5,170	4	Wood
Wabash	4,650	*	Wood
Vermont	4,150	*	Wood
Independence	3,270	6	Wood
Richmond	2,700	2	Wood
UNSERVICEABLE			
New Hampshire	4,150	6	Wood
Pensacola	3,000	*	Wood
Omaha	2,400	*	Wood
Constitution	2,200	4	Wood
Iroquois	1,575	*	Wood
Nipsic	1,375	4	Wood
St. Louis	830	*	Wood
Dale	675	*	Wood
Minnesota	4,700	9	Wood
UNDER CONSTRUCTION			
Kearsarge	11,525	22	Steel
Kentucky	11,525	22	Steel
Illinois	11,525	18	Steel
Alabama	11,525	18	Steel
Wisconsin	11,525	18	Steel
Princeton	1,000	6	Comp
Plunger	168	2	Steel
Tug No. 6	225	*	Steel
Tug No. 7	225	*	Steel
Training ship	1,175	6	Comp

SPANISH NAVY
FIRST-CLASS BATTLESHIPS

NAME	DISPLACEMENT (TONS)	GUNS IN MAIN BATTERY	HULL
Pelayo	9,900	22	Steel
Vitoria (inefficient)	7,250	**	Iron
OLD BATTLESHIPS			
Numancia	7,250	10	Iron
FIRST-CLASS ARMORED CRUISERS			
Carlos V.	9,235	28	Steel
Cisneros	7,000	24	Steel
Cataluna	7,000	24	Steel
Princess Asturias	7,000	24	Steel
Almirante Oquendo	7,000	30	Steel
Maria Teresa	7,000	30	Steel
Vizcaya	7,000	30	Steel
Cristobal Colon	6,840	40	Steel
SECOND-CLASS ARMORED CRUISERS			
Alfonso XIII	5,000	19	Steel
Lepanto	4,826	25	Steel
UNARMORED CRUISERS			
Reina Cristina	3,520	21	Steel
Aragon	3,342	24	Steel
Castilla	3,342	22	Steel
Navarra	3,342	16	Steel
Alfonso XII	3,090	23	Steel
Reina Mercedes	3,090	21	Steel
Velasco	1,152	7	Steel
C. de Venadito	1,130	13	Steel
Ulloa	1,130	12	Steel
Austria	1,130	12	Steel
Isabel	1,130	15	Steel
Isabel II	1,130	16	Steel
Isla de Cuba	1,030	12	Steel
Isla de Luzon	1,030	12	Steel
Ensenada	1,030	13	Steel
Quiros	315	**	Iron
Villabolas	315	**	Iron
- - -	935	5	Wood

TORPEDO BOATS
Armed with two and four torpedo tubes, six quick-fire and two machine guns.

NAME	DISPLACEMENT (TONS)	GUNS IN MAIN BATTERY	HULL
Alvaro de Bezan	830	**	Steel
Maria Molina	830	**	Steel
Destructor	458	**	Steel
Filipinas	750	**	Steel
Galicia	571	**	Steel
Marques Vitoria	830	**	Steel
Marques Molina	571	**	Steel
Pinzon	571	**	Steel
Nueva Espana	630	**	Steel
Rapido	570	**	Steel
Temerario	590	**	Steel
Yanez Pinzon	571	**	Steel

GUNBOATS

NAME	DISPLACEMENT (TONS)	GUNS IN MAIN BATTERY	HULL
Hernon Cortes	300	1	Steel
Pizarro	300	2	Steel
Nunez Balboa	300	1	Steel
Diego Velasquez	200	3	Steel
Ponce de Leon	200	3	Steel
Alvarado	100	2	Steel
Sandoval	100	2	Steel

TORPEDO BOAT DESTROYERS

NAME	DISPLACEMENT (TONS)	GUNS IN MAIN BATTERY	HULL
Audaz	400	6	Steel
Furor	380	6	Steel
Terror	380	6	Steel
Osada	380	6	Steel
Pluton	380	6	Steel
Prosperina	380	6	Steel

SMALL TORPEDO BOATS

NAME	DISPLACEMENT (TONS)	GUNS IN MAIN BATTERY	HULL
Ariete	**	*	Steel
Rayo	**	*	Steel
Azor	**	*	Steel
Halcon	**	*	Steel
Habana	**	*	Steel
Barcelo	**	*	Steel
Orion	**	*	Steel
Retamosa	**	*	Steel
Ordonez	**	*	Steel
Ejercito	**	*	Steel
Pollux	**	*	Steel
Castor	**	*	Steel
Aire	**	*	Steel
General Concha	520	*	Steel
Elcano	524	*	Steel
General Lego	524	*	Steel
Magellanes	524	*	Steel

The fourth ship named *Baltimore* (Cruiser No. 3) was launched in 1888 by William Cramp and Sons of Philadelphia. She was commissioned in 1890 and became the flagship of the North Atlantic Squadron in May. For the next six years, she cruised the Atlantic, Pacific and Mediterranean areas until placed out of commission on Feb. 17, 1896, at Mare Island in California. Recommissioned on Oct. 12, 1897, she sailed for Hawaii. Later, she joined Dewey's squadron at Hong Kong and participated in the Battle of Manila Bay on May 1, 1898. She remained on the Asiatic Station conveying transports and protecting American interests until May 1900. In 1907, the ship again went out of commission. Placed back in service in 1911, *Baltimore* served as a receiving ship at the Charleston Navy Yard. In 1914, she was converted to a minelayer and recommissioned in 1915. During World War One, she operated off the coast of Ireland and in 1919, joined the Pacific Fleet. In 1922 she was again decommissioned and placed at Pearl Harbor, Hawaii, where she was located during the Dec. 7, 1941, attack. In 1941 she was sold for scrap.

Typical sailors of the U.S. Navy in the 1890s. MNG

The cruiser *Nashville* of the North Atlantic squadron, headquartered at Key West, fired the first shot of the war. When the fleet was 12 miles from Sand Key Light, which lies seven miles southeast of Key West, the *Nashville* sighted a Spanish vessel. Admiral Sampson signaled from the *New York* for the *Nashville* to capture the enemy ship. The *Buena Ventura*, with a crew of 30 was bound from Pascagoula, Mississippi, to Rotterdam, Holland, with a cargo of lumber, cattle and miscellaneous freight. The *Nashville* bore down on the Spanish ship and fired a blank shot from her port guns aft, but the ship did not stop. A second solid shot was fired close to her bow and the Spanish ship immediately stopped. She was taken back to Key West, the first prize of the war. Gunner Michael Mallia had the distinction of firing the first shot of the war.

The *Brooklyn* (AC-3) was commissioned in 1896. She became flagship of Commodore Schey's Flying Squadron in March 1898. She was a key vessel in the Battle of Santiago. She was struck 20 times by whole shot with only one sailor wounded. In December 1899, the ship became flagship of the Asiatic Squadron and participated in the North China Relief Expedition. After many cruises around the world, she went into reserve in 1907. She was recommissioned in 1914 and until 1921 sailed in the Pacific waters. In 1921, she was decommissioned and sold for scrap.

The *Massachusetts* (BB-2) was commissioned in 1895. She took part in the Cuban blockade but missed the Battle of Santiago Bay on July 3 while coaling at Guantanamo Bay. On July 4, she helped force the *Reina Mercedes* to surrender and then supported the occupation of Puerto Rico. After service in World War One, she served as a target ship off Pensacola, Florida. In 1925, she was offered for sale as scrap, but no acceptable bids were received and in 1956 the State of Florida took over the remains. USN NH73767

The *Texas* was commissioned in 1895. She was part of the Cuban blockade fleet and patrolled between Santiago and Guantanamo Bay in June. She took part in the Battle of Santiago Bay, firing on four of Spain's main ships and two torpedo-boat destroyers. In late July, *Texas* returned to New York and a great reception. She served as flagship for the Coast Squadron until 1905 and became the station ship at Charleston, South Carolina. In 1911, her name was changed to *San Marcos* and she was sunk as a target ship. USN NH63506

Terror (Monitor No. 4) was an iron-hulled, twin-screw, double-turreted monitor. She was laid down in 1874 but not completed until 1896. She was sunk in the 1920s.

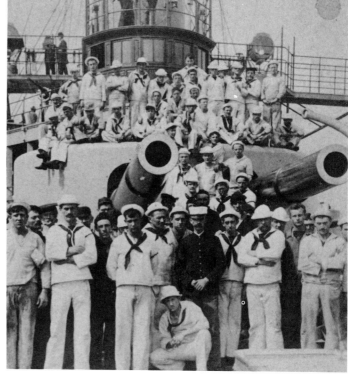

Iowa sailors pose on the 12-inch gun turret.

The Iowa (BB-04) was commissioned in 1897. She was ordered to blockade duty and on July 3, she was the first to sight the Spanish ships and fired the first shot in the Battle of Santiago. In a 20-minute battle with the Maria Teresa and Oquendo, her effective fire set both ships on fire and drove them to the beach. After sinking several more ships, she received on board Admiral Cervera and the officers and crews of the Vizcaya, Furor and Pluton. She was decommissioned in 1908 and recommissioned in 1910 as a sea training ship and served in that capacity during World War One. In 1919, she was renamed Coast Battleship No. 4, and was the first radio-controlled target ship to be used in a fleet exercise. She was sunk in 1923. USN NH739976

The USS Iowa (ex-BB-04) under fire by battleship guns, while in the last phase of her target service off Panama, March 22, 1923. The ship was sunk as a result of this shelling. USN NH96027

The *Eugenia* was a steel-hulled, single-screw schooner built in 1897, purchased by the Navy in 1898 and renamed *USS Siren*. She participated in the Cuban blockade and on Aug. 2, captured the Norwegian ship, *Franklin*, with a cargo of provisions headed for the Spanish. She also assisted in the captured of another Norwegian ship, the *Berzen*. *Siren* was struck from the Navy list in 1910.

The *Dixie*, a screw steamer, was built in 1893 as *El Rio*, purchased by the Navy in 1898, and converted to an auxiliary cruiser. She was attached to the Eastern Squadron, North Atlantic Fleet and served on blockade duty and helped capture several towns in Puerto Rico. She was decommissioned in 1922. EAC

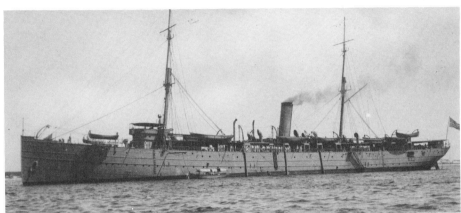

The *Helena* (PG-9) was commissioned in 1897. She saw action several times off Cuba. On July 2 and 3, she exchanged fire with enemy batteries at Fort Tunas. On July 18 she was part of the squadron which closed the port of Manzanillo by sinking eight small vessels. She also took part in the Philippine Insurrection and was struck from the Navy list in 1932.
USN NH53698

The *Relief* was built as the steel passsenger liner *John Englis* and purchased by the Army in 1898 for service as a hospital ship. It was transferred to the Navy in 1908 and served with the Great White Fleet cruise. After suffering severe damage in a typhoon near the Philippines she remained in that country until World War Two. USN NH92845

The *USS San Francisco*, a steel protected cruiser, was commissioned in 1890. She became the flagship of the North Atlantic Squadron in 1893 and in 1898, she patrolled off Florida and Cuba. During World War One she was converted to a minelayer and decommissioned in 1921. She was renamed *Tahoe* and then *Yosemite* and was finally scrapped in 1939. EAC

The *Minneapolis* (C-13) was commissioned in 1894. In April, she was dispatched for scouting duty in the West Indies, searching for the Spanish fleet as far as the coast of Venezuela. She returned to the Santiago area on May 19 and then to Key West. She was a training ship and after duty in World War One was decommissioned in 1921. EAC

The *USS Marblehead*, an unarmored cruiser, was commissioned in 1894. On May 11, 1898, she cut the cables off Cienfuegos and then patrolled off Santiago. On June 7, she captured the lower bay of Guantanamo and supported the landing of the Marines there. She helped destroy the Spanish fort of Cayo del Toro on June 15. She was decommissioned in 1920. USN NH47159

The *USS Saint Paul* was launched in 1895 as a steel passenger liner and converted to an auxiliary cruiser on April 20, 1898. Her captain was Charles Sigsbee from the *USS Maine*. She captured the British colier, *Restormel*, bound for Cuba on May 25 and took part in the naval action off of San Juan, Puerto Rico in June. She spent the remainder of the war as a transport and was used again as a transport in World War One. She was scrapped in 1923. USN NH59924

CAPTAIN A. T. MAHAN.   CAPTAIN A. S. CROWNINSHIELD.   JOHN D. LONG, SECRETARY OF THE NAVY.   REAR-ADMIRAL MONTGOMERY SICARD.

THE NAVAL STRATEGY BOARD IN CONSULTATION AT WASHINGTON.

Painted by T. V. Chominski, from a photograph by Barte & Pullis.

U.S. Naval Reservists at Port Tampa. Fifteen states had naval reserve or militia units. Approximately 4,500 served during the war with 2,600 on board ship. They provided most of the crews for the auxiliary cruisers *Yankee, Dixie, Yosemite, Badger, Rosolute* and *Prairie*.

U.S. Army engineers at Tampa's harbor paddling a canvas pontoon boat. MNHS #61407

Office of Naval Intelligence

After the *Maine* blew up at Havana, the Navy Department began negotiations for the purchase of ships and munitions of war from abroad. The negotiations were conducted through the naval attachés in Europe and through commercial agents in Washington.

The activities of the naval attachés, in addition to the purchase of war material, were devoted principally to reporting the movements of the Spanish squadrons of Admirals Cervera and Camara. The attachés also established and maintained a corps of special agents. The attaché reports were forwarded to the Office of Naval Intelligence (ONI) and formed a special information report series. The series was destroyed after the war because the reports contained much data that would have been compromising to the special agents (some of whom were in high positions in Spain) had the contents—and thus the agents' identities—ever been made public.

At the time of the sinking of the *Maine*, several ONI staff officers had already been ordered to sea duty without replacement. When Congress declared war on Spain on April 25, there remained in ONI four officers plus a retired ensign. Capt. John R. Bartlett, USN (ret.), reported on May 1 as the relief for the Chief Intelligence Officer, Cdr. Richardson Clover.

On the day after the declaration of war, ONI was transferred from the office of the Assistant Secretary back to the Bureau of Navigation by order of the Secretary.

On April 5, Ens. Arthur B. Hoff was assigned as an Assistant Naval Attaché, London, in order to aid in the extensive arrangements being undertaken by the attachés in both London and Paris to purchase ships and material in anticipation of war with Spain.

The Naval War Board was established on the day war was declared. Capt. Alfred Thayer Mahan was ordered back to active duty on the same day and reported to the board on May 9. Assistant Secretary Theodore Roosevelt was a member of the board until he severed his connection with it on May 9 and resigned as Assistant Secretary on the 10th. Rear Adm. Montgomery Sicard was president of the board. The other member was Capt. Arent S. Crowninshield, Chief of the Bureau of Navigation.

The Naval War Board was the outgrowth of an informal advisory board that had existed for some time. It was the duty of the board to advise the Secretary of the Navy about the Navy Department's strategic policy. ONI's responsibility to the board was to make available information from its files about the defenses of Cuba, Puerto Rico, and the Philippines, as well as the location of the principal ships of the Spanish fleet. During the approximately five months of war, the amount of intelligence information furnished by ONI to the Naval War Board was reported by Captain Bartlett to equal that furnished to all the bureaus of the Department of the Navy combined.

As of July 1, 1898, following successive detachments of officers to sea duty, there remained in ONI only one retired captain and one retired ensign, plus the usual borrowed clerks and messengers. Retired Capt. John R. Bartlett on July 9 was also ordered to additional duty to relieve Rear Adm. Henry Erben, USN (ret.), as Chief of the United States Auxiliary Naval Forces. Bartlett, with Lt. H.L. Satterlee as his assistant, operated the Auxiliary Naval Forces headquarters from ONI spaces in the State, War and Navy Building. Captain Bartlett also continued to serve as superintendent of the Coast Signal Service, a position he had held prior to becoming Chief Intelligence Officer.

During the war, it became apparent that the Navy had a critical need for a qualified observer of naval affairs in the Far East. This situation was rectified on Sept. 10, 1898, when Lt. Albert L. Key was ordered as naval attaché to the U.S. legations at Tokyo and Peking.

Troops Transported by Sea April 1–Sept. 15, 1898			
To Cuba	28,195	From Cuba	21,686
To Puerto Rico	17,460	From Puerto Rico	5,541
To Manila	16,405	Civilian employees	2,920
To Honolulu	629	Total	92,836

The *Gloucester*, formerly J. Pierpont Morgan's yacht *Corsair*, was built in 1891 and acquired by the Navy on April 23, 1898. She participated in the Battle of Santiago and on July 25, she entered the harbor before the fleet at Guanica, Puerto Rico, and, captured the place for the army. On Aug. 1, with the assistance of *Wasp*, she took possession of Arroyo, Puerto Rico. The ship was decommissioned in 1905 and struck from the Navy list in 1919. USN NH53600

The *USS Prairie*, an auxiliary cruiser was built in 1890 as a Morgan liner *S.S. El Sol*. She was purchased by the Navy on April 6, 1898, and served in Cuban waters. After service in World War One, she was struck from the Navy list in 1922. USN NH44056

Alfred Thayer Mahan was America's most influential naval historian and naval philosopher. He graduated from the Naval Academy in 1859 and saw service in the Civil War. He was a prolific writer on naval affairs and served as president of the Naval War College. He retired in 1896 but was recalled to active duty in 1898 to serve on the Naval Board of Strategy. He was promoted to rear admiral on the retired list in 1906. His writings had a profound effect on the navies and their strategies in many countries. Mahan died in 1914. USN NH48054

U.S. Navy Ships Named for People or Places of the Spanish American War Period

Anderson (DD-411), named for Edwin A. Anderson Jr., of the *USS Marblehead,* commissioned in 1939, and sponsored by Mrs. Mertie Anderson, Edwin's widow. Sunk at Bikini Atoll in 1946.

Bagley (Torpedo Boat No. 24), launched in 1900, sponsored by Mrs. Josephus Daniels, sister of Ensign Bagley, Commissioned in 1901 and decommissioned in 1919.

Bagley (DD-185), launched in 1918, sponsored by Mrs. Adelaide Worth Bagley, mother of Ensign Bagley. Commissioned in 1919, transferred to Great Britain and decommissioned in 1944 (?).

Bagley (DD-386), launched in 1936, sponsored by Miss Bella Worth Bagley, sister of Ensign Bagley. Commissioned in 1937 and decommissioned in 1946.

Bernadow (DD-153), named for John Baptiste Bernadow, commander of the *USS Winslow* at Cardenas, Cuba. Commissioned in 1919, sponsored by the commander's sister, Miss Cora Winslow Bernadow. She was decommissioned and sold in 1945.

Blue (DD-387), named for Victor Blue a naval intelligence officer in Cuba. He died on the *USS Juneau* in November 1942 off Guadalcanal. Commissioned in 1937, sponsored by Victor's sister Miss Kate Lilly Blue. In August 1942 she sunk off Guadalcanal.

Blue (DD-744), commissioned in 1944, co-sponsored by Mrs. J.S. Blue and Miss Eleanor Stuart Blue, widow and daughter of Victor Blue.

Clark (DD-361), named for Charles E. Clark, commander of the *USS Oregon.* Commissioned in 1936 and decommissioned in 1945.

Dewey (DD-349), launched in 1934, sponsored by Miss A.M. Dewey, great-grandniece of Admiral Dewey. Commissioned in 1934 and decommissioned in 1945.

Dewey (D16-14), launched in 1958 and commissioned in 1959.

Evans (DD-78), named for Robley D. Evans, commander of the *USS Iowa* and the Great White Fleet, 1907-08. Commissioned in 1918, sponsored by Evans' granddaughter Mrs. D.H. Sewell and decommissioned in 1944.

Evans (DD-552), commissioned in 1943 and decommissioned in 1945.

Gridley (DD-92), commissioned in 1919, sponsored by Mrs. Francis P. Thomas, Gridley's daughter. Decommissioned in 1946.

Gridley (DD-380), commissioned in 1937, sponsored by Mrs. Lewis Buddy III, another of Gridley's daughters. Decommissioned in 1946.

Hobson (DD-464), launched in 1941, sponsored by Jrs. R.P. Hobson, widow of Rear Admiral Hobson. Commissioned in 1942.

Lamberton (DD-119), named for Benjamin P. Lamberton, chief of staff of the *Olympia.* Commissioned in 1918, sponsored by Lamberton's granddaughter, Miss Isabell Lamberton. Decommissioned in 1946.

Leonard Wood (AP-25), built in 1922 as a transport. She was purchased by the U.S. Army in 1939 and the U.S. Navy in 1941. She sailed in support of British outposts in the Far East in 1941-42 and was converted to an attack transport in 1943 as APA-12. She took part in the North African and Sicilian campaigns and the Pacific campaigns in the Gilbert and Marshall Islands, Saipan, Leyte, Lingayen Gulf, Angaur Island and Mindoro Island. She was decommissioned in 1946 and scrapped in 1948.

Mahan (Destroyer No. 192), launched in 1918, sponsored by Miss Ellen K. Mahan, niece of Rear Adm. A.T. Mahan. Commissioned in 1918 and decommissioned in 1930.

Mahan (DD-364), launched in 1934, sponsored by Miss Kathleen H. Mahan, great-granddaughter of Rear Adm. A.T. Mahan. Commissioned in 1936 and sunk off Leyte in 1944.

Manila Bay (CVE-61), launched and commissioned in 1943. After extensive service in the Pacific during World War II, she was decommissioned in 1946 and sold for scrap in 1959.

Roosevelt (a three-masted schooner, built for Arctic service), launched in 1905, she was altered to ocean tug duties in 1923. She was abandoned in 1942.

Sampson (DD-63), launched and commissioned in 1916. Sold for scrap in 1936.

Sampson (DD-394), launched and commissioned in 1936. She was decommissioned in 1945.

Sampson (DDG-10), launched in 1960 and commissioned in 1961.

Schley (Destroyer No. 99), launched and commissioned in 1918. She was decommissioned in 1945 and scrapped in 1946.

Selfridge (DD-320), launched in 1919, sponsored by Mrs. Catherine Kellond granddaughter of Rear Adm. Selfridge. She was commissioned in 1921, decommissioned in 1930 and scrapped in 1931.

Siboney (ID-2999), formerly the *S.S. Oreinte,* a combination cargo and passenger vessel, she was launched in 1917. The Navy acquired her in 1918 and renamed her. Converted to an Army hospital ship in 1944, she was scrapped in 1957.

Sigsbee (DD-502), launched in 1942 and commissioned in 1943. She was decommissioned in 1947.

Theodore Roosevelt (CVN-71), a Nimitz-class aircraft carrier was commissioned in 1984.

The Soldiers and Civilians

Members of the 2nd Nebraska Volunteer Infantry posed before their tent at Camp Thomas in August 1898. WYOMING STATE ARCHIVES

Well-known novelist and sports writer, Damon Runyon was a private with the 1st Colorado Volunteer Infantry in the Philippines.

A "Buffalo Soldier" Hero

George Barry was a First Sergeant with Troop D, Tenth Cavalry. Under heavy fire, 50 feet in advance of his comrades on San Juan Hill, he planted two flags, one of the Tenth and one of the Third Cavalry, upon the works of the Spanish defenders. He had spent 30 years in the army fighting the Cheyennes, Kiowas, Arapahoes, Commanches, Apaches and Utes all over the West. He retired from the service on Nov. 1, 1898, at Huntsville, Alabama.

After the December 1890 Battle of Wounded Knee in South Dakota, the Indian Wars were officially over. With this ending and the panic of 1893, the Regular Army was reduced to a force of between 26,000 and 28,000 men. Except for the localized wars in the west with the Indians, the nation had been at peace for over 30 years.

With the sinking of the *Maine* in February 1898, a general mobilization was begun for a possible war with Spain. This was no easy task for a nation at peace for three decades and as Russell Alger, the Secretary of War stated: "The government machinery was altogether inadequate to meet the emergency."

As it turned out the three-month war was fought mainly with volunteer troops from the states and territories.

Noted orator and statesman, William Jennings Bryan was appointed colonel of the Third Nebraska Volunteer Regiment and was stationed at Camp Cuba Libre. Here he is shown with Gen. Fitzhugh Lee. The regiment, known as the "Silver Regiment," remained at camp throughout the war.

"The Spaniards call us 'Negro Soldados' and say there is no use shooting at us, for steel and powder will not stop us. We only hope our brethren will come over and help us to show to the world that true patriotism is in the minds of the sons of Ham. All we need is leaders of our own race to make war records, so that their names may go down in history as a reward for the price of our precious blood.
M.W. Saddler
First Sergeant, Co. D
25th Infantry"

Blacks in the War

Black troops had made a name for themselves in the period between the end of the Civil War and the 1890s as the "Buffalo Soldiers."

Thousands of blacks served in the Union Army during the Civil War and afterwards, became members of the regular army and provided more than half the troops for the Indian wars of the 1860s, '70s and '80s.

The Indians dubbed the black troopers "Buffalo Soldiers" because their tightly curled hair resembled that of the buffalo. It was also meant as a compliment, since the buffalo was respected by the Indian as a proud, brave and strong animal.

Organized into four regiments—the 9th and 10th Cavalry formed in 1866 and the 24th and 25th Infantry formed in 1868—they performed so admirably on the frontier that they earned 18 Medals of Honor. As seasoned troops, they had the lowest desertion rate in the army.

Considering the discrimination and racial hostility that was prevalent in the country at the time, especially in the South, the "Buffalo Soldiers" are even more deserving of respect.

One such soldier was Charles Young, who in 1889 became the third black to graduate from West Point. He served in the western campaigns and began his rise to colonel in 1917, the highest ranking black officer at the time. He saw action in the Spanish American War and the Mexican border crisis. He also served in Haiti as America's first black military attaché.

In 1917, he was forced to retire on medical grounds. Young fought to be reinstated but was recalled to duty with less than a week of World War One left. On a second tour of duty in Liberia in 1922, he became ill and died. He is buried in Arlington National Cemetery.

The 25th Infantry was the first regular army unit to be activated for war service and left its post at Fort Missoula, Montana, for Camp Thomas. The regular army units who took part in the Cuban and Philippines campaigns proved themselves very capable soldiers. Several units participated in the battles around Santiago.

Several of the black volunteer regiments gained notoriety but in a somewhat negative vein.

The Ninth United States Volunteer Infantry under the command of Col. Charles J. Cane was mustered in at New Orleans between June 18 and July 16, 1898. It sailed to Cuba on Aug. 17, arriving on Aug. 22, thus missing all the action there.

During its time in Cuba, the Ninth was stationed at San Juan Hill, San Luis, Songo, Cristo, El Cobre, Palma Sariano and Mayari. Gen. Leonard Wood, who was senior commander in the area at the time, said that he wanted it and the other black units brigaded together and out of the way for fear of trouble.

The Ninth was the recipient of probably more ill-treatment by the press than any other regiment in the war. This was in spite of the fact that Colonel Cane maintained the discipline of his men was superior to that of the other black regiments in Cuba.

A few of the regiment's members were involved in a drunken incident at San Luis in which some native military policemen were killed. Although the news reports of the time list no other disciplinary shortcomings among the Ninth or the other units of the black brigade, the dispatches from Cuba began to commonly include the words "riot" and "mutiny." Some of the more moderate press, realizing the damage being done, sought to disassociate these black volunteers from the black units of the regular army. This editorial appeared in the Nov. 17, 1898, issue of the *Boston Journal*:

"It must not be thought that the bright record of the colored regiments in this war with Spain is sullied by the misbehavior of the colored troops who have mutinied in their camp near Santiago. These miscreants, who, in drunken rage, have quarreled with and killed several of General Wood's Cuban military policemen, belong to a command that, from the first, has been disorderly and inefficient. It is one of the so-called 'immune' regiments, the Ninth U.S. Volunteers, raised in the cotton and sugar belt about the lower Mississippi. These men were hurried off to Cuba with scant opportunity for drill or discipline, and they proved so worthless that General Wood promptly drove them out of Santiago....The regiment itself had not been long enough together to develop any esprit de corps. The breakdown of its helter-skelter discipline at Santiago was...inevitable."

During the time that the culprits went uncaptured and unpunished the outcry for justice grew. This editorial in the Nov. 19, 1898, issue of the *Boston Globe* comes right to the point:

"The behavior of our colored volunteer soldiers in Cuba has been such that...the exemplary hanging of a few of them...who can be proved to be offenders might probably be the means of saving many lives later on."

The hyperbole of the Cuban independence press was picked up and amplified by some American newspapers. While there was no sympathy shown toward the radical proposal as described, its very publication shows the proportions the story had reached:

"The failure of the Americans to arrest and punish the Negro soldiers who were involved in the fatal shooting affair at San Luis ten days ago has led to a great deal of talk among the Cubans. Men who, two years ago, were in the United States recounting with horror stories of Spanish barbarity are demanding that, in the event of a failure to fix the guilt on the real perpetrators, the Americans shall summarily shoot ten out of every 100 of the black soldiers, the fate of the victims to be determined by the black bean method."

The unit returned from Cuba on April 20, 1899, and all remaining troops were discharged from the army on May 25.

Members of the 9th and 10th Cavalry at Camp Wikoff, Long Island, New York, in September 1898. The trooper in the background is holding a non-regulation keyed trumpet, probably a personal item. Note the card players in the center. USAMHI

The 9th and 10th Cavalry at the Battle of Las Guásimas in support of the Rough Riders, June 24, 1898. A Kurz & Allison lithograph, 1898. LC-USZ62-134

General Benjamin O. Davis Sr.

The first black general military officer in U.S. history was the 20th American honored in the U.S. Postal Service's Black History Stamp Series on Jan. 28, 1997.

Benjamin O. Davis Sr. was born in Washington, D.C., in 1877. He began his 50-year military career in the D.C. National Guard on April 25, 1898, as a lieutenant in Co. D, First Separate Battalion. He joined the regular army as a temporary first lieutenant of the 8th U.S. Infantry on July 13, 1898. He was mustered out on March 8, 1899, and a few months later he enlisted as a private in Troop I, 9th Cavalry. On Feb. 2, 1901, he was commissioned a second lieutenant of cavalry in the Regular Army.

After service in the Philippines he advanced through the ranks to brigadier general (temporary) in 1940. He retired in 1941 but was recalled to active duty on Aug. 1, 1941, with the rank of brigadier general.

Through the years he served in a variety of posts including military attaché to Liberia and ROTC duties at several black colleges. He was assigned to Europe in 1942 as special duty Advisor on Negro Problems. In 1944, he became Special Assistant to the Commanding General, Communications Zone, ETO. In January 1946, he became Assistant, The Inspector General, U.S. Army and retired in 1948.

Davis died in 1970. His son Benjamin Jr. is a retired Air Force lieutenant general.

HEADQUARTERS SECOND DIVISION, THIRD CORPS,
Camp George H. Thomas, Chickamauga Park, Ga., June 3, 1898.
ADJUTANT-GENERAL UNITED STATES ARMY,
Washington, D.C.

SIR: I have the honor to report that there is at this date the following-named colored men, W.W. Ruby, Company A; James A. Paris, Company L, and Randolph Cushen, Company K, enlisted and serving as privates in the First Maine Infantry Volunteers.

I make this report under an interpretation of the law that colored men shall be assigned to colored regiments, and also from the fact that two affairs have come to my knowledge which are likely to grow into detrimental and serious obstacles to the well-being of the service.

As far as I am able to learn, the trouble has arisen between the First Maine and the Second Kentucky Infantry Volunteers, in camp contiguously, by reason of, in one instance, a colored soldier of the First Maine running the guard of the Second Kentucky; arrested, and attempted rescue by the men of the First Maine; the other an altercation between one of the colored soldiers of the First Maine and a sentinel of the Second Kentucky. A friction between the two regiments has thus been engendered and is likely to increase rather than subside. I am aware that the War Department, by the mingling of troops from all States of the Union, has done much to allay the prejudices of the former conflicting sections. In this division, now camped together, are regiments from Maine, New York, Kentucky, Missouri, Arkansas, and Mississippi, with none but the most amicable feeling toward each other excepting in the instances and cases here noted.

I respectfully recommend that the colored men herein mentioned be discharged from the military service or assigned to one of the colored regiments now in service.

I deem this a matter of great importance.

Very respectfully,

C.E. COMPTON,
Brigadier-General, U.S. Volunteers, Second Division, Third Corps.

The band of the 25th U.S. Infantry while stationed at Fort Missoula, Montana.
UNIVERSITY OF MONTANA ARCHIVES #B.I. J-4 ELROD COLL.

The 25th Infantry Regiment*

One of two black infantry regiments, the 25th was stationed at Fort Missoula, Montana, prior to being called up for duty on April 10, 1898. The year before, 20 members of the regiment participated in a historic bicycle trip from Missoula to St. Louis, Missouri, in an attempt to gain military approval for the two-wheeler, but the Spanish War put an end to this effort.

The 25th Infantry was sent south to train for war, acclimatize to the heat and humidity, and remain available for war service when they were needed. With the exception of Companies A and G, who were sent to train in Key West, Florida, the 25th Infantry transferred from Montana to Camp Thomas.

Adjustment to the South's heat and humidity while wearing wool and flannel uniforms probably was not nearly as difficult as conforming to its racist climate and Jim Crow laws. The soldiers were refused service in local businesses, and whites attempted to subject the men to the same laws they enforced on the local African-American population. One soldier summed up the situation, "It mattered not if we were soldiers of the United States and going to fight for the honor of our country, we were 'niggers,' as they called us, and treated us with contempt." The troops later departed for Tampa, Florida, and finally, embarked for Cuba on June 14,

1898, where a high percentage of the men suffered from dysentery and other diseases, and food was in short supply.

The 25th Infantry took particular pride in its role in the battle of El Caney. Under heavy fire, the men worked their way to the hilltop, where the stone fort of El Viso overlooked the town of El Caney. Stories vary as to who first reached the fort when the Spanish surrendered, but there is no doubt the 25th Infantry played a critical role in the surrender of the position. An image of the stone fort became part of the infantry's regimental coat of arms.

African-American soldiers were active in all of the Cuba campaigns, and they were commended for their courage and endurance. Their bravery and dedicated service were widely reported and at first, some believed the high praise they earned would result in better acceptance of African-Americans in society. Southern whites were appalled by the acclaim heaped on the soldiers and reacted with violence.

The 25th Infantry returned to the U.S. on Aug. 13, 1898. Following the war in Cuba, the companies were split up and assigned to posts in Arizona, New Mexico and Texas, but their stay in the Southwest was brief. Most of the regiment was sent to the Philippines during the summer of 1899, where they fought in the country's rebellion.

African-American soldiers now found themselves in the ironic position of fighting against the oppressed islanders, who sought independence from foreign rule. M.W. Saddler, a member of the 25th Infantry wrote, "We are now arrayed to meet a common foe, men of our own hue and color. Whether it is right to reduce these people to submission is not a question for a soldier to decide. Our oaths of allegiance know neither race, color, nor nation."

*Excerpted from Fort Missoula's Military Cyclists: The story of the 25th U.S. Infantry Bicycle Corps, by Linda C. Bailey, published by The Friends of the Historical Museum at Fort Missoula.

Col. James A. Moss served with the 25th U.S. Infantry. He was born in 1872 and graduated from West Point in 1894. During the Spanish American War he was recommended for two brevets for gallantry and meritorious conduct at the Battle of El Caney and was awarded the Silver Star. From 1899 to 1902, he saw service in the Philippines and was with the American Expeditionary Force in France during World War I. In 1922 he retired from active duty. He was founder and president general of the U.S. Flag Association and originator of Flag Week (now Flag Day, celebrated each June 14). He was killed in an auto accident in New York City in 1941.

John Philip Sousa

While John Philip Sousa's marches have been played for almost a century, the Spanish American War was the first war where they became part of the patriotic spirit of the populace.

Sousa was born in Washington, D.C., in 1854. After studying violin and harmony, he began his professional career at the age of 17, playing in theater and dance orchestras and touring with a variety show. In 1877 he played in Jacques Offenbach's orchestra when the famous French composer toured the United States. Soon afterward, Sousa wrote an operetta, *The Smugglers*, the first of many he wrote over the next 35 years.

Sousa was appointed leader of the U.S. Marine Band in 1880 and made it into one of the finest in the world. In 1892, he was discharged from the Marine Corps and formed his own band. He toured the world with the band, playing his famous marches and became known as the "March King."

Sousa's band planned for a European tour in 1898 or '99 but plans were dropped at the outbreak of the Spanish American War. The war motivated Sousa to compose a patriotic pageant called *The Trooping of the Colors*. The band made a tour of large cities, and the composition was used in conjunction with large choruses.

Sousa tried to reenlist in the Marine Corps but there wasn't a position open for him. He volunteered his services as bandmaster in the Sixth Army Corps, completely without pay, with the understanding he be permitted to complete two tours. He was recommended for a captains rank, but he was not destined to serve.

He became very sick after his second tour and almost died. By the time he recovered the war was over.

Because Sousa was known as the "March King," his band is often thought of as a marching band. Actually, it was a concert band that marched only seven times in its nearly four decades of existence. The band happened to be in Cleveland the morning of May 5 when Troop A of the Ohio National Guard departed for war. The band escorted them to the train station. On Sept. 11, they marched in the welcome home parade for the Eighteenth Regiment, Pennsylvania Volunteers and on Sept. 30, 1899, the band participated in the great victory parade in New York City for Admiral Dewey.

The Sousa Band marched only seven times in its 39-year history. On May 5, 1898, it escorted Troop A of the Ohio National Guard to the Cleveland train depot on its way to camp.

In 1900, the American writer Rupert Hughes wrote, "There is probably no other composer in the world with a popularity equal to that of Sousa." From 1917 to 1919, Sousa served as bandmaster for the United States Navy. He died in 1932.

His marches live on in history—"Semper Fidelis, The Washington Post, El Capitan, Thunderer, The High School Cadets, Liberty Bell, Manhattan Beach, Hands Across the Sea" and "The Stars and Stripes Forever."

1st Sgt. Henry A. Dobson (1878-1898), Co. D, 1st District of Columbia Volunteers. He died of typhoid fever at Camp Wikoff, Long Island, at 20 years of age. He found the key to the San Juan Hill blockhouse, which is now on display at the Henry B. Plant Museum, Tampa, Florida.

John Philip Sousa in the 1890s.

Famous short-story writer and novelist, Sherwood Anderson was born in Camden, Ohio, in 1876. He served in the army during the war. In 1912, he started writing and his most famous short-story was *Winesburg, Ohio*, written in 1919. Many critics consider him a symbol of the rejection of materialistic middle-class values for the values of art. He died in 1941. RUTHERFORD B. HAYES PRESIDENTIAL CENTER #4972

John J. (Black Jack) Pershing (1860-1948), commander of the American Expeditionary Forces (A.E.F.) during World War One was a first lieutenant with the 10th Cavalry during the Santiago campaign. He also served in the Philippines from 1899 to 1903.

Top right: Members of the Utah Volunteer Light Artillery from Bountiful, Utah. Middle: Battery B, Utah Volunteer Light Artillery. USHS #973.89, P. 22 & P. 21

Private Kirby of the 2nd Illinois Volunteer Infantry at Camp Cuba Libre. He is holding a Model 1884 .45-.70 Springfield rifle. Lower right: Typical volunteers of the 2nd Illinois Volunteer Infantry. The rifles are all Model 1884 .45-.70 Springfields. MRS. PAUL MILLER

Robert Winslow of Co. I, 1st Illinois Volunteer Infantry at Camp Thomas. He is holding a Model 1884 .45-.70 Springfield rifle. USAMHI

Charles Sutton, NCO of Co. L, 1st Montana Volunteer Infantry, in the Philippines. He has a Model 1879 .45-.70 Springfield rifle and is carrying a .45 Colt single-action Army revolver which was converted to a 5-1/2-inch barrel length (known as the Artillery Model). It was unusual to carry this weapon as it was not regular army issue. MHS

A letter from home. HOC

Volunteers in Cuba. They are holding Krag .30-.40 rifles which was unusual as most volunteers were issued the obsolete Model 1884 .45-.70 Springfield rifle. USAMHI

First Officer Killed in the War

The state of North Carolina had the unpleasant distinction of giving up two of her sons as the first killed in a war. Henry Wyatt from Edgecombe County was the first Confederate to be killed at the Battle of Big Bethel in 1861. Thirty-seven years later, Worth Bagley from Raleigh would be the first officer killed in the Spanish American War.

Bagley was born in Raleigh in 1874, the son of an ex-Confederate soldier whose daughter would marry Josephus Daniels, Secretary of the Navy under President Woodrow Wilson.

Bagley was appointed to the naval academy in 1889 at the age of 15, but had difficulty at his age with the curriculum. He also had a physical problem as the apex of his heart had shifted to the left about two inches due to violent exercise. As it turns out this exercise was actually from playing football for the academy team, where he was a star player.

He graduated in 1895 (after being readmitted in 1891) and the next year was posted to the *USS Maine*. On July 1, 1897, he was promoted to ensign and was assigned to his last ship, the torpedo boat *Winslow*, on which he was executive officer.

After America's entry into the war the *Winslow* sailed for Cuba where on May 11, 1898, she was engaged in action near Cardenas with three Spanish gunboats.

Bagley and four of the crew were killed by a Spanish shell. *The New York Times* in referring to the death of the first American officer in the war with Spain, ended with this paragraph:

"It is worthwhile also to remember that the South furnishes the first sacrifice of this war. Ensign Bagley was a native of North Carolina. With his blood he has sealed the union in arms of the North and South. A people who once fought against the Stars and Stripes send one of their sons as the first sacrifice for the honor and glory of that flag. There is no North and no South after that. We are all Worth Bagley's countrymen."

His monument stands in Raleigh. Three naval vessels have been named for him: A torpedo boat built in 1900 and sold in 1919, a destroyer built in 1918 and a destroyer built in 1937. The

Spanish American War Veterans Camp No. 2 in Raleigh was named for Bagley.

Above: Worth Bagley as a naval ensign, and below, in his naval academy football uniform. NORTH CAROLINA COLLECTION, U OF NC LIBRARY AT CHAPEL HILL

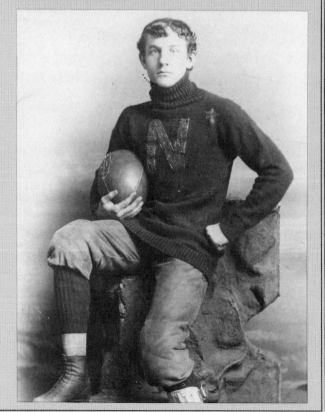

DEATH'S FIRST HARVEST IN THE AMERICAN FLEET.

Ensign Bagley and Four of Crew of the Winslow
Killed by a Shell While Seeking Spanish
Ships in Cardenas Harbor.

LITTLE TORPEDO DESTROYER OVERWHELMED BY MASKED GUNS.

Her Commander and Four Others Injured—Vessel Barely
Saved by Consort as She Drifted Helplessly in Deadly Hail
—Two Spanish Boats Sunk and the Town Partially
Wrecked by the Daring American Seamen—Unfortunate
Ensign's Calm Heroism—Navy Department to Inquire
Why Three Unprotected Vessels Were Sent on Such
a Hazardous Mission—Washington Astonished—
Dead and Injured Now at Key West.

FIRST AMERICAN VICTIMS OF BATTLE IN THE WAR WITH SPAIN.

THE DEAD:	THE WOUNDED:
BAGLEY, WORTH, *ENSIGN.*	BERNADOU, JOHN B., *LIEUTENANT.*
DENEFEE, JOHN, *FIREMAN.*	COX, R. E., *GUNNER'S MATE.*
MEEK, GEORGE B., *FIREMAN.*	GRAY, F.
TURRELL, ELIJAH B., *CABIN COOK.*	PATTERSON, L. *FIREMAN.*
VARVERS, JOHN, *OILER.*	

WINSLOW ORDERED TO PORTSMOUTH NAVY-YARD
FOR REPAIRS, WILL NOT BE READY FOR SIXTY DAYS.

LIEUT. BERNADOU, OF THE WINSLOW, TO THE WORLD.

Tells from His Cot in the Hospital How the Little
Vessel Was Riddled—Kept on Firing as She
Was Towed Out of Action.

A Father and Son

Col. Harry Clay Egbert was commander of the 6th Infantry and was wounded in the chest leading his regiment up San Juan Hill. He was born in 1839, and graduated from the University of Pennsylvania. He was an attorney until joining the Union Army in 1861.

After the Civil War he served in Washington, D.C., Arizona, New Mexico, California and New York, obtaining the rank of Lt. Colonel in 1893. On July 1, 1898, he was promoted to Colonel of the 22nd Infantry and on Oct. 1 promoted to Brig. General of Volunteers but was reverted back to colonel on Dec. 1.

On March 26, 1899, Colonel Egbert was killed in action at Malinta in the Philippines while leading the 22nd Infantry. He was shot in the abdomen and died while being evacuated from the field. His dying words were, "I must die. I am too old."

His son was a private in the 22nd Infantry at the time. He was promoted to Second Lieutenant that day.

The Tom Mix Myth

A 1st Lieutenant of a volunteer regiment at Camp Alger, Virginia. He is wearing a khaki twill uniform that he had to have purchased with his own money. At this time army issue was still wool although they had realized wool wasn't the proper material for uniforms to be worn in the tropics.

Col. John Jacob Astor IV (1864-1912), founder of Astor's Battery and Brevet Colonel on General Shafter's staff was one of the wealthiest men in America. He was the great-grandson of the family's founder. He managed real estate, wrote science fiction, built hotels in New York City and invented various mechanical devices. He died on the *Titanic* in 1912.

It has been written in many books and magazine articles that famous cowboy actor Tom Mix was in the thick of the fighting during the Spanish American War. And that he went on to fight in the Philippines, South Africa and China.

Yes, Mix was in the Spanish American War but his military career is far different than has been portrayed for years. Paul Mix in his book, *Tom Mix*, McFarland & Co., 1995, follows his career in detail.

Tom Mix enlisted at Washington Barracks, Washington, D.C. in April 1898 and was assigned to Battery M, Fourth Regiment, U.S. Army Artillery. He was then 18 years old. His first assignment was to guard the DuPont power works at Montchanin, Delaware against the possibility of Spanish sabotage or attack by a Spanish fleet.

His battery was next stationed at Battery Point, Delaware (later Fort DuPont) to protect the Delaware River. The war was over before Mix was transferred, almost a year later to Fort Monroe, Virginia. He was later transferred to Fort Hancock, New Jersey, where he was discharged on April 25, 1901.

His own reports of being wounded in both conflicts and further action in the Boer War and Boxer Rebellion do not coincide with his military record. Other aspects of Mix's life are inconsistent with his own life's story. Some speculated that his ideas about fighting in Cuba and the Philippines came from his appearance in the 1909 Selig Polyscope film, *Up San Juan Hill*. But Robert Birchard's 1993 book, *King Cowboy: Tom Mix and the Movies* by Riverwood Press states that Mix didn't even arrive in California (where the movie was shot) until 1914, so was not in the movie.

It is not a myth however, that by 1921 Tom Mix was the top paid and most popular western star and "The King of the Cowboys." In all he made 93 feature films from 1917 to 1935, was married five times and had two children. On Oct. 12, 1940, he was killed in a car accident in Arizona and is buried in Forest Lawn Memorial Park in Hollywood.

Tom Mix had many real-life adventures after his birth in 1880 and really didn't have to make up his military myth.

Poet and biographer, Carl Sandburg served with the 6th Illinois Volunteer Infantry in Puerto Rico.

The Generals and Admirals

General Nelson A. Miles

Gen. Nelson A. Miles was born in Massachusetts in 1839. He received rudimentary military instruction from a former French officer. He received commission as a captain in 1861 and served on Gen. O.O. Howard's staff. He participated in many major battles of the Civil War and was brevetted brigadier general in 1867 and received the Medal of Honor for action during the war. He commanded the District of North Carolina during Reconstruction and then spent 1869 to 1894 on the western frontier fighting the Indian wars. He was commanding general of the U.S. Army from 1895 to 1903 and conducted the Puerto Rico campaign in 1898. He was advanced to three-star rank in 1900, retired in 1903 and died in 1925.

General Fitzhugh Lee

Gen. Fitzhugh Lee was one of two ex-Confederate generals who played an important role in the war. He was born in 1835. Graduating from West Point in 1856, he was posted to Carlisle Barracks, and Texas, then was transferred back to West Point.

He entered the Confederate army in May 1861 as a first lieutenant and by the end of the war, the then major general was in command of the remains of the cavalry of the Army of Northern Virginia. Fitzhugh was the nephew of Confederate General Robert E. Lee.

After the war he became a farmer and in 1885, governor of Virginia. In 1896 he was named consul-general to Havana, the most important American official in the country. When war was about to break out he returned to the U.S. and was commissioned major general of volunteers on May 5, 1898.

He was assigned to the V Army Corps which was the chief combat force in the Cuban campaign. The capture of Santiago ended the campaign but Lee took his command to Cuba, established his headquarters near Havana and established order in the country.

Lee retired in 1901 and died in 1905. He was a superior soldier, politician and great public speaker. He is buried in Richmond, Virginia.

General William Rufus Shafter

Shafter was born near Galesburg, Michigan, in 1835. He entered the army during the Civil War as a private and in 1895 was awarded the Medal of Honor for his gallant fighting at Fair Oaks, Virginia, in 1862.

He stayed in the army after the war taking part in the western Indian campaigns and eventually attaining the rank of major general. He was one of the few Spanish American generals who did not attend West Point.

Shafter was assigned to head the Fifth Army Corps assembling at Tampa for the planned invasion of Cuba. At 63 years of age, a weight of over 300 pounds and suffering from gout, he seemed to be a poor choice to lead an army. A naval academy cadet at Tampa stated: "The camp is supposedly under the command of Gen. William Shafter but there seems to be no discipline whatsoever. I caught a glimpse of the general. He is an enormous man and must weigh over 300 pounds. I can't imagine him leading troops in the tropical jungles of Cuba."

But the general did go to Cuba and eventually took Santiago, the major campaign in the Cuban war. This in spite of the heat, gout, and fever which partially immobilized him.

After accepting the surrender of Santiago and sending his troops back home, he returned to the states where he retired from the army in 1901. Shafter died in 1906.

General Joseph Wheeler

Gen. Joseph Wheeler was one of two ex-Confederate generals who led the American army in the Spanish American War. He was born in Georgia in 1836 and graduated from West Point in 1859. He served in the New Mexico Indian campaigns before joining the Confederate army in April 1861.

He was colonel of the 19th Alabama Infantry but soon commanded the cavalry of the Army of Mississippi and eventually commanded, as lieutenant general, all cavalry in the western theater of operations. He was an outstanding leader and earned the nickname "Fighting Joe."

After the war he became a cotton planter and lawyer and served in Congress from Alabama for over 17 years. His chief public contribution was his untiring advocacy of reconciliation between the North and South.

President McKinley appointed Wheeler a major general of volunteers and he commanded the cavalry division of Shafter's Santiago expedition. He was present at Las Guasimas and San Juan Hill and at the end of the war commanded Camp Wikoff on Long Island.

He was sent to the Philippines for a brief period and finally retired as a brigadier general in the regular army in 1900. He died in 1906 and is buried in Arlington National Cemetery. Wheeler was a true son of both the North and South.

The Louisville Legion

In 1877 a serious riot occurred in Louisville, Kentucky. Early the next year John B. Castleman, an ex-Confederate soldier, who was captured as a spy in 1864, was asked to organize a regiment to protect the community. The Louisville Legion was mustered into service and many prominent citizens of the city served through the years.

On Feb. 7, 1898, eight days before the *USS Maine* blew up, now Colonel Castleman sensing the impending war mood in the country, filed the following resolution:

"Resolved, that the Louisville Legion, First Regiment, Kentucky State Guard, requests the Governor of Kentucky to tender to the National Government its services in this or any foreign country where it may be needed.

"The members ask to be assigned to duty amongst the first called for, should the emergency arise.

"The Regiment of seven hundred, rank, file and officers—two battalions—is sufficiently equipped for active service. They are armed with Springfield, Model 73, 45-70 rifles. The men are instructed in rifle practice. Each company is also instructed in drill of 83 model Gattlings, of which the regiment has four. One company is drilled in the use of three-inch rifles, model 64, Muzzle loaders, of which the regiment has four as part of its equipment.

Jno. B. Castleman,
Colonel.
Louisville, Feby. 7, 1898."

A large percentage of its members were sons of Confederate veterans. The Legion was sent to Camp Thomas and then to Newport News, Virginia, where they embarked for the campaign in Puerto Rico. They served until Dec. 4, 1898, and was the last volunteer regiment to leave the Caribbean area.

While in Puerto Rico, Castleman organized "The Patriotic Society of Porto Rico." The objections of the society were as follows:

"First. To stimulate respect for Government of the United States; for the enforcement of the laws and customs usual in the United States in protection of life, liberty and property, and for the maintenance of the right of the individual to worship God according to the dictates of his own conscience.

"Second. To encourage increased modesty among citizens by demanding that no nude person of any age shall appear in any public place, street or highway. When this end may not be accomplished by persuasion of committee of this society, and by creation of proper public sentiment, then there shall be invoked the aid of general and municipal laws to punish offenders and compliance.

"Third. To encourage marriage everywhere in Porto Rico, not only in the young but among all people who live together as man and wife. And where this result may not be accomplished by persuasion of the committee of this society, then the general and municipal laws shall be enforced to compel compliance and punish noncompliance."

John Castleman was born in 1841 near Lexington, Kentucky. After service in the Civil War he graduated in law from the University of Louisville. With his love of horses he founded the American Saddlebred Horse Association in 1891 and the same year founded the Louisville Park Department. He was prominent in the Democratic Party and in 1892 was credited with securing the presidential nomination for Grover Cleveland.

He was twice Adjutant General of Kentucky and had to intervene in the bitter gubernatorial race of 1899. In 1913, a statue was unveiled at the entrance to Cherokee Park in Louisville to honor the city's most noted citizen.

General Castleman had just completed his memoirs, *Active Service*, when he died on May 23, 1918. His two sons, one who served with him in Puerto Rico, preceded him in death.

Gen. John B. Castleman at the time of the Spanish American War.

General Frederick Funston

The war produced many interesting characters but none could match the adventures, either before, during or after the war, of Frederick Funston.

He was born on Nov. 9, 1865, in New Carlisle, Ohio. His family moved to Allen County, Kansas, where he graduated from high school in 1886. He went on to attend the University of Kansas.

As a special botanical agent for the Department of Agriculture he joined a trip to Death Valley, California, in 1891 to collect specimens. Soon recognized as a competent botanist he made a trip to Alaska and Canada in 1892 to collect flora samples for the U.S. government. He made a 3,500-mile trip from the McKenzie River to the Bering Sea, wintering in the Klondike area alone in 1893-94 and undertaking a solo canoe expedition 1,500 miles down the Yukon River. He returned in 1894 to lecture on his adventures.

After holding several newspaper jobs and working for the Santa Fe Railroad he happened to hear a speech by Civil War Gen. Daniel Sickles who pled the cause of Cuban Independence at Madison Square Garden in New York City. Funston immediately signed up with the Cuban insurgents and went to Cuba in 1896.

He was accepted for artillery service on the strength of having seen a salute fired for President Rutherford B. Hayes at a county fair in Kansas. He served 18 months under generals Gomez, Garcia and others and proved to be a quick learner and brave soldier.

After participating in 22 engagements, being wounded several times and being captured and condemned to death by the Spaniards, he escaped late in 1897 and returned to the United States in January 1898.

When war was declared in April 1898, Governor Leedy of Kansas, recalling Funston's exploits in Cuba, asked him to command the 20th Kansas Volunteer Infantry Regiment. While the regiment was encamped at San Francisco, Funston met and married Eda Blankart on Oct. 25, 1898.

The regiment arrived in the Philippines too late for the war but there were heavily involved in the Malolos Campaign against the Filipino insurrectionists in 1899. For his part in an action at Calumpst on the Rio Grande de Pampanga River on April 27, 1899, Funston was promoted to brigadier general of volunteers and awarded the Medal of Honor.

Although the 20th Kansas served only a year, Funston returned to the Philippines in December 1899 to command the 4th District of the Department of Northern Luzon. He personally led the small cadre of American soldiers and Macabebe scouts in the capture of Emilio Aquinaldo, the leader of the Filipino insurrectionists.

In recognition of this, Funston was commissioned a brigadier general in the regular army in 1901 at the age of 36, the youngest in the army. From 1901 to 1905 he commanded the Departments of Colorado, Columbia and the Lakes and the Southwestern Division.

In 1905 he took over command of the Department of California in San Francisco. On April 18, 1906, San Francisco was struck by a disastrous earthquake and fire. Funston immediately ordered federal troops into the city to assist in the rescue and firefighting efforts and to prevent looting. His forceful, but unauthorized, actions were credited with reducing the loss of life and property, but he was criticized for his decision to dynamite fire breaks in the city.

Frederick Funston in the uniform of the Cuban Insurgent Army. KSHS

After the earthquake, with the exception of brief service with the government's commission to settle a factional dispute in Cuba, his assignments were routine. He served as Commandant of the Army Service Schools at Fort Leavenworth and two additional years back in the Philippines. In 1913 he was transferred to command the Hawaiian Department and in 1914 was the military governor of Vera Cruz, Mexico, during the Mexican border crisis. He was in command of the Southern Department along the Mexican border when Pancho Villa attacked Columbus, New Mexico. Funston recommended that Gen. John J. Pershing be sent after him.

At age 51, on Feb. 19, 1917, General Funston died suddenly in the lobby of the St. Anthony Hotel in San Antonio, Texas. He was buried at the Presidio of San Francisco on Feb. 24.

Had he lived, Funston would have probably been called upon to command the American Expeditionary Forces (A.E.F.) in France instead of Gen. John J. Pershing.

Funston and officers who captured Emilio Aquinaldo in 1901. KSHS

Funeral ceremony for Gen. Frederick Funston at San Antonio, Texas, Feb. 21, 1917. KSHS

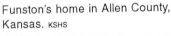

Funston's home in Allen County, Kansas. KSHS

General Irving Hale

One of Colorado's most distinguished citizens was born in 1861. In 1865 his parents moved to Colorado and Hale was in the first graduating class of East Denver High School.

He entered West Point in 1880 and graduated four years later with the highest record that has ever been achieved in the history of the school. He was commissioned in the Corps of Engineers and later taught engineering at the military academy.

After a few years in the army, he resigned and worked for the Edison Company in Denver. He renewed his interest in the military in 1897 and became a lieutenant colonel in the Colorado National Guard. At the outbreak of war he was appointed colonel of the First Colorado Infantry and eventually was sent to the Philippines.

Hale was cited for gallantry and distinguished service and promoted to brigadier general of the Second Brigade, Second Division, Eighth Army Corps, for his action against Manila on Aug. 13, 1898.

On March 26, 1899, he was wounded in the knee at Meycauyan and was recommended for a brevet major general for his gallant service throughout the campaign. He was also awarded the Silver Star.

On Dec. 1, 1899, he called a meeting of his former comrades and organized the Colorado Society of the Army of the Philippines. It merged with the American Veterans of Foreign Service in 1913. The name was changed to the Army of the Philippines, Cuba and Puerto Rico and in 1914, the name Veterans of Foreign Wars (VFW) was adopted.

In 1906, at the centennial celebration in Colorado Springs, General Hale, representing the U.S. Army, officially christened Pike's Peak. He was engaged in engineering work and many civic activities in Denver until suffering a paralytic stroke in 1911 from which he never fully recovered.

Hale died in 1930 and is buried in Denver. Camp Hale, the training site for the 10th Mountain Division during World War II, was named for General Hale.

General Charles King

Gen. Charles King had the distinction of serving longer in the military than any soldier in American history. He wore campaign medals from the Civil War, Indian Wars, Spanish American War, Philippine Insurrection and World War One. His career spanned 70 years, from 1861-1931. He graduated from West Point in 1866 and was awarded a Silver Star for action against the Apaches in 1874. His service with the regular army was ended in 1879 by severe wounds received in combat but in 1880 he joined the Wisconsin National Guard. He rose to the position of adjutant general of the state and brigadier general of volunteers during the Spanish American War. He commanded the 1st Brigade, 1st Division, VIII Corps in the Philippines. King was also a noted author of fiction, military history and over 250 articles for magazines and newspapers.

Brig. Gen. Irving Hale, 1st Regiment Colorado Volunteer Infantry. USAMHI

General Arthur MacArthur

The father of Gen. Douglas MacArthur was born in 1845 in Springfield, Massachusetts, and raised in Milwaukee, Wisconsin. In 1862, he was commissioned a first lieutenant in the 24th Wisconsin Infantry and mustered out in 1865 as a lieutenant colonel. He had a distinguished career in the war and in 1890 was awarded the Medal of Honor for his actions at Missionary Ridge in 1863.

Between the wars he served in various army positions, and, at the start of the war in 1898, he was appointed adjutant-general of the troops at Tampa and later of the III Army Corps at Chickamauga. On May 27, he was promoted to brigadier-general and assigned to the Philippine expeditionary forces, landing there on July 25.

He took part in the occupation of Manila and was appointed provost-marshall general and civil governor of the city. Until he left the Philippines in July 1901, MacArthur led troops in battle during the insurrection, was given command of the Department of Northern Luzon, and became commander of the Division of the Philippines and military governor of the Islands.

He retired from the army as a lieutenant general in 1909. At the time of his sudden death on Sept. 5, 1912, he was national commander of the Loyal Legion of the United States, a Civil War veterans organization.

Brig. Gen. William C. Oates. MICHAEL JONES COLL.

Gen. Arthur MacArthur

Brigadier General William C. Oates

General Oates was one of very few Confederate veterans appointed to brigadier-general in the Spanish American War.

Oates was a colonel in the Confederate Army and led the 15th Alabama Infantry at the Battle of Gettysburg. He had been a lawyer in Abbeville, Ala-

bama, before the war and raised a volunteer company that became Company G, 15th Alabama. He participated in most of the battles with the Army of Northern Virginia until Aug. 16, 1864, when he lost his right arm in a battle near Richmond.

After the war, he returned to Alabama and served that state in Congress for 14 years and was governor of the state.

During the Spanish American War he was frustrated in not being allowed to lead his Alabama troops into battle. He concluded that the War Department was deliberately discouraging regionalism. "State pride was rebuked. The Republican Policy was to ignore the states and nationalize everything," he wrote.

Oates spent the war commanding troops from northern states at Camp Meade, Pennsylvania. He resigned from the army on Jan. 11, 1899. He wrote his memoirs in 1905, *The War Between The Union and The Confederacy* in which he defended the right of the southern states to form a new country.

General Elwell S. Otis

He was born in Frederick, Maryland, in 1838 and graduated from Harvard Law School in 1861. In 1862 he joined the 140th New York Infantry and saw action throughout the war. He was wounded in the head at Petersburg and was mustered out in January 1865, receiving the brevet ranks of colonel and brigadier general of volunteers.

He rejoined the regular army after the war and served in numerous commands including the establishment of the Army school at Leavenworth, Kansas. On May 4, 1898, he was made major general of volunteers and left for the Philippines where he was placed in command of the VIII Army Corps. On Aug. 29, he relieved General Merritt in command of the Department of the Pacific and as military governor of the Philippines. On May 5, 1900, he turned his command over to General MacArthur and returned home. He retired in 1902 and died in 1909.

Henry W. Lawton (1843-1899) won a medal of honor in the Civil War and commanded the 2nd Division of the 5th Army Corps as a brigadier general of volunteers. He was military governor of Santiago and participated in the Philippine Insurrection and was killed at the town of San Mateo on Dec. 19, 1899.

General Wesley Merritt

He was born in New York City in 1834 and graduated from West Point in 1860. He served in Utah until the outbreak of the Civil War, and rose quickly through the ranks. Serving with distinction, Merritt was advanced to brigadier general of volunteers just prior to the Battle of Gettysburg and by the end of the Civil War, had attained the rank of major general. He mustered out of the volunteers on Feb. 1, 1866, and continued in the regular army primarily in the western Indian campaigns. He was also commandant of West Point. In 1898, Merritt led the American army in support of Admiral Dewey's victory at Manila Bay and received the surrender of Manila. He died in 1910.

Samuel B.M. Young (1840-?) after extensive service in the Civil War, he fought in the western Indian campaign. He commanded the 2nd Brigade, Cavalry Division of the 5th Army Corps as a major general of volunteers. In 1903 and 1904, he was commanding general of the U.S. Army.

Frederick Dent Grant (1850-1912) was the eldest son of President Ulysses S. Grant. During the Civil War, he accompanied his father in the field and was wounded at Vicksburg. He graduated from West Point in 1871 and participated in the western Indian campaigns. For two years he was New York's commissioner of police and was mustered into service as colonel of the 14th New York Infantry on May 2, 1898. On May 27, he was appointed brigadier general of volunteers. He commanded a brigade at Camp Thomas and was stationed in Puerto Rico. For four years, 1899-1902, he fought in the Philippine Insurrection. At the end of the conflict, Grant returned to the U.S. and was appointed a major general in the regular army in 1906 after various commands across the country. He died in 1912 and is buried at West Point.

John R. Brooke was born in 1838 and in April 1861 entered the army as captain of the 4th Pennsylvania Volunteer Infantry. He had a distinguished career in the Civil War and was brevetted major-general in 1864. After the war, he held various command positions in the West. He was named commander of Camp Thomas, Georgia, at the outbreak of the Spanish American War plus commander of the Department of the Gulf and 1st Army Corps. He led troops in the Puerto Rico campaign and was made military governor of the island in October. In December he was appointed military governor of Cuba until General Wood replaced him in December 1899. He was forced to retire in 1902 and died in 1926, the next to last Union general to die.

General Brooke.

Civil War Generals (regular and brevet) who also served in the Spanish American War

Adelbert Ames (1835-1933) was born in Maine and graduated from West Point in 1861. He fought throughout the Civil War and brevetted to Major General. He was later a senator from Mississippi and governor of the state. He served six months in the Spanish American War as a brigadier of volunteers. When Ames died in 1933, he was the last surviving general officer, other than brevet, from either side.

Guy Vernor Henry (1839-1899) graduated from West Point in 1861. He had a distinguished career in the Civil War, earning the Medal of Honor for action at Cold Harbor and brevetted brigadier general of volunteers in 1865. He participated in several Indian campaigns and was brevetted a brigadier general in the regular army, serving in that rank in the Spanish American War. Henry led troops in the invasion of Puerto Rico and died on active duty in 1899.

Joseph Warren Keifer (1836-1932) was a general officer by brevet during the Civil War. Afterwards, he was a banker, legislator and congressman from Ohio. Keifer became a major general of volunteers during the Spanish American War.

Alexander Cummings McWhorter Pennington (1838-1917) was an 1860 graduate of West Point from New Jersey. He served in the cavalry during the Civil War where he held brevets as a colonel of regulars and brigadier general of volunteers upon his muster out in August 1865. After serving as a brigadier general of volunteers in the Spanish American War, Pennington retired in 1899.

Roy Stone (?-1901) participated in many battles during the Civil War and was commander of the prisoner-of-war prison at Alton, Illinois. He received a brevet as brigadier general of volunteers for action at Gettysburg and was commissioned a brigadier general of volunteers during the Spanish American War.

James Harrison Wilson (1837-1925) was an 1860 graduate of West Point. He served extensively in the Civil War as an engineer and a cavalryman. He was brevetted a major general at the end of the war. Wilson left the army in 1870 but served again as a general officer of volunteers during the Spanish American War and the Boxer Rebellion in China. He retired as a brigadier general in 1901.

Admirals of the U.S. Navy Who Participated in the Spanish American War*

Charles Johnston Badger (1853-1932) was a graduate of the Naval Academy in 1873 and during the war was the navigator on the cruiser *Cincinnati*. He was superintendent of the Naval Academy from 1907-09 and was promoted to admiral in 1911. He later became commander of the Atlantic Fleet and was heavily involved in naval affairs during World War One. Badger retired in 1921.

Mark Lambert Bristol (1868-1939) was an 1887 graduate of the Naval Academy. He was a lieutenant (j.g.) on the battleship *Texas* at Guantanamo Bay and the Battle of Santiago. He was an ordnance specialist and an accomplished diplomat, especially in Turkey. In 1913, Bristol became director of naval aviation and was promoted to rear admiral in 1918. He commanded the Asiatic Fleet in the 1920s. He retired in 1932.

William Banks Caperton (1855-1941) graduated from the Naval Academy in 1875. He commanded the schooner-rigged gunboat *Marietta* which accompanied the *Oregon* on her famous run. He became executive officer of that battleship in August 1898. Appointed rear admiral in 1913, Caperton commanded the Pacific Fleet during World War One. He retired in 1919.

French Ensor Chadwick (1844-1919) was an 1865 graduate of the Naval Academy. He participated as a midshipman on anti-Confederate raider patrol during the Civil War and in 1882 became America's first naval attaché. He was involved in the battleship *Maine* investigation and was chief of staff to Admiral Sampson during the Cuban campaign. Chadwick was promoted to rear admiral in 1903 and retired in 1906. From 1909-11 he wrote three volumes on the Spanish American War.

Charles Edgar Clark (1843-1922) graduated in 1864 from the Naval Academy. He participated in the 1864 Battle of Mobile Bay then commanded a variety of ships until March 1898 when he took command of the battleship *Oregon*. His 67-day trip around the Horn to reinforce the fleet blockading Cuba was one of the most famous incidents of the war. Clark was promoted to rear admiral in 1902 and retired in 1905.

Robert Edward Coontz (1864-1935) was a graduate of the Naval Academy in 1885. In 1898, he was an officer on the *Charleston* which captured Guam and fought in the Philippines. He participated in the Mexican and Haitian conflicts and World War One. He was promoted to rear admiral in 1918 and CNO in 1919. Coontz retired in 1928.

Charles Henry Davis Jr. (1845-1921) was an 1865 graduate of the Naval Academy. He was involved with the Naval Observatory for many years and was noted for his scientific work. In command of the converted auxiliary cruiser *Dixie*, he accepted the surrender of Ponce, Puerto Rico, in July 1898. Davis was promoted to rear admiral in 1905 and retired in 1908.

Edward Walter Eberle (1864-1929) graduated from the Naval Academy in 1885. As a lieutenant (j.g.) he served on the *Oregon,* commanding her forward turret during the Battle of Santiago and participated in the Philippine Insurrection. Superintendent of the Naval Academy from 1915-19, Eberle was promoted to rear admiral in 1918. He was CNO from 1923 to 1927 and retired in 1928.

Robley Dunglison Evans (1846-1912) was an 1864 graduate of the Naval Academy. He was in the navy during the Civil War and commanded the battleship *Iowa* during the Battle of Santiago. Promoted to rear admiral in 1901, Evans retired in 1908.

Bradley Allen Fiske (1854-1942) was a graduate of the Naval Academy in 1874. He was a noted naval inventor, reformer and intellectual. During the war he was the navigator of the gunboat *Petrel* at the Battle of Manila Bay and participated in the Philippine Insurrection. Promoted to rear admiral in 1911, Fiske retired in 1916. From 1911 to 1923, he was president of the Naval Institute.

Frank Friday Fletcher (1855-1928) graduated from the Naval Academy in 1875. From May to July 1898, he served as assistant chief of the Bureau of Ordnance and, briefly, on the *St. Louis*. He also commanded the gunboat *Kanawha* in the Caribbean in 1898. Promoted to rear admiral in 1911, Fletcher served in World War One and retired in 1919.

Albert Gleaves (1858-1937) was an 1877 graduate of the Naval Academy. He invented a device which improved the accuracy of torpedoes and patrolled the Cays during the war. He was promoted to rear admiral in 1915 and helped develop the convoy system during World War One. Gleaves retired in 1922.

Casper Frederick Goodrich (1847-1925) was a graduate of the Naval Academy in 1865. He was a founder of the U.S. Naval Institute and the Naval War College. He commanded the *St. Louis* during engagements off Cuba. In August 1898, he took over command of the *Newark* and shelled Manzanillo, Cuba, the last naval action of the war. Promoted to rear admiral in 1904, Goodrich retired in 1909.

Thomas Charles Hart (1877-1971) was an 1897 graduate of the Naval Academy. He had one of the longest naval careers in history stretching from 1897 to his retirement in 1942. He was on the *Massachussetts* at the start of the war and on the converted yacht *Vixen* at the Battle of Santiago. Hart served in many positions throughout his career including submarines and Commander-in-Chief Asiatic Fleet in 1942. He was promoted to rear admiral in 1929. In 1945, he assumed a vacated senatorial seat from Connecticut.

Charles Frederick Hughes (1866-1934) graduated from the Naval Academy in 1888. He participated in the final bombardment of Manila in August 1898 and the Philippine Insurrection. He was promoted to rear admiral in 1918 after service in World War One. Hughes was CNO in 1927 and resigned and retired in 1930.

William Wirt Kimball (1848-1930) was a graduate of the Naval Academy in 1869. He was on the *Dupont* during action off Cuba. He was promoted to rear admiral in 1908 and in 1909 commanded the Nicaragua Expeditionary Squadron. Kimball retired in 1911 but returned to active duty during World War One.

Ernest Joseph King (1878-1956) was a 1901 graduate of the Naval Academy. He was a naval cadet on the *San Francisco* during patrols off the coast of Florida and Cuba during the war. He served in many capacities through the years including submarines and aviation. He was promoted to rear admiral in 1935. During World War Two, he was Commander-in-Chief United States Fleet and Chief of Naval Operations (CNO). King retired in 1945.

Austin Melvin Knight (1854-1927) graduated from the Naval Academy in 1873. He was the navigator on the monitor *Puritan* off Cuba and Puerto Rico. He was promoted to rear admiral in 1911. He directed American naval operations during the Allied intervention in the Russian Civil War. Knight retired in 1918.

William Daniel Leahy (1875-1959) was a Naval Academy graduate in 1897. One of several high-ranking World War Two naval commanders who served in the Spanish American War. He was a naval cadet on the *Oregon* on its historic trip around the Horn and fought at the Battle of Santiago. He was promoted to rear admiral in 1927 and during World War Two, he was Chief of Staff to President Roosevelt and Chairman of the Joint Chiefs of Staff. Leahy's 56-year naval and diplomatic career ended in 1949.

Alfred Thayer Mahan (1840-1914) was an 1859 graduate of the Naval Academy. He is considered America's most influential naval historian and naval philosopher. He served in the Civil War and later as president of the Naval War College where he wrote some of his most important naval books. He retired in 1896 but was recalled to active duty on the Naval Board of Strategy in 1898. Mahan was promoted to rear admiral on the retired list in 1906.

Henry Thomas Mayo (1856-1937) graduated from the Naval Academy in 1876. He was navigator on the gunboat *Bennington* during the war but saw no action. He was promoted to rear admiral in 1913. Mayo controlled all American warships in Atlantic and European waters during World War One. He retired in 1920.

Bowman Hendry McCalla (1844-1910) was an 1865 graduate of the Naval Academy. He commanded the cruiser *Marblehead* in the North Atlantic and during the capture of Guantanamo Bay. Promoted to rear admiral in 1903, McCalla retired in 1906.

William Adger Moffett (1869-1933) was a graduate of the Naval Academy in 1890. He was on the *Charleston* during the capture of Guam and the final bombardment of Manila. He was the port captain on the salvage of the sunken Spanish warships. Moffett is considered the father of naval aviation and died in the crash of the airship *Akron* in 1933. Moffett Field in California is named for him.

Albert Parker Niblack (1859-1929) graduated from the Naval Academy in 1880. He was on the gunboat *Topeka* in the Cuban campaign. He also participated in the Philippine Insurrection. Promoted to rear admiral in 1917, Niblack retired in 1923.

William Veazie Pratt (1869-1957) was an 1889 graduate of the Naval Academy. He served aboard the converted yacht *Mayflower* during the war. He was promoted to rear admiral in 1921 and Chief of Naval Operations in 1930. Pratt retired in 1933.

Joseph Mason Reeves (1872-1948) was a Naval Academy graduate in 1894. He was in charge of the *Oregon*'s main engines on her voyage around Cape Horn. He was promoted to rear admiral in 1927. During World War Two, he served on numerous boards including the Roberts Pearl Harbor investigation. Reeves was released from active service in 1946 ending 52 years of naval service.

Hugh Rodman (1859-1940) was an 1880 graduate of the Naval Academy. He served on the *Raleigh* at the Battle of Manila Bay. Promoted to rear admiral in 1917, Rodman retired in 1923.

William Sowden Sims (1858-1936) graduated from the Naval Academy in 1880. He directed American wartime secret service operations in Spain, Italy and Russia. Sims was promoted to rear admiral in 1917 and retired in 1922.

William Harrison Standley (1872-1963) was an 1895 graduate of the Naval Academy. He was on the gunboat *Yorktown* in the Philippines. He was promoted to rear admiral in 1927 and retired in 1938. Recalled to active duty in 1939, Standley served throughout World War Two in various capacities including ambassador to the Soviet Union. He retired again in 1945.

Yates Stirling Jr. (1872-1948) was a graduate of the Naval Academy in 1892. He was an assistant equipment officer at Newport News, Virginia, and served on the cruiser *Dolphin* during the war. Promoted to rear admiral in 1926, Stirling retired in 1936.

Joseph Knefler Taussig (1877-1947) graduated from the Naval Academy in 1899. He was a naval cadet on the *New York* at the Battle of Santiago. His father took command of Wake Island in 1899 as commander of the gunboat *Bennington*. Promoted to rear admiral in 1932, Taussig retired in 1941. Returning to active duty in 1943, he served on various boards until 1947.

Henry Clay Taylor (1845-1904) was an 1864 graduate of the Naval Academy. He saw service in the Civil War and commanded the *Indiana* in the Spanish American War, bombarding Puerto Rico, convoying troops from Tampa to Cuba and sinking two destroyers in the Battle of Santiago. Promoted to rear admiral in 1901, Taylor died on active duty in 1904.

Richard Wainwright (1849-1926) was a graduate of the Naval Academy in 1868. He was the great-great grandson of Benjamin Franklin. He was the executive officer of the *Maine* and survived her destruction in Havana harbor. In May 1898, he took command of the converted yacht *Gloucester* and sank a Spanish destroyer in the Battle of Santiago. He also took two coastal positions in Puerto Rico. Promoted to rear admiral in 1908, Wainwright retired in 1911.

Cameron McRae Winslow (1854-1932) graduated from the Naval Academy in 1875. He served on the gunboat *Nashville* from which he led a boat expedition which cut the underwater cable off Cienfuegos, Cuba. He was promoted to naval aide to President Theodore Roosevelt in 1902 and to rear admiral in 1911. Retiring in 1916, Winslow returned to active duty in 1917 and retired again in 1919.

Harry Ervin Yarnell (1875-1959) was an 1897 graduate of the Naval Academy. He was on the *Oregon* on her voyage around the Horn and participated in the Philippine Insurrection. He was promoted to rear admiral in 1928 and retired in 1939. Returning to active duty in 1941, Yarnell served in World War Two, retiring again in 1944.

*Information for these biographies was obtained from *Famous American Admirals* by Clark G. Reynolds, Van Nostrand Reinhold Company, New York, 1978.

Spanish American War Sailors Who Were Admirals in World War Two

Thomas Charles Hart
Ernest Joseph King
William Daniel Leahy
Joseph Mason Reeves
William Harrison Standley
Joseph Knefler Taussig
Harry Ervin Yarnell

Commanders of U.S. Capital Ships

USS Iowa – Capt. Robley D. Evans
USS Indiana – Capt. Henry C. Taylor
USS Texas – Capt. John W. Philip
USS Oregon – Capt. Charles E. Clark
USS Olympia – Capt. Charles V. Gridley
USS Massachusetts – Capt. Francis J. Higginson
USS Minneapolis – Capt. G.H. Wadleigh
USS New York – Capt. French E. Chadwick
USS Brooklyn – Capt. Francis A. Cook

Admiral George Dewey

George Dewey was born in Montpelier, Vermont, in 1837 and graduated from the Naval Academy in 1858. He served extensively during the Civil War at New Orleans, Port Hudson, Charleston, James River, Fort Fisher and finally, as the executive officer of the screw sloop *Kearsarge*.

After the war he held various positions on ships and at the Naval Academy (1867-70). He commanded the hospital ship *Supply* in a relief voyage to aid victims of the Franco-Prussian War and served at the Boston Navy Yard and the Newport torpedo station.

He was appointed commander in 1872 and spent many years as a lighthouse inspector and Lighthouse Board member. In 1896, he was promoted to commodore and in November 1897, took command of the Asiatic Station.

Commodore Dewey hoisted his flag on the *Olympia* at Nagasaki, Japan, in January 1898 and in February, moved his squadron to Hong Kong. From there he headed into his now famous battle at Manila Bay on May 1.

Dewey became an admiral in 1899 and retained command of the Asiatic Station until October 1899. The next March he became president of the newly created General Board.

Congress commissioned Dewey in the specially created rank of admiral of the Navy, unique in the history of the Navy, retroactive from March 1899. With this rank he remained on active duty until he died on Jan. 16, 1917.

Admiral Dewey's home, across from the state capitol in Montpelier, Vermont. It is no longer in existence.
VHS #2930

Admiral William Thomas Sampson

Sampson was born in 1840 in Palmyra, New York, and graduated from the Naval Academy at the head of his class in 1861. His participation in the Civil War was varied from service with the blockade fleet, instructor and acting master of a training ship at the relocated Naval Academy at Newport, Rhode Island, service on a monitor off of Charleston, South Carolina, and cruising on the European Station until the summer of 1867. His interest was science which he taught at the Naval Academy and as assistant superintendant of the Naval Observatory. He was one of the principal figures in the early days of the U.S. Naval Institute and from 1898 to 1902 its president. He was appointed head of the *Maine* Court of Inquiry but did not participate in all the hearings. In April 1898, he held the rank of acting rear admiral and instituted the blockade of Cuba which resulted in the destruction of the Spanish fleet at Santiago. However, he was on his way to a meeting with General Shafter on July 3 when the great battle commenced and his ship did not take part in the battle. Since Schley gave the initial orders, a quarrel developed over which commander was responsible for the victory. Sampson's promotion was delayed until April 1899.

After the war he was a commissioner to Cuba and commander of the North Atlantic Squadron from December 1898 to October 1899. He retired in February 1902 after commanding the Boston Navy Yard. He died on May 6, 1902. Sampson's illness incapacitated him for periods of time from 1895 until his death in 1902. At the time it was not known what he suffered from. It is now thought that he had repeated small strokes which caused him to suffer multiple infarct dementia (brain damage symptoms).

Admiral Winfield Scott Schley

Schley was born in 1839 in Frederick, Maryland, and graduated from the Naval Academy in 1860. He participated in the homeward voyage of Japan's first diplomatic mission and from May 1861 to 1864 served on various blockade ships along the Atlantic coast and later on the Mississippi River against Port Hudson. From 1864-66, he patrolled in the Pacific and up to the Spanish American War saw service in Korea, China, Central America and several tours at

the Naval Academy.* He was promoted to Commodore in February 1898 and took command of the Flying Squadron on his flagship the *Brooklyn.* He led the fleet in the great Battle of Santiago but was censured by the Navy Department for vacilating in his conduct of the campaign in which Admiral Sampson claimed credit for the victory. His promotion to rear admiral was also delayed until August 1899. After the war he served on the Puerto Rico commission, was president of the retirement board and commander-in-chief of the South Atlantic Squadron (1899-1901). He retired in 1901 and died in 1911.

*He commanded the expedition that rescued the Arctic explorer Adolphus W. Greely in 1884.

Admiral Sampson

Admiral Schley

Theodore Roosevelt had been itching for a fight. As Assistant Secretary of the Navy he had already set in motion the ability of the United States Navy to wage war at sea on two fronts.

When President McKinley issued his call for 125,000 volunteers plus the formation of three regiments of frontiersmen and cowboys, Roosevelt decided he would be of more use in the army than waging war from a desk.

He immediately went to see Secretary of War, Russell Alger to volunteer his services and was offered his own regiment. As Roosevelt himself admitted, he had no real military experience and proposed that his friend, Leonard Wood take command with the rank of Colonel. Roosevelt would be second in command in the rank of lieutenant colonel.

Thus was born the First United States Volunteer Cavalry or as they would go down in history—"The Rough Riders" or "Roosevelt's Rough Riders."

The call went out to men from the southwest and even the Ivy League schools of the east. In a few weeks approximately 1,000 men were selected from 20,000 volunteers and congregated in San Antonio, Texas, for training and outfitting.

After a few weeks, the regiment was orderd to Tampa, Florida, for possible use in the invasion of Cuba. There they were thrown into the chaos of the expanded U.S. Army trying to equip and train thousands of volunteer troops.

When the call came to begin loading the transports for the trip to Cuba, Roosevelt had to forceably take over the *Yucatán* and could take only 542 of his troopers and none of the horses, except his two mounts.

The regiment went on to glory in Cuba and would become one of the best-known units in the history of the U.S. Army. Roosevelt was propelled to the New York governship and eventually President of the United States.

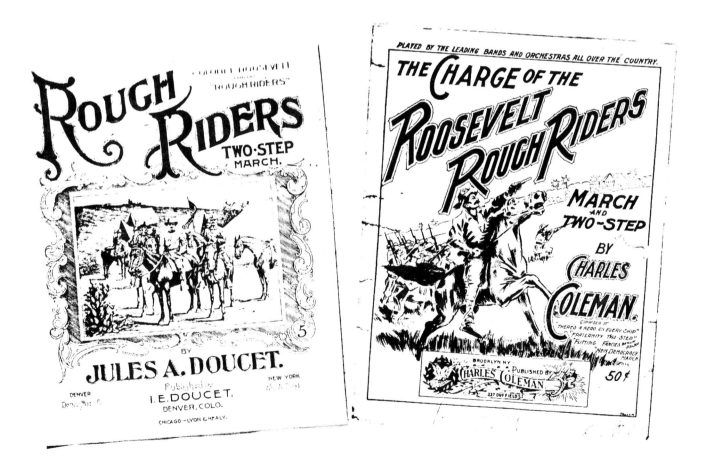

Theodore Roosevelt

No other personality who participated in the war is as identified with it as Theodore Roosevelt. First as Assistant Secretary of the Navy before the war and then in command of the Rough Riders.

Roosevelt was born in New York City in 1858, the second of four children of Theodore and Martha Bullock Roosevelt. Like his father, Teddie, as he was called, had great energy, curiosity and determination. He enjoyed an active childhood although he was puny and frequently ill.

He entered Harvard University in 1876 and graduated in 1880. That same year he married Alice Hathaway Lee but she died two days after the birth of their daughter, also named Alice, in 1884.

In 1881 he was elected to the New York state assembly and was heavily involved in politics. After the death of his wife he left politics and bought two ranches on the Little Missouri River in the Dakota Territory. He married a second time in 1886 to his childhood friend, Edith Kermit Carow.

When Roosevelt's friend, Benjamin Harrison was elected president in 1888, he was appointed to the Civil Service Commission. In 1895, he was appointed president of the Board of Police Commissioners in New York City and fought tirelessly to stamp out dishonesty on the police force.

Newly elected President William McKinley appointed Roosevelt Assistant Secretary of the Navy in 1897. He again fought tirelessly for an expanded, modern navy and due to his efforts the United States fleet overwhelmed the Spanish fleet in the ensuing war.

Roosevelt was impatient with McKinley's attempts to avoid war with Spain. In private he complained that the President had "no more backbone than a chocolate eclair." Once war was declared Roosevelt resigned from the government and helped form the First Volunteer Cavalry Regiment with Col. Leonard Wood as commander.

The Rough Riders and San Juan Hill made Theodore Roosevelt a household name in America. Twenty years later he declared, "San Juan was the great day of my life."

San Juan Hill propelled Roosevelt into the governor's seat in New York in 1898 and his efficient and independent administration would be his trademark the rest of his political career.

McKinley ran for a second term in 1900 and put Roosevelt on the ticket as the vice-presidential candidate. Their ticket defeated the Democratic ticket of William Jennings Bryan and Adlai Stevenson. Only six months after his second inauguration, McKinley was shot in Buffalo, New York, and died a few days later. Roosevelt became the youngest American president at age 43.

The rest is history. He served for two terms and ran again, unsuccessfully in 1912. He literally molded the course of American history in the first two decades of the 20th Century. He died of a blood clot on Jan. 6, 1919.

Roosevelt Historic Sites

- Theodore Roosevelt Birthplace NHS, New York City
- Sagamore Hill NHS, Oyster Bay, Long Island, New York
- Theodore Roosevelt National Park, Medora, North Dakota
- Theodore Roosevelt Inaugural NHS, Buffalo, New York
- Theodore Roosevelt Island, George Washington Memorial Parkway, McLean, Virginia
- Mt. Rushmore National Monument, Keystone, South Dakota

Roosevelt's uniform, hat and gloves on display at the Theodore Roosevelt Birthplace National Historic Site in New York City.

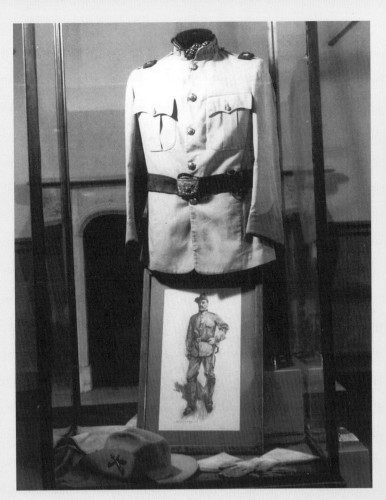

One of Roosevelt's Rough Riders uniforms on display at Sagamore Hill.

Sagamore Hill was the home of Theodore Roosevelt and his family for over 30 years. He built it in 1884-85 and used it as the "Summer White House." He died here on Jan. 6, 1919. His wife, Edith lived here until her death in 1948. In 1950 the site was purchased by the Theodore Roosevelt Association, and in 1963 the Association presented it and Roosevelt's birthplace in New York City to the American people. Sagamore Hill, Old Orchard Museum, Memorial Park and the gravesite and Sanctuary at Oyster Bay, Long Island, New York, are now national historical sites of the National Park Service.

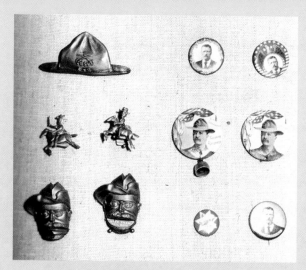

Campaign memorabilia emphasizing his Rough Riders fame.

A regimental bugle, cavalry sword and Cuban-style machete from the Cuban campaign.

Bronze equestrian statue of Roosevelt in Lion's Room. Cast from the working mode the heroic size statue creation of A. Phimister Coe, presented by Henry Waldo Coe, M.D., to the city of Portland, Oregon. The bronze was a gift from Dr. Coe to the Roosevelt Memorial Association in 1924.

Roosevelt's canteen used in Cuba.

All items on display at the Theodore Roosevelt Birthplace National Historic Site at 28 East 20th Street, New York City. PHOTOS BY MERV BLOCH, NEW YORK CITY.

FOR GOVERNOR.

FOR LIEUT· GOVERNOR

COL·THEODORE ROOSEVELT· TIMOTHY L·WOODRUFF·

Roosevelt's fame as a Rough Rider propelled him into the New York governor's chair in 1898.

General Leonard Wood

Gen. Leonard Wood was born in Winchester, New Hampshire, in 1860. He graduated from Harvard Medical School in 1886, and practiced for slightly more than a year before receiving a commission in the United States Army.

He took part in the arduous campaign against the Apache Chief Geronimo as an assistant army surgeon. For his part in the campaign he was awarded the Medal of Honor.

Wood was a colonel when war broke out with Spain. He was asked to organize and train a volunteer cavalry unit which subsequently became the Rough Riders. When he was appointed brigadier general of volunteers, Lt. Col. Theodore Roosevelt assumed command of the regiment and his name has forever been associated with the famous unit.

In 1899, now General, Wood was appointed governor general of Cuba after serving as governor of Santiago. During his tenure as governor, he worked tirelessly to bring the fledgling nation's standards in line with the rest of the world. He inaugurated a medical research program which led to the discovery of how yellow fever was transmitted and how it could be controlled.

From 1906 to 1909 he commanded army troops in the Philippines and served as Chief of Staff of the United States Army from 1910 to 1914. In this position he tried to advocate American preparedness for the coming war but was sharply criticized. When war did come in 1917 he was in charge of training troops and was sent on a tour of the European Front. He was seriously wounded and spent a number of weeks in a French hospital. At war's end, he was in command of the 10th Division.

In 1920 he was a leading candidate for the Republican presidential nomination but Warren Harding was chosen instead.

Wood next accepted the presidency of the University of Pennsylvania but soon left to take over as governor general of the Philippines. He served there until his death in 1927.

Fort Leonard Wood in Missouri was established as a basic training center in 1940. Today, it is the home of the U.S. Army Engineering School.

Roosevelt, left, Wood, center, and an unknown trooper at the San Antonio fairgrounds. NA #111-SC-93573

Wood wrote his wife from the train to Tampa: "New Orleans was very enthusiastic, streets full of people and best of all an American flag in the hands of all. The cost of this war is amply repaid by seeing the old flag as one sees it today in the South. We are indeed once more a united country."

General Wood, his family and staff. Front row, left to right: Luisita Wood, Osborne Wood, the General, Mrs. Wood, Leonard Wood Jr. Back row, left to right: Henzman, his orderly, Capt. Matthew E. Hanna, Capt. Edward Carpenter, Capt. Frank R. McCoy. NA #111-SC-93576

Gen. Leonard Wood as governor general of the Philippines in the 1920s. NA #111-SC-84786

Swearing in of Rough Riders by Capt. Charles L. Cooper, U.S. Army, in front of the Palace of the Governors, Santa Fe, New Mexico, May 7, 1898. MNM #6051, CHRISTIAN G. KAADT PHOTO

A crowd sending off
Rough Riders recruits
from Las Vegas, New
Mexico, to San Antonio.
MNM #66657 CHARLES DOLL PHOTO

Rough Riders recruits
marching to the railroad
depot at Santa Fe, New
Mexico, to embark for San
Antonio, May 7, 1898. MNM
#14294

Officers of Troop A, Rough
Riders, leaving Santa Fe
New Mexico for San
Antonio, May 7, 1898. MNM
#14293, DR. G.A.NEEFF PHOTO

The historic Menger Hotel in San Antonio is located adjacent to the Alamo. The hotel was built in 1859 by William A. Menger. It has been added to through the years and now has 350 rooms. It is a member of Historic Hotels of America. In 1887 a new taproom was built within the hotel as a replica of the House of Lords Pub in London. It was located facing Alamo Plaza. The bar still features the original brass spittoons for tobacco chewing and snuff dipping. It was in this bar that Teddy Roosevelt recruited many of his Rough Riders including some of the East Coast millionaires such as: Hamilton Fish, Reginald Ronalds and Woodbury Kane. Carry Nation also visted the bar in 1917 and attacked it with her infamous axe to foster her temperance beliefs. During Prohibition, the bar was disassembled and moved to its present location within the hotel.

An oak tree at the Riverside Golf Course in San Antonio. This was supposedly a campsite for the Rough Riders while they were training in San Antonio.

Recruits mobilizing in Prescott, Arizona. SHM #MIL218PA

The gazebo in Prescott, Arizona, where the Rough Riders mobilized before being sent to San Antonio, April 1898. SHM #MIL218PE

The Rough Riders encamped at the fairgrounds in San Antonio. MNM #6035

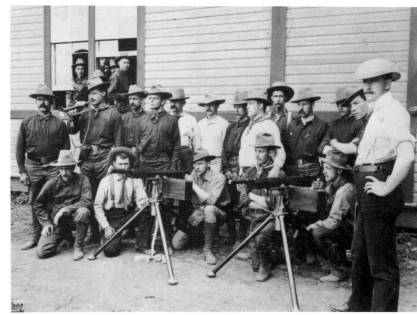

Pvt. Gordon Johnston, mounted orderly to Colonel Roosevelt, hands his colonel a dispatch during a training exercise at San Antonio. ITC

Top right: Rough Riders gathered behind two Colt automatic rifles presented to the regiment in San Antonio. HU Middle: Officers take a break from a meal to pose for this photo at their training camp. SHM #MIL121PA

Troopers of Troop G and I pose at San Antonio, May 16, 1898. MNM #71213 A.A. BRACK PHOTO

Scenes of the Rough Riders at San Antonio.

Troop I in camp. MNM #5998

Colonel Wood and
Roosevelt with Rough
Riders officers and their
mountain lion mascot. MNM
#152654 BROCKMEIER PHOTO

Troop E at San Antonio.
MNM #13899

Occupations of Rough Riders*

Accountants 1	Farriers 10	Packers 2
Actors 2	Firemen 9	Painters 6
Architects 1	Florists 2	Pharmacists 1
Army 29	Football Players 10	Photographers 1
Artists 2	Foreign Legion 2	Physicians 8
Assessors 1	Furriers 2	Planters 1
Associated Press 1	Gardeners 3	Plasterers 1
Attorneys 16	Golfers 5	Plumbers 8
Bakers 5	Grocers 2	Policemen 6
Bandmasters 2	Guards 1	Polo Players 15
Barbers 6	Half-milers 1	Postal Clerks 1
Baseball Players 7	Harnessmakers 1	Printers 14
Bicyclists 1	High-jumpers 1	Prospectors 6
Blacksmiths 17	Horse Dealers 1	Railroad Men 31
Bookbinders 1	Hotel Clerks 2	Ranchers 44
Bookkeepers 2	Hotelkeepers 1	Rangers 2
Brakemen 1	Hunters 6	Real Estate Dealers 2
Bricklayers 2	Indian Agents 1	Reporters 11
Brickmakers 1	Insurance Agents 3	Recorders 1
Bridge Builders 1	Internal Revenue Agents 1	Saddlers 11
Butchers 8	Ironworkers 1	Sailors 3
Cabinet Makers 1	Jewelers 2	Salesmen 5
Car Inspectors 1	Jockeys 1	Scouts & Indian Fighters 5
Carpenters 13	Journalists 3	Sculptors 1
Car Repairers 1	Judges 1	Shoemakers 2
Cattlemen 14	Justice Dept. Agents 3	Singers 2
Chaplains 2	Laborers 34	Song Writers 1
Cigar Makers 1	Lawyers 16	Speakers of House 1
Civil Engineers 1	Linemen 1	Stage Drivers 3
Clerks 44	Liverymen 2	Steeplechase Riders 1
Coaches 2	Locksmiths 1	Stenographers 2
Collectors 1	Locomotive Engineers 2	Stock Exchange 3
Conductors 2	Locomotive Firemen 1	Stonemasons 2
Confectioners 1	Machinists 6	Students 26
Congressmen 4	Mailmen 2	School Superintendents 2
Contractors 3	Manufacturers 1	Surveyors 2
Cooks 13	Marshals or Sheriffs 8	Teachers 15
Coopers 1	Mechanics 2	Teamsters 13
Cowboys 160	Merchants 3	Telegraph Linemen 3
Crewmen 4	Miners 87	Telegraph Operators 3
Cuban Insurgents 3	Ministers 5	Telephone Operators 1
Deserters 7	Moulders 1	Tennis Players 4
Detectives 1	Musicians 14	Tinners 3
Druggists 3	Navy 3	Traders 1
Editors 1	Newsdealers 1	Trainmasters 1
Electricians 4	Newspapermen 11	Trappers 8
Engineers 12	Nurses 1	Veterinary Surgeons 3
Expressmen 1	Nurserymen 2	Watchmakers 4
Farmers 53	Orators 1	Weather Observers 1
		Yachtsmen 2

*SOURCE: VIRGIL CARRINGTON JONES, *ROOSEVELT'S ROUGH RIDERS*

The Rough Riders had a 21% casualty rate in the entire Cuban Campaign—23 killed, 104 wounded in battle and over 100 died of disease. The highest casualty rate of any unit in the war.

Rough Riders of Some Note

William Tiffany of the famous jewelry family was a 34-year-old and a grandnephew of Commodore Oliver H. Perry. He died of yellow fever upon his return to the United States.

David M. Goodrich was the captain of the Harvard crew team and one of the most noted college athletes in the country. He later became chairman of the Board of the B.F. Goodrich Rubber Co.

Stanley Hollister, at 24, was a champion half-miler from Santa Barbara, California. He died on Aug. 17, of typhoid fever.

Dudley Dean, 27, was a great football player from Harvard University.

Bob Wrenn was another Harvard football player.

John McIlhenny from New Orleans, a 2nd Lieutenant in Troop E, later owned the Tabasco Sauce Co.

Charles Younger, a private in Troop C, was the son of the outlaw, Bob Younger.

Woodbury Kane, at 38, was a noted polo player and horseman and later a noted yachtsman.

Hamilton Fisk Jr. was a New York playboy, captain of the Columbia University crew team and grandson of Hamilton Fisk, President Grant's Secretary of State. After college Fisk worked on the railroad in Utah. At the start of the war, he wrote home: "I am going into the fight with my stripes." At 25, he was killed in the battle at Las Guasimas.

Frank Knox became a prominent publisher and politician after the war. In 1928, he became general manager of all the Hearst newspapers. He bought controlling interest in the *Chicago Daily News* in 1931. In 1936 he was the Republican Vice-Presidential candidate against the Roosevelt ticket. In 1940, President Roosevelt appointed Knox Secretary of the Navy and he became one of the few party leaders in U.S. history to serve in a cabinet formed by a President of the opposing party. He served in this post until his death in 1944, directing the Navy's war against the Axis powers.

Dr. James Rovert Church, son of the U.S. Senate Librarian, Alonzo W. Church, was the regimental surgeon. He played on the Princeton University football team and was an expert horseman.

Joseph Sampson Stevens of Newport, Rhode Island, was the son of the Duchess de Dino of Paris and a crack polo player.

Thirteen Rough Riders joined Buffalo Bill's Wild West Show in 1899.

The Rough Riders
Where They Were From*

States				Territories	
Alabama	15	Montana	1	Arizona	35
Arkansas	14	Nebraska	8	Indian	103
California	42	New Hampshire	5	New Mexico	120
Colorado	24	New Jersey	12	Oklahoma	12
Connecticut	3	New York	90		
Delaware	1	North Carolina	6	Foreign Countries	
Florida	17	North Dakota	3		
Georgia	10	Ohio	46	Alsace	1
Illinois	81	Oregon	3	Australia	1
Indiana	28	Pennsylvania	45	Canada	10
Iowa	42	Rhode Island	3	Denmark	1
Kansas	52	South Carolina	5	England	13
Kentucky	18	Tennessee	17	Germany	14
Louisiana	16	Texas	127	Ireland	5
Maine	3	Utah	5	Monaco	1
Maryland	7	Vermont	4	Russia	2
Massachusetts	25	Virginia	15	Scotland	7
Michigan	21	Washington	1	Sweden	5
Minnesota	3	West Virginia	10	Switzerland	2
Mississippi	6	Wisconsin	16	Wales	1
Missouri	63	Wyoming	3		

*SOURCE: VIRGIL CARRINGTON JONES, *ROOSEVELT'S ROUGH RIDERS*

Rough Riders with their mascots, *Cuba* the dog and *Florence* the mountain lion. SHM #MIL215PC

Middle photo: How the Rough Riders rode to Port Tampa. This photo appeared in *Harper's Weekly.* Bottom photo: Roosevelt and Captain Lee of the British Army confer in Tampa. USF ENSNINGER BROS. PHOTO

Artist Bernard Partridge's view of Theodore Roosevelt for the British publication *Punch*. Roosevelt took two horses with him to Cuba. "Rain-in-the-Face" drowned at the initial landing. "Little Texas" was his mount through the campaign.

Officers of the Rough Riders posed with Maj. Gen. Joseph Wheeler (front) in Tampa. From left: Maj. George Dunn, Maj. Alexander Brodie, Chaplain Henry Brown, Colonel Wood and Lieutenant Colonel Roosevelt. KE

"THE ROUGH RIDER."

Left to right: Leonard Wood, John Greenway and Theodore Roosevelt. Greenway was a graduate of Yale, an ex-college athlete, and an officer in Troop G. After the war, he became a prominent Arizona mining man and his sculptured likeness is in the U.S. Capitol. ASHS

Who Really Took San Juan Hill?

by Blaine Taylor (reprinted with slight editing
from *War Classics* magazine, Fall 1990 issue)

It is July 1, 1898, and U.S. Army Gen. William R. Shafter's troops are sweltering under the broiling Cuban sun.

Part of General Shafter's command is one of the most famous cavalry units in American history, the legendary "Rough Riders," commanded by the notable veteran of the Geronimo Wars, Leonard Wood and his able subordinate, Theodore Roosevelt. In time, both would be nominated by the Republican Party as the GOP standard bearers for the Presidency—and one, Roosevelt, would actually make it to the White House.

But now, in the hot summer of 1898, Roosevelt and Wood are chagrined at what Roosevelt tells Massachusetts Sen. Henry Cabot Lodge is the "criminally incompetent" conduct of the campaign by General Shafter. They are itching to take the Spanish-held Cuban city of Santiago, but first the Americans must get past fortified Spanish blockhouses atop El Caney, San Juan Hill and Kettle Hill, the defensive positions ringing the city.

The day before, Wood had placed Roosevelt in charge of the Rough Riders, who occupied nearby El Pozo Hill. There, German, English and Japanese war correspondents fled with the rest as Roosevelt's artillery came under very accurate Spanish gunfire, and Teddy himself was hit: "One of the shrapnel bullets dropped on my wrist, hardly breaking the skin, but raising a bump about as big as a hickory nut," he later wrote.

The American artillery returned fire onto San Juan Hill, but the telltale black powder smoke from their guns gave the U.S. positions away, to the intense satisfaction of the enemy's gunners.

Author Stephen Crane was reporting the fighting for the newspapers back home, and wrote, "The American battery thundered behind the men with a shock that seemed likely to tear the backs of their heads off. The Spanish shrapnel fled on a line to their left, swirling and swishing in supernatural velocity. The noise of the rifle bullets broke in their faces like the noise of so many lamp-chimneys or sped overhead in swift, cruel spitting, and at the front the battle-sound, as if it were simply music, was beginning to swell and swell, until the volleys rolled like a surf."

A young American officer attached to the Black 10th Cavalry—1st Lt. John J. "Black Jack" Pershing recalled that "The road...follows tortuous and narrow, along the river through the swampy jungle, then crosses the river and passes toward and between San Juan Hills...The regiment moved slowly along this road under the scorching sun and sweltered.:.A converging fire from all the works within range opened fire upon us that was terrible in its effect; the 71st New York, which lay in a sunken road near the ford, became demoralized and well-nigh stampeded; our mounted officers dismounted, the men stripped off at the roadside everything possible, and prepared for business...."

It was soon decided by the American command that the key to the entire position was the blockhouse straddling the most immediate height in front: San Juan Hill. Roosevelt was given the order to attack it, and told his cheering men, "Don't cheer—but fight—now's the time to fight!"

As they maneuvered into position to begin the assault, all the American troops present—including the aid stations—came under intense Spanish shellfire, a frustrating experience inasmuch as they were not yet allowed to fire back....

As Rough Rider Frank Knox later wrote home, "The enemy were slowly withdrawing from the brush into the bottoms of the trenches on the hills. As they withdrew, we advanced on our hands and knees, crawling on our stomachs at times and—where the ground permitted—with a rush, until we had driven them all to the hilltops. Now began the serious work of the day. We had to dislodge an enemy our equal or superior in numbers from a strongly fortified and entrenched position on the ranges of hills that surround the city."

It was now around 1 p.m. on July 1, and, as nearby Kettle Hill came under American assault, Roosevelt conspicuously pranced back and forth on horseback in front of his men—and in full view of the entrenched Spanish opposite them. He gave the order to begin the famous "Charge up San Juan Hill" that would help catapult him to the Oval Office a little more than three years later.

"By this time," he recalled after the war, "we were all in the spirit of the thing, and greatly excited by the charge. The men cheering and running forward between shots...I...galloped toward the hill, passing the shouting, cheering, shooting men, and went up the lane, splashing through a small stream. When I got abreast of the ranch buildings on top of

Kettle Hill, I turned and went up the slope.

"Being on horseback, I was, of course, able to get ahead of the men on foot, except my orderly, Henry Bardshar, who had run ahead very fast in order to get better shots at the Spaniards—who were now running out of the ranch buildings...some 40 yards from the top. I ran into a wire fence and jumped off *Little Texas*, turning him loose. He had been scraped by a couple of bullets, one of which nicked my elbow, and I never expected to see him again. As I ran up the Hill, Bardshar stopped to shoot, and two Spaniards fell as he emptied his magazine. These were the only Spaniards I actually saw fall to aimed shots by any one of my men, with the exception of two guerrillas in trees."

Continuing, Colonel Roosevelt wrote, "Almost immediately afterward, the Hill was covered by the troops, both Rough Riders and the colored troops of the 9th, and some men of the 1st... One Spaniard was captured in the buildings, another was shot as he tried to hide himself, and a few others were killed as they ran.

"No sooner were we on the crest than the Spaniards from the line of hills in our front, where they were strongly entrenched, opened a very heavy fire upon us with their rifles. They also opened upon us with one or two pieces of artillery, using time fuses which burned very accurately, the shells exploding right over our heads.

"On top of the Hill was a huge iron kettle—or something of the kind—probably used for sugar refining. Several of our men took shelter behind this. We had a splendid view of the charge on theSan Juan blockhouse to our left, where the infantry of Kent, led by Hawkins, were climbing the Hill."

Thus it was that, in fact, Roosevelt and his Rough Riders took *Kettle* Hill—not *San Juan* Hill—unless Kettle is accorded to be part of the San Juan Hills complex—as, indeed, some historians have done. What of San Juan Hill itself, though?

A Gatling gun detachment under the command of Lt. John H. Parker unleashed the "coffee grinders" at the Blockhouse with "Three guns simultaneously at 1:15 p.m. using ranges of 600-800 yards," reminisced Parker subsequently. "The enemy at first concentrated his fire upon us, but soon weakened, and in five minutes was clambering from his trenches and running to the rear. We fired as rapidly as possible upon the groups thus presented until I saw a white hankerchief [sic] waved by someone of my own

Regiment--the 13th Infantry...I ordered the fire to cease..."

A trembling captured Spanish officer told Parker, "It was terrible when your guns opened—always. They 'B-r-r-r,' like a lawn mower cutting the grass over our trenches. We could not stick a finger up when you fired without getting it cut off!"

Crane remembered the actual charge up San Juan Hill thus: "Yes, they were going up the Hill, up the Hill. It was the best moment of anybody's life! An officer said to me afterward, 'If we had been in that position and the Spaniards had come at us, we would have piled them up so high the last man couldn't have climbed over!' but up went the Regiments with no music save that ceaseless fierce crashing of rifles."

Correspondent Richard Harding Davis recalled: "I have seen many illustrations and pictures of this charge on the San Juan Hills, but none of them seem to show it just as I remember it. In the picture-papers, the men are running up hill swiftly and gallantly, in regular formation—rank after rank—with flags flying, their eyes aflame and their hair streaming, their bayonets fixed, in long, brilliant lines, an invincible, overpowering weight of numbers. Instead of which I think the thing which impressed one the most, when our men started from cover, was that they were so few! It seemed as if someone had made an awful and terrible mistake! One's instinct was to call them to come back...."

The foreign military observers present agreed: 'It is very gallant, but very foolish.' 'Why, they can't take it, you know! Never in the world!' 'It is slaughter!' are just some of the later remembered comments made at the time, in the very heat of the fighting.

Davis rejoined, "They had no glittering bayonets, they were not massed in regular array. There were a few men in advance, bunched together, and creeping up a steep, sunny Hill, the tops of which roared and flashed with flame. The men held their guns pressed across their breasts and stepped heavily as they climbed. Behind these first few, spreading out like a fan, were single lines of men, slipping and scrambling in the smooth grass, moving forward with difficulty...It was much more wonderful than any swinging charge could have been. They walked to greet death at every step, many of them, as they advanced, sinking suddenly or pitching forward and disappearing in the high grass, but the others waded on, stubbornly, forming a thin blue line that kept creeping higher and higher up the Hill. It was as inevitable as the rising tide.

"It was a miracle of self-sacrifice, a triumph of bulldog courage," continued Davis, "which one watched breathless with wonder. The fire of the Spanish riflemen, who still stuck bravely to their posts, doubled and tripled in fierceness, the crests of the Hills crackled and burst in amazed roars, and rippled with waves of tiny flame, but the blue line crept steadily up and on, and then—near the top—the broken fragments gathered together with a sudden burst of speed, the Spaniards appeared for a moment outlined against the sky and poised for instant fight, fired a last volley and fled before the swift-moving wave that leaped and sprang after them."

And what of Teddy Roosevelt and his men on captured Kettle Hill meanwhile?

As they saw the Americans take San Juan after the final rush over the top, Roosevelt rose and ordered his Rough Riders to take the "Next line of Spanish trenches on the Hills to their front: Thinking that the men would all come, I jumped over the wire fence in front of us and started at the double, but—as a matter of fact—the troopers were so excited, what with shooting and being shot, and shouting and cheering, that they did not hear, or did not heed me...After running about a hundred yards, I found I only had five men along with me!" Sheepishly, he returned to organize the delayed advance....

"We started across the wide valley which lay between us and the Spanish entrench-ments...Long before we got near them, the Spaniards ran, save a few here and there, who either surrendered or were shot down. When we reached the trenches, we found them filled with dead bodies in the light blue-and-white uniform of the Spanish Regular Army....

"I was with Henry Bardshar, running up at the double, and two Spaniards leapt from the trenches and fired at us, not 10 yards away. As they turned to run, I closed in and fired twice, missing the first and killing the second. My revolver was from the sunken battleship *Maine*.

"There was very great confusion at this time, the different regiments being completely intermingled—white regulars, colored regulars, and Rough Riders...We were still under a heavy fire, and I got together a mixed lot of men and pushed on from the trenches and ranch houses which we had just taken, driving the Spaniards through a line of palm trees, and over the crest of a chain of hills. When we reached these crests, we found ourselves overlooking Santiago."

The San Juan Hills had, indeed, been taken, but the battle for Santiago was far from over. In fact, the American high command—surprised by the suddenness of its own, swift victory—thought at first that it would not be able to hold against the expected Spanish counterattack. But hold they did, and the resultant, overall American victory in Cuba—personified later in the public imagination by Roosevelt and his Rough Riders "taking" San Juan Hill—gave the nation our first and only "cowboy" President, Teddy himself.

But for the men present, there was a more important and immediate result of the Battle of San Juan Hill: "To help erase lines of section and color," as noted by author Frank Friedel.

As he quotes Rough Rider Frank Knox, "...In justice to the colored race, I must say that I never saw braver men anywhere! Some of those who rushed up the Hill will live in my memory forever." Pershing agreed, adding, "White regiments, black regiments, regulars and Rough Riders, representing the young manhood of the North and the South, fought shoulder to shoulder, unmindful of race or color, unmindful of whether commanded by ex-Confederate or not, and mindful only of their common duty as Americans."

It was a fitting epitaph for a battle that helped propel the "cowboy" United States of America onto the global stage of world power—just as former Under Secretary of the Navy Theodore Roosevelt had envisioned it would from the very start....

Capron's Battery firing on El Caney, July 1, 1898.

Capt. William "Buckey" O'Neill of Troop A. He had been mayor of Prescott, Arizona, a sheriff and a fighter in the Indian wars. On July 1, he was killed in action while deploying his troop before Kettle Hill. His earlier remark that "the Spanish bullet has never been molded that will kill Buckey O'Neill" would prove untrue, however, the legend that he would calmly walk around in a hail of bullets has had many versions through the years. SHM #P0112P

Upper right: Rough Rider Frank Knox, a private in Troop D, would eventually become one of the principal men in America's fight against the Axis in World War II as Secretary of the Navy.

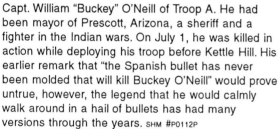

Col. Henry L. Turner of the 1st Illinois Volunteer Infantry confers with Lieutenant Colonel Roosevelt the morning of July 12, 1898. After an all-night rain, Turner was barefoot while his shoes and socks were drying. Roosevelt called upon Turner, whose troops occupied trenches on the Rough Riders right, to see if he could be of any service to the Illinois' troops. Later two boxes of hardtack were sent to Turner.

The Rough Riders resting
before Santiago. KE

Chaplain Henry Brown
conducts a service in the
field. Brown was the
pastor of St. Luke's
Episcopal Church in
Prescott, Arizona, when
the call came for volun-
teers. He was an avid
proponent of Cuban
independence and asked
Governor McCord to
appoint him as chaplain of
the First United States
Volunteer Cavalry. KE

Officers of the
Rough Riders.
AHSL

William Dunwiddie's famous photo of the Rough Riders on the top of San Juan Heights, July 1, 1898. Roosevelt carried a pistol salvaged from the *Maine.*

Sgt. Albert Wright from Yuma, Arizona, was the tallest trooper at 6'6". He was attached to headquarters as the regimental color bearer. He carried the silk banner of the Arizona Squadron presented to the Arizona Rough Riders by the ladies of the Women's Relief Corps of Phoenix. HU

Scene along a part of the line before Santiago, held by the Rough Riders, showing the tents and huts in which they tried to avoid the frequent rains. HU

Rough Riders cheering at the rear of the trenches dug on the heights overlooking Santaigo after the famous charge up San Juan and Kettle hills. This was the day the Spanish surrendered the city. HU

Wounded troopers recuperating in the field hospital set up in the jungle. An attendant, with arm band, waits in the background while one of them drinks from a cup. HU

A statue to fallen Rough Rider and ex-mayor of Prescott, William "Buckey" O'Neill was dedicated at the Court House Square in Prescott, Arizona, on July 5, 1907. It was executed by Solom Borglum, the brother of Gustav Broglum who sculpted Mount Rushmore in South Dakota. SHM #MISC 238P

The Rough Riders were portrayed in a variety of advertising mediums while still stationed in Cuba. Wood and Roosevelt appeared on this New York tobacconist's cigar box. The Rough Riders became one of the most recognizable military units in American military history and it propelled both Wood and Roosevelt into national prominence.

According to Nofi's *The Spanish-American War, 1898,* the Rough Riders sustained 23 killed and 104 wounded in the entire Cuban campaign. Several troopers died on the way home or at Camp Wikoff.

PLUCKY RIDERS

GENERAL WOOD.   COL. ROOSEVELT.

LOUIS E. NEUMAN & CO.,   No. 1292—INS. $1.70 per 100 Net   ALSO BLANKS
Park Avenue & 130th Street, N. Y.   No. 1293—OUTS $0.80 per 100. Net   Special Prices in lots of

SMOKE PLUCKY RIDERS CIGARS

Rough Riders parade on horseback at Camp Wikoff, something they could not do as a unit in Cuba. SHM #MIL240 PA

Returned Rough Riders clean their weapons at Camp Wikoff, never to fire them in anger again. SHM #MIL 240PB

Roosevelt said goodbye to his men at Camp Wikoff on Sept. 13, 1898. A hollow square was formed around him and a reproduction of Frederick Remington's bronze sculpture, the "Bronco Buster" was presented to him by the men he led. Roosevelt praised his men from the West when he said: "The cowpuncher was the foundation of the regiment, and we have got him here in bronze." He then shook hands with every man in his regiment and each member of the Ninth and Tenth Cavalry regiments who was in attendance.

The Castañeda Hotel in Las Vegas, New Mexico, was the headquarters for the first Rough Riders reunion in 1899. Roosevelt, who was governor of New York by this time, was in attendance. MNM #77367 & #14292

Montana Rough Riders upon their return to Butte, Montana, in late 1898. MHS #77-35

Roosevelt greets his Rough Riders in an uncharacteristic outfit of tails and top hat. Date and location unknown but likely sometime during his presidential tenure (1901-1908). SHM #M.1 217P

Reunion of Rough Riders at Colorado Springs, Colorado, date unknown. DPL #P537 H. POLEY PHOTO

Six ex-Rough Riders marched in a 1901 Memorial Day parade in Trinidad, Colorado. MNM #71211

In 1899 some Rough Riders met in Deadwood, South Dakota, with Capt. Seth Bullock, center between the two Indian chiefs. Bullock was captain of Troop A, Third U.S. Volunteer Cavalry and a noted frontiersman who was the sheriff of Helena, Montana, and Deadwood. He became a leading developer of the Black Hills region. DPL #F46419

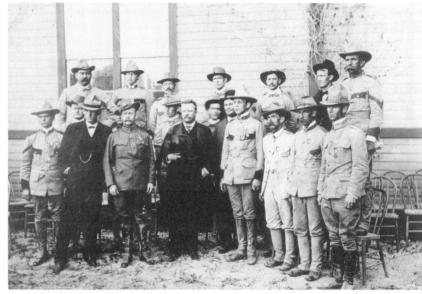

Theodore Roosevelt returned with a group of former Rough Riders to their training site at the San Antonio fairgrounds in April 1905. MNM #71212

G.A. Rapp, left, E.G. Le Stourgeon and F.W. Walff gather in San Antonio to reminisce of their adventure in 1898. This photo was taken in 1934. ITC #0193-B

In 1955 the last officer of the regiment died— Robert Patterson of Troop C.

These two well-known paintings depict a dramatic charge up San Juan Hill by the Rough Riders on horseback. Of course the charge was made on foot as the troopers had to leave their horses in Tampa and only Roosevelt was on horseback. The top painting was by W.G. Read in 1898 (LC-USZC4-826), the bottom an 1899 Kurz & Allison lithograph (LC-USZC4-1316).

WILLIAM H. WEST'S BIG MINSTREL JUBILEE

THE CHARGE OF SAN JUAN HILL

WM. H. WEST IMPERSONATING COL. ROOSEVELT, LEADING THE FAMOUS "ROUGH RIDERS" TO VICTORY.

Las Vegas, New Mexico
Before the Rough Riders were discharged, they agreed their first reunion would be held in New Mexico, where the largest contingent of troopers had originated. Las Vegas won the bid to hold the reunion. In late June 1899, the veterans arrived along with Roosevelt. The Castañeda Hotel was the reunion headquarters. In the years that followed, the men met in other cities until their 50th reunion in 1949 when they returned to Las Vegas. They came again in 1952 and '54 and finally made the city their permanent reunion headquarters until the last reunion in the late 1960s. Many veterans donated artifacts and a museum was established by the city which is now called the Rough Riders Memorial and City Museum.

The Charge of San Juan Hill: Wm. H. West impersonating Colonel Roosevelt, leading the famous "Rough Riders" to victory. Copyrighted by Strobridge Lith. Co., Cincinnati and New York, 1899. LC-USZ62-26060

This poster was produced during World War II. McElroy was supposedly a member of one of the black regiments which fought in Cuba with the Rough Riders, and in the Philippines. ITC #68-959

HUGH McELROY, AGE 54, WORLD WAR SERGEANT, PHILIPPINE CAMPAIGNER, DECORATED FOR HEROISM. HE GAVE TWO SONS TO THE NAVY, PROVIDES FOR A FAMILY OF FIVE, IS AN ELLINGTON FIELD CIVILIAN EMPLOYEE, AND BUYS A WAR BOND EVERY MONTH

Grigsby's Cowboys

In early 1898, even before the *Maine* was destroyed, Melvin Grigsby, then attorney general of South Dakota purposed the idea that cowboys from the West would make good and ready cavalrymen in case of war with Spain. He went to Washington, D.C., in March and got an amendment attached to the Volunteer Army Bill, passed by Congress, to call up a regiment of cowboys if so needed.

After war was declared three regiments were authorized, the First, Second and Third regiments of the United States Volunteer Cavalry. The First Regiment would muster in men at Prescott, Arizona, Santa Fe, New Mexico, Muskogee, Indian Territory and Guthrie, Oklahoma Territory and be under command of Col. Leonard Wood. The Second Regiment would muster in men at Casper and Cheyenne, Wyoming and be under the command of Judge Jay Torrey. The Third Regiment would muster in men at Sioux Falls, South Dakota, and be under the command of Melvin Grigsby.

The Third Regiment would consist of 12 troops, five from South Dakota, four from Montana, two from North Dakota and one from Nebraska. They were all mustered into federal service between May 12 and 23 in Sioux Falls. Grigsby was made colonel and commander of the regiment and it was subsequently shipped to Camp Thomas, Georgia.

Unfortunately for the Second and Third Regiments, the First, under Wood and Roosevelt would be the only one to go to Cuba and come under enemy fire. The rest of the cowboy cavalrymen would languish at Camp Thomas for the duration of the war and many of its members would succumb to typhoid fever. The regiment was finally mustered out from Camp Thomas in September 1898.

Will Cave, a prominent citizen of Missoula, Montana, had the distinction of being the first volunteer in the country for the war as he began organizing Troop F on March 30, 1898.

Troop A — South Dakota
Troop B — South Dakota
Troop C — South Dakota
Troop D — South Dakota
Troop E — South Dakota
Troop F — Montana
Troop G — North Dakota
Troop H — North Dakota
Troop I — Montana
Troop K — Nebraska
Troop L — Montana
Troop M — Montana

Field and staff officers of Grigsby's Cowboys. Colonel Grigsby is sitting in the middle.

The Camps

Soldiers of the 16th Infantry entering Fort Sherman in Coeur d'Alene, Idaho, for the war. The 16th garrisoned the fort in 1894 but did not return after the war. Fort Sherman was named for Gen. William Tecumseh Sherman who established the site in 1878. It was closed in 1901 and its remaining buildings are now located on the campus of North Idaho College.

Camp and Fort Locations in the United States During the War

Fort Adams, R.I.
Camp Alger, VA
Fort McPherson, GA
Fort Baker, CA
Camp Black, NY
Fort Caswell, NC
Fort Macon, NC
Fort Clinch, FL
Camp Cuba Libre, FL
Clarks Point, MA
Columbus Barracks, OH
Dutch Island, RI
Fort Point, CA
Fort Point, TX
Fort Grant, AZ
Fort Griswold, CT
Hilton Head, SC
Camp Hamilton, KY
Fort Hamilton, NY
Jackson Barracks, LA
Jefferson Barracks, MO
Key West, FL
Fort Knox, ME
Long Island Head, MA
Fort McHenry, MD
Camp McKenzie, GA
Miami, FL
Fort Mott, NJ

Camp Meade, PA
Fort Morgan, AL
Fort Monroe, VA
Fort Pickens, FL
Fort Preble, ME
Plum Island, NY
Fort Popham, ME
Fort Snelling, MN
Fort Sheridan, IL
Sheridan Point, VA
Sullivans Island, SC
Fort Slocum, NY
San Diego Barracks, CA
Fort St. Philip, LA
Fort Schuyler, NY
Camp Shipp, AL
Camp Thomas, GA
Tampa, FL
Tybee Island, GA
Fort Trumball, CT
Fort Wadsworth, NY
Washington Barracks, DC
Fort Washington, MD
Camp Wheeler, AL
Willets Point, NY
Winthrop, MA
Camp Wikoff, NY

The staff of Gen. Fitzhugh Lee at Camp Cuba Libre included Lt. Col. Curtis Guild Jr., Inspector-General, publisher of the *Boston Commercial Bulletin*, Maj. Russell B. Harrison, Assistant Inspector-General, son of ex-President Benjamin Harrison, Major Hobart, Assistant Adjutant-General, a nephew of the Vice-President, Lieutenant Sartoris, grandson of ex-President U.S. Grant, Maj. Gary Evans, former governor of South Carolina and his own son, Lt. Fitzhugh Lee Jr.

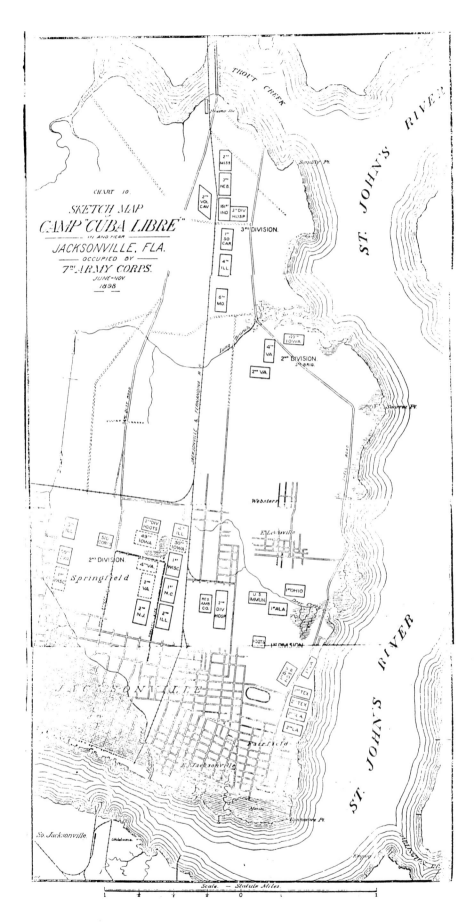

Russell Harrison, son of
ex-President Benjamin
Harrison was Provost
Guard Marshall at Camp
Cuba Libre. USAMHI

A militiaman at Camp Cuba Libre.

Camp Cuba Libre was located on the St. John's River
in a heavily wooded area five miles north of
Jacksonville.

Camp Thomas

As war appeared to be inevitable, the most pressing need of the army was to concentrate the Regular Army infantry, cavalry and artillery units in one place for organization and training.

The recently established National Military Park at Chickamauga, Georgia, site of an 1863 battle was selected for this concentration. It had rail lines, adequate water, terrain and a climate that would aclimate the troops to Cuban conditions.

All 7,300 Regulars had arrived at Camp Thomas, named for Gen. George H. Thomas, by April 27. Maj. Gen. John R. Brooke was placed in command of the camp.

By May 14 all units had departed this camp for Tampa and other ports. The next day the first of the volunteer regiments had arrived, the vanguard of close to 60,000 troops and 10,000 to 15,000 horses. It was a chaotic time with a lack of proper facilites for this many people and the fact that the supplies did not keep up the numbers arriving daily. In addition, most of the men who had a uniform were wearing hot, dark blue woolen ones that had been standard since the Civil War.

There was also racial tension, especially in the adjacent cities and towns with the regular and volunteer black troops. Chattanooga which was only nine miles from camp did welcome the white troops on leave and especially the money they spent.

The troops were eager for combat but unfortunately only a small percentage of them ever left camp. Disease and sickness had been present in camp since the first arrivals and as the summer wore on it got worse. The *New York Herald* published an account by a member of the Eighth New York, who described Camp Thomas as:

"...a perfect Hell on Earth. War itself would have been a paradise compared with the peace of this camp. I saw many awful sights there—men dying under the trees for want of a glass of water. I found men who had been sick with typhoid fever for days, and who had not received any medical attention. No one had even taken their temperature. It was awful...The water from the creek was simply mud, and yet the boys had to bathe in it and drink it. Everything about the camp was badly managed."

The War Department took alot of heat for the camp conditions and a number of investigating boards were appointed to look into the situation. On Aug. 8, Secretary Alger ordered the camp to begin closing. Troops were sent to other sites or discharged and sent home. The Eighth U.S. Volunteers stayed until early 1899 to clean up the camp and guard the tons of supplies and equipment that remained.

A Congressional investigation after the war determined that 752 soldiers at the camp died of disease. Camp Thomas claimed more victims than any other camp or battlefield of the war. The park would take years to recover. A new Camp Thomas just north of the park was established by 1902 and lasted through World War Two.

Camp Life at Chickamauga

PUBLISHED BY THE INDIANA WOMAN, INDIANAPOLIS, IND.

Price 25 Cents

The nearly 40,000 volunteers encamped here, many of them from Northern States, wearing heavy woolen clothing, suffered greatly today from the intense heat and the ambulance corps were kept busy carrying off the victims of prostration.

Eighteen members of the 5th New York Volunteers were prostrated this afternoon while marching into the camp through the Roseville Gap. Other arrivals today have been the 2nd Missouri, 1087; the 1st New Hampshire, 1,090; and Battery B, Pennsylvania Light Artillery. The 14th New York arrived here in the night and was taken to Chickamauga late this afternoon.

F.K. McBrady, a private in the 12th New York, died this morning of delirium tremors. He was buried within three hours of death in the National Cemetery here by a detachment from his regiment.

Lt. Col. John Jacob Astor and General Breckenridge are expected to arrive here tonight.

Some of the soldiers are giving the police great trouble. The officers are very lenient with the men, a large number of whom proceed to become intoxicated soon after arrival. Owing to the hot climate they cannot gauge their drinking. The city police are powerless to preserve order.

It is claimed that two members of the 12th New York last night held up a prominent physician and rifled his pockets. They were arrested but released by request of the colonel commanding.

The New York Journal, May 20, 1898

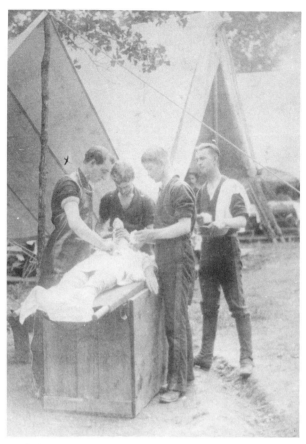

Soldiers of the 1st Regiment Georgia Volunteer Infantry apparently practicing a field operation at Camp Thomas. USAMHI

A regimental band on the porch of a hotel at Point Lookout near Camp Thomas.

The volunteer hospital system is a disgrace to civilization. The men are said to die from disease. I say they are being murdered by this wretched system. I have seen fever patients with their dry tongues hanging from their mouths, with flies swarming over their faces, with maggots in their bed sores, with no medical attention, with no water fit to drink, with no milk, with no stimulant—simply left to die, and then lie dead for hours alongside of other sufferers. It's too horrible to talk about! Tell of Spanish atrocities, of American massacres, of tortures at the stake, but for God's sake don't imagine that anything can be more terrible than any destruction of our volunteer army under the miserable hospital system. It is even more fearful than Mauser bullets!

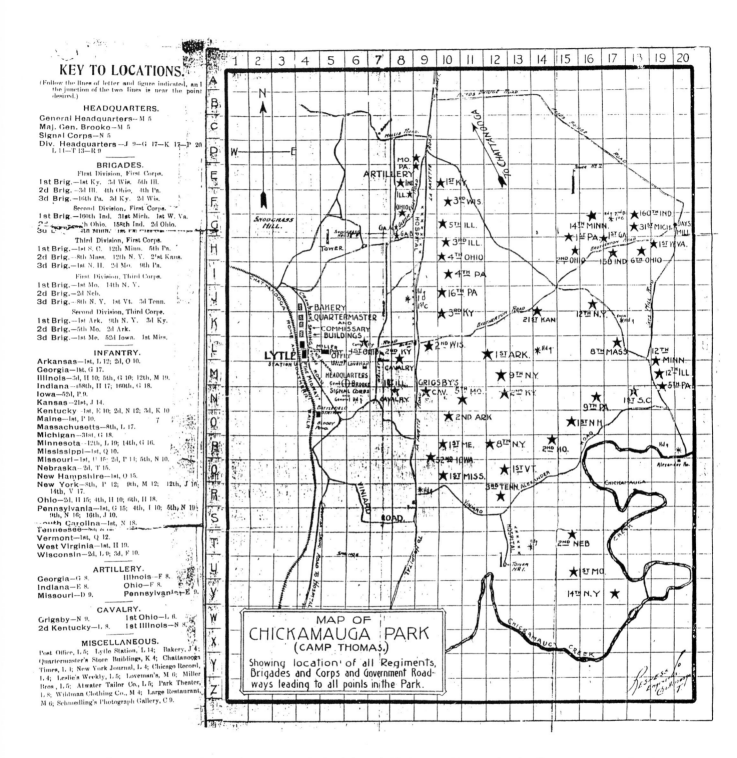

Between 1890 and 1899 Congress authorized the establishment of four national military parks associated with the Civil War. Chickamauga and Chattanooga was the first followed by Shiloh, Gettysburg and Vicksburg. The park was officially dedicated on Sept. 18-20, 1895, with most of the present-day monuments and historical markers in place. The War Department administered all national military parks until 1933 when they were transferred to the National Park Service. NPS

BOTH MAPS COURTESY CHICKAMAUGA AND CHATTANOOGA NATIONAL MILITARY PARK

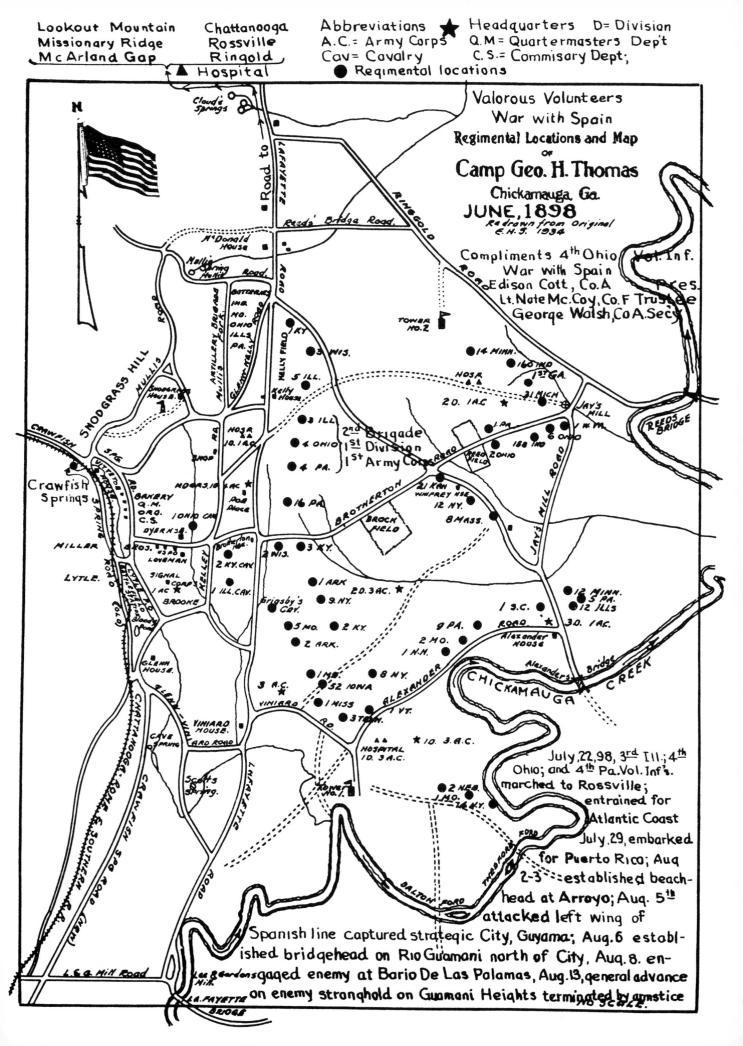

Lookout Mountain   Chattanooga   Abbreviations   ★ Headquarters   D= Division
Missionary Ridge   Rossville   A.C.= Army Corps   Q.M.= Quartermasters Dep't
Mc Arland Gap   Ringold   Cav= Cavalry   C.S.= Commisary Dept;
▲ Hospital   ● Regimental locations

Valorous Volunteers
War with Spain
Regimental Locations and Map
of
Camp Geo. H. Thomas
Chickamauga, Ga.
JUNE, 1898
Redrawn from Original
E.H.J. 1934

Compliments 4th Ohio Vol. Inf.
War with Spain
Edison Cott, Co. A   Pres.
Lt. Nate McCoy, Co. F Trustee
George Walsh, Co. A. Sec'y

July 22, 98, 3rd Ill.; 4th
Ohio; and 4th Pa. Vol. Inf's.
marched to Rossville;
entrained for Atlantic Coast
July 29, embarked
for Puerto Rico; Aug
2-3 established beach-
head at Arroyo; Aug. 5th
attacked left wing of
Spanish line captured strategic City, Guyama; Aug. 6 established bridgehead on Rio Guamani north of City, Aug. 8 engaged enemy at Bario De Las Palamas, Aug. 13, general advance
on enemy stronghold on Guamani Heights terminated by armistice
NO SCALE

A cavalry regimental barber shop at Camp Thomas. The barber was apparently also the regimental bugler.
MNHS, EDWARD A. BRUMLEY PHOTO, *MINNEAPOLIS TIMES* #62084

Members of the 14th Minnesota Volunteer Infantry at Camp Thomas, grouped on a Civil War cannon at the Chickamauga battlefield. MNHS #64829

Col. Adna R. Chaffee with his staff. Chaffee fought in the Civil War and the Indian wars. In May 1898, he was commissioned a brigadier general of volunteers and colonel of cavalry in the regular army. He was in command of the 3rd Brigade, 2nd Division, 5th Army Corps. At the battle of El Caney he became known as the "Hero of El Caney" and was promoted to brigadier general. Involved in both the Philippine Insurrection and the Boxer Rebellion, Chaffee became chief of staff of the army in 1904.

The headquarters of Gen. John Brooke, left, commander of the camp from April 25 to July 23, 1898, when he left for the campaign in Puerto Rico. Gen. J.E. Wade succeeded him as camp commander.

Gen. Frederick Dent Grant at his Camp Thomas headquarters. He was colonel of the 14th New York Volunteer Infantry and commanded a brigade at the camp. USAMHI

When Company I of the 1st Montana Infantry received its temporary issue of rifles for drill in the manual of arms, it found that one of the boxes was stencilled, "Inspected. Oct. 29, 1868." Even more disconcerting, some of the hardtack ration boxes were dated "1863."

Cooking dinner for Co. B, 9th U.S. Infantry, Camp Thomas. KE

Sutler's store at Camp Thomas. The army had a hard time supplying the basic necessities for the thousands of troops reporting to the camps so private individuals set up shop in or near the camps to supply those items not usually found in army inventory—tobacco, toiletries, reading materials, etc. The same system had been used during the Civil War period.

An officer of the 1st Regiment Georgia Volunteer Infantry at Camp Thomas with his mount held by an enlisted man, possibly his "striker" or servant.

Staff of the 2nd West Virginia Volunteers at Charleston, July 1898. A chaplain on the left, two surgeons on the right. Some wear the regulation uniform coats, others have modified coats, tailor-made with exterior pockets. WEST VIRGINIA STATE ARCHIVES

Newspaper row at Camp Black in New York provided local papers and war bulletins for the encamped troops. BA

Hospital at Camp Thomas. USAMH'

Christmas arch of Co. G, 15th Minnesota Volunteers at Camp McKenzie, Augusta, Georgia, December 1898. This was also typical of camps in the Civil War period. MNHS #7292-A

Minnesota troops assembled at Camp Ramsey (Minnesota State Fairgrounds) in St. Paul before being shipped south. MNHS #64830

A company of the Third Regiment of the 14th Minnesota Volunteer Infantry (Minnesota National Guard) at Camp Ramsey (Minnesota State Fairgrounds), St. Paul, April 1898. A classic appearance of a militia unit at the start of the war. MNHS #64828

A lieutenant whose knowledge of drill was limited to what he had learned within the week had a peculiar experience one day. His company was nearing the board fence that bounds the camp on the west. He realized they needed to be turned or a collision would be inevitable however, he couldn't remember the command. The company walked right into the fence and stood there marking time expecting to be commanded to scale the fence. Fortunately, another officer came to the rescue and right about faced the company.

Trooper Russell Moore of the 13th Regiment Minnesota Volunteers in his stall at Camp Ramsey, St. Paul. Troops were housed in the horse barns at the Minnesota State Fairgrounds. Model 1884 .45-.70 single-shot Springfield rifles with slings with webb cartridge belts are stacked against a stall. His tablecloth is a wool blanket and newspapers. MNHS #64838

A Minnesota trooper eating at a camp in Mobile, Alabama, April 1898. The boxes were made of eastern white pine and held 1,000 rounds of .45 caliber ammunition. MNHS #64836

Regimental Band of the 15th Minnesota Volunteers at Camp McKenzie, Augusta, Georgia, 1898. Note the special painting on the base drum, the crossing of the American and Cuban flags. MNHS, FLYNN PHOTO CO., AUGUSTA, GEORGIA #62087

Co. G, 15th Minnesota Volunteers at Camp Ramsey, St. Paul, Minnesota, 1898. The spring temperatures probably forced them to shed their jackets. MNHS #7802

A member of the First Battalion, Nevada Volunteer Infantry at Camp Clark, Carson City, Nevada. He has a Model 1884 .45-.70 Springfield rifle, straw-filled mattress sacks, an A-tent with sides rolled up and 1880s blanket bags serving as knapsacks. NSM

Middle: First Battalion, Nevada Volunteer Infantry at Camp Clark, Carson City, Nevada. NSM

Bottom: Co. B, 1st Infantry, Arizona National Guard, notice the unusual dress-white gloves they are wearing with their khaki tropical duck uniforms. AHSL #44457

Camp Merritt with
Parnassus Heights and
the University of California
medical school in the
background. NPS

Another view of the expanse of Camp Merritt. NPS

Camp Merritt, the major camp on the West Coast for troops destined for the Philippine campaign, was adjacent to the Presidio of San Francisco in an area called the Outside Lands or "Sand Dune Waste" in the Richmond District. MHS

Additional views of Camp Merritt showing some of the artillery pieces (top) and spartan living conditions of the troops (middle). TOP: DPL #F27562 W.C. BILLINGTON PHOTO, MIDDLE: ISHS #1153

Nevada and Utah cavalry camps at Camp Merritt, California. NPS

Tents pitched among the established buildings at the Presidio of San Francisco are examples of how the flood of troops overtaxed the existing facilities. The island of Alcatraz is in the background. NPS

Middle: Troop F, Fourth Cavalry at the Presidio of San Francisco. ISHS #60-142.28

Bottom: The Presidio of San Francisco in 1898, showing the main parade ground, encampment, the bay and Fort Mason in the background. Alcatraz Island can just be seen in the bay. NPS

Inside a tent at Camp Merritt, California. The sleeve insignia is unknown, but these are infantry troops. NPS

Co. F, 1st California Infantry at the Presidio. A good example of the mixture of uniform components worn by troops going to tropical climates. CSL #22,580

Sgt. Murray, Co. A, and Corp. Stocking, Co. B, 8th U.S. Infantry, in a barracks at the Presidio of San Francisco. Notice the picture of Admiral Dewey on the wall and the pattern 1880 "solar helmet." This photo was probably taken upon the soldiers' return from the Philippines. NPS

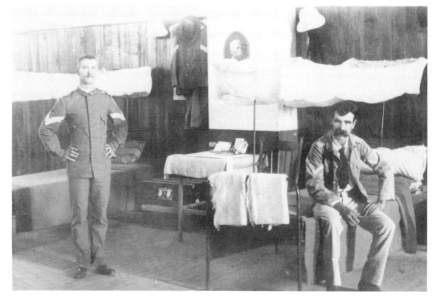

First Idaho Regimental band. They apparently have returned from the Philippines. ISHS #77-10.1

Co. A, First Idaho Volunteers. ISHS #61-86.0

Idaho troops encamped at Boise Barracks, 1898. Photo taken from present Fort Street. ISHS #60-108.56K

Payday in camp for Washington State Volunteer troops. WSHS

Idaho militia at mess. ISHS #3326-A

Co. L 1st Montana Volunteers in Helena. Notice the golden eagle mascot. MHS

Butte, Montana Company, 3rd Squadron, 3rd U.S. Volunteer Cavalry at Camp Thomas. MHS

"Admiral Dewey" was the mascot of the 1st Montana Volunteer Infantry. The golden eagle was apparently between two and three years old, and quite tame. He had spent most of his life in a cage in Helena's Central Park. Some time before the war he was given to the Grand Army of the Republic chapter which in turn gave him to the 1st Infantry. Accompanying the regiment to San Francisco, he was placed in a zoo when the soldiers left for the Philippines. His fate is unknown. MNG

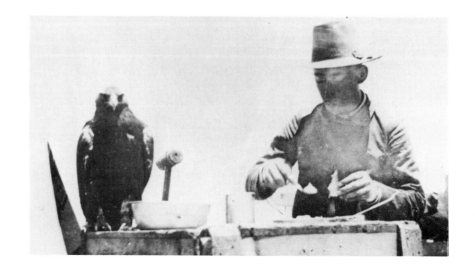

The medical staff of Colorado Volunteers. There are three surgeons, two hospital stewards and 13 stretcher bearers. DPL #10431

Members of the guard mount from Alfred University at Harnellsville, New York, April 30, 1898. They were part of the 47th Separate Co., 3rd New York Infantry. USAMHI

Troopers of the 2nd U.S. Infantry who were stationed at Fort William Henry Harrison, Helena, Montana, with their families before leaving for Camp Merritt. MHS

Recruits of the 2nd Oregon Infantry in front of a statue of President Garfield, location unknown. USAMHI

Dismounted saber drill, 6th U.S. Cavalry at Tampa. KE

A letter from home. The other trooper appears to be playing a harmonica. KE

Co. D., 1st Regiment, Illinois Volunteer Infantry at Camp Tanner, Springfield, Illinois, May 1898. Note the soldier seated on the left with the fez-like cap and the "D" on his shirt. USAMHI

Entrance gate for camp of Co. C, 8th Pennsylvania Volunteer Infantry at Camp McKenzie, Georgia. USAMHI

A private in the cavalry at Camp Lincoln in Springfield, Illinois. Notice the wooden wiping rods in the barrels of stacked carbines in the background. KE

Artillery practice at Newport News, Virginia. The men are not wearing regulation uniforms. These look as if they were copied from the Spanish or Cuban uniforms. KE

Review day at Camp Alger, Virginia, with President McKinley in attendance. Members of the Regimental band are in the front. KE

Camp Conrad hospital at Columbus, Georgia, December 1898. USAMHI

Troops of the 3rd Nebraska Volunteer Infantry march on the beach at Pablo Beach, Florida. USAMHI

U.S. regulars getting supper at Camp Merritt. KE

The long and short of Co. K, New Jersey Volunteers, Jacksonville, Florida. KE

This photo was probably taken at a California camp. There are many civilians with bicycles visiting the troops. The photo was taken by famous photographer William H. Jackson. DPL

Battery A, Wyoming National Guard ready to leave for Manila. DPL

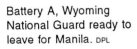

Wash day at Tampa. KE

Regular army cavalrymen cleaning their Model 1896 .30-.40 Krag carbines for inspection. KE

Troop I, 6th U.S. Cavalry at Tampa showing the continuing tradition of matching horses in a troop. KE

A letter home. Note the twisted band on his campaign hat. A personal touch by a citizen-soldier. KE

7th Army Corps review at Jacksonville, Florida. USAMHI

4th Illinois Provost Guard, Jacksonville, Florida. USAMHI

Probably New York National Guard troops in camp as they commonly had "separate companies" stenciled on their merriam packs. AHC #5099.21

Passing in review, dipping the colors at Tampa. KE

Payday at Camp Tampa. Notice the paymaster is using a biscuit box for his table. KE

Emergency hospital of the 2nd Arkansas Volunteer Infantry at Anniston, Alabama. Note the rock garden arranged in the cross of the medical department. AHC #2109

Grand review of the 4th
Missouri Volunteers at
Camp Meade,
Pennsylvania, before
heading to southern
camps. USAMHI

Grand review at Camp
Meade, Pennsylvania.
USAMHI

Troop B, Third U.S.
Cavalry ready for Cuba.
The Senior NCO on the
right is amazingly heavy
for cavalry service. KE

Tampa and the War

No city in the United States was more tied to the troubles in Cuba than Tampa on Florida's west coast. Hundreds of her citizens, born in Cuba, had fled from the island because of the tyranny imposed by Spanish authorities. Ybor City and West Tampa, sections with high percentages of Cuban inhabitants, and the centers for cigar making were especially affected by the situation in Cuba.

When Cuban hero, Jose Martí came to Tampa to plead for funds for the revolutionaries, he received a tremendous welcome. Almost every cigar maker pledged a day's pay each week for the cause.

The city was also a major port for trans-shipment of arms and personnel sent to the insurgents in Cuba. Filibusterers' ships often left the port at night to deliver the weapons.

Early in 1896 Spanish General Weyler in Cuba declared an embargo on tobacco exports from Cuba to the United States. This hit Tampa especially hard and the major industry of cigar making was about to be shut down, which coincidentally, would dry up funds being sent to the Cuban insurgents.

Leading cigar makers persuaded H.B. Plant to send two ships, the *Olivette* and *Mascotte* to Havana to buy up all the tobacco they could carry before the embargo was put into effect. The ships brought back a huge cargo, even their staterooms were piled high. This saved the local cigar industry until the war was over.

Tampa and especially Ybor City became a hotbed for Cuban revolutionaries to expound their views on their country's situation. In the time between the sinking of the *Maine* on Feb. 15, 1898, and the declaration of war on April 25, the area was swarming with government agents checking out the harbor, transportation and docking facilities and business firms. Two 50-ton cannons were taken from Tampa to protect the Key West area.

On March 28, survivors of the *Maine* were brought to Tampa by Plant's steamship *Olivette*. Refugees from Cuba started pouring into Port Tampa bringing in stories of Spanish oppression.

On April 9, Consul-General Fitzhugh Lee, stationed in Havana, arrived in Tampa to a welcome of over 1,000 people. He would later return to the city to command a portion of the Cuban Expeditionary Force. Five companies from Fort McPherson, Georgia showed up and were camped at DeSoto Park. They were soon joined by the 69th Regiment from New York.

War fever was at a high pitch and would become even greater after McKinley's war declaration of April 25. Tampa had been selected as a point of concentration for the army because it was the nearest city to Cuba with port and rail facilities.

The developer of Tampa, Henry Bradley Plant used his political influence to bring the troops to town using his own railroad. At Port Tampa, nine miles from town, he had built an immense wharf almost a mile long with warehouses nearby. Only one track led to the wharf, a situation that would soon lead to chaos.

With the thousands of troops converging on the area, camps were set up all over town. The largest was on a 250-acre tract on Tampa Heights. Plant's Tampa Bay Hotel was taken over by the high-ranking officers. It was from this hotel that the phrase "The Rocking Chair War" originated because of the slowness to join the action and the disarray in the city.

The largest military expedition to ever leave the shores of the United States up to that time pulled away from Port Tampa on June 8. On board the transport ships were 819 officers, 15,058 enlisted men, 30 civilian clerks, 272 teamsters, 107 stevedores, 89 newspapers reporters and photographers, 11 foreign officers, 952 horses, 1,336 mules, 114 six-mule army wagons, 81 escort wagons, seven regular wagons and seven ambulance wagons. Artillery consisted of two Colt cannons, a dynamite gun, 16 light guns, four 7-inch howitzers, four 5-inch siege guns, one Hotchkiss revolving cannon, eight 3.6-inch field mortars and four Gatling machine guns. Due to the mistaken belief the Spanish navy was in the area, the ships did not start for Cuba until June 12.

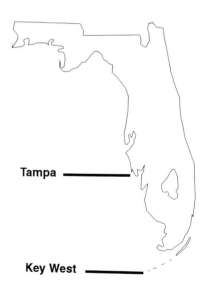

Tampa ———

Key West ———

MINISTER POLO NOW IN CANADA.

With Members of His Legation He Arrives in Niagara Falls and Is Quickly Carried Across the River.

SAYS WE WAGE INIQUITOUS WAR.

Declares It Will Be a Case of Robbery if the United States Is Successful.

NO CAUSE TO TAKE CUBA.

Left Bills In Washington for Which He Will Still Have to Write Checks.

HIS STAY IN CANADA SHORT.

Announces That He Will Sail from Montreal or Halifax After a Few Days.

NIAGARA FALLS, N. Y., Thursday.—Señor Polo y Bernabe, the Spanish Minister, with members of his Legation, arrived here early this afternoon, over the New York Central Railroad, in a private car. In the party were Señor Pablo Soler, First Secretary of the Legation; Señor Acquaront, Second Secretary; Señora Pia and Almeida, attaches; Captain De La Concha, Military Attache; Lieutenant De Carranha, Naval Attache, and two servants. They were in charge of George F. Foster and Charles La Salle, of the United States secret service, who were detailed by the President to see that the Minister and his suite were landed safely in Canada.

Carriages were then taken at the railroad station and driven to the Canadian side of the river, where rooms had been reserved for the visitors in the Hotel Lafayette, at the Canadian end of the upper bridge.

Chief of Police Dinan detailed a sergeant and two officers at the station to see that order was preserved. Señor Bernabe caused some merriment by switching the legs of some youngsters who persisted in following too closely beside him.

Looking on Our Flag.

After reaching the Lafayette and being shown their rooms, which looked out on the American Falls and the American side of the river, with the American flag floating from the flag pole on the State Reservation in Prospect Park, the party had lunch and then took a drive through the park on the Canadian side.

Minister Polo visited the post office and telegraph offices and received several despatches. These seemed to put him in very good humor, and when he returned to the hotel he bounded from his carriage and greeted the crowd of newspaper men with a smile and bow.

Before Bernabe told me it would not be right in his position as a diplomat to give any official utterance at this trying and critical time.

"It is necessary to be very careful," he said, "and I would prefer not to express any opinion which might be construed as an official utterance.

"I will say, however, that it is an iniquitous war the United States seeks to wage with Spain. It is unjust. That nation has no cause to try to rob us of Cuba, for it is simply a case of robbery if the United States does succeed."

"There are my sentiments as a citizen of Spain, and are not to be considered as official utterances.

Lesson in the Falls.

"If the American nation was as great and powerful as those wild waters (pointing to the falls) they would not seek this war; but they are not. Surely Nature teaches them a mighty lesson here."

"Is there any information you have received from Madrid which you can give out?" I asked.

"None whatever," he answered; "most of my despatches are pertaining to Militia at Washington. I have quite a lot of business in connection with my Legation which demands my attention, and a number of bills yet for which I will have to write checks."

"How long will you remain at the falls?"

"I will be here for a few days, possibly, and will then go to Toronto, to remain a week. I will go to Montreal and will either sail from there or Halifax for Europe, probably going by way of Kingland. I intend to go direct to Spain and Madrid, unless otherwise ordered by my government."

"What do you think will be the outcome of the war?"

"I beg to be excused from answering that question, although as a Spaniard, you know what my hopes and belief are."

It is known that very important messages were received by cable via Halifax last night and sent to Washington. They were from Madrid, and were forwarded to the Minister at Suspension Bridge. They were in Spanish and cipher code. It is also learned that messages were received from the secret intelligence of Spain in various localities of the United States and Canada. Minister Bernabe received numerous despatches from Washington at a late hour.

WANTED ALL LIGHTS OUT.

Minister Polo Found Himself No Match for a Sleeping Car Porter.

PITTSBURG, Pa.,—During his hurried trip to Canada last night Señor Polo y Bernabe "went against" an American colored porter of a sleeping car and came out second best. H. A. Allen, a travelling man of New York, told the story here to-day. Mr. Allen was on the Northern Central train that carried Señor Polo and his suite

from Washington to Harrisburg. They changed cars at Harrisburg and Señor Polo was nervous. He ordered the porter of the Northern car to turn out all the lights, but the porter refused. He said after the party retired all but two lights would be turned out.

"But I want them all out now," said the Spanish Minister.

"I cannot help that, sir," replied the porter. "I am under orders to keep two lights burning all night. After everybody in the car has retired all lights but two will be turned out. The lights left burning will be turned down. This is the best I can do for you."

Another passenger on the train from Washington to Harrisburg was John Hane, of Washington, who said that in Baltimore and Harrisburg large crowds were at the stations. Very little discourtesy was shown, although in Baltimore when the Spanish occupants of the car were seen several persons in the crowd shouted "Remember the Maine!" and "Hang the dogs!"

CAN PROHIBIT EXPORT OF COAL.

Both Houses of Congress Pass a Resolution Authorizing the President to Stop Fuel and Other War Material from Being Taken Abroad.

WASHINGTON, D. C., Thursday.—Mr. Quay, of Pennsylvania, introduced this resolution in the Senate to-day:—

"That the President is hereby authorized, in his discretion and with such limitations and exceptions as shall seem to him expedient, to prohibit the export of coal or other material used in war from any seaport of the United States until otherwise ordered by Congress."

After an amending the resolution so as to enable the President not only to lay but to raise the embargo, the resolution was passed without division.

When the resolution was called up on the House, later in the day, and unanimous consent asked for its immediate passage, Mr. Dinsmore, of Arkansas, and Mr. Bailey, of Texas, and Mr. Virginia, said much coal was produced in his district, and he was not prepared to allow a measure of such importance to go through without due consideration.

He was appealed to by members on both sides of the House not to object, but refused to withdraw his objection. Members labored with Mr. Walker for ten minutes, and finally induced him to withdraw his objection, and the resolution was passed without division.

THE PROBABLE HEADQUARTERS OF GENERAL MILES AT TAMPA.

STEAMSHIPS MAY DEFY BLOCKADE.

The Arkadia Sails for Porto Rico, and the Aloedene, Clearing for Cuba, May Leave To-Day.

LOADED WITH SUPPLIES.

Both Vessels May Be Liable to Seizure if They Try to Enter Spanish Ports.

One steamship sailed yesterday from this port and another is scheduled to sail to-day with cargoes which may be seized as contraband of war should the vessels attempt to put in at the ports for which they have cleared.

The Arkadia got away yesterday for Porto Rico. The Aloedene will probably leave this morning for Cuba. Although both fly the British colors they are under the control of American shipping firms. The Arkadia belongs to the New York and Porto Rico Steamship Company, which is operated by Miller, Bull & Knowlton. The Aloedene is under charter with James E. Ward & Co., proprietors of the New York and Cuba Mail Steamship Company, generally known as the Ward line.

The Aloedene cleared yesterday for Havana, Cienfuegos and Santiago. She was expected to sail yesterday, but could not get her cargo aboard in time. In her hold and on deck is freight which, if it succeeds in discharging at any Cuban port, will materially fortify the authorities of the island in holding out against a siege and also further their efforts in resisting an armed invasion.

Steel Railway Cars for the Spanish.

Not only has the Aloedene on board tons of provisions, but also two steel military railway cars. These cars are consigned to F. G. Cantio, of Manzanillo, and are intended for the Spanish forces under General Pando.

The cars are each twenty-five feet long and about nine feet high. They are built of wood and iron, with armored steel, seven-eighths of an inch thick. They are entirely closed with the exception of fifteen small inverted T shaped port holes on each side. Three openings are for rifles. Along the string, the top of the month. "Fort's carry military rations of the cars are underlined by Mr. Kirwood, Peartt & Co., whose foundry is in the Erie Basin, Brooklyn. The cars and their machinery are making the most of their opportunity, and have shipped their plates of business with most tempting displays. Hedges bearing designs of the Cuban flag have suddenly grown popular. They are worn on every hand, and after these in the public favor come buttons with catch words referring to Spain, Cuba or the Maine.

Street Hawkers' Harvest.

Swarms of street hawkers during the last few weeks have decorated their trays for New York, Broadway, Fulton street and the approaches to the ferries, loudly proclaiming innumerable devices that play upon the Spanish-American difference. Some of them, with mysterious winks, ask sealed envelopes, in which are proclaimed to contain the solution of the blowing up of the Maine.

"The popular hero of the day is evidently General Lee, whose likeness, in lithographs and half tones, can be seen on every hand, framed by colored bunting. Lee's portraits may be seen in the windows of many apartment houses.

MAY MOBILIZE HER NATIONAL GUARDS.

Pennsylvania Authorities Expected to Order Concentration of Militia at Mt. Gretna.

PHILADELPHIA, Pa., Thursday.—Another day of expectancy was put in by the National Guardsmen to-day. There is no doubt that the entire divisin of the State will be concentrated at Mount Gretna as a preliminary to volunteering for the federal service.

One of the officials of the Pennsylvania Railroad Company had an officer yesterday that the company expected to have the three brigade at that point by Sunday night.

Governor Wolcott Orders Massachusetts Militia Put on War Footing.

BOSTON, Mass., Thursday.—Governor Wolcott to-day issued orders to raise the Massachusetts militia to a war footing at once. Company commanders have been ordered to increase the strength of their companies to the men. The present authorized strength is sixty enlisted men and three officers. The forty additional men will be carried on the rolls of the companies, but will not be enlisted into the service of the State until further orders.

Little Rhody Will Appropriate $150,000 for Equipping Its Militia.

PROVIDENCE, R. I., Thursday.—The General Assembly to-day adopted a resolution appropriating $150,000 for militia equipment. This resolution was prepared by Governor Dyer and was passed without a dissenting voice amid intense enthusiasm.

Delaware National Guard To Be Placed on a War Footing.

DOVER, Del., Thursday.—The Legislature to-day enacted a law placing the Delaware National Guard upon a war footing.

John A. Logan Wants to Recruit a Regiment for Cavalry Service.

CHICAGO, Ill., Thursday.—John A. Logan has received authority from the War Department at Washington to recruit a regiment of 1,200 men and equip them for light cavalry service. The work of organizing has been quietly progressing for several weeks.

PRICE OF FLOUR RAISED.

One Dollar a Barrel Increase by Haverhill, Mass., Wholesale Dealers.

HAVERHILL, Mass., Thursday.—Wholesale flour dealers in Haverhill have made an advance of one dollar a barrel on flour, and a still further increase in price is expected on the breaking out of hostilities.

RIGHTS OF PRIVATEERING.

President McKinley Accused of Exceeding His Constitutional Powers in Declaring That United States Would Not Resort to It in the War with Spain.

HERALD BUREAU,
CORNER FIFTEENTH AND G STREETS, N. W.,
WASHINGTON, D. C., Thursday.

President McKinley is accused of exceeding his constitutional powers yesterday in authorizing the official declaration by the State Department that the United States would not resort to privateering during the war with Spain.

The constitution of the United States expressly reserves to Congress the right to grant letters of marque and reprisal, and Senator Money inquired in the Senate to-day from the Committee on Foreign Relations if the President had really taken it upon himself to invade this constitutional power of Congress. He got no satisfactory answer, for the reason that the committee had no official information.

He raised the point, however, that the decision as to whether or not letters of marque and reprisal are to be issued during the war with Spain rests with Congress. There is no disposition on the part of Congress to resort to this system of warfare.

Privateering is looked upon as merely legalized piracy, but at the same time there is a feeling that the United States should not declare that it will not be resorted to in this war unless a similar declaration is made by Spain.

It is understood that the Spanish government proposes to resort to privateering unless prevented by the action of the European Powers, and the members of the Senate and House committees with whom I talked to-day thought it a good plan not to declare at this time that this nation would not retaliate by similar action if Spain should go to any great length in privateering.

"I believe in fighting the devil with fire," said Representative Clark, of the House Committee, to me. "And if Spain harasses us with privateers we might have to employ them against her, much as we might dislike the general policy of resorting to this method of warfare."

FLAGS AND BUNTING DECK NEW YORK

Big Buildings in the Business Sections and Many Private Houses Hung with Streamers.

CUBAN FLAG IS POPULAR.

Displayed in the Shopping District Side by Side with the Stars and Stripes.

War excitement pervaded the city yesterday. From City Hall Park to Herald square, the streets and the lobbies of public resorts were filled with gesticulating groups.

War fervor and patriotism are seeking their outlet by the flying of flags and banners. The big office buildings down town vie with one another in waving the largest expanse of Stars and Stripes. Many fresh rows of flags appeared floating from roofs and window ledges all along Broadway yesterday, and the fluttering of colored silk and bunting transformed the city into a scene of gayety and excitement.

Cuban flags, with the red triangle, white star and blue and white stripes, are next in favor with the national colors, and never fail to cause comment. From Herald square one can see big flags floating from the flag poles on more than a dozen buildings, of which five are hotels, one a bank and one an apartment house.

Barnesmen, too, are in abundance. In Fourteenth street two big flags face each other from opposite sides of the street, connected by a line crossing the street, from which is suspended a third flag. Dry goods merchants along Sixth avenue are also beginning to drape their stores. Some of them have displayed a United States and a Cuban flag side by side.

Flags of All Sizes.

Patriotic occupants of offices are displaying flags of all sizes from windows along the fronts of buildings. There is hardly a break in the popular outburst of patriotism. Flags appear from the fronts of almost every residence and apartment houses. There are many tiny ones in sight, evidently placed there by childish hands.

Three flags and streamers in the residential portion of the city are sign of the patriotic sentiments of private citizens, and are not to be confounded with the draping of restaurants and public resorts with the national colors with the idea of swelling the plate of water.

Flag dealers along Park place and adjacent thoroughfares are making the most of their opportunity, and have draped their plates of business with most tempting displays.

THE MIANTONOMOH READY.

PHILADELPHIA, Pa., Thursday.—The monitor Miantonomoh is ready to sail from League Island.

Her orders are to proceed to Key West, touching at Charleston. Her engines and ammunition holsts were tested to-day and found to be in first class condition. The gunboat Vixen will be ready for sea in forty-eight hours. She will receive a crew of seventy-four men from the receiving ship Richmond to-morrow.

Sailed Under Sealed Orders.

"It is reported that Captain Lloyd had received sealed orders, which were to be opened when his vessel was well out to sea. There is believed to direct Captain Lloyd to put in at St. Thomas for orders before proceeding to Porto Rico.

THE CORSAIR TO JOIN THE NAVY.

J. Pierpont Morgan's Handsome Craft Has Been Purchased by the Government for Use in Cuban Harbors.

THE COMANCHE ALSO BOUGHT

She is H. M. Hanna's Yacht, on Which President McKinley Cruised in the Lakes Last Summer.

OTHER CRAFT RECOMMENDED

Labors of Cruiser Board Nearing a Close and Several Members Will Be Detailed to Other Duty.

Three yachts—the Corsair, the Penelope and the Comanche—have been bought by the government. The Auxiliary Cruiser Board yesterday recommended the purchase of two others—the Vergana and the Aileen.

The Corsair is one of the best yachts which have been secured. She was owned by J. Pierpont Morgan, and was one of the largest and best equipped vessels of the fleet of the New York Yacht Club. She measures 569 tons gross and 273 tons net. She is 165 feet over all, 264 feet at the water line, 27 feet in beam and draws 12 feet of water.

Of about the same size is the yacht Penelope, which was owned by H. E. Converse, of Boston. Her gross tonnage is 341 tons. She is 216 feet long, 27 feet in beam and draws 14 feet 4 inches of water.

Advices received by the Herald from Cleveland, Ohio, last night said that the government has purchased the Comanche. She is a fast steam yacht, which was owned by H. Melville Hanna, a brother of the Senator. She is one of the finest vessels on the Great Lakes. She was built in 1891 at the Globe Iron Works, in Cleveland. She is 185 feet over all, 25 feet in beam and 12 feet and 7 inches deep. President McKinley cruised in the Comanche last summer.

The Vergana and Aileen.

There is little doubt that the Vergana and the Aileen will soon be in the service of the United States.

The Vergana, owned by Frederick H. Benedict, is 146 feet over all and has a draught of 7 feet. The Aileen, whose owner is Richard Stevens, is 146 feet over all, 20 feet in beam and 16 feet 1 inches deep.

Members of the Board have inspected the following yachts:—

The Brisenger, owned by Mr. George Lewis, which is 187 feet long, 22 feet in beam and 11 feet deep.

The Felicia, a new yacht owned by E. W. Bliss, which was launched on April 2. She is 135 feet long.

The Huntress, a wooden yacht, owned by Jacob Impson, of Buffalo. She is 109 feet long, 25 feet in beam and draws 8 feet 8 inches of water.

The Sapphire, owned by J. J. Albright, of Buffalo, 118 feet long, 19 feet in beam and 10 feet 3 inches in draught.

Passed Engineer Danforth inspected the tug Robert H. Rathbun.

Arrangements have been practically completed for the purchase of Michael Moran's new tug, the Albert W. Booth, which will soon be completed at the yards of Neafie & Levy, in Philadelphia. She is a fast steel craft.

E. D. Morgan and August Belmont were in conference with the Board yesterday afternoon. They declined to say anything for publication concerning the object of their visit, as I learned that the conference had no definite result.

Emil L. Boas, the agent of the Hamburg-American line, also called. He decided that the Board would inspect the Furst Bismarck, and said that he had called to ask a technical question of Captain Rodgers, the chairman of the Board.

Vernon H. Brown denied yesterday that the government had bought the Cunard line steamers Umbria and Etruria.

No orders for the disbanding of the Board have yet been received, but it is evident that their labors are near a close. Lieutenant Commander Sneder has been ordered to command the fourth division of the coast defence fleet. Passed Engineer Danforth will be sent to the Brooklyn Navy Yard. Naval Constructor Tawresey is now in Philadelphia superintending the construction of the American harbor into auxiliary cruisers. The whole board also making up preparing reports for the Navy Department.

HOMING PIGEON VOLUNTEERS

Owners Asked to Give Their Services and Those of Their Birds.

Superintendent Howard Carter, of the United States Naval Homing Pigeon service of the Navy Yard, is organizing a company of homing pigeon fanciers, who will give their services together with their pigeons, to transmit despatches from patrol boats, cruisers and battle ships in case of war with Spain.

Suppose an army is fighting by a patrol boat 150 miles from port, pigeons will be liberated with duplicate and triplicate messages, reaching their respective lofts in three and a half hours, thus warning the department five hours before the arrival of the fastest despatch boat.

The owners of the pigeons will receive a compensation, not yet determined, for the use of their birds under their individual training. This service will necessitate a training these birds over water and along the coast.

Mr. Carter requests all owners of a No. 1 homing pigeons who wish to serve the United States in case of war with Spain to write to him at the Brooklyn's Navy Yard, and their names will be enrolled and mustered into the government service should war be declared.

REFUSED TO CALL COAL CONTRABAND

Mr. Balfour Declared the British Government Cannot Lay Down the Principle Suggested.

OUR COURSE IS CHEERED.

Applause Greeted the Announcement That We Shall Observe the Treaty of Paris.

AUDAZ NOT TO BE DETAINED.

The Disabled Spanish Torpedo Boat May Leave England Even After Hostilities Begin.

LONDON, Thursday.—Replying in the House of Commons to-day to Sir Arthur Bower Forwood, conservative member for the Southwest division of Lancashire, Mr. A. J. Balfour, the government leader and Acting Secretary of State for Foreign Affairs, said, in regard to neutral vessels, that the government had received from the United States this morning a notification that it would adhere to the principles of the Treaty of Paris. The announcement was greeted with cheers. Mr. Balfour added that no answer on the subject had yet been received from Spain, but he declared, "I confidently expect the same answer from Spain."

Answering the question which Mr. Dalziel gave notice yesterday of putting to-day—whether steps are to be taken to retain the Spanish torpedo boat Audaz, now docked at Queenstown for repairs, in the event of war breaking out before the repairs are completed, so as to "prevent a repetition of the Alabama case"—Mr. Balfour said that if, as he understood to be the case, the Audaz is a commission of ship of the Spanish navy, it would be contrary to international practice to detain her.

Treaties Still in Force.

"The treaties of 1796 and 1819 between Spain and the United States," Mr. Balfour added, "affirming between themselves the principle that a neutral flag covers the enemy's goods, are still in force. Whether a steamer carrying an American or Spanish official despatches after war is declared is liable to seizure may depend upon the facts in the case. No general answer can be given."

Mr. Michael Davitt, Irish nationalist, member for South Mayo, asked whether the government would consider the advisability of notifying the British colonies and British merchants that coal must be considered contraband of war during the continuance of the hostilities between Spain and the United States. Mr. Balfour replied:—

"Her Majesty's government cannot lay down the principle that coal is contraband in the way suggested. There is no doubt that in very frequently is contraband, but not of necessity so under all circumstances."

Replying to Rear Admiral Lord Charles Beresford, conservative, member of Pallabam for York, Mr. Balfour said he did not believe the interests of British shipowners were threatened more in this case than in other cases of maritime warfare, adding that he did not believe it possible to give an exhaustive definition of contraband of war.

Experts No Interference.

The Attorney General, Sir Richard Webster, replying to Mr. James H. Dalziel, liberal, member for the Kirkcaldy district of Scotland, said that in view of the declarations of the United States and the acts of Spain upon previous occasions, the government could not contemplate that there would be any interference with British goods on board ships belonging to the belligerents or interference with goods belonging to the belligerents on board British ships, except confiscation of contraband of war.

The action of privateers, the Attorney General added, if the employment of such vessels is sanctioned, will depend upon the views of the belligerents in regard to their rights of interference with neutral commerce.

WAR RISKS ADVANCE.

LIVERPOOL, Thursday.—Marine insurance concerns advanced the rates of war risks to-day five shillings on British vessels and £3 (£10) on Spanish and American vessels.

VESSELS CANNOT CLEAR FOR CUBA.

HERALD BUREAU,
CORNER FIFTEENTH AND G STREETS, N. W.,
WASHINGTON, D. C., Thursday.

When President McKinley to-morrow proclaims the ports of Cuba in a state of blockade no more vessels will be allowed to clear from the ports of the United States for any of the blockaded ports.

Up to the present time all vessels leaving the United States for Spanish ports have done so at the risk of being intercepted by any blockade which might be established before their arrival.

As soon as the blockade has been extended to the ports of the island of Porto Rico vessels will be refused clearance to those ports, and the same rule will be followed as to other Spanish ports that may be blockaded during the progress of the war.

FOLLOW THE FLAG, SAYS MR. CLEVELAND.

Former President Tells Princeton Students and Townspeople to Respond to the Call of Our Country.

Former President Grover Cleveland was visited last evening at Princeton, N. J., by a large body of undergraduates and townspeople and asked to make a speech. After several "Three times three" and Princeton "locomotives," with Mr. Cleveland's name attached to the cheers, the former President stepped out on his front veranda.

"I suppose this demonstration is in the interest of the present national crisis," said Mr. Cleveland, when silence was restored. "It is impressive in these exciting times to follow our country, no matter whether it may be right or not. Patriotism makes us love our native land and fills us with willingness to stand by it even until death. We hope our country is now in the right. May we in after years, when matters are all settled, look back and say, 'We were right and fought for a good cause.' But we should be conservative in our actions and not let our feelings get the better of our judgment. Gentlemen, I thank you for the honor you have shown me."

There will be a mass meeting of the university men this evening for the purpose of forming a company of undergraduates to volunteer its services in time of war.

Henry B. Plant and the Tampa Bay Hotel

The U.S Army procured the elegant Tampa Bay Hotel for Fifth Army Corps headquarters in Tampa while gathering troops for the invasion of Cuba.

The hotel was built in 1891 by Henry B. Plant who was the founder and president of the Plant System of railways, steamship lines and hotels. He was also the organizer and president of the Southern Express Company, Texas Express Company, Plant Investment Company and Plant Improvement Company. He developed and promoted the west coast and central sections of Florida. His railroad empires transported the thousands of troops to Tampa in the spring of 1898.

Plant was born in 1819 and died the year after the Spanish American War ended. His legacy lives on in Tampa. The hotel building itself is Tampa's quintessential Victorian building. It was built in the Moorish Revival architecture and included 500 rooms, most with their own baths, telephones and electricity. Total cost was three million with furnishings costing an additional $500,000.

The hotel was a lively place with balls, tea parties and hunts during the busy winter season. After Plant's death in 1899 the hotel operated off and on but failed to prosper and was eventually purchased by the City of Tampa. The city refurbished the building during the Florida land boom of the mid-1920s, but the end of the boom and ensuing depression ended its era as a hotel. In 1933 the University of Tampa leased the building for offices and classrooms. The south wing of the first floor was set aside as the Tampa Municipal Museum, now known as the Henry B. Plant Museum. One can wander through the interior or sit on the veranda and feel the elegance much as visitors did in 1898.

Tampa Bay Hotel and Grounds, Tampa, Fla.

OF THE VERANDAS,
BAY HOTEL,
PA, FLORIDA.

Maj. Gen. W.R. Shafter and his staff on the veranda of the Tampa Bay Hotel prior to their departure for Cuba. TL 271/32544

General Wade and his staff on the Tampa Bay Hotel grounds. TL 276/32551

Gen. Fitzhugh Lee and his staff on the Tampa Bay Hotel grounds. TL 256/32545

Interior of the Tampa Bay Hotel, General Shafter's headquarters.

TAMPA BAY HOTEL

Henry B. Plant built this ornate Moorish structure at a cost of $3 million. Opened in 1891, it became the social and cultural center of early Tampa. During the Spanish American War it was headquarters for troops going to Cuba and housed such visitors as Col. Theodore Roosevelt, Clara Barton, Richard Harding Davis and Gen. Nelson Miles. Purchased by the City of Tampa in 1905, it has served as the main building of the Univ. of Tampa since 1933.

The Tampa Bay Hotel as it looks today. UNIVERSITY OF TAMPA

War Memorial Cannon

This 6-inch Q.F. Armstrong Rifle was erected in 1898 at Fort Dade on Egmont Key. After the sinking of the *USS Maine* in Havana harbor many citizens of Tampa feared that the Spanish navy would capture the islands at the mouth of Tampa Bay, and from there, attack Tampa. Henry B. Plant demanded to some of his political friends in Washington that Tampa Bay must be protected. The city would be the staging area for the American expeditionary force to invade Cuba. Congress quickly passed a bill and allotted money for the fortification of Tampa Bay.

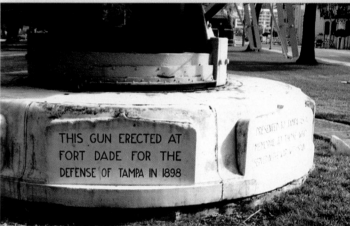

Construction hastily began in April 1898 at Egmont Key and eventually Forts DeSoto and Dade came into being. The forts were surplused in the 1920s and this gun was moved to the campus of the University of Tampa on the north side of West Kennedy Boulevard in 1927. Although erected by the Gen. Joe Wheeler Camp No. 2, Dept. of Florida, United Spanish War Veterans as a memorial to that war's veterans, it is now a memorial to those who gave their lives in the past.

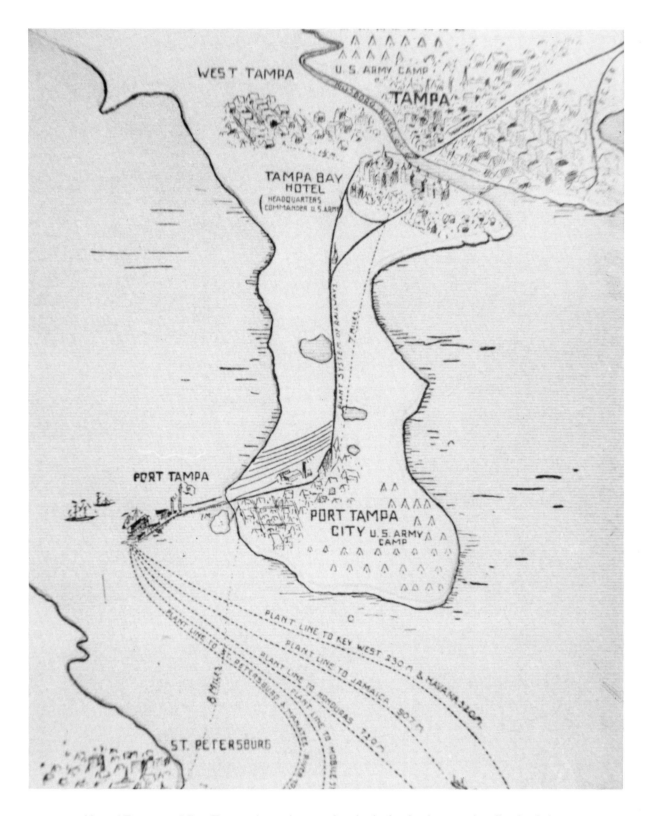

Map of Tampa and Port Tampa, the main port of embarkation for the army heading for Cuba.

An evening at the hotel. Tampa. Florida.

Drawn by
W. Bengough.

Street scene in Tampa, 1898. TL 274A/R273

TROOPS WILL SOON CAMP IN TAMPA

Three Regiments of Infantry Ordered to Move Direct to This City.

GATEWAY OF GULF CHOSEN BY GENERAL

Supplies for the Army Will Soon Begin to Arrive in Quantities.

WHOLE ARMY PREPARING FOR WAR

Twenty Three Regiments of Infantry Ordered to Gulf Ports, and All Cavalry and Light Artillery to Chattanooga and Chickamagua—Money Allotted for Ordnance Supplies.

Special to the Tribune.

New York, April 15.—Twenty-three regiments of infantry have been ordered by Gen. Miles, commander of the army, to be distributed between Tampa, Mobile and New Orleans.

The Fifth, Ninth and Twenty-first regiments of infantry were ordered to-day to proceed direct to Tampa, and remain there until further orders.

The quartermaster's department for the three regiments ordered to Tampa, will precede the troops and make all arrangements for their accommodation. The proximity of Tampa to Key West and Tortugas has impressed General Miles favorably, and if satisfactory arrangements can be made for the rapid transportation of troops from Tampa to Key West and Tortugas, or to Cuba in the event of hostilities, then Tampa will be made the basing point of the army, and all supplies will be shipped through that port.

The orders issued to-day were for practically the whole army to move to the department of the Gulf at once.

All cavalry and light artillery were ordered to go to Chickamauga and Chattanooga, and the remaining 23 infantry regiments to the Gulf ports.

Secretary Alger has decided that the six companies of the Twenty-fifth infantry, which should reach Chicka-

Major Brodie (left) and Colonel Wood (right) of the Rough Riders confer with General Wheeler, commander of the Cavalry Division at Tampa. USF

TAMPA MAY TRIUMPH.

But the Base of Supplies Has Not Yet Been Selected by War Department·

MOBILE IS STILL MIGHTY

But Florida's Delegation is Moving Mountains and Tampa May Secure the Plum.

ADVANTAGES ARE FULLY ADMITTED.

Deep Water In Tampa Bay is a Big Card in Our Favor, and Also the Nearness to the Scene of Possible Hostilities Cuts a Big Figure

It has not yet been officially settled as to which of the Gulf ports will be selected by the war department as a base of supplies for the army and navy in event of war.

The Washington correspondent of the Times-Union and Citizen says:

"Every effort and influence is being now put forward by the Florida delegation in Congress to induce the military authorities to locate the proposed great military and naval supply station at Tampa. Three cities are in the race, the authorities having decided that this immense base of supplies will be located either at New Orleans, Mobile, or Tampa. The naval military strategic board to whom the matter has been referred has eliminated all other places, and is is probable that a final decision will soon be made.

"The natural advantages of Tampa, its deep harbor, adaptability to fortification, its railway facilities and above all its comparative nearness to Cuba, have been pointed out to the strategic board, and it is an even chance now that it will be either Tampa or Mobile, as far as can be learned, New Orleans having been practically declared to be too far from the actual scene of possible hostilities. The Florida Congressmen and Senators are working manfully to induce the board to select the Tampa site, but whatever action may be taken will be based solely upon the military features involved. No outside influence will have one jot of weight with the board.

One of the cannon set up at DeSoto Park for the protection of Tampa Bay. USF, WEHMAN COLL.

Army wagons loaded at Ringgold, Georgia, headed for Tampa. Supplies were coming in from all over the country, swamping the inadequate rail facilities into Tampa. USF, O.S. WAMSLEY COLL.

Gen. Nelson Miles and Joseph Wheeler and their staffs at army headquarters on Picnic Island. This was an area where soldiers practiced close order drills and simple maneuvers. It was also a resort with parks, a dance pavilion and bathing beach, where they enjoyed their off-duty hours. The original island was later dredged in and became part of the mainland. TL 272/32546

Camp at Tampa Heights at the present location of Ross and Central avenues. TL

A regimental barber shop of the 21st Infantry, Regular Army at Tampa. Notice the Cuban flag tied to a surveyor's stadia rod on the right. USF, WEHMAN COLL.

Cavalry drill at West Tampa. USF, WEHMAN COLL.

Hundreds of horses were quartered at West Tampa. Because of the lack of transport, most of these had to be left behind and most of the cavalry fought on foot. USF, WEHMAN COLL.

The faces of the men who
would soon go to war.
Troopers of the 3rd Illinois
Volunteer Infantry at
Camp Tampa.

Camp of the 69th New
York Volunteers at Tampa.
TL 273A/32547-1

Co. C, 71st Regiment, New York National Guard at Tampa. They participated in action at San Juan Hill and El Caney and sustained many casualties from enemy fire and later from tropical diseases. USF, O.S. WAMSLEY COLL.

Troops at Tampa Heights, the main campground in the Tampa area. USF, TONY DIZZO COLL.

Seventeen volunteer nuns of the Academy of the Holy Names rose at 4 a.m. each day to prepare three meals a day for hundreds of soldiers during their stay in Tampa. They are photographed with members of the Second Brigade's medical corps. USF

COLORED TROOPS COMING.

But they will Not Arrive Here To-day. The Sheriff's Joke.

It was currently reported all day yesterday that the 25th Regiment of United States Infantry would arrive here last night or this morning en route from Montana to Key West and Tortugas. The regiment is composed of colored troops, but officered by white men, and the news of that it was expected caused great interest among the colored residents of Tampa, a large number of whom went to the Plant System depot last night to see the colored soldiers.

The railroad officials stated last night that they had received no information concerning the troops, and did not expect them before to-morrow or next day, as the regiment did not get orders to leave Fort Missoula, Mont, until last Thursday.

Sheriff Spencer had considerable fun yesterday over the report that the colored troops would arrive to-day. He informed one or two colored men that he had orders to enlist 40 colored residents of Tampa to fill the ranks of the regiment. The news spread rapidly, and the colored men kept out of sight of the sheriff all day for none of Tampa's colored citizens are anxious to fight.

April 3, 1898

Top photo: An unusual sleeping arrangement. The photo caption reads: "The boys slept this way to keep above water." USF, O.S. WAMSLEY COLL.

Buglers practicing their calls. USF, O.S. WAMSLEY COLL.

These Indiana troops are camped at the state fairgrounds in Indianapolis. The center soldier, 2nd Lieutenant Kerr of Co. B, 1st Indiana Volunteer Infantry, died of yellow fever at Port Tampa. USF, O.S. WAMSLEY COLL.

The Signal Corps practicing with their hot air balloon at Tampa. The balloon was used before the San Juan Hill defenses with mixed results as the device, when inflated, tended to draw enemy artillery fire. A new road, however, was discovered from the air, which did relieve some troop congestion before the battle.
USF, O.S. WAMSLEY COLL.

This fence of loose barbed wire wound into the tree tops was erected to simulate the obstacles at Santiago. It was used for practice by troops camped at Tampa. USF, O.S. WAMSLEY COLL.

Major General Shafter at the Tampa docks. His size (over 300 pounds) is quite obvious in this photo. It would prove to be debilitating in his command of troops in Cuba.

Ships at the Tampa dock loading troops for Cuba on June 8. MHS #64841

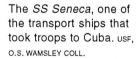

The port facilities at Tampa were a sea of troops, supplies and ships in June. On June 12 and 13, 36 transport ships finally left for the expedition to Santiago. USF AND USAMHI

The *SS Seneca*, one of the transport ships that took troops to Cuba. USF, O.S. WAMSLEY COLL.

Troops loading on transports at Port Tampa for the Cuban campaign. USF, O.S. WAMSLEY COLL.

Troops of the 71st New York Volunteers at Port Tampa. USF, ENSMINGER BROS.

The *SS Mohawk* was loaded with 1,100 troops of the 11th U.S. Regulars, 1,100 mules and 200 horses when she left the harbor for Cuba on July 24. USF, O.S. WAMSLEY COLL.

Transports at Port Tampa, part of a
fleet of 36 that would take the
troops to Cuba.

One of the transport ships leaving
Port Tampa on June 8. MNHS #64840

More views of the troops preparing to load on transports at Tampa for the invasion of Cuba. On June 8, the ships left the port but were held in the bay due to a mistaken belief that Spanish ships were between Florida and Cuba. It wasn't until the 12th that the flotilla actually started for Cuba.

Key West

Key West, Florida, is located only 90 miles from the Cuban coast. In 1898, it was the main coaling and supply base for the North Atlantic Squadron. Naturally, it would play a key role in the Spanish American War.

Before the war started, it was a busy anchorage for American naval ships. As there was a telegraph cable connecting the city of Havana, it was a natural gathering place for newspaper and magazine correspondents reporting the happenings in Cuba.

The *USS Maine* left Key West on Jan. 25, 1898, for her fateful journey to Havana. The Navy Court of Inquiry was held in Key West's federal custom house after the sinking.

The Dry Tortugas, 68 miles west of Key West, was used as a "drill ground" for the fleet. Fort Jefferson on Garden Key was called the "Gibraltar of the Caribbean." Fort Taylor was built in 1832 to guard the entrance to Key West Harbor. It is now a state park.

The old Custom House in downtown Key West was the site of the *Maine* Court of Inquiry in 1898. It was built in 1891 of brick and granite and used as a federal custom house, post office and naval office building. The building has been restored to its 1891 appearance.

Scenes at Key West, clockwise from left: 1st U.S. Artillery at the Key West barracks; captains of the *Detroit, Cincinnati* and *Nashville* on the way to visit the captain of the *Puritan*; on board the *Puritan*, letters from home and barracks room for the 1st Artillery with protective mosquito bar over each cot.

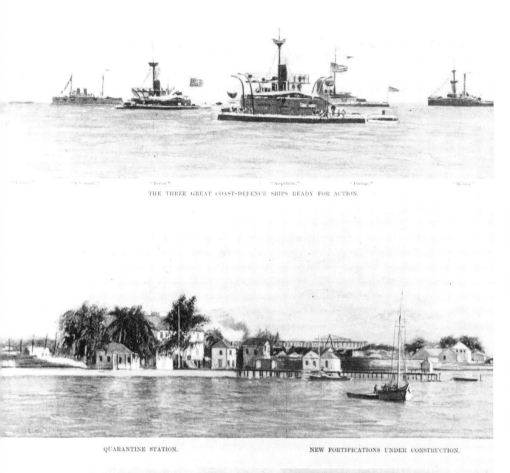

"Cincinnati." "Terror." "Ampnitrite." "Puritan." "Helena."

THE THREE GREAT COAST-DEFENCE SHIPS READY FOR ACTION.

QUARANTINE STATION. NEW FORTIFICATIONS UNDER CONSTRUCTION.

THE GOVERNMENT DOCK-UNLOADING STORES FOR THE FLEET.

U. S. MARINE HOSPITAL.

KEY WEST BARRACKS-OFFICERS' QUARTERS.

Scenes of Key West in 1898.

The North Atlantic Fleet at Key West. Top, left to right: *Castine, Cincinnati, Terror, Ampnitrite, Puritan* and *Helena*. Middle: the Quarantine Station and fortifications under construction. Bottom: gun practice on the *Marblehead*.

A 1916 photo of the *Maine* monument and graves of some of the lost crewmen at the Key West Cemetery.
USN NH 2142

U. S. S. "HELENA" COALING AT GOVERNMENT DOCK, APRIL 9, 1898.

Showing Boats sent in from the Battle-Ships when they were stripped for active Service.—Drawn by Carlton T. Chapman, Special Artist for "Harper's Weekly."

Top left: government seawall. Top right: government storehouse. Bottom left: government dock, storehouse and post office. Bottom right: coaling a ship. Middle: *USS Helena* coaling at the government dock on April 9, 1898.

Plaque of the *Maine* cemetery plot.

In the historic Key West Cemetery is a monument (left) to the victims of the *USS Maine* and to memory of the Cuban martyrs (right) who fought for Cuban independence.

Key West Today

ALL PHOTOS BY RICHARD WEATHERWAX, KEY WEST, FLORIDA

In Bayview Park is a monument to Jose Marti, the great apostle of Cuban liberty.

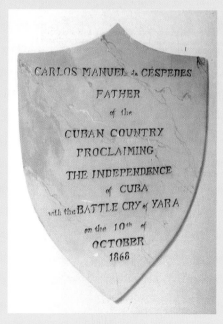

This painting of Carlos Manuel de Cespedes is on the wall at the San Carlos building, known as the "cradle" of Cuba's liberty because of the many activities of patriotic Cubans that took place here.

Off to War

It had been 33 years since the end of the Civil War and 37 years since the boys of '61 had been ushered off to what they thought would be a short and marvelous adventure. Other than the regular army troops who had battled the Indians on the western frontier, America's youth had not experienced warfare. Only the older officers who had gone through the bitter Civil War knew what lay ahead.

When McKinley made his call for troops, an outpouring of patriotism, not unlike 1861, was seen throughout the country. Once again volunteer regiments were formed, this time drawn mostly from state national guard units.

There was great fanfare in hundreds of towns and cities across the country, sending "their boys to war." It was of course not known then that a great percentage of the troops would languish in camps in the United States, far from battle, dying of disease.

But for now, in the spring 1898, another great adventure was about to begin.

Departure of the 13th Minnesota Volunteers marching down Washington Avenue in Minneapolis. They are dressed in their tan felt campaign hats, dark blue wool coats and light blue wool trousers, and are carrying .45-.70 Springfield rifles. MNHS #8954

Adjutant General's Office.

Washington April ~~xx~~, ~~xxxx~~.

Colonel Harry C. Kessler,

Butte, Montana.

Governors of States will be called upon to furnish volunteers. Suggest you communicate with Governor Montana respecting tender of services of your regiment.

Assistant Adjutant General.

4 Sent - Apl 22, 98 -

THE WESTERN UNION TELEGRAPH COMPANY.

INCORPORATED

21,000 OFFICES IN AMERICA. CABLE SERVICE TO ALL THE WORLD.

This Company TRANSMITS and DELIVERS messages only on conditions limiting its liability, which have been assented to by the sender of the following message. Errors can be guarded against only by repeating a message back to the sending station for comparison, and the Company will not hold itself liable for errors or delays in transmission or delivery of Unrepeated Messages, beyond the amount of tolls paid thereon, nor in any case where the claim is not presented in writing within sixty days after the message is filed with the Company for transmission.

This is an UNREPEATED MESSAGE, and is delivered by request of the sender, under the conditions named above.

THOS. T. ECKERT, President and General Manager.

NUMBER	SENT BY	REC'D BY	CHECK
593 Ch	XD	DA	53 paid 18 Ex

Apl 20 189

RECEIVED at Wyatt Building, Cor. 14th & F. Streets, Washington, D. C.

Dated Butte mont To

To Genl H C Corbin
Adjt Genl. U S A
Washn D C

By permission of the Governor of the state of montana I have the honor to tender to the Prest of the U S the services of the first regiment infantry natl guard montana as Volunteers.

Harry C Kessler Col,
Comdg 1st Infty N G M and
late 1st Lieut 104th Penna
Volunteers

Troops of the 1st Montana Volunteer Infantry line up at the Presidio in San Francisco before leaving for the Philippines. MNG

Form No. 168.

THE WESTERN UNION TELEGRAPH COMPANY.
——— INCORPORATED ———
21,000 OFFICES IN AMERICA.   CABLE SERVICE TO ALL THE WORLD.

This Company TRANSMITS and DELIVERS messages only on conditions limiting its liability, which have been assented to by the sender of the following message.
Errors can be guarded against only by repeating a message back to the sending station for comparison, and the Company will not hold itself liable for errors or delays
in transmission or delivery of Unrepeated Messages, beyond the amount of tolls paid thereon, nor in any case where the claim is not prosecuted in writing within sixty days
after the message is filed with the Company for transmission.
This is an UNREPEATED MESSAGE, and is delivered by request of the sender, under the conditions named above.
THOS. T. ECKERT, President and General Manager.

RECEIVED at

9 W TV KP 44 Paid. 345 P

Helena, Mont. June 2.

Meiklejohn, War Dept., Washington, D.C.

Kessler Colonel first Montana applying for Brigadier Generalship, is on
ground, acquainted with men and situation. His was first volunteer regiment mustered in. Merritt already practically given him command as
Brigadier and most strongly urge you use your influence have him nominated and confirmed.

A. J. Seligman.

The *City of Para* leaves San Francisco on June 26, 1898, for the Philippines. On board are members of the 13th Minnesota Volunteer Infantry. MNHS #64832

THE WAVE

L. XVIII. NO. I   SAN FRANCISCO, JULY 2, 1898   PRICE 10 CENTS

THE THIRD EXPEDITION TO MANILA
THE "CITY OF PARA" WITH THE MINNESOTA VOLUNTEERS ON BOARD ABOUT TO SAIL FOR THE PHILIPPINES

The *City of Para* on the way to the Philippines. MNHS #25000

Officers of the 13th Minnesota Volunteer Infantry at lunch in Honolulu en route to Manila, July 1898. MNHS #64833

South Carolina troops
marching off to war in
Columbia. UNIVERSITY OF SOUTH
CAROLINA

Co. C, 13th Minnesota
boarding the train on their
way to San Francisco. MNHS
#22240

A parade in Minneapolis,
Minnesota, for troops
leaving for camp. This
group is probably a boys'
militia from a military
school. The photo is
looking down Hennepin
Avenue from 6th Street.
MNHS #64837

The First New York Volunteers at San Francisco, on their way to Manila.

Volunteers in their civilian clothes sign up at Laramie, Wyoming. DPL #10431

Embarkation of troops at San Francisco bound for the Philippines. NPS

Departure of the First
Idaho Volunteer Regiment
at the old Union Pacific
depot on Front Street in
Boise on May 19, 1898.
Notice the banner on the
side of the Oregon Short
Line passenger car. ISHS
#60-108.56/L & 72-47.3

The 7th Regiment of the
U.S. Army troops
marching on 17th Street
(between Champa and
Curtis) in Denver,
Colorado, on April 20,
1898. DPL #10431

The transport *Pennsylvania* leaving San Francisco for the Philippines. It carried 1,300, mostly troops from the western states. KE

Washington State troops leaving Seattle for the camps in the South, April 1898. WSHS

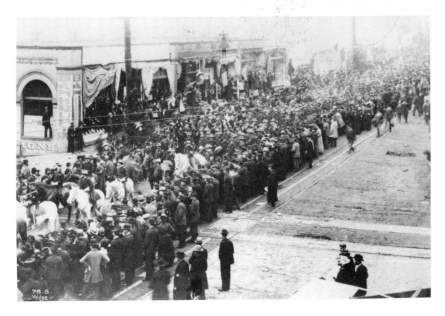

Ohio troops leaving Newport News, Virginia, for the Puerto Rico campaign. KE

During the consumption of a beef ration on board the *Pennsylvania* one of the Montana boys actually found a horse shoe nail in his plate, and another found an ear that strongly sustained the suspicion they were getting horse meat...in the place of beef.

The 51st Iowa leaving the main gate of the Presidio of San Francisco. NPS

A Marine battalion parades through the streets of Portsmouth, New Hampshire, 1898. USN
NH 46345

The Cuban Campaign

The first plan to drive the Spanish from Cuba was to land American troops somewhere on the northwest shore of Cuba near Havana. This would happen after Adm. Pascual Cervera's Caribbean squadron had been neutralized or destroyed.

Cervera brought his fleet into Santiago under the protection of the forts guarding the bay, thus avoiding battle. A new American plan was formulated to land an army near Santiago, attack the forts and expose the Spanish fleet to attack from the blockading American fleet.

On June 22, General Shafter's V Corps began landing at Daiquiri and Siboney, east of Santiago with 17,000 troops. The troops were unopposed although landing facilities were practically non-existent.

Spanish Gen. Arsenio Linares attempted to block the American army's advance to Santiago at Las Guasimas on June 24 but was forced to withdraw to his main defensive position on the San Juan heights.

General Shafter scheduled a frontal assault on July 1 on the heights using General Wheeler's dismounted cavalry. A simultaneous assault on the left was led by Gen. Jacob Kent's infantry division.

In a coordinated operation General Lawton's infantry was to size the town of El Caney, two miles to the north of the heights, and then return to support Wheeler's right wing. Lawton's troops encountered stiff resistance and returned too late to participate in the battle on the heights.

The troops of Wheeler and Kent did not receive adequate artillery support and for a time were pinned down by intense fire from Spanish troops in their trenches. Eventually troops of the 10th and 19th Cavalry along with the Rough Riders succeeded in taking Kettle Hill. A little later, after a Gatling gun battery had driven some of the Spanish from their trenches, Kent's infantry took the main Spanish position on San Juan Hill.

On July 3, the Spanish fleet was destroyed in Santiago Bay and this put the Spanish troops in the city in a hopeless position. On July 17, they surrendered and on Aug. 12, Spain agreed to an armistice.

The Cuban Campaign cost 379 American lives but thousands more succumbed to tropical diseases.

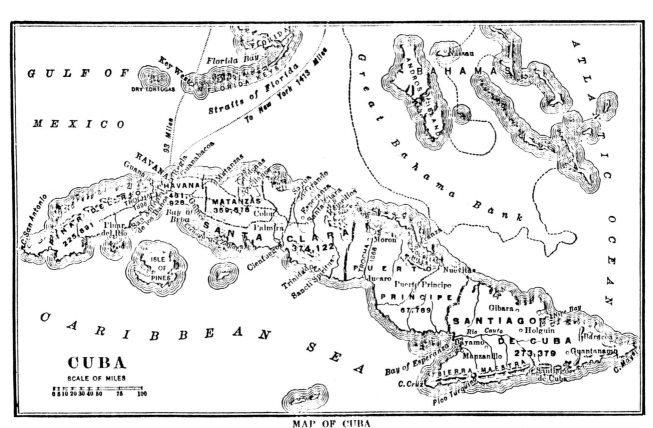

MAP OF CUBA
Showing its Provinces, population of each, principal points, etc.

REAR ADMIRAL SAMPSON'S SQUADRON OFF THIS MORNING FOR CUBA.

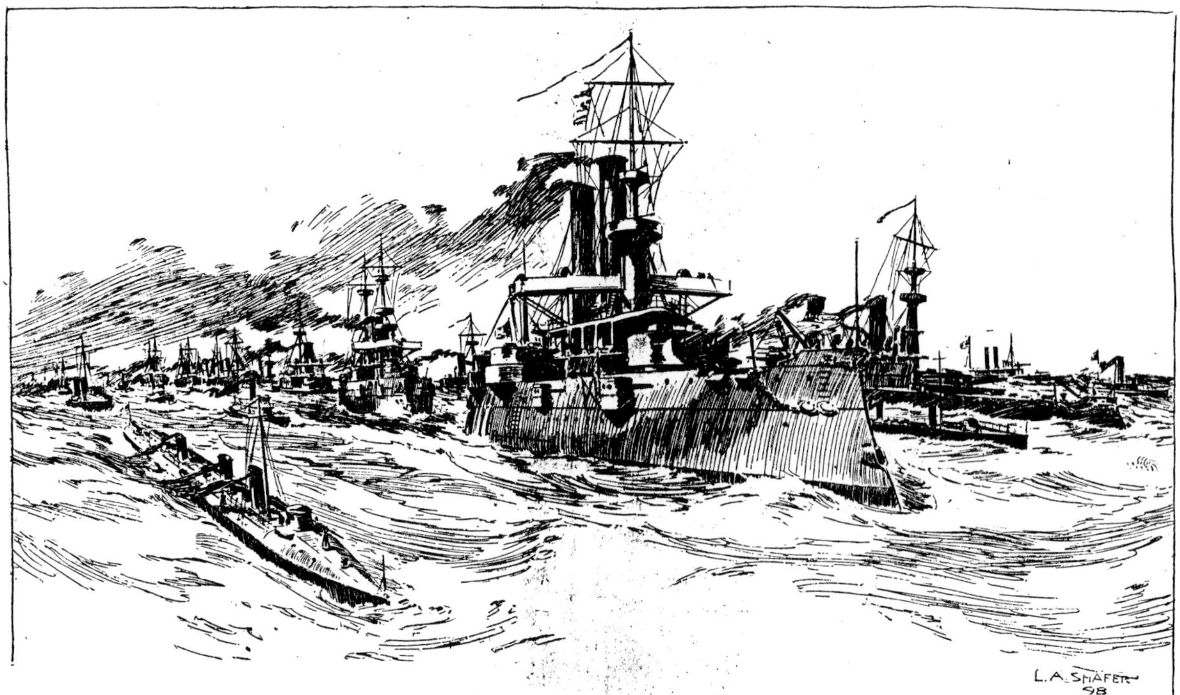

DUPONT. NEWARK. DETROIT. HELENA. MARBLEHEAD. PORTER AND MEMBERS OF AUXILIARY FLEET. PURITAN. NEW YORK. TERROR. IOWA. INDIANA. CUSHING. OSCEOLA. UNCAS.

"FULL STEAM AHEAD—REMEMBER THE MAINE."

WAR BEGINS TO-DAY WITH THE BLOCKADE OF HAVANA.

Minister Woodford's Dismissal Before He Had an Opportunity to Present McKinley's Ultimatum at Madrid Construed as a Declaration of War.

GENERAL BLANCO HAS ISSUED A CALL TO ARMS IN HAVANA.

War between the United States and Spain has begun. The squadron at Key West received orders yesterday afternoon to move at once to blockade Havana. The start will be made early this morning.

There has been no formal declaration of war by either country as yet. Spain, as exclusively foreshowed in yesterday's HERALD, refused to receive the ultimatum prepared by President McKinley.

Before Minister Woodford had an opportunity to follow the cabled instructions, the Spanish Foreign Minister sent him his passports, with the information that diplomatic relations between the two nations were at an end. He turned over the Consulate to the British Ambassador, notified the consuls in Spain, and left Madrid.

Congress Decides on Hostilities.

When the news of Spain's act reached Washington, President McKinley called an extraordinary session of the Cabinet. It was decided that Minister Woodford's dismissal was nothing else than a declaration of war.

The Cabinet decided to begin hostilities at once. After the meeting adjourned the Secretaries of War and Navy began issuing war orders.

Rear Admiral Sampson has instructions to capture or destroy every Spanish war vessel in Cuban waters that attempts to break the blockade he will establish to-day. The Flying Squadron at Hampton Roads is ready to sail at a moment's notice. The Asiatic squadron at Hong Kong will sail to-day to invest the Philippines.

Spain, too, is ready for war. A semi-official note issued in Madrid says Spain will make no further reply, but await the time mentioned in the ultimatum before opening hostilities.

Blanco's Call to Arms.

Havana is making ready to repel an attack. General Blanco has issued a call to arms. The newspapers yesterday published official notices of the alarm signal that will tell the people to assemble for protection. The stations of the regular troops, the volunteers and the firemen, if called upon to prepare for an attack, were published.

Great demonstrations are taking place in Havana streets. In the churches are throngs praying for victory. A crowd assembled in front of the palace and pledged their lives and money to defend Spain's honor.

It is expected that a land force will be landed near Havana next week. General Miles will be in the field himself then. The first division of the army of invasion will consist of 12,000 regulars.

Call for Volunteers To-Day.

As it looks now, President McKinley will call for volunteer forces to-day. The bill authorizing this action was amended in the Senate yesterday.

There is every indication that the bill as amended will be passed by both houses to-day. Immediately after its passage the President will sign it, then requisitions will be made upon the Governors of the States to furnish 80,000 volunteers. The volunteers will be formed into divisions and be moved to the Gulf points, where corps will be organized. In each corps there will three divisions of volunteers and one division of regulars.

All the United States infantry, whose route Southward can without difficulty be deflected to Chickamauga National Park, were ordered by Secretary Alger to concentrate at that rendezvous under the command of Major General John R. Brooke.

Congress has passed a resolution authorizing the President to prohibit the export of coal or other war material, in his discretion.

AWAITING FIRST SHOT.

HERALD BUREAU,
CORNER FIFTEENTH AND G STREETS, N. W.,
WASHINGTON, D. C., Thursday.

And now it is war in earnest.

Momentous events have passed quickly within the last twenty-four hours. But while history has been made to-day, the events of to-morrow may cast into obscurity those which have led up to the crisis. A peaceful blockade of Havana harbor under existing conditions seems impossible, and no one supposes for a moment that the American fleet under command of Rear Admiral Sampson, now engaged in blockading Havana harbor, can remain in those waters an hour without the first shot being fired that will precipitate a conflict which may go down to posterity as the greatest sea battle of modern history.

The guns from our American vessels may open up the pathway to peace and prosperity in Cuba, but one day's work will only be the beginning and not the ending of the Hispano-American war. Dropping all talk of the causes which have led us to make the fatal plunge, the military and naval strategists have come to the front and will occupy the field of speculation for the future—how long no one can tell.

They already differ in their views as to the duration of the war. They all agree that swift and vigorous will be the stroke delivered by the American navy to put an end to Spanish misrule in Cuba. But the loss of Cuba to Spain does not mean an end of the war with Spain. Members of the Strategic Board who have been watching Spanish movements do not anticipate a vigorous resistance in defence of Cuba. The real strength of Spain's navy will be kept far away from Cuba, and in positions which will enable her to prey upon vulnerable points along our coast and upon our commerce, and thus harass us in prolonging the war indefinitely in retaliation for forcing her out of Cuba.

The events of the day in Washington and Madrid, which have severed diplomacy and culminated in war, will long be [illegible] in the history of both countries. Here, as in Madrid, the war spirit is intense, and every step taken on both sides has been for waging war vigorously and with all the forces at the command of the respective countries.

Up to this time neither country has made a formal declaration of war. Yet both countries recognize that a state of war exists. When Minister Woodford received his passports this morning, before he had an opportunity to present the ultimatum demanding that Spain pick up her goods and chattels and leave Cuba, the President considered that Spain threw down the gauntlet. He promptly picked it up by issuing orders for our military and naval forces to begin operations for carrying out his plans for intervention.

Congress May Declare War.

The proclamation which the President will issue to-morrow calling for volunteers, and the notification to foreign Powers of the existence of a blockade of Havana harbor, will be evidence enough that war is upon us. If necessary, however, the Congress of the United States, which under the constitution has the sole power of declaring war, will within five minutes after the first shot has been fired pass the required resolution. Some of the members of the Foreign Relations Committee with whom I talked to-day said that this course would probably be necessary to avoid any future complications with foreign powers in regard to neutrality.

The question of privateering also received some consideration by members of the Foreign Relations Committee to-day. Generally Congress fully agrees with the President that the policy of this country should be against a resort to that of legalized piracy.

If Spain should persist in pursuing warfare of this character, Congress may feel called upon later to exercise the authority granted by the constitution, which permits the granting of letters of marque and reprisal.

The whole tendency of both the administration and Congress, however, is violently opposed to anything of this kind, and should Spain seek to prolong war by engaging in it it is believed that the principal Powers of Europe will combine to prevent it, and that in this way Spain may be forced to give up the fight after we have ousted her from Cuba.

REBELS WOULD NOT LISTEN TO THEM.

Representatives of the Autonomista Who Went to Persuade the Insurgents to Accept Armistice Are Returning to Havana Unsuccessful.

[SPECIAL CABLE TO THE HERALD.]
[FROM A SPANISH CORRESPONDENT.]

HAVANA, Cuba, Thursday.—The committee that went early in the week to Santa Cruz del Sur, as agents of the autonomists, to try to persuade the insurgents to accept the armistice offered by Spain, will be back in Havana Sunday, it is expected.

Its mission was a failure. It did not even get a chance to speak to the insurgent leaders whom it was seeking to turn to peace.

SPAIN'S RESERVES OUT

London, Friday.—A special despatch from Madrid says the government has authorized Lieutenant General Correa, Minister of War, to call out eighty thousand reserves. Three vessels loaded with troops left Cadiz yesterday (Thursday) for a destination [illegible] disclosed.

SQUADRON ORDERED TO SINK SPAIN'S WAR SHIPS.

Rear Admiral Sampson Has Been Instructed to Capture or Destroy All War Vessels of the Enemy in Cuban Waters and Reports of Naval Engagements Are Expected To-Day.

HE WILL RUN NO RISKS OF MINES IN THE HARBORS.

HERALD BUREAU,
CORNER FIFTEENTH AND G STREETS, N. W.,
WASHINGTON, D. C., Thursday.

Resistance attempted by the Spanish vessels now in Cuban and Porto Rican waters to the blockade instituted by the North Atlantic squadron will be followed by their destruction.

Under the instructions given him, it will be the duty of Rear Admiral Sampson, as he has been officially designated, to capture or destroy every ship Spain has in Cuban waters, and, when this has been accomplished, to impose the blockade contemplated by the government's plan of campaign.

Naturally, it is not expected that the execution of this instruction will be performed without damage to the American vessels, and it is anticipated by the officials that by to-morrow evening reports will reach the department of engagements which have been fought by the American and Spanish vessels.

Although Spain has a total of fifty-eight ships distributed in Cuban and Porto Rican waters, no doubt exists in official circles of the ability of the North Atlantic squadron to easily destroy those which it will meet in the vicinity of Cuba.

Largest Cruiser Disabled.

Of the Spanish force, its largest cruiser, the Alfonso XII., of 3,900 tons displacement, lies in a disabled condition in Havana Harbor, and it is expected that it will remain there until the American flag displaces that of Spain.

Spain's next largest ship in Cuban waters is the cruiser Reina Mercedes, of 3,000 tons, built in 1887, which is regarded as a very good vessel of her type. The only other ships which American men-of-war have to fear are seven torpedo cruisers, the Filipinas, of 750 tons and 20 knots; the Jorge Juan, of 935 tons and 13 knots; the Nueva Espana, of 60 tons and 18.6 knots, and the Galicia, the Marques de Molins, the Martin Alonzo and the Vincente Yanez, each of 571 tons and 18.6 knots.

Four cruisers of between eleven and twelve hundred tons are distributed around the island. In addition to this force, Spain has stationed in Cuban ports a large number of gunboats, ranging in displacement from 500 to 20 tons.

Not to Attack Fortifications.

It is recognized by the officials that Captain General Blanco, in view of the hostile parade being made by Rear Admiral Sampson's fleet, will not direct the confinement of the Spanish vessels to Cuban ports, where they will be protected by the land batteries, and it is the expectation of the authorities that these ships will attempt to do as much damage to the blockading squadron as possible.

Rear Admiral Sampson is expected to take measures to destroy any vessels making an attack, and while he will not bombard any fortifications, he is expected to direct the commanding officers of the vessels of his fleet to capture or destroy any Spanish men-of-war which they may meet.

It is believed that at least twelve or fifteen of these are in the harbor of San Juan awaiting the arrival of the flying squadron, which will leave Hampton Roads for that point just as soon as it becomes apparent that the Northern patrol squadron, under Commodore Howell, is in condition to defend the coast should an attack be attempted by Spanish men-of-war.

To Avoid Harbor Mines.

Information which has reached the authorities shows that the Spanish officials in Cuba and Porto Rico, anticipating the arrival of the American fleet, have placed mines in the harbors of these islands and have taken every precaution possible to defend them against attack. It is not proposed to risk any vessels of the North Atlantic squadron by sending them into a harbor in order to attack the cities or any men-of-war that may be lying therein.

LINING UP FOR STARTING.

[FROM THE HERALD'S SPECIAL CORRESPONDENT.]

Key West, Fla., Friday, 3 A. M.—The monitor Terror and the gunboat Helena are now moving out toward the flagship. Rush orders have been sent in calling all the men to their ships

FLEET TO SAIL THIS MORNING.

All Officers and Men of the Key West Squadron on Their Ships Prepared for Prompt Action.

FILLING UP THE BUNKERS WITH COAL.

Everybody, from Rear Admiral Sampson Down, Enthusiastic Over the Prospect of Fighting.

CAPTAIN M'CALLA DELIGHTED

He Expects to Make a Record with the Marblehead to Wipe Out Criticism.

TORPEDO BOAT CREWS ANXIOUS.

Eager for the Fray, in Order to Show What They Can Do in Action.

[FROM THE HERALD'S SPECIAL CORRESPONDENT.]

Key West, Fla., Thursday.—The announcement that Spain considered the President's ultimatum equivalent to a declaration of war caused the greatest sensation in Key West since the destruction of the Maine. The further announcement that the fleet had been ordered to proceed to Cuba sent all officers scurrying for their ships.

The Herald's despatch boats Dewey and Sommers R. Smith led the fleet of newspaper boats from the dock at five o'clock this evening. This fleet consists of ten fast boats, and will remain outside Sand Key light all night, though it is now very well understood that the fleet will not sail before to-morrow.

To Sail This Morning.

The Marblehead has orders to coal at daybreak, and as she is expected to follow the New York, Iowa and Indiana out, the fleet can hardly get away before nine o'clock in the morning.

The Indiana has been coaling at Dry Tortugas, and is now on her return trip. She is expected at her anchorage alongside the Iowa at midnight. The Cincinnati is now coaling from a barge alongside.

Change from the lethargic condition of last month to one of intense activity is apparent on every ship, and seems to have created enthusiasm in the hearts of all, from Rear Admiral Sampson to the crews.

Final target practice was indulged in by all the ships early this afternoon. Then preparations were made for instant sailing.

Captain McCalla Happy.

Captain McCalla, of the Marblehead, is probably the most delighted man in the entire fleet. It is no secret that he hopes to retrieve all that is lost when he was censured for keeping his men aloft and abusing them...

SAMPSON MADE A REAR ADMIRAL.

Captain Commanding the North Atlantic Squadron Promoted by the President.

HERALD BUREAU,
CORNER FIFTEENTH AND G STREETS, N. W., }
WASHINGTON, D. C., Thursday. }

President McKinley to-day authorized Captain W. T. Sampson, Commander in Chief of the North Atlantic squadron, to hoist the flag of a rear admiral.

"RALLY ROUND THE FLAG."

BLANCO ISSUES A STIRRING CALL TO ARMS.

OUR DOGS OF WAR READY FOR FIGHT

United States Forces Eager to Pounce Upon Their Prey and Successfully Execute the Offensive and Defensive Plans.

ATTACK TO BE MADE ON THE PHILIPPINES.

HERALD BUREAU,
CORNER FIFTEENTH AND G STREETS, N. W., }
WASHINGTON, D. C., Thursday. }

With the North Atlantic squadron investigating the waters of Cuba, with the Asiatic squadron under orders to sail to-morrow from Hong Kong for the Philippines, and with the flying squadron champing at the bit at Hampton Roads, ready to move on Porto Rico the moment it is announced that Commodore Howell's patrol squadron is ready for effective service in connection with the defence of the coast...

"WE WILL THROW THEM INTO THE SEA!"

General Blanco Makes a Rather Wild Promise to His Excited Followers in Havana.

[BY THE ASSOCIATED PRESS.]

Havana, Cuba, Thursday.—Havana is preparing for defence against the forces of the United States. Captain General Blanco issued to-day a call to arms, and to-night a great public demonstration was made in the streets in response to a proclamation from the palace.

If the United States Wants Cuba, the Captain General Declares, Let Its Forces Try to Take It—His Summons to Spaniards in Cuba.

[BY THE ASSOCIATED PRESS.]

Havana, Cuba, Thursday.—The Official Gazette publishes an extra, containing the following manifesto:—

"The General Government of the Island of Cuba to the Inhabitants of the Island of Cuba:—

"Without any reason or legal right, without the least offence on our part, and at a time when they have received from us only proofs of friendship, the United States are forcing us into war, just at the moment when questions began to settle over the country, when production was flourishing, commerce taking courage and peace approaching, with the co-operation of all classes and all parties under the new institutions granted by the mother country.

"Such a proceeding is without precedent in history. It evidently manifests the bogus politics of the Republic, demonstrating the tricky policy and purposes that have always been nourished again Spain's sovereignty in Cuba, which the enemy has been conspiring for nearly a century to destroy. Our foes now carry their hypocrisy and falsehood to the extent of demanding immediate peace in a war provoked and sustained by themselves. Her prudence and moderation have been of no avail to Spain, though she has carried her concessions to the extreme limit of toleration in order to avoid a rupture.

"She still deplores the state of affairs, but she accepts it with all the energy inspired by a glorious national identity and the pride of her people, a pride which will never yield to the stranger's haughtiness nor consent to see Spain's right and reason trampled upon by a nation of nobodies.

"If the United States wants the island of Cuba let them come and take it. Perhaps the hour is not far distant in which these Carthaginians of America will find their Zama in this island of Cuba, which Spain discovered, peopled and civilised, and which will never be anything but Spanish.

"It is our turn to have the honor of defending her, and we will know how to do it with decision and to affront many a time put forth. I count upon you for this with absolute certainty. I believe there is no sacrifice you are not prepared to make in defence of the national territory, whose integrity is sacred to all Spaniards, of whatever origin.

"I am sure that every one in whose veins runs Spanish blood will respond readily to the call which, in these solemn moments, I address to all, and that all will group themselves around me to contribute as much as they can to repel a foreign invasion, without allowing dangers, sufferings or privations to weaken the heart of courage.

"To arms, then, fellow countrymen, to arms! There will be a place for all in the fight. Let all co-operate and contribute with the same firmness and enthusiasm to fight the eternal enemy of the Spanish name, emulating the exploits of our ancestors, who always exalted high their country's fame and honor.

"The moment has come in which we shall be able, once for all, to deliver this country's ultimatum.

"Long live Spain with the honor and integrity of her territory! To arms!

"The eternal cause of the Spanish nation is become known abroad. At the White House, the State, War and Navy departments and throughout the city generally...

"To arms! Cry a thousand times, 'Viva Espana!' 'Viva el Rey Alfonso XIII.!' 'Viva la Reina Regente!' 'Viva Cuba always Spanish!'

"Your Governor General,
"RAMON BLANCO.
"Havana, April 21, 1898."

CABINET DECIDES TO BEGIN WAR.

Eventful Day at the White House Opened with the Announcement of Minister Woodford's Dismissal.

LOOKED UPON AS A DECLARATION.

HERALD BUREAU,
CORNER FIFTEENTH AND G STREETS, N. W., }
WASHINGTON, D. C., Thursday. }

National history was made at the White House to-day with lightning like rapidity. This has been one of the most eventful days at the Executive Mansion in the history of this government.

The first sensation of the day was the announcement that the Spanish government had given our Minister at Madrid his passports.

Proclamation Will Probably Be Issued by the State Department To-Day Announcing Its Inauguration.

SUCCESS DEPENDS ON THE SQUADRON.

Purpose of This Government Is to Starve the Spanish Insular Troops Into Submission.

POWERS TO BE NOTIFIED.

Cablegrams Will Be Sent to Our Diplomatic Representatives Throughout the World.

EFFECT UPON NEUTRAL VESSELS.

Those in Port Will Be Allowed a Certain Length of Time to Leave Unmolested.

HERALD BUREAU,
CORNER FIFTEENTH AND G STREETS, N. W., }
WASHINGTON, D. C., Thursday. }

Upon the success of the efforts of the North Atlantic Squadron to establish and maintain an effective blockade will depend in a great measure the fall of Cuba. Any ineffectiveness of blockade will result in its non-observance by neutrals and the consequent resumption of commerce between them and the ports of Cuba.

As it is the purpose of this government to starve the Spanish troops into a state where they will be comparatively easy prey for the American army, which it is proposed to land in a short time, the shipments of supplies into Cuba would be most disastrous to the plans of this government.

What a Blockade Requires.

Secretary Mason's instructions stated that:—

"A lawful maritime blockade requires the actual presence of a sufficient force stationed at the entrance of the ports sufficiently near to prevent communication..."

ENGLAND'S ATTITUDE.

The Paris Temps Asks if She Is Separating from Germany.

Paris, Thursday.—The Temps this afternoon is much exercised over the Anglo-American relations...

MAP OF HAVANA'S DEFENCES.

Drawn From Official Diagrams and Information in the Possession of the Navy Department, Much of Which Was Furnished by Lieutenant Jenkins, of the Maine.

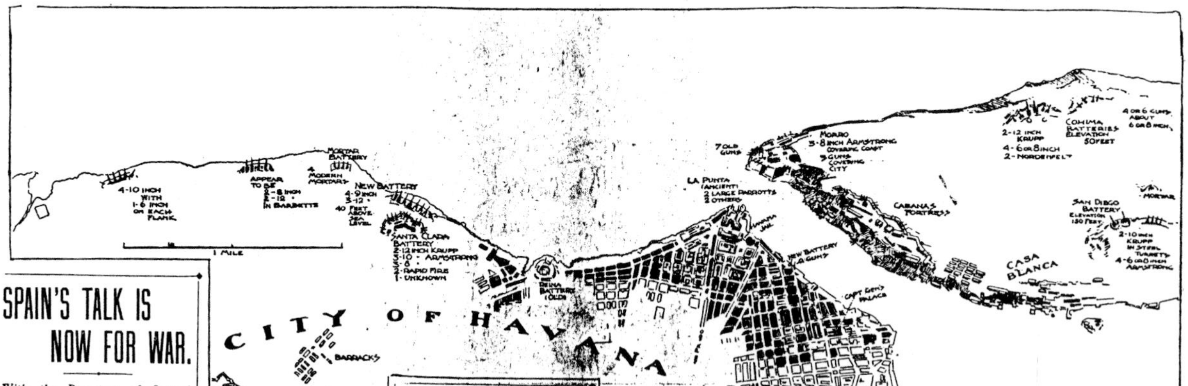

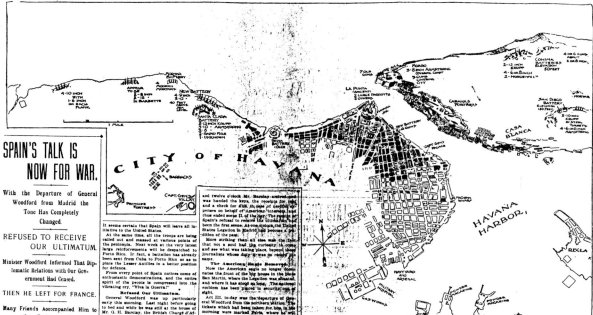

SPAIN'S TALK IS NOW FOR WAR.

With the Departure of General Woodford from Madrid the Tone Has Completely Changed.

REFUSED TO RECEIVE OUR ULTIMATUM.

Minister Woodford Informed That Diplomatic Relations with Our Government Had Ceased.

THEN HE LEFT FOR FRANCE.

Many Friends Accompanied Him to the Train to Say Goodby.

BRITISH FLAG ON OUR LEGATION.

Archives Turned Over to the English Ambassador, Who Will Care for Our Interests.

[SPECIAL CABLE TO THE HERALD.]

The HERALD's European edition publishes the following from its correspondent:—

MADRID, Thursday.—At last the varying phases of the Cuban question have been merged into a concrete issue, with war as the arbiter. Even those who most dreaded such a solving of the problem are glad that the strain is over, that there is no more hesitation possible, and that, in fact, the ball has been set rolling. The Spanish government has broken off diplomatic relations with the United States.

Irritation at Mr. Woodford's Stay.

For the last couple of days there has been a noticeable feeling of restlessness, and even some little irritation, over the continued stay in Madrid of General Woodford. As I told you last night, the Spanish government had firmly decided to receive no ultimatum. One Minister said to me that it was an insult for any nation to demand from another the performance within forty-eight hours of a physically impossible task—namely, the withdrawal of her huge military and naval forces from any point—so they determined to avoid the necessity for reply by refusing further communication with the United States, and, as it was certain that General Woodford would carry out his instructions to the letter, a sort of deadlock began to be feared.

Sagasta's Cabinet Embarrassed.

The most serious question that could possibly confront a country even threatened to take on a faintly grotesque aspect, and the presentation of the ultimatum to degenerate into a process resembling the serving of a writ on the government. An intimation was conveyed to General Woodford that the negotiations were at an end between the two countries when Señor Moret called upon him to bid him adieu. When this somewhat broad hint had no effect they were quite nonplussed. Finally last night, shortly before the arrival of the cable message to General Woodford from President McKinley containing the ultimatum, the Cabinet despatched a note to the United States Minister officially informing him that diplomatic relations were broken off, and that no further communications were possible between the two governments. An end was thus put to the situation that was rapidly becoming strained to the danger point.

Spain Eager for War.

With the going away of General Woodford all lethargy has left the people. War specials are being cried in the streets. All the talk is of war, every one wondering where the first blow will be struck and by whom.

It seems certain that Spain will leave all initiative to the United States.

At the same time, all the troops are being called out and massed at various points of the peninsula. Next week at the very latest large reinforcements will be despatched to Porto Rico. In fact, a battalion has already been sent from Cuba to Porto Rico so as to place the Lesser Antilles in a better position for defence.

From every point of Spain notices come of enthusiastic demonstrations, and the entire spirit of the people is compressed into the vibrating cry, "Viva la Guerra!"

Refused Our Ultimatum.

General Woodford was up particularly early this morning. Last night before going to bed and while he was still at the house of Mr. G. H. Barclay, the British Chargé d'Affaires, where he had dined, he was quietly informed that the Spanish government would not accept the ultimatum sent by the United States, that it considered such to be a pure insult, for it was understood that the Spanish troops should be removed in forty-eight hours, which, to begin with, was a physical impossibility, and secondly, that the idea of removing the forces was untenable.

Found the Ultimatum at Home.

But General Woodford had returned to his almost abandoned home scarcely believing that the news which the HERALD announced yesterday could be true. When he got home quite late the ultimatum was there. When he woke in the morning a big official Spanish note was handed him stating that diplomatic relations had been broken off and that Spain considered all official intercourse with the United States ended. That meant, naturally, that the Spanish government refused to accept the ultimatum.

This General Woodford at once telegraphed to President McKinley, stating that Spain's note had arrived before he could present the ultinmatum, and adding that he had applied for a safe pass to the frontier. And he started this afternoon by the express at four o'clock.

America Must Declare War.

Thus the first two points in the game of "who shall begin the fighting" have gone to Spain. She has neither accepted the ultimatum nor handed General Woodford his passports. It is he who asked for them. If Spain can have it so it will be the United States that will declare war.

Scenes at the Legation.

At ten o'clock the places, five in number, were booked on the express, with small compartment for General Woodford and Captain Bliss, the military attaché and the last remaining official member of the Legation, besides the Minister himself. Other seats were for Señor Moreno, who for many years has been shorthand and type writer to the Legation, and for James Hunter, the long, thin, soft toned colored man, who has been popularly considered in Madrid as the keeper of the conscience of Minister Woodford.

I saw the Minister at an early hour in what may be termed the wreck of his home, for his handsome apartment, No. 13 Nunez de Balboa, presented a most desolate appearance, being full of cases, discarded deal boxes and every symptom of hasty packing. General Woodford said he had decided not to make any statement for publication.

At half-past eleven o'clock he was at the Legation. He had come down with Captain Bliss, the only incident on the road being that a small group, composed among others of a few women, hissed as he passed, but as showing how little any demonstration was feared the guard had been diminished here, as also at his residence.

Our Archives in Safe Keeping.

The office was well crowded with journalists. All the archives of value had been removed, though the rent of the office had been paid up to July, as also the salaries of the staff hired to guard the place until that date, and the Department of State notified. Toward twelve o'clock Mr. Barclay arrived and was handed the keys, the receipts for rent and a check for £100, in case of needful expenses on behalf of American interests, and thus ended scene II. of the day. The receipt of Spain's refusal to receive the ultimatum had been the first scene. At one o'clock the United States Legation in Madrid had become a tradition of the past.

More striking than all else was the fact that not a soul had the curiosity to come and see what was taking place, beyond those journalists whose duty it was to record the same.

The American Eagle Removed.

Now the American eagle no longer dominates the front of the big house in the plaza San Martin, where the Legation was situated, and where it has stood so long. The national emblem has been placed in security out of sight.

Act III. to-day was the departure of General Woodford from the northern station. The tickets which had been taken for him in the morning were marked Paris, where he will stop at the Hotel Binda. It was just ten minutes before four. There were two or three hundred friends and others assembled in front of the station when a closed brougham drawn by one horse and followed by a detachment of cavalry rattled down, and General Woodford briskly stepped out. He was offered every civility by the employes of the railroad and the Governor of Madrid and other officials there. He wore a round hat and his favorite suit, with a tinge of red in it, and in his buttonhole the badge of the Loyal Legion. With him came Captain Bliss, and following closely was noticeable the form of James Hunter, his colored factotum, carrying the General's yellow bag, in which probably the ultimatum lay.

Seeing General Woodford Off.

There was a great deal of handshaking, and the General made his way as quickly as possible to the platform. There I noticed, among others, Mr. and Mrs. Berkeley, of the British Embassy, and Sir Donald Mackenzie. Mr. Wallace Sickles, Secretary of the Legation, who is leaving with the Minister, and Mrs. and Miss Sickles. One officer and eleven privates, fully armed, quietly and quickly made their way into one of the carriages. They are to guard General Woodford, for Spain is determined that no affront shall be offered to America's representative, and fear lest the accounts published in this morning's papers stating that the Spanish escutcheon had been torn down in Washington might excite public feeling here, not perhaps in Madrid, but more likely in Valladolid and other places on the road where patriotic feeling runs high.

Mr. Woodford and the Spanish Public.

General Woodford, in reply to a remark I made to him about the attitude of the crowd, replied:—

"Yes, they have behaved admirably throughout," a tribute which the public here richly deserves.

It was three minutes past four when General Woodford had said the last word to the Spanish people, which was simply, "Goodby," and he desired it to be especially understood in case the sensational minded newspaper correspondents should seek to add anything to it.

The captain of the guard who accompanied the General had been duly introduced and all the officials had said adieu to him. Mr. Sickles stood on the car platform, saying the last words to his other sister, and the sound of a military fanfare streamed through the doors from the street without, when the bell rang and the train began to move out of the station.

An Anxious Moment.

It was an anxious moment. General Woodford, pale and worried, but firm, glanced up from reading a paper, which seemed to interest him immensely. It was the first issue of a war special, the first of thousands to come probably, called "The Correo de la Guerra," and its last sentences were "Death to the United States!" "Long live Spain with honor!" "Glory to the army and navy, in whose hands is the honor of the fatherland!" and as the train began to move out hats were waved, arms were raised, and there came forth ringing cries in unison of "Viva España con honore!"

General Wodford simply sat back and closed his mouth somewhat firmer. Just as the train was out of sight there was a rush by the biggest man in Madrid, its Governor. He was heard speaking at the top of his powerful lungs. He was invoking the crowd. He was telling the people collected that, now America's representative had gone, Spain's feelings might be given full vent to without indecorum, and the people echoed his words with renewed cheers for Spain, but, after all, it was a very good natured crowd and it uttered not a single cry against the United States, General Woodford or President McKinley.

There are indications in the streets of rising popular excitement.

SPAIN'S HOME FLEET IS AT TWO PORTS.

Four of Her Cruisers and a Torpedo Flotilla Are at Anchor at Cadiz, Four Cruisers Are at Carthagena and Precautions Are Taken at All Ports.

[SPECIAL CABLE TO THE HERALD.]
[COPYRIGHT, 1898, BY JAMES GORDON BENNETT.]

CADIZ, Thursday.—I obtained here to-day a list of all the war ships now at Spanish ports.

Four cruisers are here. They are the Carlos V., the Princess de Asturias, the Don Juan de Austria and the Reina Cristina. With them is a torpedo flotilla.

At Carthagena are the Alfonso and Ferrol and the cruisers Cardenal Cisneros and Lepanto.

There are no war ships at Barcelona.

I was told that strict orders had been issued that no information about the ships or their destinations should be given and that agents of the govenment are watching at all the ports to see that no information is obtained by representatives of the United States.

BITTER FEELING AGAINST ENGLAND.

Spaniards Show Resentment Against Her Attitude on Contraband of War and Privateering.

MADRID, Thursday.—There is a bitter feeling here again Great Britain, especially on the contraband of war and privateer questions. It is the belief of the general public that Great Britain is playing, in an underhand manner, the game of the United States.

MOBS FILL THE STREETS OF MADRID.

Outburst Against the United States Causes Crowds to Collect and Show Displeasure by Destroying an American Eagle in Front of the Equitable Insurance Building—Demand Made for the Expulsion of All Foreigners, Especially American Newspaper Correspondents.

THE SUPPLY OF COAL IS SHORT, BUT THE QUEEN STANDS BY THE CABINET.

MADRID, Thurday.—A mob gathered in front of the building of the Equitable Life Insurance Company, to-night and insisted upon the removal of the American Eagle, which was thrown down and smashed to bits.

The fragments were then carried through the streets by a cheering, yelling mob to the Military Club, where the members appeared upon the balcony and enthusiastically cheered the demonstration, shouting "Viva Espana!" and "Down with the Yankees!" The police mixed with the crowd and allowed the demonstrations to go on without restraint.

The police mixed with the crowd and allowed the demonstrations to go on without restraint.

The Civil Governor of Madrid, Señor Aguilera, instead of prohibiting, allowed complete liberty of action, going among the demonstrators. He was loudly cheered, especially when the American escutcheon was thrown from the balcony of the Equitable Building and fell at his feet.

Spanish Lion Aroused.

Señor Aguilera, as if trampling upon the escutcheon, addressed the populace amid enthusiastic applause. He said:—

"The Spanish lion is roused from its slumber. We will shake his mane and dispose of the rest of the brute creation."

The demonstration continued, a part of the mob proposing a demonstration in front of the American Legation, which is now under the British flag. It is hoped at the time this despatch is sent that the crowd will disperse exhausted, having nothing upon which to wreak its vengeance.

La Correspondencia Espana suggests the expulsion of all foreigners, especially the newspaper correspondents, "whose presence is dangerous." It says the censorship is inadequate, as the correspondents have other means of "keeping up their calumnies against Spain, especially the American correspondents."

The paper demands that a date shall be named for their expulsion, giving them time only to reach the frontier. "Let them follow their profession elsewhere," it says, "and we are confident that no Spaniard worthy the name will act as a substitute for Yankee press correspondents."

Cuban Congress at Work.

At the outset of proceedings in the Congress (the Lower House of the Cortes), the President, Marquis Vega d'Armijo, urged the necessity of the quickest possible organization of the House, "to enable us to defend the honor and flag of our country."

The Chamber commenced forthwith the election of committees, and it is believed that the work of organization will be completed by Saturday.

In the lobbies Deputies of all parties were unanimous in saying that America must be resisted to the utmost.

Hoisted the Spanish Flag.

The mob hoisted the Spanish flag over the Equitable Life Insurance Company's building and replaced the American shield by another, indicating that the edifice had been hypothecated in favor of the company's insurers.

They then moved to other buildings bearing the arms of the United States, all of which were either taken down or will be taken down to-morrow. The crowd then visited the railway station and gave an ovation to a couple of departing battalions of marines. From this point they went to the military club.

The demonstration finally divided into two processions. The first moved to the French Embassy to express gratitude to France for taking charge of Spanish affairs in Washington. The second, numbering 5,000, went to the National Theatre, which was crowded. Vast throngs were on the outside unable to get admission. Those outside finally dispersed, still shouting "Viva Espana!" and "Death to the Yankees!"

QUEEN STANDS BY THE CABINET.

MADRID, Thursday.—The Queen Regent has consulted with the respective political leaders and with the President of the Senate. They advise her that the existing Cabinet without any modification ought to continue to meet the difficulties of the situation.

Señor Montero Rios and the Marquis d'Armijo, in substantially the same terms as Marshal Campos, declared to the Queen Regent their opinion that it was reasonable and patriotic that the Crown should continue to give full confidence to the liberal party, which expects co-operation and unanimous support from all other parties in the defence of the honor, integrity and dignity of the country.

SPAIN VIRTUALLY DECLARES WAR.

MADRID, Thursday.—By refusing to receive the ultimatum of President McKinley and handing Minister Woodford his passports Spain, by her own act to-day, cut off all diplomatic relations with the United States. General Woodford has left Madrid and his departure was made the occasion for a great jingo demonstration at the station.

Madrid newspapers this afternoon print highly colored accounts of how General Woodford was handed his passports, and efforts are made to place him in a bad light. The facts are that the government, having received the text of the ultimatum of the United States from its own sources, did not wait for the United States Minister to present the ultimatum, but sent him his passports.

It is not expected that there will be any formal declaration of war. Spain's action is considered a virtual declaration of war, and hostilities may begin immediately. Both nations, however, may make to their own people and to all neutrals what is termed "the notification of war."

There was a slight fall in prices on the Spanish Bourse as a result of the severance of diplomatic relations between Spain and the United States, but there was no panic.

The news of the rupture was received calmly. There is no excitement apparent anywhere.

The Queen Regent presided this afternoon at the Cabinet Council. Senor Sagasta, the Premier, announced the departure of Senor Polo de Bernabe from Washington, and that the United States Minister, General Woodford, had been informed that it would be useless to present any note.

United States Consul R. M. Bartleman, has started from Malaga for Gibraltar. The escutcheon and the American flag over the Consulate have been removed and the archives transferred to the British Consulate.

FAILED TO PROVIDE COAL FOR SHIPS.

LONDON, Thursday.—A despatch to the Daily Telegraph from Barcelona, via Paris, says:—

"Grave apprehensions are entertained in the highest government circles that the issue of war may be decided not by valor and enthusiasm and dogged perseverance, qualities of which the Spaniards possess abundance, but by reserves of coal and victuals, of which they have made but a scanty provision in Cuba. It apears that in respect of coal in particular they are incomparably worse off than they have hitherto imagined.

"The Spanish government, firmly believing down to the very last moment that peace would be preserved through the intercession of the Pope and the Powers, neglected to lay in sufficient provision of coal, despite the representations made to them by one or two farseeing naval officers. Besides, it is believed that they never once inquired of the British or other neutral governments whether coal would be regarded as contraband of war. The result is said to be a state of things which may be fraught with unpleasant surprises and bring hostilities to a premature end.

"Those in the secret were anxious to overthrow the Cabinet on other grounds before the beginning of war, for patriotic considerations forbade a public discussion of the country's weak point on the eve of hostilities. The short time allowed for the deliberations of Parliament rendered this intention difficult of execution, and the Liberal Cabinet, which conducted the negotiations, will be allowed to bear the responsibility for the results during a conflict. This alarming story comes from an excellent source, quite above all suspicion, even of hostility to the Cabinet."

WOODFORD TOLD TO GO

Text of the Note from Senor Gullon Informing Him That the Action of Congress Was a Declaration of War and That Diplomatic Relations Had Ceased.

MADRID, Thursday.—Following is the text of the note received this morning by General Woodford from Señor Gullon, Minister of Foreign Affairs:—

"DEAR SIR:—

"In compliance with a painful duty, I have the honor to inform you that there has been sanctioned by the President of the Republic a resolution of both Chambers of the United States which denies the legitimate sovereignty of Spain and threatens armed intervention in Cuba, which is equivalent to a declaration of war.

"The government of Her Majesty have ordered her Minister to return without loss of time from North American territory, together with all the personnel of the Legation.

"By this act the diplomatic relations hitherto existing between the countries and all official communications between their respective representatives cease.

"I am obliged thus to inform you so that you may make such arrangements as you think fit. I beg Your Excellency to acknowledge this note at such time as you deem proper. Taking this opportunity to reiterate to you the assurances of my distinguished consideration.

"P. GULLON."

THE CHICAGO TIMES-HERALD.

EIGHTEENTH YEAR. FRIDAY MORNING, JULY 15, 1898. PRICE IN CITY CARRIER DISTRICTS ONE CENT. OUT OF TOWN AND ON TRAINS TWO CENTS.

SHOULD VICTORS RETAIN SPOILS?

Question of the Hour Discussed by Illinois Lawyers at the Session of the Bar Association.

WAR AND CONQUEST AND AMERICA'S FUTURE.

Some See a Military Government Rising on the Foundations of the Present Republic—Views of A. E. Stevenson, Judge Grosscup and Others.

EMINENT lawyers of Illinois, gathered at the Chicago Beach Hotel for the Bar Association's meeting, took occasion with the fall of Santiago to discuss the end of the war and the immense amount of new territory which the United States will have at its command. Should all of this territory be retained? Should it be held merely for indemnity and released when that indemnity is paid? Ought not new coaling and naval stations be secured even if the territory seized be not kept? Is territorial expansion a necessity or an evil? These questions were discussed by the lawyers, and what they said is given herewith. There was a majority sentiment in favor of coaling and naval stations; a wide divergence as to whether outside of this the rest of the new territory should be held for indemnity or kept forever as a part of the union. Some lawyers saw a military government rising on the foundations of the present republic; others felt that to make the Philippines, the Ladrones, Cuba and Porto Rico, with their mixed and curious populations, American states was a grave error. The Nestor of the Chicago bar, Judge Tuley, said of this, in one sentence: "The rule of the republic has been that its peoples should become part of this republic unless they themselves consented. By conquest we cannot bring in the new races whose land we now hold. If these races do not wish our rule how can we in fact upon it?"

ADLAI E. STEVENSON (former Vice President of the United States)—It would seem that the policy of expansion is being forced upon the people of the United States and that we shall be compelled to adopt it. It is a very difficult problem that is presented to the nation. Hawaii has become a part of our government by the consent of her people and in accordance with the wishes of the people of this country. We have practically conquered Cuba, and the understanding is that her people shall have a republican form of government of their own. It requires no prophet, however, to foretell that in the course of time Cuba will become one of the states of the union. I have not given the subject sufficient thought to warrant my saying whether I am in favor of territorial expansion at present.

JUDGE PETER S. GROSSCUP—I do not regard territorial expansion as implying that the republic is drifting into militarism; that we shall have in the end a military republic. The commercial element of this country, in which I include the manufacturers, is growing. Commerce has always followed the flag. That is the reason why with such growth there is always a decided movement for the acquisition of new territory in which to operate. This is the reason why England to-day is the most powerful commercial agent in the world. England's government stands as a sort of advertising agency for every British product. Her products are in every port. Her consular headquarters are conspicuous at the entrance to every port. In other words, the English government maintains in all parts of the world a standing advertisement for the products of her people. England is ready to act always for her commercial interests, and to that position we are coming very rapidly and naturally at the present time.

JUDGE MURRAY F. TULEY—The commercial element is now in control of this country. There can be no question of that. The commercial element elected McKinley. The commercial element did not advocate this war and in fact did all it could to prevent it, but after it was on it took control of it, has conducted it, and will dictate the terms of peace. The commercial element is now on top of the farmer, and the end of such control, in my opinion, will be a military republic—the man on horseback. I cannot, without being pessimistic at all, see any other end of the republic than a military government. The people have practically no voice in the government to-day. Four or five men in this state dictate all the legislation. Resistance to acquisition of new territory is impossible. The commercial element demands such territory, and having acquired it, an army and a navy of great proportions will be necessary to protect it. Having acquired that army and navy, there is provided the strong arm of the government for the future that the commercial element needs to carry out its designs. I have not favored new territorial acquisitions. The policy of the government has been to develop within itself and to leave the outside world to itself. We are now about to expand and to enter the congress of nations in a vital factor. The change presented upon our people by this will be wonderful and I believe it will alter the whole character of the republic from what it was originally proposed to be.

ALFRED ORENDORFF (president State Bar Association)—I am in favor of commercial expansion, which amounts to about the same thing as territorial expansion. I oppose, and the maintenance of an army and navy which will support such a policy. This nation should have coaling stations in every part of the world, and that is as far as we need go in the acquirement of new territory. Our national policy can be enlarged without any very radical departure from our traditions. As for Cuba and the Philippines, I am in favor of holding all the territory acquired until the war indemnity is paid in full.

JUDGE OLIVER H. HORTON—In my judgment the new territory which we have acquired should be held for indemnity. The land should remain ours until Spain has footed the expense bills—if this war which we have incurred. At the time the payment is made that we hold, then all the territory should relinquish the territory to which she is legally entitled. I do not mean that we should merely keep little bays in which one ship may anchor. We should hold immense naval stations, where a whole fleet may evolute as it sees fit, where coal is abundant so that any ship, flying the American flag may have under all circumstances a haven. This it appears to me should be the proper outcome of this war, one that will be satisfactory to all the people. I cannot believe that we should take into the union as part of it the races of the lands that we now hold, races in which the savage predominates and which can have no conception of our form of government or appreciation of its principles. We ought to make them American citizens. This is wrong to the bona fide American. They should not be forced upon us and never can be. Citizenship, as we understand it, never can be conferred upon them. They land is ours only until we have been paid for this war. From them we want nothing but ample harbor shelter for our men-of-war and our merchantmen.

JUDGE JOHN BARTON PAYNE—I do not see that the question of territorial expansion has been forced upon us. I look upon its approach as a natural thing; something which was bound to come. The time for territorial expansion is at hand, and the nation must face it as it has all other problems with the full consciousness that the right is with us and that ultimately the policy of the government has been against entangling foreign alliances. Territorial expansion is not an entangling foreign alliance. The territory has come to us through force of arms. We have acquired it by the right of battle and we should hold it. The keeping of it does not involve entanglement with any foreign nation except possibly the one which has just given up Santiago. With this new territory we shall go on minding our own business, just as we have in the past. Our fleets and our merchant marine. That is my idea of territorial expansion.

[CONTINUED ON FIFTH PAGE.]

PORTO RICO NEXT

American Army of Occupation to Leave Next Week.

GENERAL BROOKE TO LEAD

Summoned From Chickamauga to Washington for Instructions—His Force to Number 33,000.

"Next is Porto Rico; then, if need be, Havana."—Secretary Alger.

[SPECIAL TO THE TIMES-HERALD.]

WASHINGTON, July 14.—Porto Rico next. The army of occupation will leave the United States next week if plans do not miscarry. An official dispatch to a southern camp to-

day gave warning that the expedition should be ready to move in eight days.

General John R. Brooke, commanding at Chickamauga, is to lead the invading force. He has been ordered to come to Washington to receive instructions, and is now on the war here.

The government will profit by its experience. It will avoid some of the mistakes of the past. It will not underestimate the defensive strength of the enemy, and it will send 33,000 to 35,000 men to the conquest of Porto Rico. It will not attempt to feed all from one port. The troops will go from Tampa, Mama and Fernandina, and perhaps from Charleston, Newport News and New York.

Cruisers as Transports.

Some of the transports are loaded already. Others are on the way to points of departure. The auxiliary cruisers Yale, Harvard, St. Paul and St. Louis have been placed at the service of the army, and if used will expedite the shipment of troops because of their speed and large carrying capacity.

The government has yet all the machinery of the army in motion, and the intention is to hasten the departure of this expedition as much as possible. It will contain about 25 of volunteers. The plan to use most of the regulars has been abandoned because of the yellow fever among the troops in Cuba. The disease is not of the malignant type and the cases are not numerous but the authorities will take no chance of infecting the fresh troops from the north by bringing them into contact with men who have been exposed in Santiago.

The plan to use Santiago as a base of operations against Porto Rico has been abandoned for that reason. The troops will be sent direct to Porto Rico from its coast. The work of the volunteers in Cuba proves that they can be depended on for the task before them in Porto Rico. There is said to be relatively little danger of yellow fever in the eastern island, and the climatic conditions are altogether more favorable than in Cuba.

Troops Now in Florida.

There is an abundance of good military material for another army without moving on General Shafter for a single man. There are nearly 8,000 troops at Chickamauga, 8,000 at Tampa, 3,000 at Camp Alger, 15,000 at Jacksonville and 7,000 at Miami. There are enough men at the Florida camps alone for the proposed force.

Tampa has the following organizations of the Fourth corps under Major General J. J. Copinger:

FIRST DIVISION, MAJOR GENERAL SNYDER—First Brigade, Colonel Vincent United States infantry: First Louisiana. Second Wisconsin, Sixteenth Pennsylvania. Second Brigade, First Massachusetts, Ninth Ohio and Fifth Illinois.

SECOND DIVISION, MAJOR GENERAL WILLIAM A. BANCROFT—First Brigade, Wisconsin, Fifteenth Iowa and Fourth Illinois.

THIRD DIVISION—First Ohio, First Florida, Third Georgia and Fourth Virginia and Forty-ninth Iowa.

THIRD DIVISION (details)—Second Missouri infantry and Terre s ninth corps.

General Lee's First division is at Tampa and is made up as follows:

FIRST BRIGADE, GENERAL W. W. MARSTON—First Texas, First Alabama and First Louisiana.

SECOND BRIGADE, GENERAL W. W. GORDON—Second Georgia and First Louisiana and Second Alabama.

Sent From Chickamauga.

Major General J. H. Wilson has been ordered to forward two brigades of his division from Chickamauga to Charleston for the voyage to Santiago. One of them has arrived, but he was instructed to-day to stop at Fernandina or Miami, take his men and horses off for a rest and have his heavy freight aboard. He was told he would be sent to Porto Rico within a few days.

BEREFT OF HOPE.

Futility of Resistance to Shafter Pointed Out to Toral.

VISITED BEFORE SURRENDER

Conference Between Opposing Leaders at Santiago, in Which General Miles Takes Part.

[ASSOCIATED PRESS DISPATCH.]

PLAYA DEL ESTE, Guantanamo Bay, July 14, 2 p. m.—(Copyright, 1898 by the Associated Press.)—General Toral, commanding the Spanish forces in Santiago de Cuba, this morning sent a communication to General Shafter, indicating his willingness to accept the terms of surrender proposed yesterday.

FRENCH GUNBOAT IS FIRED ON.

Quickly Brought to Terms at Guantanamo for Refusing to Stop.

[ASSOCIATED PRESS DISPATCH.]

PLAYA DEL ESTE, Guantanamo Bay, July 14.—(Copyright, 1898, by the Associated Press.)—A French gunboat of about 12 tons, and endeavored to come into the harbor about dusk to-night with-r permission and met with a surprise part-

The cruiser Marblehead fired a blank shot at the gunboat came into the entrance to the harbor, but no attention was paid to it, and a shot from a gunboat was sent over her bows, Then, too, was disregarded, the gunboat coming along under full steam.

For a few minutes it looked as if a row was possible. The impetus on the Marblehead rang out a call to quarters and another shot was sent across the French gunboat's bows, this time in unmistakable manner. That warning was subsequent, however, and the Frenchman stopped with extreme suddenness.

There is a naval custom for a war vessel of one nation to enter a port which vessels of another nation are blockading upon permission is given. The captain of the French gunboat was either in ignorance of the American occupation or chose to disregard it until formally reminded of the fact by Commodore Watson. The gunboat was allowed to anchor in the lower harbor for the night.

Futility of Resistance Shown.

[ASSOCIATED PRESS DISPATCH.]

GENERAL WHEELER'S HEADQUARTERS BEFORE SANTIAGO DE CUBA, July 13, 4 p. m., via Kingston Jamaica, July 14.—White flags still flutter over the opposing lines. The truce has been extended until to-morrow noon, and negotiations looking to the surrender of Santiago are progressing. Both sides have prided somewhat. General Toral, the Spanish commander, realizes the hopelessness of further resistance. This morning General Shafter, at the request of the terms which he at first proposed to impose upon the enemy.

It appears that on Monday General Shafter did not again demand the unconditional surrender, which General Toral had refused on Sunday, but offered as an alternative proposition to allow the capitulation of the enemy and to transport the Spanish officers and troops to Spain, they to leave all their arms behind and he to accept their parole. It was this proposition which General Toral declined yesterday.

Conference Held With Toral.

This morning it was decided to hold a personal interview with General Toral. Generals Miles and his staff, who are no further than General Shafter's headquarters last night, accompanied by General Shafter and his staff, rode out to the front shortly before o'clock under a flag of truce. A request for a personal interview with the Spanish commander-in-chief was made and secured to, and about ½ o'clock Generals Miles, General Shafter, General Wheeler, General Gilmour, Colonel Morse, Captain Wiley and Colonel Maus rode up, passed over our intrenchments and went down into the valley beyond. They were met by General Toral and his chief of staff under a spreading mango tree at the bottom of the valley about half way between the lines. The interview that followed lasted an hour.

The situation was placed frankly before General Toral and he was offered the alternative of being sent home with his garrison or leaving Santiago province, the only condition imposed being that he should not deprive his remaining fortifications and should leave his arms behind.

Given No Discretion by Spain.

This latter condition the Spanish general, who does not speak English, explained, was against his interpreter was impossible. He said the laws of Spain gave a general no discretion. He might abandon a place when he found it untenable, but he could not leave his arms behind without subjecting himself to the penalty of being court-martialed and shot. His government, he said, had granted him permission to evacuate Santiago. That was all. Further than that he was powerless to go.

Without saying so in words, General Miles said the tenor of General Toral's remarks betrayed that he could not hold out long. When General Shafter explained that our reinforcements were coming up, that he was completely surrounded, and that new batteries were being posted, General Toral simply shrugged his shoulders.

Spanish Leader's Bravery.

"I am but a subordinate," said he, "and I obey my government. If it is necessary we can die at our posts."

General Toral is a man of 60 years of age, with a strong, rugged face and fine, soldierly bearing. His brave words inspired a feeling of respect and admiration in the hearts of his American antagonists. His frank Spanish general's anxiety to avoid further sacrifice of life in his command was manifest, and he did not hesitate to ask for time to communicate the situation to Madrid, al-

[Continued on Fourth Page.]

GENERAL MILES PAYS TRIBUTE TO SHAFTER

BEFORE SANTIAGO, via Playa del Este, July 14.—Secretary of War, Washington: General Toral formally surrendered the troops of his army—troops and division of Santiago—on the terms and understanding that his troops shall be returned to Spain.

General Shafter will appoint commissioners to draw up the conditions of arrangements for carrying out the terms of surrender. This is very gratifying, and General Shafter and the officers and men of his command are entitled to great credit for their sincerity and fortitude in overcoming the almost insurmountable obstacles which they encountered.

A portion of the army has been infected with yellow fever, and efforts will be made to separate those who are infected and those free from it, and to keep those who are still on board ship separated from those on shore.

Arrangements will be immediately made for carrying out further instructions of the President and yourself.

NELSON A. MILES, Major General of the Army.

TROOPS LAND AT CIENFUEGOS.

Soldiers Go Ashore Under Cover of the Montgomery's Guns.

[ASSOCIATED PRESS DISPATCH.]

LONDON, July 14.—The Madrid correspondent of the Daily Mail says:

"A dispatch from Havana to El Imparcial says that 1,000 Americans have landed near Cienfuegos under cover of the guns of the United States cruiser Montgomery.

"El Correo doubts the truth of this report, but the government has no news upon it."

WAR HISTORY OF ONE DAY.

Thursday, July 14, 1898.

GENERAL TORAL, commander of the Spanish forces at Santiago de Cuba, surrenders. The Spanish troops are to be sent to Spain under parole. The surrender includes all the fortifications and the eastern end of Cuba.

THE UNITED STATES GOVERNMENT will turn its attention to the conquest of Porto Rico. An expedition is to be started at once. Porto Rico, and thence to Havana if necessary.

AN IMPORTANT ARTICLE in the Cologne Gazette declares that there is no truth in the report that a German cruiser hovered in air with the operations of Admiral Dewey at Manila.

THE FLORIDA and the Fanita, conveying the gunboat Peoria, have landed large expeditions at Palo Alto, on the south coast of Cuba, in the fighting which took place at Tunas near Manzanillo, three were killed and Winthrop Sargent of the Rough Riders and several wounded. The Peoria was landed.

SANTIAGO AND EASTERN CUBA SURRENDER

Toral Capitulates to Shafter, Giving Up Vast Territory Besides the Beleaguered City.

HIS SOLDIERS TO BE SENT HOME ON PAROLE.

Captured Forces Number 13,500 and Include All Spaniards in the Eastern End of the Island Except Garrisons at Holguin and Manzanillo.

PLAYA DEL ESTE, July 14.—Adjutant General, Washington: Have just returned from interview with General Toral. He agrees to surrender upon the basis of being returned to Spain.

This proposition embraces all of eastern Cuba, from Acerraderos on the south to Sagua on the north via Palma, with practically the Fourth army corps. Commissioners meet this afternoon at 2:30 to definitely arrange the terms.

W. R. SHAFTER, Major General.

PLAYA DEL ESTE, July 14.—General Greely, Washington: Santiago has surrendered. JONES.

[SPECIAL DISPATCH TO THE TIMES-HERALD.]

WASHINGTON, July 15.—Aside from the brief dispatch from General Shafter announcing that General Toral had agreed to surrender Santiago and practically all of eastern Cuba to the American troops, the officials of the war department had, up to 2 o'clock this (Friday) morning, received no details on the consummation of capitulation or the time of occupancy of the city by Shafter's forces. Secretary Alger stayed at the White House with President McKinley until shortly before that hour in hopeful but disappointed expectation of having further news to communicate to the President, who anxiously awaited additional advices. Their time was pleasantly occupied in a measure, though, by the reading of numerous telegrams from all parts of the country conveying hearty congratulations on the first great victory for American soldiers during the present war.

[SPECIAL DISPATCH TO THE TIMES-HERALD.]

WASHINGTON, July 14.—Santiago de Cuba has surrendered. General Toral bowed to the inevitable to-day and accepted President McKinley's ultimatum. The Spanish commander surrendered unconditionally, and the United States on its own motion promised to send his troops to Spain. They will go as prisoners of war on parole, pledged not to take up arms against this government. General Toral made a gallant effort to dodge humiliation, but fate had delivered him into General Shafter's hands. He sought to escape with honor and liberty, but gives up more than was expected. He surrendered not only the troops in Santiago, but a large section of the eastern end of Cuba. He gives up his munitions of war and abandons the fortifications about the harbor of Santiago. He will only be permitted to take away the side arms of his officers. Washington understands that this includes about 10,000 troops in the city of Santiago. There are said to be about 2,000 at Baracoa and 1,500 at Guantanamo. These garrisons are included in the surrender, and a message from General Shafter says the captured force will include most of the Fourth army corps.

The territory yielded by the Spaniards is bounded on the west by a line drawn from Acerraderos north to Palma, thence and thence northeast to Boca del Sagua. Acerraderos is on the southern coast of Cuba, about twenty miles west of Santiago Bay. It was near that place that General Shafter and General Garcia had their first interview. Palma is about twenty-five miles north of Acerraderos. Sagua is on the north coast of Cuba, about seventy miles west of Cape Maisi, the easternmost point of the island. Baracoa is on the northern coast, about twenty-five miles west of the cape. This territory takes in the eastern end of Cuba, including about one-third of the province of Santiago de Cuba, but it does not include Manzanillo or Holguin, which have Spanish garrisons. General Shafter had about 24,000 troops in all, but his effective force now is not over 20,000.

The truce expired at noon to-day. It was 11 o'clock when Adjutant General Corbin received a dispatch from General Shafter and started with it toward the White House. General Corbin has truly said: "General Shafter is a fighter and not a writer." His dispatches prove he is not a writer, for many of them have been provokingly ambiguous or obscure. This morning's dispatch was of that kind, and neither the President nor his advisers were able to determine whether Toral had surrendered or was about to surrender. The President is said to have asked General Shafter for a more intelligible message, and shortly after 12 o'clock General Corbin posted the following bulletin on the first dispatch, which gives a good illustration of how General Shafter gave Washington an uncomfortable half-hour: "Cable just received from General Shafter says General Toral has asked that commissioners be appointed to arrange terms of surrender. Toral already having appointed his." The general tenderly of events led to the conclusion that Toral had surrendered, but neither Secretary Alger nor General Corbin was prepared to assert with confidence that the moment of victory had arrived. The Spaniard was suspected of a crafty design to gain more time by another parley between commissioners, and Washington was in great doubt as to the meaning of General Shafter's message. General Corbin pointed to the President's ultimatum as a decree that would bar further delay, and he thought General Shafter too good a soldier to disobey orders. He explained that it was not an exceptional thing to designate commissioners to arrange the minor details in the case of a surrender, and said that office was not so great at the same might imply. But even General Shafter for a more intelligible message, and shortly after 12 o'clock General Corbin admitted that General Shafter's message left the situation at Santiago in doubt, and would not accept it as evidence of a surrender.

It was after 1 o'clock when another dispatch arrived from General Shafter, but even this message was so worded as to leave a shred of doubt in Washington. Gen-

Types of U.S. naval ships, 1898. (1)
Cruiser *Detroit*, (2) Cruiser
Montgomery, (3) Cruiser
Marblehead, (4) Barbette turret
coast-defense Monitor *Puritan*, (5)
Practice Cruiser *Bancroft*, (6)
Gunboat *Mackias*, (7) Gunboat
Castine, (8) Cruiser *New York*, (9)
Cruiser *No. 13*, (10) Cruiser
Columbia, (11) Battleship *Oregon*,
(12) Battleship *Indiana*, (13)
Battleship *Massachusetts*, (14)
Harbor-defense ram *Katahdin*, (15)
Second-Class Battleship *Texas*,
(16) Double-turreted Monitor
Monterey, (17) Cruiser *Raleigh*,
(18) Cruiser *Cincinnati*.

SUNDAY INSPECTION BY CAPTAIN EVANS ON BOARD THE IOWA.

The battleship *Indiana* leads the transport from Tampa, bound for Cuba.

Spanish prisoners of war captured on April 29 were confined at Fort McPherson, Georgia. Lt. J.A. Moss of the 25th Infantry was in charge of the prisoners.

Richmond Pearson Hobson was born in 1870 in Greensburg, Alabama, and graduated from the Naval Academy in 1889. After duty on the *Chicago*, he underwent additional training and was appointed an Assistant Naval Constructor in 1891. He served at various Navy yards and became an Academy instructor. At the start of the war he was serving on board the *New York*. In order to bottle up Cervera's fleet, Hobson took temporary command of the collier *Merrimac* and attempted to sink it in the Santiago channel as an obstruction. On June 3, under heavy Spanish fire an attempt was made to sink the ship but its steering gear was disabled by gunfire. Hobson was able to sink the ship but was unable to move her to the shallowest part of the channel. He and his six crewmen were picked up by Admiral Cervera's ship, interned for a time and later released. The Spanish admiral even commended Hobson for his gallant actions. After the war, Hobson was advanced 10 numbers in grade and in 1933 was awarded the Medal of Honor for his heroic attempt. He worked repairing and refitting captured Spanish ships at Cavite and at various shore stations of the Navy. Resigning from the Navy in 1903, Hobson served as a Congressman from Alabama from 1905 to 1915. In 1934, by a special act of Congress, he was advanced to Naval Constructor with a rank of Rear Admiral. Hobson died in 1937.

Sinking of the *Merrimac*

The *Merrimac* sunk in the Santiago channel on June 3. USN NH46244

The heroes of the sinking of the *Merrimac*. Hobson was finally awarded a Medal of Honor in 1933 by President Roosevelt. Normally officers were awarded a brevet or honorary promotion rather than the Medal of Honor.

"CORKING THE BOTTLE"

ASSISTANT NAVAL CONSTRUCTOR HOBSON'S ...

When the narrowest part of the Santiago channel was reached, Lieutenant Hobson put her helm hard-to-port, stopped the engines, dropped anchor, opened the sea connections and touched off the torpedos that sunk the *Merrimac*, but the sinking had missed its mark and did not block the channel.

Blowing up the *Merrimac* at 4 a.m. on June 3. A press dispatch read: "The water was foaming with the commotion made by the shells and bullets. Hobson and his men floated down stream 150 yards dragging the wires out after them. This was the distance for the contact to be made and it was done."

Cell in which Lieut Hobson was Confined. Morro Castle

Cell in which Lieutenant Hobson was confined in Morro Castle in Santiago. He and his crew were exchanged on July 6 for a Spanish officer.
USN NH001482

Lt. Richmond Hobson.

Camp McCalla at Guantanamo Bay. USN NH 001762

Guantanamo Bay, about 45 miles east of Santiago, was seized by U.S. Marines in early June to serve as a coaling station for the blockading fleet at Santiago. After several days of fighting and the deaths of six Americans, the Spanish troops retreated. The Marines established a permanent camp on the eastern shore of the bay on a low, flat hill. It was named Camp McCalla after the commander of the *USS Marblehead.*

Hoisting the first American flag over Camp McCalla by Lieutenant Jenkins and his men from the *USS Abarenda* (AC-13), June 1898. USN NH 1136

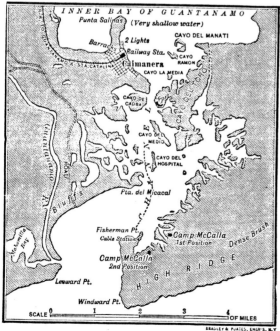

ENTRANCE TO HARBOR OF GUANTANAMO.
(Showing Camps of the Marines.)

Capt. Bowman H. McCalla of the *USS Marblehead* supervising the raising of the Spanish gunboat *Sandoval* in Guantanamo Bay, Aug. 30. It would later become a U.S. Navy ship. USN NH 80790

The sunken
Reina Mercedes.
USN NH 61233

Bottom left: The
Reina Mercedes,
the day after her
raising in
Santiago Harbor.
USN NH61270

The *Reina Mercedes* was a 3,090-ton steel-hull, Spanish cruiser with 21 guns of various caliber. She was in Santiago Bay with other Spanish ships. On June 6, Sampson on the *New York* and Schley on the *Brooklyn* approached the channel into the bay and began a bombardment. Shells landed at the battery on the Socapa Heights and in the inside harbor. The first-class armored cruiser *Vizcaya* was hit twice, the torpedo boat destroyer *Furor* once. The *Reina Mercedes* was hit 35 times and sunk. The ship's executive officer Commander Emilio Acosta was killed. His right hand and leg were torn off but he continued to give orders to care for the wounded until he died. The Spanish had five killed and several wounded. The Spanish troops guarding Santiago stripped the guns from the ship and emplaced them in earthworks batteries. An attempt was made on July 4 to resink the *Reina Mercedes* in the narrow Santiago channel to prevent the American fleet from gaining entrance. It, however, was too far to the eastern edge of the channel to be an obstacle. After the Americans took Santiago, the ship was raised and later commissioned in the U.S. Navy.

The Spanish first-class armored cruiser *Vizcaya*. The *Brooklyn* sent an 8-inch round into her bow detonating a torpedo in her forward tube. Another round hit her bridge and the resulting fire set off ammunition. She headed toward the beach and struck her colors. EAC

WINSLOW.　　　　HUDSON.　　　WILMINGTON

The Battle of Cardenas – gunboat *Wilmington*, revenue cutter *Hudson* and torpedo boat *Winslow* under fire.

Action at Cardenas

Eighty miles east of Havana was the port of Cardenas. Three Spanish gunboats lay in the shallow harbor. The *USS Wilmington* stood outside, but on May 22 she attempted to enter the harbor, guided by the revenue cutter *Hudson* and the torpedo boat *Winslow*.

The American ships came under fire from the Spanish gunboats and the *Winslow* was hit. Her steering gear was disabled and her forward conning tower smashed. Her rudder was also jammed.

The *Hudson* took the *Winslow* in tow but it was soon cut loose. Ensign Worth Bagley and four crewmen, John Barbenes, G. Deneije, George Meek and E.B. Tunnell, were on deck when a Spanish shell hit and killed all five – the first casualties of the short war.

The *Winslow* was again taken in tow and all three American ships withdrew, leaving two of the enemy gunboats sunk and a large part of Cardenas in flames.

Action at Cienfuegos

Two underwater cables came together at Cienfuegos on the south coast of Santa Clara Province. It was determined that these should be cut to deny the Spanish the ability to communicate within the island and with Madrid.

On May 11, a party from the cruiser *Marblehead* attempted to cut the two cables. Covering fire was given by the *Marblehead*, the gunboat *Nashville* and the revenue cutter *Windom*. In addition, two boats full of Marines provided additional firepower.

Lt. Cameron Winslow led the cutting party close in to shore to try and grab the cables and cut them with axes, chisels and finally hacksaws. They were under fire from Spanish troops on shore but they were kept down by fire from the Marines.

The first cable was cut but the second, which was closer to shore, proved harder due to heavy fire from the Spanish. It was finally cut and then a third, smaller cable was found. While trying to cut this cable a Marine was killed and several others wounded, including Winslow.

The intense enemy fire finally forced the sailors and Marines to retire back to the *Marblehead*. This action resulted in 52 participants receiving the Medal of Honor.

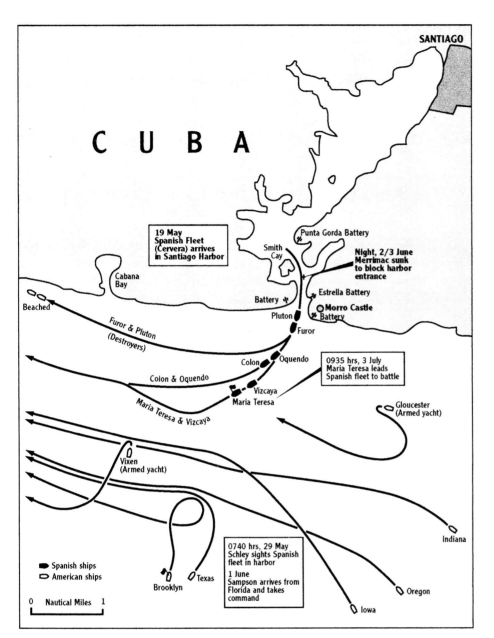

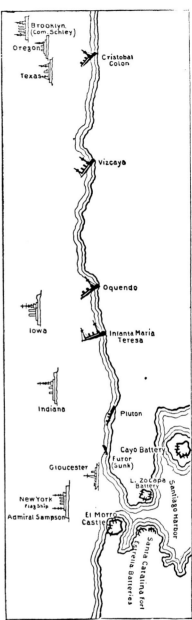

APPROXIMATE POSITIONS OF THE OPPOS-
ING VESSELS AT THE CLOSE OF THE
BATTLE.

After the Battle of Santiago, Admiral Sampson sent the following message to Washington: "The fleet under my command offers the nation, as a Fourth of July present, the whole of Cervera's fleet." Secretary of War Alger commented on the news: "At two o'clock on the morning of July 4th I walked home, with the newsboys crying in my ears the joyful tidings of 'Full account of the destruction of Spanish fleet!' I also had with me the last message from General Shafter, received at a quarter past one. It contained but a single sentence—

"'I SHALL HOLD MY PRESENT POSITION.'"

— The Battle of Santiago —

On the morning of July 3, 1898, the U.S. Navy maintained its close blockade of Santiago Harbor. Since May 29, 1898, five cruisers and two torpedo boats of the Spanish Navy lay trapped within, unable to impede the American invasion. Two days earlier U.S. soldiers of V Corps commanded by General Shafter had captured the San Juan Heights overlooking the city and harbor. It would only be a matter of time before the Americans brought up their siege guns and forced the Spanish fleet to surrender, scuttle their ships or try to break out past the formidable U.S. fleet.

A critical moment in the campaign was rapidly approaching. General Shafter had lost nearly 2,000 men and wanted the navy to force their way past the harbor defenses and sink the Spanish ships at anchor as Dewey had done at Manila. Admiral Sampson, commanding the U.S. Fleet, wanted Shafter's troops to assault Santiago to avoid the possibility of losing any of his virtually irreplaceable armored ships. Sampson however, was fully aware of the high standard Dewey had set at Manila Bay. With the best and most powerful ships of the U.S. Navy at his command anything less than an overwhelming victory would not be good enough.

Admiral Cervera, commanding the Spanish squadron understood the situation. Unwilling to meekly surrender or scuttle his ships, he resolved to try to race past the slow U.S. battleships. The Spanish cruisers were low on coal and not steaming well but since the U.S. ships would need time to work up to speed, they might get through to reach Havana or a neutral port.

Admiral Sampson had sailed in the cruiser *New York* to a meeting with General Shafter when Cervera's squadron of four cruisers and two torpedo boats rushed past the Morro Batteries. Commodore Schley was in command of the U.S. fleet and while engaging the Spanish cruisers performed a maneuver that nearly resulted in disaster.

When the enemy squadron left the harbor in a westerly direction, the cruiser *Brooklyn*, Schley's flagship, was the closest American ship. Schley decided that to close with the Spanish would subject him to a ramming or an even more feared attack by torpedo boats. In addition, his position west of the fleet would make the *Brooklyn* the sole target of all the enemy's fire. His solution was to swing east and then south and finally west to continue the chase.

According to Schley, "Immediately (Captain)

Battle of Santiago Bay. EAC

Cook gave the order to port the helm. I did not. I should have done it in a second...I have never seen a ship turn more rapidly than she did; and her turn was absolutely continuous; there was no easing of her helm."

However, the turn put the *Brooklyn* in the path of the *Texas* which was steaming west towards the Spanish. Schley stated that the *Texas* "...was so far away that she never entered my head as a menace or danger..." Captain Phillips of the *Texas* saw it differently, "The smoke (from the firing) began to hang so heavily (that) we might as well have had a blanket tied over our heads." Phillips said that when the smoke cleared somewhat from a lull in the firing, "(the *Brooklyn*) seemed so near that it took our breath away." The *Texas* backed both engines and a collision was avoided.

The *Brooklyn* was slowed by its turn and the *Texas* lost speed trying to avoid the big cruiser. The *Iowa* was hit forward at the waterline and was falling back. For a moment it seemed that the Spanish cruisers would escape. But the "slow" *Oregon*, forcing on steam to reach 18 knots, came up and the Spanish ships, withering under the frantic fire of the American gunners were disabled and run aground. All the Spanish ships were destroyed and over 300 Spanish sailors were killed. No U.S. ships were lost or even seriously damaged and only Chief Yeoman George Ellis was killed by Spanish fire.

The destruction of the Spanish fleet should have made the propriety of Schley's loop a moot point. However, it did become a point of contention after the war. Admiral Sampson, stung by having missed the battle because he was en route to the meeting with General Shafter, was eager to bring discredit upon Schley. The dispute was fully covered in the press and even Mark Twain commented that he saw no reason for the fuss, "one admiral wasn't there and the other was doing his best to get away." Schley was amazed by the criticism and hoping to clear his conduct of the battle of any suspicion he called for a court of inquiry. The court found against Schley who appealed the decision to the President. Theodore Roosevelt let the decision stand.

It was a hollow victory for Sampson who, suffering from Alzheimer's Disease, died in 1902. Schley retired from the navy in 1902 after the inquiry, and died in 1911. Like his unconventional tactic in the face of the enemy, Commodore Winfield Scott Schley's fame in destroying Cervera's squadron faded quickly.

Morro Castle, Western Battery and Estrella, Santiago Bay, July 1898. USN NH001135

NAVAL BATTLE O

, JULY 3rd, 1898.

USS Indiana
BB-01

Drawn and rendered by R. Detyna 1997

USS Oregon
BB-03

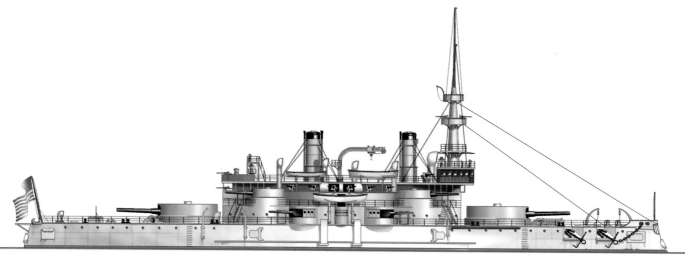

Drawn and rendered by R. Detyna 1997

Ship profiles produced digitally by Roman Detyna of
Glendale, New York.

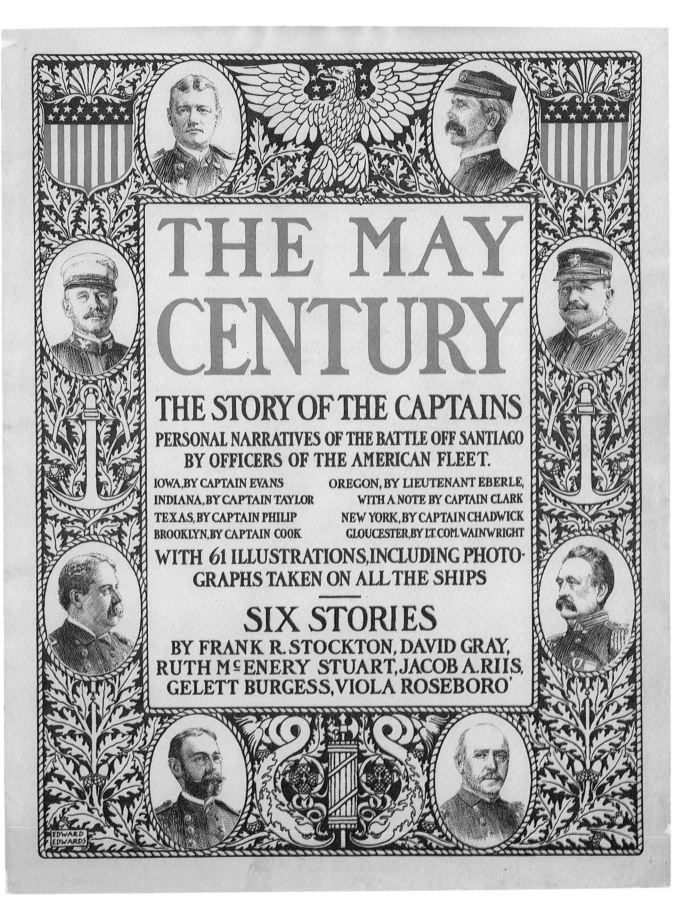

THE MAY CENTURY

THE STORY OF THE CAPTAINS

PERSONAL NARRATIVES OF THE BATTLE OFF SANTIAGO
BY OFFICERS OF THE AMERICAN FLEET.

IOWA, BY CAPTAIN EVANS
INDIANA, BY CAPTAIN TAYLOR
TEXAS, BY CAPTAIN PHILIP
BROOKLYN, BY CAPTAIN COOK

OREGON, BY LIEUTENANT EBERLE,
WITH A NOTE BY CAPTAIN CLARK
NEW YORK, BY CAPTAIN CHADWICK
GLOUCESTER, BY LT. COM. WAINWRIGHT

WITH 61 ILLUSTRATIONS, INCLUDING PHOTO-GRAPHS TAKEN ON ALL THE SHIPS

SIX STORIES

BY FRANK R. STOCKTON, DAVID GRAY,
RUTH McENERY STUART, JACOB A. RIIS,
GELETT BURGESS, VIOLA ROSEBORO'

EDWARD EDWARDS

The first American troops to set foot on foreign soil since the Mexican War land at the inadequate docks at Daiquirí on June 22, 1898. Over 6,000 troops were landed that day.

Twenty minutes before the battle for San Juan Hill, this photograph was taken of American troops on the way to the front.

Arrival of wounded from around El Caney and San Juan Hill.

The 16th Infantry

On April 6, 1869, the 11th Infantry merged with the 34th Infantry to form the 16th. It fought in the Indian wars and in 1898 was transferred to Tampa and then to Cuba.

During the advance on Santiago on July 1, the lead element of the army panicked and refused to advance past a well-placed Spanish ambush. The soldiers of the 16th had to surge through and establish the forward lines. After his troops deployed for the assault, Brigadier General Hawkins rode out in front and announced, "Boys, the time has come. Every man who loves his country, forward and follow me."

The regimental bugler sounded the charge to attack the fort atop the hill. With fixed bayonets, the troopers pushed the Spaniards off the hilltop. The 16th had 14 killed and 115 wounded by enemy artillery fire while crossing the San Juan River. The 16th applied pressure and continued forward capturing the San Juan Hill.

When the regiment returned home with the rest of V Corps less than a month later, not even half of its original strength remained. The next year the regiment was posted to the Philippines to fight the insurgents.

In the following years, the regiment served in South Dakota, took a second tour of the Philippines, Alaska, California, the Mexican border area and was the first American regiment to see combat in World War One.

The regiment had a distinguished career in World War Two fighting in North Africa, Sicily, France, Belgium and Germany. The regiment is still in existence today.

The 16th U.S. Infantry under Spanish fire from San Juan Hill on July 1. The photograph was made just before the 16th and 6th Infantries began their climb up the slope of San Juan Hill. Foreign attachés commented that the charge "was very gallant, but very foolish." An American officer later said: "If we had been in that position and the Spaniards had come at us, we would have piled them up so high the last man couldn't have climbed over."

The Gatling Gun

The inventor of the forerunner of the modern machine gun, Richard Jordon Gatling, was born in 1818. He was a prolific inventor but also took time to complete medical school in 1850. While never practicing medicine, he became a millionaire with his inventions by age 36. In 1860 Gatling was granted patents on five inventions: a rotary plow, a cultivator for cotton plants, a lath-making machine, an improved hemp brake and a rubber washer for tightening gears.

The dramatic events of 1861 had a profound effect on Gatling and the outbreak of the Civil War suggested the invention that was to make him famous—the gun that bears his name.

His first model, patented in 1862, had many design problems but his 1865 model was the forerunner of all later guns. The Gatling Gun used in the Spanish American War was the .30 caliber 1895 model.

The 1895 model was different from the 1893 model only in the painting of the bronze parts an olive drab color. On May 20, 1898, 18 Model 1895 guns were purchased by the U.S. Army and an additional 31 were delivered on Aug. 29, 1898.

The troops that landed at Daiquiri included the Gatling Gun Detachment, V Army Corps, commanded by John Henry Parker, an 1888 graduate of West Point and a first lieutenant in the 13th Infantry. Four of the guns were used in the capture of San Juan Hill on July 1, 1898. For the first time, the U.S. Army employed close-support machine guns in an attack. Parker describes the formation of the detachment and its subsequent actions in his book: *Tactical Organization and Uses of Machine Guns in the Field*, (1899).

"At the outbreak of the war between the United States and Spain, April 26, 1898, there were about 150 Gatling guns and about half as many Gardner guns of the two-barreled type in the land service of the United States. The Government had some time before ordered from the makers, a private firm, 100 of the Gatling guns, to be of the .30 caliber adopted for the new magazine rifle, and to use the same ammunition. A consignment of 15 of these new guns reached Tampa while the expedition was being fitted out for the Santiago campaign. A detachment of four pieces was formed, under command of a lieutenant, as an independent organization, under the direct orders of the general commanding. The detachment was not decided on until the 14th of June, after the expedition had already embarked, and as one result of this delay, the men were imperfectly equipped, not having any revolvers, and being hampered by having to carry the rifle, which was more of a burden than otherwise. There was no time to look after the proper equipment of the guns in the matter of spare parts for repairs, etc., and the pieces were taken into the campaign without any tools for repair, or possibility of overhauling a disabled piece, unless the enemy should furnish such necessaries out of a rare spirit of generosity. The men to serve the guns were taken from infantry regiments, without special instruction of any kind until the day after they had been rushed to the extreme front of the lines, within 5,000 yards of the enemy. Even then only four days were available for special instruction, and it became necessary, after the pieces were on the skirmish-line, to instruct men in the art of feeding the guns.

"The guns were pushed right up in the hottest place there was in the battle-field, at "the bloody ford" of the San Juan, and put into action at the most critical moment of the battle, after part of the troops had already been forced back by the strong fire of the defenders, and so successfully subdued the Spanish fire that from that time to the capture of this practically impregnable position was only eight-and-one-half minutes. The expenditure of ammunition during this time, in which a continuous fire was kept up from three guns, was 6,000 rounds per gun. The remaining ammunition, with the guns, was pushed up at once on to the captured position, which enabled the now exhausted troops to hold it without reinforcements against two counterassaults of the Spaniards."

Parker outlined in his book the definitive procedures for machine gun tactics but unfortunately the U.S. Army did not adopt them. The guns were used with some effectiveness in the Philippine Insurrection and in later actions around the world.

Gatling guns in front of Santiago.

Las Guasimas Battle

Las Guasimas Ridge was about three miles north of Siboney and was reportedly held by 2,000 Spanish troops with some artillery. Maj. Gen. Joe Wheeler was the commander of the American force with Generals Lawton and Young under him.

Wheeler had been instructed by overall commander, General Shafter, to stay in Siboney if the enemy forces offered any opposition. However Wheeler, possibly feeling that so many enemy troops that close to Siboney posed a real threat, ordered a reconnaissance in force for July 24. The American force consisted of the 1st and 10th Cavalry Regiments, U.S. Regulars plus the Rough Riders, and help from the Cuban insurgents. The total was about 1,300 troops.

General Young was in command and split his force in two columns later to unite before the ridge. The going was tough with the heat and the cavalry units (most used to horses) were forced to walk. Swarms of insects also impeded travel.

The Spanish had 1,500 men on the ridge in three successive lines. Their intention was to conduct a delaying action as long as possible and then retreat toward the defenses of Santiago.

The Americans had to advance through thick woods and for a time could not locate the enemy, who were using smokeless powder in their rifles. The Americans finally spotted them and in a heated battle forced the Spanish to retreat.

In this action the Americans lost 16 killed and 52 wounded with the Rough Riders taking half of the casualties. The Spanish losses were considerably less.

Because the Spanish had been forced to retreat, it can be called an American victory and provided the Rough Riders their first baptism of fire. In a side note it was reported that General Wheeler who showed up at the thick of the fighting forgot for a moment where he was and supposedly shouted, Come on! We've got the damned Yankees on the run!

W.A. Rogers' painting from *Harper's Weekly*, depicting the heroic stand of the Rough Riders.

Map drawn by Leonard Wood of Las Gausimas Battle.

Shortly after Las Gausimas battle. The body of Sgt. Hamilton Fish lies shrouded on the ground. In the background are General Lawton, Richard Harding Davis, Colonel Wood and Lieutenant Colonel Roosevelt.

Colonel Wood on El Paso Hill on the morning of July 1, taking his first view of the San Juan Heights.

Artillery just before going into action behind the hill above San Juan Heights.

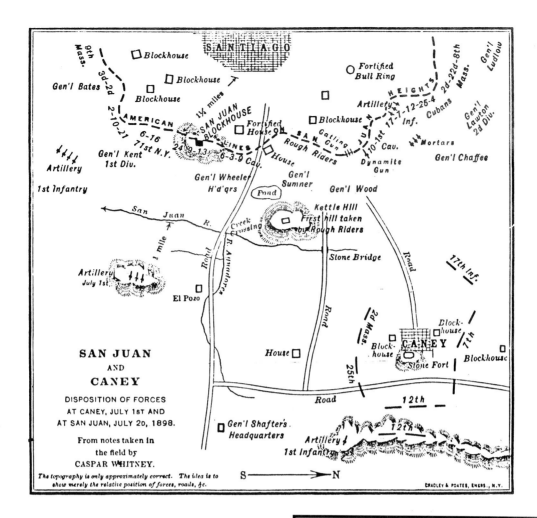

SAN JUAN
AND
CANEY

DISPOSITION OF FORCES
AT CANEY, JULY 1ST AND
AT SAN JUAN, JULY 20, 1898.

From notes taken in
the field by
CASPAR WHITNEY.

The topography is only approximately correct. The idea is to
show merely the relative position of forces, roads, &c.

BRADLEY & POATES, ENGRS., N.Y.

Conference soon after the fight at Las Guasimas,
from left: Richard Harding Davis, General Wheeler,
Colonel Wood, General Lawton, Caspar Whitney and
Lieutenant Colonel Roosevelt.

Casualties of the Santiago Campaign

According to Lt. John Parker, *The Gatlings at Santiago*, there were 22 officers and 208 enlisted men killed, 81 officers and 1,203 enlisted men wounded and 79 missing (later accounted for). This was out of approximately 12,000 men on the firing line on July 1.

Roosevelt states in his, *The Rough Riders*, that there were approximately 6,600 American troops in the attack on the San Juan hills and the total loss in killed and wounded was 1,071. The cavalry division which included 2,300 officers and men sustained 375 killed and wounded. He further states there were about 4,500 Spaniards defending the area.

According to Noji, the American force before Santiago numbered 19,438 of which 244 were killed and 1,347 wounded.

Spanish numbers and losses are very imprecise ranging from 13,700 to 14,500 with unknown losses.

It was during the Battle of San Juan Hill, on July 1, 1898, that the Rough Riders, under the command of Lieutenant Colonel Roosevelt, made their mark in American military history. Ordered to seize Kettle Hill in support of the main attack, the Rough Riders fought their way to the top despite heavy enemy fire. New Mexico E and G troops (the 1st New Mexico Cavalry entered Federal service as the 2nd Squadron, 1st U.S. Volunteer Cavalry) were among the first to reach the top of Kettle Hill. After taking the hill, the Rough Riders continued their attack, seizing the heights overlooking the city of Santiago. The American victory led to the Spanish surrender two weeks later.

FROM THE ORIGINAL PAINTING *THE ROUGH RIDERS* BY MORT KÜNSTLER © 1984 MORT KÜNSTLER, INC.

THE WERNER COMPANY. AKRON, O.

O TO GENERAL SHAFTER—JULY 13th, 1898

The heroic dash of the 71st New York Volunteers to the blockhouse on San Juan Hill along with the 16th and 6th Regiments of U.S. Regular troops.

Killed at Las Guasimas—Top, left to right: Capt. Allyn K. Capron, 1st U.S. Volunteer Cavalry; Sgt. Hamilton Fish Jr., 1st U.S. Volunteer Cavalry; Sgt. Marcus D. Russell, 1st U.S. Volunteer Cavalry; Cpl. Alex Lhennoc, 1st U.S. Volunteer Cavalry; Edward Marshall, correspondent, *New York Journal* (wounded); Pvt. Gustave A. Kolbe, 1st U.S. Volunteer Cavalry; Pvt. Emil Bjork, 1st U.S. Volunteer Cavalry and Pvt. Peter H. Dix, 1st U.S. Volunteer Cavalry.

COL. CHAS. A. WIKOFF, U.S.A., 22d U.S. Infantry.

LT.-COL. J. M. HAMILTON, U.S.A., 9th U.S. Cavalry.

MAJOR A. G. FORSE, U.S.A., 1st U.S. Cavalry.

CAPT. T. W. MORRISON, U.S.A., 16th U.S. Infantry.

CAPT. WM. O. O'NEILL, "Rough Riders."

LIEUT. JULES G. ORD, U.S.A., 6th U.S. Infantry.

LIEUT. D. M. MICHIE, U.S.A., 17th U.S. Infantry.

LIEUT. CHAS. H. FIELD, U.S.V., 2d Massachusetts Volunteers.

CORP'L GEORGE H. DOHERTY, Troop A, "Rough Riders."

CORP'L GEORGE L. IMMEN, Co. C, 71st New York Volunteers.

Killed at Santiago—Top, left to right: Col. Charles A. Wikoff, 22nd U.S. Infantry; Lt. Col. J.M. Hamilton, 9th U.S. Cavalry; Maj. A.G. Forse, 1st U.S. Cavalry; Capt. T.W. Morrison, 16th U.S. Infantry; Capt. William O. O'Neill, 1st U.S. Volunteer Cavalry; Bottom, left to right: Lt. Jules G. Ord, 6th U.S. Infantry; Lt. D.M. Michie, 17th U.S. Infantry; Lt. Charles H. Field, 2nd Massachusetts Volunteers; Cpl. George H. Doherty, 1st U.S. Volunteer Cavalry and Cpl. George L. Immen, 71st New York Volunteers.

Killed at Santiago—Top, left to right: Capt. John Drum, 10th U.S. Infantry; Capt. James Fornance, 13th U.S. Infantry; Capt. Maximilian Luna, 1st Volunteer Cavalry; 1st Lt. W.M. Dickinson, 17th U.S. Infantry; 2nd Lt. A. Wansboro, 2nd U.S. Infantry; Bottom, left to right: 2nd Lt. William A. Sater, 13th U.S. Infantry; 2nd Lt. Clark Churchman, 13th U.S. Infantry; 2nd Lt. E.N. Benchley, 6th U.S. Infantry; Sgt. Henry Anderson, 2nd U.S. Cavalry and Sgt. Frank W. Scofield, 71st New York Volunteers.

CAPT. JOHN DRUM, 10th U.S. Infantry.

CAPT. JAMES FORNANCE, 13th U.S. Infantry.

CAPT. MAXIMILIAN LUNA, 1st Volunteer Cavalry.

1st LIEUT. W. M. DICKINSON, 17th U.S. Infantry.

2d LIEUT. THOS. A. WANSBORO, 2d U.S. Infantry.

2d LIEUT. WILLIAM A. SATER, 13th U.S. Infantry.

2d LIEUT. CLARK CHURCHMAN, 13th U.S. Infantry. Photograph by Pach.

2d LIEUT. E. N. BENCHLEY, 6th U.S. Infantry. Photograph by Pach.

SERGT. HENRY ANDERSON, 2d U.S. Cavalry. Photograph by Powell.

SERGT. FRANK W. SCOFIELD, 71st N.Y. Volunteers.

Tampa Fla.
June 23, 1898
"after taps"

Dear Mamma:

I am not so sleepy tonight as usual, so will try to write a short letter. I am iying on my blanket, (a hard position to write from), it is 11 PM. "Taps" were over hour & ½ ago. It is 12 at home and you are all probably asleep. I am better. We changed cooks yesterday, and the result is apparent, good food including bacon. He, Yeatman, cooks bacon so that it is fine. My stomach seems well. Night before last I was carried to the hospital with the strangest illness I ever had a sick-headache and a weakness that was awful but they got my stomach cleaned out, (I vomited scraps of bacon that I know I ate at Camp Alger, and lots of grease etc,) Now I feel better, internally, then at any time since leaving home. I've got some cuts on my feet of course but they don't count----nothing to speak of. This is a terrible place for whiskers. Today I shaved off a weeks growth; the hair was as long as   every bit. Before I shaved I looked 30 years old. Most all of the boys have half-beards. Mr. Ritchey received another letter from home today (that makes two) and was as happy as a clam ect. He wants to be remembered to you, as do Sgt. Dickinson and all the rest including some that never saw you.

I saw a strange and beautiful sight this evening. It was while we were standing at inspection (Which takes the place of dress parade): We face the east and it is just before the sun leaves us in the strange dark twilight of the south.

A few clouds had come into view, and presently right before us there appeared a beautiful clear, full arched rainbow, then above it another and above that still another----a triple bow.

But then the strange part came. The lower and brighter bow became four or rather a quadruple repetion of the colors. The bow itself remained unchanged but beneath it were narrow lines of color adding to it in regular order, four times repeated the violet at the bottom.

Altogether it was the most beautiful "sky piece" I have ever seen.

The rainy season is on us sure. It rained 8 times today rain, clears, rains, clears, ect all the time. You people must not be worried at any reports of sickness from here. There has been no real sickness at all here, in our regiment only cramps etc, nothing bad. Very beautiful place it seems. If I get taken sick-bad—I'll telegraph, of if I'm not able Wooldridge or the Captain will, so never worry. Wooldridge is well and is looking better I think than at Alger.

Please don't kick when I don't write because I really am awfully worked and go to sleep as soon as possible. I'll try though to write more often.

I asked for another picture of Col. Harries first parade, can't I have it? I also would like to have one of our group at Camp Alger, the one Carolie and Rosalie call "Your Chevrons." We are now ordered to be in readiness to move at any hour, but will not go until 30th or later I know.

Well I really must stop, so again telling you that I'm in excellent health. I'll say good bye

your loving son (who won't cry when the war is over)
Henry A Dobson

Love to all

Tell Dot---now that the show is over that sisters letters are nice--even if I don't always answer

H.A.D.

San Juan Heights
Santiago Cuba
July 28, 1898

Dear Mamma:

All O.K. Received Papa's letter with note from you attached, also one from Carolie.

Fever rages here, but not "yellow jack." The feaver lasts from four days to two weeks but is not dangerous. 13 men had it yesterday 20 today in our company. "K" has 35. Some of my men are getting well, others are coming down with it. I guess we all will eventually tumble to it. Otherwise things are improving, we get enough to eat, all right now. It rains every day, is very hot when it don't rain. A breeze though, 12 hrs. out of 24. Nights very cool. Have slept out doors in my blankets on stray mats in preference to sleeping on the ground in shelter tent. Sleep well, only thing that bothers me is reveille. Sounds to loud. Well, I've got to stop writing for a while as I'm called as witness in "Court martial" of one of my men charged with sleeping on post. I'm to give his character and career in company. I think he will be cleared. I believe him to be O.K. and innocent-------
August 1st-----I am writing by moonlight---it is after taps. We have our larger tents up now. I am sitting in front of mine, taking my first opportunity in several days to finish your letter. The moon is very brilliant, you can read a newspaper easily. Rec'd letter from Papa----Dot and you. Send more, all reach me eventually. I guess one reason that you don't see Mable Anderson in Sabbath school is that she is in Michigan.

I took six men day before yesterday and went down into a sunken road on the field. Two boys of the 6th Inf. had been killed there and had simply been covered with earth as they had fallen. The rain had washed the earth away and the buzzards were starting their work. We finished the uncovering and dug two Christian graves and put them in. Terrible work Got official news today of Towners death. Food getting better. I'm holding my own now. Stomach O.K. I got the fever day before yesterday. After taking medicine knocked it. Little weak yet. But I didn't give in. Expect that we will move soon. Rations for tomorrow. Coffee, Sugar, Fresh Beef, Bacon, Soft Bread (baked in Sausage and tomatoes.) An extra issue. Bread 3 times per wk.....by themselves. Each squad together. Breakfast today for Sgts. Mess----Rice cakes, bacon, "slum gullion," coffee and bread. Dinner. good soup---boiled beef, coffee and bread (I ate 1 qt. soup 1 qt. coffee. lots of meal and bread) But that was because my meal was interrupted and I had to take a half hour recess. Supper. Steak, rice, coffee, & bread and tomatoes. I'll write more about our mess some other time. Well for the present good bye. Give love and regards to everybody. You'll hear from me again soon.

H.A.D.

All Spaniards Look Alike to Me.

COMPOSED BY PAUL BERLACK, ORLANDO, FLA.

Tune "All Coons Look Alike to me."

Talk about a nation having trouble,
    Uncle Sam has enough of his own;
It was all about the Battleship Maine,
    Into thousands of pieces she was blown.
There's a first class general from the South, sir,
    In the army he's the leader of the day;
Pretty soon he'll be ordered down to Cuba,
    And to him uncle Sam will say:
"Just use them rough, and and treat them tough,
Don't try to bluff, but give them hot stuff."

      CHORUS:—All of you Spaniards look alike to me.
    I am sorry, but we can't agree;
    We wont quarrel, but let it be
    Till we fight upon the sea:
    We're going to send General Lee
    Down there to set Cuba free.
    And I don't like you no how,
    All you Spaniards look alike so me.
So there are no Spaniards allowed.
No Spaniards allowed.
This place is ruled by Americans, that is all.
We don't want none your trecherous kind,
So keep out Spaniard, don't cross the line;
No Spaniards wanted here at all.

The Spaniards deny the accusation,
    It is like ——— that ———
But they will wish they had do.
    Before the war is through they had owned it.
Their fleet can do some good
    Probably almost as good as ———
But our fleet will have them for a target,
    And will send them to the bottom of the sea.
I am proud to say, but then I say;
There they will lay, until they decay.   CHO.

General weyler wants to come back to Cuba,
    But if he does he will wish he'd never tried:
I will advise you, butcher Weyler to stay just where you are,
    If you want to save your hide.
They have got such dreadful guns over here
    Laid up for you and your boys.
Why the ball would not have to hit you
    They would kill you from the noise.
You would be slain, for the Battleship Maine;
You would never see Spain, no, not never.   CHO.—

Little Cuba is begging and imploring
    With tears streaming from her little eyes.
She says uncle Samuel, come and help us
    Before every one of us dies,
Uncle Sam would have kept quiet
    But the Spaniards got to raising cane:
But they put their heads in a hornet's nest
    When they blew up the Battleship Maine.
They raised much cain, So I repeat again:
They must be slain. To revenge the ———

After the war is ended
    Spain will be sore clear through,
She will hate it to her heart, but her lips she dare not part;
    For she'll be beaten by the boys in blue.
Hurrah! for the boys that defend the stars and stripes,
    Their freedom is already bought,
Spain wont have to learn a lesson
    For she has already been ———
By the United States it's no disgrace,
Spain set the pace, But lost the race.   CHO.—

Raising the American flag at the Governor's Palace in Havana, Jan. 1, 1899. MRS. PAUL MILLER

Parade of the Army of Occupation in Havana, Jan. 1, 1899. MRS. PAUL MILLER

Occupation troops at Camp Columbia, Havana, March 1899. MRS. PAUL MILLER

A monument at Camp Columbia, Havana, 1899. Apparently erected to honor Indiana troops. USAMHI

Civilians in Havana at a patriotic celebration, no date. USAMHI

The 7th Cavalry's last time to lower the flag at Columbia Barracks, May 19, 1902. USAMHI

The Phillipine Campaign

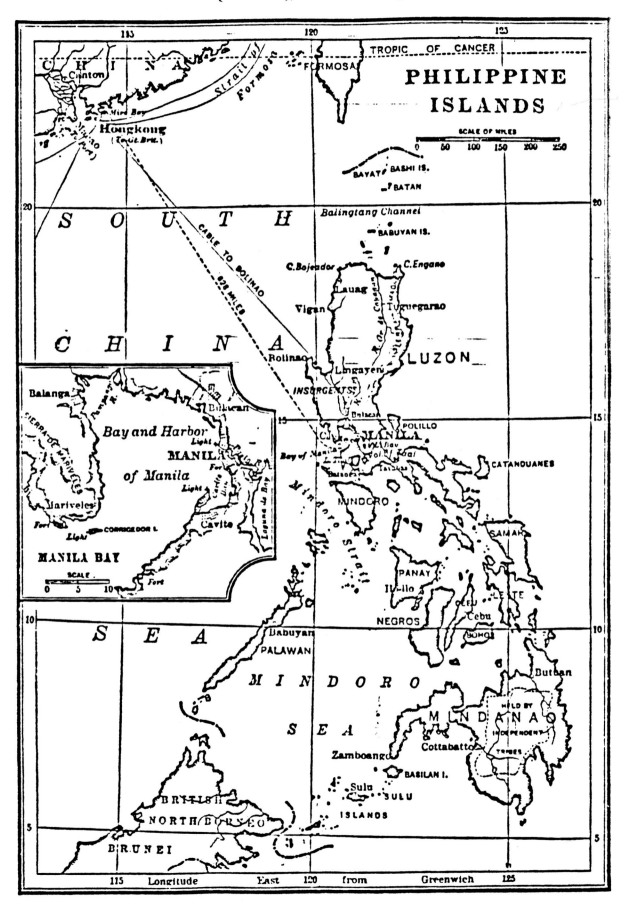

USS Olympia

USS Olympia, 1908.

The Olympia and the USS Becuna are now on display at Penn's Landing, Philadelphia, Pennsylvania. The Becuna was commissioned in 1944 and decommissioned in 1969.

The circle shows the *Olympia*'s only visible battle scar. Published in *Harper's Weekly*, Sept. 30, 1899.
USN NH 43353-A

Capt. Charles V. Gridley took over command of the *Olympia* on Jan. 8, 1898. He was an 1864 graduate of the Naval Academy and took over 30 years to make captain and become commander of a major naval ship. Gridley was sick with cancer at the Battle of Manila Bay and after the battle, which took a terrible toll on his health, he was ordered home. He set sail by way of Japan but five weeks after the battle he died in Kobe, Japan, aboard the passenger liner *Coptic*. He had made the statement: "The Battle of Manila killed me, but I'd do it again."

The *USS Olympia* (C-6) was laid down in 1891 by Union Iron Works of San Francisco. She was commissioned in 1895 with Capt. John J. Read in command. For three years, she cruised the Far East. With Captain Gridley in command, she flew the flag of Commodore Dewey from Jan. 8, 1898.

After the Battle of Manila Bay she took part in the blockade and capture of Manila and spent a year in the Philippines before returning to the United States in October 1899. She was decommissioned in Boston in November 1899.

Recommissioned in 1902 she spent the next four years roving the Caribbean, Atlantic and Mediterranean, protecting American interests. She was out of commission for the next six years and then served as a barracks ship in Charleston, South Carolina.

During World War I, she became the flagship, Patrol Force Atlantic Fleet and participated in Allied intervention of the Russian Revolution. In 1921, she became the flagship of the Train, Atlantic Fleet.

In the fall of 1921, she brought home the remains of the Unknown Soldier for interment in Arlington National Cemetery. After training midshipmen in the summer of 1922, she was decommissioned at Philadelphia on Dec. 9, 1922. She was reclassified 1X-40 in 1931, the Navy's oldest steel ship afloat.

Congress ordered the *Olympia* scrapped in 1954, but a group of public-spirited Philadelphians saved her from destruction and began the enormous job of restoring her.

In 1957, title was transferred to the Cruiser Olympia Association and she is now on permanent display at the Penn's Landing historical area in Philadelphia.

An incident during the Manila Bay battle demonstrated the ardor of *Olympia*'s crew. On learning of Dewey's decision to give the crew a break for breakfast, a gun captain commented to Captain Lamberton, "For God's sake, Captain, don't let us stop now. To hell with breakfast."

A Comparative View of the American and Spanish Fleets Engaged at Manila				
AMERICAN FLEET				
Name	Class	Armament	Men and officers	Built in
Olympia	Protected Cruiser	Four 8-in., ten 5-in., 24 R.F	466	1892
Baltimore	Protected Cruiser	Four 8-in., six 6-in, 10 R.F	395	1888
Boston	Par. Protected Cruiser	Two 8-in., six 6-in., 10 R.F	272	1884
Raleigh	Protected Cruiser	One 6-in., ten 5-in., 14 R.F	295	1892
Concord	Gunboat	Six 6-in., 9 R.F	150	1891
Petrel	Gunboat	Four 6-in., 7 R.F	100	1888
McCulloch (not in action)	Revenue Cutter	Four 4-in.	130	1888
SPANISH FLEET				
Reina Cristina	Steel Cruiser	Six 6.2-in., two 2.7-in., 13 R.F.	352	1887
Castilla	Wooden Cruiser	Four 5.9, two 4.7, two 3.4, two 2.9, 12 R.F.	349	1881
Don Antonio de Ulloa	Iron Cruiser	Four 4.7, 5 R.F.	159	1875
Don Juan de Austria	Iron Cruiser	Four 4.7, two 2.7, 21 R.F.	179	1887
Isla de Luzon	Steel Protected Cruiser	Six 4.7, 8 R.F.	156	1887
Isla de Cuba	Steel Protected Cruiser	Six 4.7, 8 R.F.	156	1887
Velasco	Iron Cruiser	Three 6-in., two 2.7, 2 R.F.	147	1881
Marques del Duero	Gunboat	One 6.2, two 4.7, 1 R.F.	96	1875
General Lezo	Gunboat	One 3.5, 1 R.F.	115	1885
Argos	Gunboat		87	

Two torpedo boats and two transports, practically not in action.
El Cano is mentioned in Admiral Dewey's list of May 4, but is omitted in that given in his despatch of July 9.

President McKinley upon learning of Dewey's victory at Manila Bay confessed that "he could not have told where those darned islands were within 2,000 miles."

USS Olympia (C-6) Protected Cruiser

Named for the city of Olympia, Washington. She was launched in 1891 at Union Iron Works, San Francisco, and commissioned in 1895.

Displacement — 5,870 tons
Length — 344 feet
Beam — 53 feet
Mean Draft — 21.5 feet
Maximum Speed — 23 knots
Twin Screws — three-cylinder triple expansion engine, 18,000 hp, six Scotch (fire tube) boilers
Complement — 34 Officers and 440 men, including Marine Guard
Armament — Four eight-inch, 10 five-inch, 14 six-pounders, six one-pounders and six 18-inch torpedo tubes.

Dewey on the bridge of the *Olympia* during the Battle of Manila Bay.

This 1926 photo shows the painted footprints of Admiral Dewey on the bridge deck where he stood when he issued his famous command, "You may fire when you are ready, Gridley." The famous American warship, *USS Constellation* is in the background. Photo taken at the Philadelphia Navy Yard. USN NH 43378

Dewey on the *Olympia* in 1899. MNHS #64839

Dewey at Manila Bay: "Fire When Ready, Gridley!"
by Blaine Taylor

On May 1, 1898, the United States Navy gave the delighted American public its first victory of the war, in a stunning naval battle at Manila Bay in the Philippines.

The President himself was so stunned by the unexpected triumph that he confessed that he could not even tell where the victory had taken place within a 2,000-mile accuracy, and had to consult a White House globe to learn Manila Bay's location. But U.S. Navy Commodore George Dewey, commander of America's Asiatic Squadron, knew well enough where it was.

At the time hostilities were announced, Dewey and his command of five cruisers and two gunboats were anchored in the British Crown Colony of Hong Kong's harbor waters. Certain that war was coming, Dewey had prepared for combat by purchasing extra supplies of coal and food for his spanking American battle fleet, and his being there ready for action was no accident, either. It was, however, part of a long-time, well-thought-out plan by Theodore Roosevelt and Massachusetts Republican Senator Henry Cabot Lodge.

As Secretary of the Navy John D. Long later recalled, "Seven hours only were required by the American Squadron to place the Philippine Archipelago at the mercy of the United States, and relieve this government of anxiety for the Pacific Slope and its trans-Pacific trade, but more than seven years, however, had been needed to provide the ships and perfect the personnel which accomplished this result."

Indeed, the Navy Department had been quietly gathering data on both the Spanish Fleet at Manila Bay and the land defenses since the summer before in preparation for just a battle as was about to transpire, and Dewey was sent out in the fall of 1897 to take command.

Following the obliteration of the battleship *Maine*, Roosevelt, acting on his own initiative, sent Dewey orders to mobilize his fleet at Hong Kong, and the latter set to the task with zeal. He purchased a collier, full of coal, and even arranged for an emergency base on the south China coast. As war became imminent, he waited impatiently for the cruiser *Baltimore* to arrive with ammunition.

The reason for his anxiety was simple, since under international law Dewey was required to leave British waters as a belligerent within 48 hours. Fidgeting nervously, he meanwhile received a cable from the Navy Department ordering him to destroy or capture the Spanish Fleet in the Philippines.

The *Baltimore* arrived on April 22 from the port of Yokohama in Japan, and hastily made herself ready for combat at sea. Finally Dewey was ready to set sail on his journey to an historic rendezvous with destiny that would make his country a world power to be reckoned with in the 20th Century.

An eyewitness described the Fleet's departure thus: "The fleet was ordered to leave Hong Kong Harbor on Sunday, Apr. 24th...The departure made no little stir in Hong Kong, the sympathy of the English there being with us. As the *Olympia* passed the English hospital ships, they gave us three hearty cheers. Three steam launches filled with Americans followed us down the harbor, waving flags and wishing us God-speed!"

And yet, the Americans there feared Dewey's flagship *Olympia* and the rest of his squadron would meet with defeat at the hands of the Spanish, as Dewey himself later noted, "In the Hong Kong Club, it wasn't possible to get bets—even at heavy odds—that our expedition would be a success. The universal remark among our hosts was to this effect: 'A fine set of fellows, but we shall never see them again!'"

Roosevelt felt otherwise, though, and had cabled Dewey back in February in this confident tone: "Order the squadron except *Monocacy* to Hong Kong. Keep full of coal. In the event of declaration of war with Spain, your duty will be to see that the Spanish squadron does not leave the Asiatic coast and then begin offensive operations in Philippines Islands. Keep *Olympia* until further orders."

And now, at 2 p.m. on the 27th, Dewey stood confidently on the bridge of the sparkling *Olympia* and meant to prove his British hosts wrong as his units proceeded to battle.

With the fleet underway, Dewey assembled the crews on the decks of their vessels so that they could hear the proclamation from their Spanish enemy, Basilio Augustin Davila, Captain-General of the Philippines: "A squadron manned by foreigners, possessing neither instruction nor discipline, is prepar-

February 25, 1898.

Dewey, Hong Kong .

~~Secret and Confidential~~

Order the Squadron except Monocacy to Hong Kong. Keep full of coal. In the event of declaration war Spain, your duty will be to see that the Spanish squadron does not leave the Asiatic coast and then offensive operations in Philipine Islands. Keep Olympia until further orders.

Roosevelt

Roosevelt's cable to Dewey.

ing to come to this archipelago with the ruffianly intention of robbing us of all that means life, liberty and honor...Vain designs! Ridiculous boastings!"

As Dewey had foreseen, the reading had the desired effect on both officers and ratings present, as a reporter noted: "A roar of derisive laughter went up from the whole berth deck."

The fleet arrived off Subic Bay on the Philippine island of Luzon on Saturday, April 30, 1898, early in the morning, about 50 miles north of the capital city of Manila. As in the days of British seadog Admiral Horatio Nelson at Trafalgar, Dewey now ordered his ships' crews to prepare for action.

The whole squadron began its final preparations for the battle that everyone knew was near at hand. Aboard the *Olympia* and *Baltimore* the sheet chain cable was 'bighted' or coiled around the ammunition hoists so as to give them considerable protection. Nets of tough, pliable manila rope, about as thick as one's little finger, were stretched beneath all the boats (to serve as splinter nets). All unnecessary material was thrown overboard, dangerous woodwork, mess chests, mess tables, ditty boxes, chairs, wardroom bulkheads, and a vast quantity of other impedimenta.

As it turned out, though, Subic Bay was found to

be empty of any Spanish naval presence. The Spanish fleet, commanded by Admiral Patricio Montojo, had arrived there only two days earlier, but when he discovered that the shore batteries were not yet ready for action, Montojo decided to stand and fight the Americans at Manila Bay instead.

Dewey now decided to call a Nelsonian council of war of his captains, and, as they started to arrive aboard the stately *Olympia*, some sailors were overheard talking.

"'They're comin',' said one of the old seamen, 'to hear the 'old man's last words before we go at the Dons.' 'Not his last word,' said one of the younger men. 'Perhaps not his,' was the reply, 'but it's near our last words some of us are. There'll be many an eye will look at that sunset tonight that'll never see another.'"

Dewey's "council" of war was, in reality, merely the occasion for the Commodore's transmission of already-decided-upon courses of action for his captains, not a time for discussion or debate. The vessels, darkened for the night except for a single light in each stern for the next ship in line to follow proceeded under cover of darkness on the evening of April 30 to take their battle stations for the next morning's action. At 9:45 p.m., by word of mouth quietly from one hand to the next so as not to alert the waiting Spaniards, the men were sent to their guns aboard each ship.

By 11:30, Manila Bay's entrance was sighted, as a reporter later wrote for his paper: "Two dark headlands, one on either side of the entrance, show up gloomy. In the space between the smaller mass shows where the dreaded Corregidor lies. It was understood the heaviest guns of the Spanish were at Corregidor. The entrance was also said to be planted with mines, and it was known that there were torpedoes waiting for the ships. The *Olympia* turns in and steers directly for the center of the southern and wider channel. The *Baltimore* follows and in regular order the rest of the fleet slide through the night toward the entrance.

"Still, there is no firing from the forts, and it is hoped that the daring maneuver may not be discovered."

Standing tensely on his bridge aboard the *Olympia*, Commodore Dewey, a distinguished-looking gentleman with the fashionable walrus-like moustache of the era and grandfatherly white hair, nervously eyed both Corregidor and its sister fortress, El Fraile, which straddled Manila Bay's entrance.

Suddenly, a flame shot up from the funnel of his ship *McCulloch*, and a single rocket was fired from Corregidor, but no sustained volleys followed, miraculously, it seemed. Dewey again held his breath as yet another flame shot out from *McCulloch*'s stack piercing the eerie darkness of the night.

Still, the Spanish guns on Corregidor were silent as the fleet glided by noiselessly, but at 12:15 a.m., May 1, a volley broke forth from El Fraile, which the Americans answered in turn. Silence returned, but on the *McCulloch*, Chief Engineer Randall died of heat prostration in the engine room, the first casualty of the action that was to follow.

Meanwhile, Dewey's ships proceeded in a leisurely pace down 23 miles of the Bay toward the waiting Spanish "Dons," reaching their location at sunup. Again, Dewey was to be surprised, for the Spanish Fleet, known to be smaller, slower, and with less firepower than his own, was absent from under the protection of the formidable Spanish shore batteries. Having survived both the non-existent Spanish mines and the twin forts behind them, the Americans were now anxious for action against the enemy.

To spare Manila the hazards of sea bombardment, however, the Spanish commander, Rear Admiral

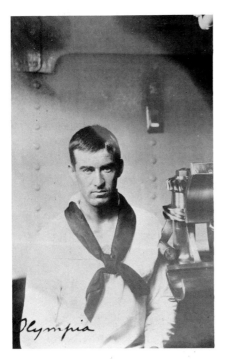

William Sneath served on the *USS Raleigh*. He was one of the eight slightly wounded sailors during the Battle of Manila Bay. This photo taken on board the *USS Olympia*.

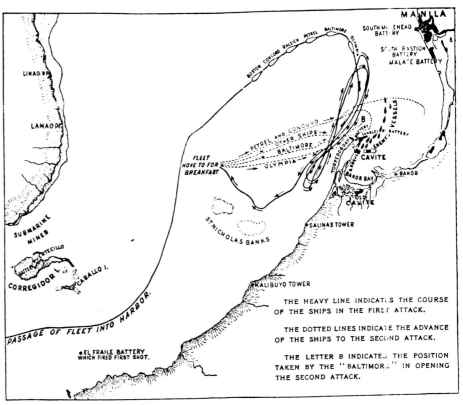

THE HEAVY LINE INDICATES THE COURSE OF THE SHIPS IN THE FIRST ATTACK.

THE DOTTED LINES INDICATE THE ADVANCE OF THE SHIPS TO THE SECOND ATTACK.

THE LETTER B INDICATES THE POSITION TAKEN BY THE "BALTIMORE" IN OPENING THE SECOND ATTACK.

The Battle of Manila Bay

Patricio Montojo y Pasarón, arrayed his fleet in shallow but almost unprotected waters at Cavite, several miles away.

Now, six miles from Manila herself, Dewey's men ate their breakfast of coffee and hardtack as dawn streaked the skies beginning at 4:00 a.m., as the fleet lined up for battle: the flagship *Olympia*, followed by the cruisers *Baltimore, Raleigh, Petrel, Concord* and *Boston*. As they passed Manila, her shore batteries opened up, consisting of four 9.4" guns, two 5.9" guns, four 5.5" guns, and two 4.7" guns at 4:50 a.m.

The seven Spanish fleet vessels were now sighted, like the Americans opposite them, drawn up in the close order line of battle prescribed in the naval war colleges of the day: *Cristina, Castilla, Isla de Cuba, Luzon, D.A. de Ulloa, D.J. de Austria* and *Duero*, and to their right middle, the smaller ships *Argos* and *El Cano*, with the *Velasco* and *Lezo* behind the main battle line, sheltering behind Cavite's point of land jutting out into the Bay.

Wrote the *Olympia's* navigator, Lt. Carlos Gilman Calkins, "The Spanish ships were ready. They were cleared for action, and their crews animated by rounds of regulation cheers and the display of battleflags, before the action began."

For the first time since Trafalgar 93 years earlier, the Spanish Navy was about to engage the enemy, while for the Americans, their last naval action had been during the Civil War a quarter of a century before. What would happen? Nobody really knew for sure.

A shore battery on nearby Sangley Point fired the first round of the Battle of Manila Bay, but this fell short by over a mile. More wild Spanish shots followed, some falling more than six miles distant. Heartened by this inaccuracy, the American sailors watched in grim silence as the *Olympia* steamed ahead toward the shellbursts and the geysers of water shooting higher and higher into the water ahead of them.

Suddenly, the tension was broken when there was a shellburst directly overhead of *Olympia*, spraying the bridge and decks with debris. Almost in unison, her 500-man crew cried out "Remember the *Maine!*" With this cry ringing in his ears, Dewey, unflappable, calmly turned to *Olympia's* Captain and uttered a single sentence that was to go down in history: "You may fire when ready, Gridley."

At 5:41 a.m., at 5,500 yards' distance, *Olympia's* forward turret eight-inch starboard gun did so, soon joined by those of the *Baltimore* and *Boston*, which sent "Two hundred and fifty-pound shells hurtling toward the *Castilla* and the *Reina Cristina.*"

Noted one eyewitness, "The Spaniards seemed encouraged to fire faster, knowing exactly our distance, while we had to guess theirs. Their ships and shore guns were making things hot for us. The piercing scream of shot was varied often by the bursting of time fuse shells, fragments of which would lash the water like shrapnel or cut our hull and rigging. One large shell that was coming straight at the *Olympia's* forward bridge fortunately fell within less than 100 feet away. Another struck the bridge gratings in line with it. A third just passed under Commodore Dewey and gouged a hole in the deck."

Wrote Lt. Fiske of the *Petrel*: "The American fleet paraded back and forth before the Spanish fleet, firing as rapidly as they could with proper aim. The whole thing looked like a performance that had been well-rehearsed. The ships went slowly and regularly, seldom or never getting out of their relative positions, and only ceased firing at intervals when the smoke became too thick. For a long while, I could not form an opinion as to which way fortune was going to decide. I could see that the Spanish ships were hit a number of times, especially the *Cristina* and *Castilla*, but then it seemed to me that our ships were hit many times also, and from the way that they cut away boats from the *Raleigh*, I concluded that the *Raleigh* was suffering severely. I could see projectiles falling in the water on all sides of all our ships."

Lt. Fiske continued, "Two of the ships in the Spanish column were evidently much larger than the others...and the Captain naturally seemed to direct the fire at them. I could see also that the Spaniards directed their firing principally at the *Olympia* and *Baltimore*, which were our largest ships. Our practice was evidently much better than that of the Spaniards, but it did not seem to me that it was at all good...

"About the decks of the *Petrel* things were entirely different from what I had expected. I had seen many pictures of battles and had expected great excitement. I did not see any excitement whatever! The men seemed to me to be laboring under an intense strain and to be keyed up to the highest pitch; but to be quiet, and under complete self-control, and to be doing the work of handling the guns and ammunition with that mechanical precision which is the result we all hope to get from drill."

If anything, when those men below decks had time, they calmly strode over to the portholes to look outside for a view of the raging battle. Recalled a gunner on the *Boston*, "All my men were naked except for shoes and drawers, and I wore only a cotton shirt in addition. Three in the after powder division fainted from the heat but none of my force was overcome. The heat was really fearful. The powder smoke settled down, choking us and half-blinding some, and only the love of the work kept us going. The Chinese stood the heat better than we did."

Remembered a stoker on the *Olympia*, the temperature was 116 degrees in the forward berth deck, but in the engine room, men claimed it was 200 degrees! "We could tell when our guns opened fire by the way the ship shook. We could scarcely stand on our feet, the vibration was so great...The ship shook so fearfully that the soot and cinders poured down on us in clouds. Whenever a Spanish ship would make a move toward us some of the boys on deck would shout down that they were coming for us full tilt. We knew it meant sure death if the *Olympia* got shot through her anywhere in our vicinity."

He concluded, "I shall never forget those few hours. It seemed to me the longest day I ever lived."

Gradually, as the ships made succeeding passes, the range grew less and less, from three miles to under a mile. Despite the heavy smoke, "gun crews could watch the fall of their shots with the naked eye and many an exultant cheer went up from every ship. Naked to the waist and grimy with the soot of powder, their heads bound up in water-soaked towels, sweat running in rivulets over their glistening bodies, these men who had fasted for 16 hours now slung shell after shell and charge after charge, each weighing 100-250 pounds, into their huge guns under a tropical sun which melted the pitch in the decks."

And what of the Spanish? Incredibly, two of their vessels were firing from a moored position, while the others, said Lt. Calkins, "Steamed about in aimless fashion, often masking their comrades' fire, occasionally dodging back to the shelter of the arsenal and now and then making isolated and ineffectual rushes in advance, which had no rational significance except as demonstrations on the point of honor, flourishes of desperation inspired by defeat..."

By now—after several hours of firing—the *Cristina* was ablaze forward and aft, with flames and smoke leaping out of both portholes and skylights. Then came a jet of white steam from around her after smokestack high into the air, and she swayed onward upon an irregular course toward Cavite until aground under its walls.

Beached and out of action, the Spanish Admiral transferred his colors from the *Cristina* to the *Isla de Cuba*, while the Americans continued to shell heavily both vessels. Next, *Duero* was also afire and forced to retreat. By 7:30 a.m., all of the Spanish ships with the exception of *Ulloa* were skulking in safety behind the mole at Cavite, from where they could not escape.

Five minutes later, Commodore Dewey decided to temporarily suspend the fierce action and issued two terse orders: "Withdraw from action," and "Let the people go to breakfast." As the ships stood out to sea and out of range of the Spanish shore guns, the men clamored topside at last while their commanders huddled aboard *Olympia* to discuss the next move.

At 11:05 a.m., the battle was rejoined, this time with *Baltimore* leading the stately parade of American combat craft into Manila Bay's embattled waters. At a range of 2,500 yards from the beach, the cruiser began an artillery duel with the shore batteries that was later described as a "magnificent spectacle," by one of the onlookers. At times, *Baltimore* seemed to be on fire, while every shell she fired was placed in the earthworks as accurately as if she were at target practice.

Canacao battery was the first to fall under this deadly fire, its embankments of sand, backed by boiler iron, torn up and flung into the faces of the gunners until panic took hold of them. Hauling down their flag, they tumbled into an ambulance and drove madly to the protection of Fort Sangley. The whole fire of the squadron was then concentrated upon this fort. At last the Spanish flag came down and a white flag was raised in its place.

Now, only the badly riddled *Ulloa* was still resisting, although nearly every gun was either dismounted or disabled. At length, the crew swarmed over her unengaged side and swam for shore. Then she gave a slow roll toward her executioners and sank beneath the waves.

The shallow draft *Petrel* raced into Cavite Arsenal, impervious to Spanish fire that never came. At 12:20 p.m., she signalled *Olympia* that "The enemy has surrendered." Dewey left his chief-of-staff to formally accept the Spanish surrender aboard the *Petrel*, while *Olympia* and the rest of the fleet sailed for Manila, where, reportedly, the squadron anchored off the city as unmolested as if in time of peace. The sun went down amid the usual evening concert and one could scarcely realize that he had just participated in the most complete naval victory of modern times.

Incredibly, Dewey's Asiatic Squadron had destroyed 11 Spanish ships, for comparative casualties of 167 Spaniards killed and another 214 wounded, while the Americans suffered only one dead (the *McCulloch*'s engineer) and eight slightly wounded, and not a ship was seriously damaged.

In addition, the fleet had captured the valuable Spanish naval yard at Cavite, and ultimately the United States would receive all of the Philippines as a virtual protectorate until after the end of the Second World War four decades later.

As in every war, far differing fates awaited both victor and vanquished. Americans at home "Instantly elevated Commodore Dewey to their gallery of heroes. In chromos and sculpture, his became the face of the hour. He returned home to a hero's welcome, and Congress elevated him to the special rank of Admiral of the Navy.

And what of the defeated Spanish Admiral Montojo? He was later accused of cowardice and poor strategy.

DEWEY'S MARVELOUS VICTORY.

NO AMERICAN SHIP OR MAN LOST.

COMPLETE MASTER OF MANILA.

The Press, Philadelphia, Sunday Morning, May 8, 1898.

Painting of the *USS Olympia* by Jim Flood, Miami Springs, Florida.

Adm. Patricio Montojo y Pasaron was commander of Spanish naval forces in the Philippines. He went to sea as a midshipman in 1855 and served in the Philippines, Peru and Cuba, before assuming his last command which ended in defeat, a court martial and brief imprisonment. He died in 1917 at age 78.

Battle Casualties

Spanish
167 killed, 214 wounded
American
One dead (the engineer on the *McCulloch* died of heat prostration), eight slightly wounded

When Dewey struck the Spanish fleet at Manila, a Spanish gunboat, the *Callao* steered into the bay. She had been in the southern islands for the previous 16 months patrolling the river. Her commander didn't know that the battle was on or that war had been declared. When the American fleet began firing, he thought it was target practice and turned to get out of the way. A few shots over the bow informed him of what was up and he lowered his flag. The captured boat was added to Dewey's flotilla.

The World.

1,011,068

1,011,068
GAIN in Three Years ... 461,206

NEW YORK, MONDAY, MAY 2, 1898.

DEWEY SMASHES SPAIN'S FLEET

VICE-ADMIRAL MONTOJO.

The Deemed Commander of the Spanish Fleet

CONNODORE DEWEY.

Great Naval Battle Between Asiatic Squadron and Spanish Warships Off Manila.

THREE OF THE BEST SPANISH VESSELS WIPED OUT, OTHERS SUNK.

The Damage Done to the American Boats Engaged Only Nominal---Hundreds of the Enemy Slain in the Encounter.

LISBON, Portugal, May 1, 11 P. M.—The Spanish fleet was completely defeated off Cavite, Philippine Islands, according to trustworthy advices received here.

WASHINGTON, May 1, Midnight.—President McKinley expresses entire satisfaction over the reported battle between Commodore Dewey's squadron and the Spanish fleet. He accepts the news as true, but believes it is worse for the Spanish than they will admit. There has been no official confirmation of the news. Nothing official is expected for forty-eight hours.

THE THREE SPANISH CRUISERS COMPLETELY DESTROYED.

CASTILLA.

DON JUAN DE AUSTRIA.

SPANISH FLAG SHIP.
REINA MARIA CRISTINA.

ADMIRAL MONTOJO ADMITS HIS UTTER ROUT.

In His Report to Spain He Says Many Ships Were Burned and Sunk and the Losses in Officers and Men "Numerous."

MADRID (via Paris), May 2.—The time of the retreat of the American squadron before the merchantmen was 11.30 A. M. The American squadron forced the port before daybreak and appeared off Cavite. Night was completely dark.

The Naval Bureau at Manila sends the following report, signed "Montojo Admiral: In the middle of the night the American squadron forced the forts and before daybreak the night was completely dark. At 7.30 the bow of the Reina Christina took fire, ... on board the Isla de Cuba. The Reina Maria Christina ... Some had to be sunk to prevent ... —Capt. Cadarso

---

NIGHT SPECIAL.

SATURDAY'S 1,408,200 CIRCULATION.

NEW YORK JOURNAL

NEW YORK, MONDAY, MAY 2, 1898.

PRICE ONE CENT.

WAR SURRENDERS! DEWEY'S FLEET TAKES MANILA.

THE SPANISH FLAGSHIP ON FIRE.

WASHINGTON GETS NEWS OF THE CITY'S FALL

WASHINGTON, MAY 2.---IT IS REPORTED THAT AMBASSADOR HAY THROUGH THE MEDIUM OF THE BRITISH FOREIGN OFFICE HAS SECURED NEWS OF THE SURRENDER OF MANILA, BUT CONFIRMATION OF THIS REPORT CANNOT BE MADE. THE STATE DEPARTMENT SAYS THAT IT HAS NOT RECEIVED OFFICIAL NOTICE AND SECY LONG OF THE NAVY IS ALSO WITHOUT DEFINITE NEWS.

When the cable service from Manila ceased the city was being bombarded.

Official reports to Great Britain announce that the Spanish fleet at Manila was annihilated.

Admiral Montijo admits that his fleet has been demolished.

Madrid has been declared under martial law.

Don Juan de Austria was blown up.

AND THEY GOT IT AS DEMANDED.

THE HOME COMING.

WHEN THIS CRUEL WAR IS OVER.

In the middle of the fight, the Spaniards say...

Dewey's squadron entered Manila Bay at night. Fighting began in early morning.

Spanish Admiral deserted his flagship, Maria Cristina, then on fire.

Captain Cadarso, commander of Spanish flagship, was killed.

Besides fighting the enemy's ships American forces sustained a hot fire from Spanish forts.

PRAYER OF THANKS IN THE SENATE.

ADMIRAL DEWEY'S GRE

CTORY AT MANILA.

"City of Peking" with troops aboard going out of San Francisco bay

FIRST REGIMENT CALIFORNIA VOLUNTEERS EMBARKING ON THE "CITY OF PEKING."—DRAWN BY J. A. CAHILL.

"Good-by"

The *SS China* leaving San Francisco on June 15, 1898, with the 1st Colorado Volunteer Infantry and Battery A and B of the Utah Artillery. USHS #386.2

MAJOR TOMPSON, SIGNAL CORPS.   MAJOR SIMPSON, CHIEF OF ARTILLERY.

Drawn by
G. W. Peters.

ON THE WAY TO MANILA—OFFICERS OF S. S. NEWPORT PLAYING CARDS.

The U.S. Army transport *Valencia* took troops to the Philippines in June 1898 and brought them back home in September 1899. MHS

1898 Philippines Expeditions from San Francisco

1st Expedition—left on May 25 under command of General Anderson, with 2,491 troops on the *City of Sydney, Australia* and *City of Peking*.

2nd Expedition—left on June 15 under command of General Greene with 3,586 troops on the *China, Colon* and *Zealandia*.

3rd Expedition—left on June 25, 27, 28, and 29 under command of General Merritt, with the command of General McArthur, with 4,847 troops on the *Senator, Morgan City, City of Para, Indiana, Ohio, Valencia* and *Newport*.

4th Expedition—left July 15 under command of Gen. Elwell S. Otis with 1,682 troops on the *Peru* and *City of Pueblo*.

5th Expedition—left July 23 and 29 under command of Gen. H.G. Otis with 1,735 troops on the *City of Rio de Janeiro* and *St. Paul*.

The *Tacoma* left on Aug. 6 with 30 troops, 19 civilian teamsters, 210 horses and mules, 44 wagons and ambulances and six months' supply of subsistence and forage.

On Aug. 21 the *Arizona* left with 490 troops and four female nurses and on Aug. 29, the *Scandia* left with troops for Hawaii and 173 troops for the Philippines. In total 16,405 people, their equipment and supplies were transported to the Far East.

Emilio Aguinaldo was the leader of Philippine independence. In 1896, he took part in an unsuccessful revolt against Spanish rule, and was forced to flee to Hong Kong. He returned to lead a Filipino army against the Spanish in 1898. In June he was made president of a revolutionary government and president of the Philippine Republic in 1899. He waged a three-year war against the American occupation army before being captured in 1901. On April 19, 1901, he took the oath of allegiance to the United States and retired to private life. In 1942 the Japanese brought Aguinaldo out of retirement to urge, by radio broadcast, Gen. Douglas MacArthur to surrender. His appeal went unanswered. In 1950, President Quirino appointed him a member of the council of state. Aguinaldo died in 1964 at age 96.

Aguinaldo's hideout in the mountains. USAMHI

Fort San Antonio de Abad defending the City of Manila. It was bombarded for 30 minutes by the American fleet on Aug. 13, 1898, and was eventually occupied by American troops. USMHI

First Colorado Volunteer band in the Philippines. H.T. Irvine was the bandmaster of his "Hot Time in the Old Town," regimental band. By this time there was a lot of latitude in the type of uniform worn by army personnel and the amount of facial hair acceptable within army regulations. DPL #F27564

Group of officers relaxing in the Philippines, 1898. Colonel Kessler of the 1st Montana Volunteer Infantry is on the left. V. Tokizama, a Japanese military attaché is in the background along with Major Fitzhugh and Lieutenant Knowlton. KE

Adm. Manuel de Camara was ordered on June 15, 1898, to sail from Cadiz, Spain, to the Philippines to engage Dewey's fleet. His fleet consisted of the *Pelayo, Carlos V, Patriots, Rapido, Audqz, Osado, Prosepina,* 4,000 troops on the *Buenos Aires* and *Panay* and four colliers. However, on July 7, Camara's fleet was recalled to Spain because of the loss of Cervera's ships at Santiago.

The 1st Colorado Volunteer Infantry advancing to attack Fort San Antonio de Abad on Aug. 13. At 10:35 a.m. the Spanish flag was hauled down and the Stars and Stripes raised. DRAWN BY T. DE THULSTRUP

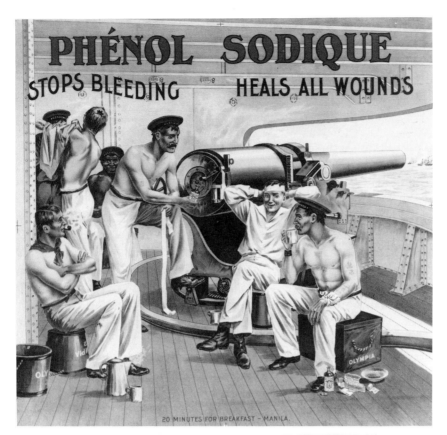

Even patent medicine manufacturers captalized on the great victory at Manila Bay. LC-USZ62-24209

MANILA IS OURS ?

Washington, May 7.—Authentic news has been received from Dewey, and it shows that the victory was complete. About 700 Spaniards were either killed or severely wounded and the entire fleet was sunk while on the American side no one was killed.

Only six were injured and our ships were unharmed.

In view of this fact, it is believed, even by the most conservative, that Commodore Dewey is now in full control of Manila, and that one more such a decisive battle with the squadron which recently left Capt Verde will cause Spain to ask for peace on some equitable basis.

Atherton.

Newspaper cartoon printed in American newspapers soon after the victory at Manila Bay. LC-USZ62-96566

The Battle of Manila

Dewey had won the great naval battle of Manila Bay but at that time had no troops to take over the city. In the meantime Aguinaldo, leader of the Filipino insurgents, had landed at Cavite, united his guerrillas and surrounded Manila.

The Spanish governor-general, Don Basilio Augustín Dávila was replaced on July 24 by Gen. Firmín Jandenes y Alvarez. Jandenes seeing that further resistance would only destroy his army and the city, proposed a surrender plan. In order to save some honor for his troops and country, he would surrender the city after a sham battle on both land and sea.

He was adamant, however, about surrendering only to the Americans, not the insurgents who surrounded the city.

To make certain this would be an American-Spanish battle, Aguinaldo's forces were promised some heavy weapons in exchange for letting Merritt's troops occupy some of their positions. While the promises were never kept, the Americans were in place to carry out the battle scenario.

On Aug. 13, the American Navy bombarded Fort San Antonio de Abad and eventually the Spaniards ran up the white flag. General Merritt's troops entered the city but not before there were some casualties on both sides due to poor communications.

The Filipino's were excluded from the takeover and even from the surrender ceremonies. This would do much to further the ill will between the two forces and eventually lead to all out war between them.

The sham battle and city surrender were actually fought three days after the "Peace Protocol" had been signed by Spain and the United States. It took time for messages to get from Washington to Hong Kong (Dewey's communication base) and then to the *Olympia* in Manila Bay.

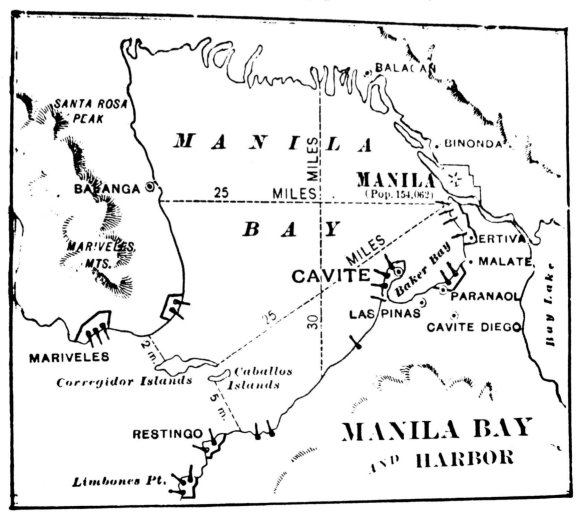

Surrender scenes at Manila. Clockwise from upper left: Spanish guns on the Luneta; Church at Paranaque destroyed by the insurgents; a dismounted Spanish gun; American troops guarding the bridge over the River Pasig on the afternoon of the surrender; old monastery near Malete, just inside the American lines, used by General Greene as his headquarters; burning of the Spanish gunboat, *Subig*; Spanish guns on Fort San Antonio where the American flag was first raised; natives transporting stores along the beach from Camp Dewey to Manila; in the insurgents trenches—firing a big gun and the entrance to Fort San Antonio.

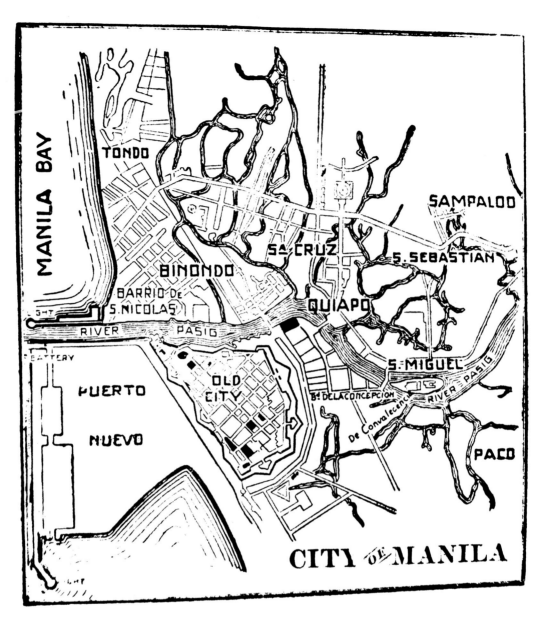

Spanish troops firing at American troops in Manila. It appears they are set up for some period of time with their Mauser rifles and extra clips on the floor. USAMHI

(Letter reprinted here as written, all errors in spelling and grammar are original.)

Manila P.I.
October 19th

Dear Willie

You no doubt will be pleased to receive a letter from Manila & to hear how the Oregon boys are. I may be mistaken but the day we left Portland for the front I thought I caught sight of you standing on Washington Street, I should have been too happy to have met you again.

I send you by this mail my photo which is pretty fair work for Philipinoes & shows that they are not altogether savages. Manila is a city of some three hundred thousand souls, & is built on both banks of a rapid & very muddy stream called the Rio Passig, we, that is the Colonel & staff with myself started up the river last Sunday in a steam launch to visit the Lapu de Bay, a large lake but were stopped by the insurgent outposts. We shall have to give those fellow's a good drubbing yet. On August 13th we landed on the water front & during the bombardment were on the "SS Quong Hoi" where we had a good view of everything that was going on. At 5:45 we took a turn around the U.S. warships & I assure you it was an inspiring sight to see those vessels cleared for action; On landing we marched up the river to the walled city, on reaching which the draw bridge at the main gate was lowered & the Commanding officer of the Spanish garrison stepped forward & saluted, we then entered & marched to the Governor General's palace. The streets were lined on both sides with Spanish troops standing at "attention" with their rifles & litterally loaded down with amunition; them began the work of disarming the rank & file, the officers were permitted to retain their arms; it was a sight never to be forgotten. The city proper is enclosed by massive stone walls some 35 feet high & about 25 feet wide on top on the outer side is also another wall built up about 6 feet & on top of this again they have placed square timbers raised above the wall about 6 inches the wall is a good breastwork & they fire between the top of it & the bottom of the log; of course it is nearly impossible to hit a man behind such works; the wall is or rather was also used as a prison as it is honey combed with dungeons.

The famous "Black Hole of Manila" is also to be seen, this is a dungeon where the Spaniards placed nearly 300 people mostly women & children & next morning over 200 were found sufocated; oh the devils, my blood boils when I think of the outrages they have perpetrated. We released women that had been confined to jail for 12 years on absolutely no legal grounds; one case I remember was of a Philipine woman who refused to let the Governor have wood from the farm without payment, she stood off a small guard of soldiers & was arrested for "Resisting the Armed Forces of Spain" she had already served over 11 years, & Blesses her stars that the "Americans" ever came here. I could cite hundreds of such cases & by Heaven if Uncle Sam gives these islands back to Spain I for one would never take up arms again in defense of "Old Glory." Our mission is accomplished, our task is done, the Maine has been avenged & now we are ready to return to old Oregon. Being the first out here we should be first home in fact the 2nd Oregon has been first all through the war & the other commands are jealous of us that accounts for the news paper correspondence from NY Sun. We leave our reputation with the Generals commanding being perfectly satisfied to abide by their decision. With very best wishes to your Mother & Sister & also your Grandmother.

Wishing you all a Merry Xmas & Prosperous New Year.

I am,
Yours Sincerely,
Harold G. Stanley

A Nervy Correspondent

John F. Bass was a special war correspondent for *Harper's Weekly* in the campaign against Manila. This letter was written by General Hale to Governor Adams of Colorado giving a summary of the work of the troops of that state: "Several of the correspondents followed the attack quite closely, but the only one, so far as I know, who was actually in the first line of the assault, at least in our brigade, was Mr. Bass of *Harper's Weekly*, who was very enterprising and nervy, accompanying us on the first firing-line, and taking snap-shots with his kodak – 'on the run,' so to speak. In fact, he became so enthusiastic after we forded the river and were advancing by alternate rushes up the beach, that he, in company with Major Bell of the Information Department, unconsciously got out in front of our firing-line, and I had to order them back."

Group of Spaniards (soldiers) Sketched from Life at old Manila
Oct: 14 (98)

THE GRAVES OF OUR FALLEN

Drawings by a member of the 1st California Volunteer Infantry in the Philippines. USAMHI

Yours Very Truly,
[signature]

B
California U.S. [Volunteer] Infantry
Manila, Philippines
1898

.RG.25-1898 Survey — 1st Calif. Vol. Inf. — 1898-82

ER BOYS IN MANILA   [signature]
Manila Oct. 20/98

The principal vessels of the German Asiatic Squadron in Manila Bay. On the left the 2nd Class battleship, *Kaiser*, in the middle the 2nd Class Protected Cruiser, *Irene* and on the right the 2nd Class Protected Cruiser *Kaiserin Augusta*. The captain of the *Irene* attempted to prevent the seizure of Isle Grande in Subic Bay by the Americans. The German government had possible territorial acquisitions in mind in the Philippines and interferred to a degree with the American blockade of Manila. In the end, with the presence of American troops in the islands, they withdrew from the area.

This drawing by T. De Thulstrup shows the Filipino Insurgent Army marching into Manila. The float, drawn by natives, flies the Insurgent flag.

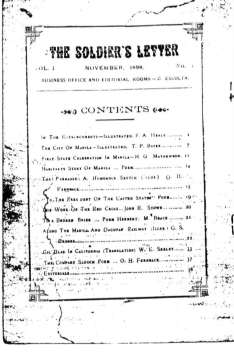

MNG

NCOs of the First Montana Volunteer Infantry in Manila. MNG

Members of the 13th Minnesota Volunteers in trenches before Manila, August 1898. MNHS #20711

The Philippine Insurrection

Tensions arose almost immediately between the Filipino troops that fought against the Spanish and the American Expeditionary Force that landed after Dewey's victory.

The Filipino rebel leader, Gen. Don Emilio Aquinaldo y Famy, was treated with contempt and disrespect. American troops prevented the insurgents from taking part in the occupation of Manila and they were not included in the Paris Peace Talks, where Spain ceded the Philippines to the United States for $20 million instead of granting her independence.

Escalating tensions exploded on the evening of Feb. 4, 1899, when three American soldiers shot three "insurrectos." Heavy firing between the two camps followed and many Filipinos and American soldiers were killed. The incident began the three-year "Phillipine Insurrection."

As the insurgents effectively used terror and violence to control the local population, the American forces soon discovered that they could not control the territory they occupied. It did not take long for the American troops to respond with similar barbarity against the rebels and the local population, returning cruelty for cruelty. Despite strict censorship, news of the violent nature of the war reached the homefront when soldiers, writing home, told stories of wanton destruction and indiscriminate violence. One rare public case received national attention; that of a lieutenant convicted of murder whose sentence was commuted to a fine and a loss of 35 places on the promotion list.

Further, Gen. J. Franklin Bell conducted a scorched-earth policy and instituted a policy to reconcentrate civilians into large camps. Touted as models of good sanitation and humanity, the camps proved to be full of disease, starvation, and death. The press naturally compared General Bell to the Spanish General, "the Butcher" Weyler of Cuban infamy.

The Puerto Rico Campaign

On April 22, after receiving orders from President William McKinley, Rear Adm. William T. Sampson, commanding the North Atlantic Squadron from *New York* (Armored Cruiser No. 2), deployed his fleet in preparation for a blockade of the Cuban coast. Three days later, the United States declared war on Spain. The monitor *Terror*, which had arrived off Cardenas, Cuba, on the 24th, captured a Cuban vessel—*Almansas*—on the first day of hostilities, but later released her. Over the next two days, the monitor took two Spanish ships, *Ambrosia Bolivar* and *Guido*, and sent the prizes to Florida.

Meanwhile, the whereabouts of the Spanish fleet under Admiral Cervera prompted concern in naval circles in Washington. Intelligence estimates which reached Sampson noted that the Spanish fleet had departed the Cape Verde Islands on the morning of April 29. Sampson reacted by deciding to meet Cervera's fleet at San Juan, Puerto Rico, the nearest Spanish base in the West Indies. With his flag on *New York*, Rear Admiral Sampson scraped together a makeshift squadron—which included *Terror* and a sistership, *Amphitrite* (Monitor No. 2), as well as battleships *Iowa* (Battleship No. 4) and *Indiana* (Battleship No. 1), *Porter* (Torpedo Boat No. 6), two auxiliaries and a collier—and departed Key West on May 3.

Terror and *Amphitrite* broke down frequently en route and materially delayed Sampson's passage. At one point, *New York* took both *Terror* and *Porter* in tow. Upon arrival off San Juan on May 12, the Americans found no Spanish ships in the harbor. In order to "develop their positions and strength," Sampson decided to conduct a brief bombardment of the shore defenses. The squadron stood in for their target at 0400, on May 12, 1898, with the ships cleared for action and the lights of the town clearly visible in the predawn darkness. Sounding general quarters at 0500, the Americans opened fire within 15 minutes, and the Spanish began returning fire at 0523.

Terror stood in, fifth in column, duelling with the Spanish shore batteries in a spirited engagement for the next three hours. As the action wore on, a tremendous volume of white smoke restricted visibility and caused the Admiral to signal "use large guns only" to cut down on the volume of smoke.

Terror expended 31 10-inch shells in three firing passes against the fortifications at San Juan, and scored a direct hit on a battery which the monitor's commanding officer, Capt. Nicholl Ludlow, considered "the most vicious." *Terror*, which had moved close inshore to gain a better firing position, kept up a spirited fire until 0815, when she broke off action and rejoined Sampson's squadron retiring to the northwest.

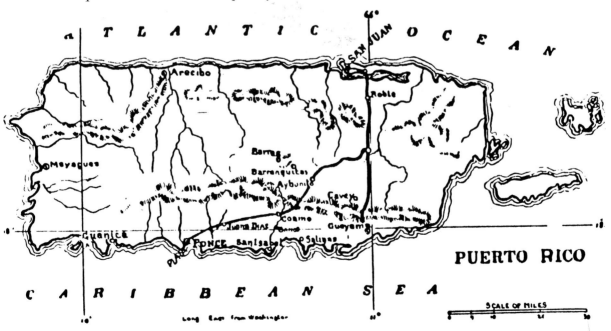

Puerto Rico had a strategic position in the Caribbean and economic ties to the United States. In addition the navy had eyed it as a possible base of operations before the war. The island was a semi-autonomous possession of Spain and did not have the intense insurgent activity as in Cuba.

With the fall of Santiago, the occupation of Puerto Rico became the next strategic necessity. General Miles had proposed to invade the island before taking Cuba but when the Spanish fleet was blockaded in Santiago harbor plans changed, and Cuba became the first priority.

Miles was already in Cuba and left Guantanamo on July 21 with approximately 4,000 troops. The expedition landed at Guanica on July 25. The port of San Juan was also blockaded at the same time by the navy.

To alleviate the past embarkation confusion, elements of the army left from their nearest ports such as New York, Tampa, Jacksonville and Newport News.

Miles' troops were reinforced by General Schwann's brigade, part of General Wilson's division and part of General Brooke's Corps, numbering over 16,000 troops.

On July 27, the troops occupied the island's most important southwestern city, Ponce, from which the rest of the campaign was directed.

With the exception of encounters with the enemy at Guayama, Hormigueros, Coamo, Yauco and Cape San Juan.

The island campaign ended abruptly on Aug. 13 when a general armistice was declared between the American and Spanish forces. Fifteen thousand United States troops were already engaged and occupied about one-third of the island. More troops were ready to land to invest San Juan and battle the remaining Spanish troops.

The 19-day campaign had cost the Americans nine killed and 46 wounded. The Spanish had 28 killed and 125 wounded. By Oct. 18, all Spanish troops had been evacuated from the island.

The invasion and occupation of Puerto Rico was better organized than the previous Cuban campaign due to better trained troops who had not been exposed to disease, a regular port for the off-loading of men and supplies, and climate conditions which reduced the threat of disease.

The USS Yale was an armed ship but was used in the Puerto Rico campaign as a troop transport. LC USZ61-76

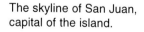

The skyline of San Juan, capital of the island.

The Mission of Lt. Henry H. Whitney

A little-known incident of the Puerto Rico Campaign occurred in mid-May 1898. Lt. Henry H. Whitney, a 31-year-old graduate of West Point and a member of the Fourth U.S. Artillery was asked to conduct a dangerous intelligence mission. The Bureau of Military Information sent him to Puerto Rico to report on enemy troop strength, port defenses and facilities, public opinion and enemy communications of the southern and western portions of the island.

Whitney would pose as a British subject, an act that would probably mean his death if captured. Secretary of War Alger gave him the direct order for the mission but as Alger later recalled:

"Certain newspapers, with a criminal disregard for his personal safety to say nothing of the government's plans, took pains, as soon as he had sailed, to publish, with the utmost attention to detail, not only the fact, but the purpose of his mission. The result was, of course, that when the foreign merchantman, with Whitney on board, touched Puerto Rico, she found the Spanish officials awaiting her. The ship was boarded and carefully searched, but the American officer was hard at work in the furnace room, 'stoking' like a professional, and thoroughly disguised in sweat and coal dust. He landed at last, and, under a different disguise, made a thorough inspection of the southern part of the island."

Whitney returned with valuable information that showed the Spanish forces as small with hardly any artillery support. He returned to the island in July as a captain on General Miles' staff.

Capt. Henry H. Whitney was born in 1866 in Pennsylvania. After graduation from West Point in 1892, he became proficient at map-making and later was appointed military attaché to Argentina—two reasons for his selection as a spy. He left on April 12 for a mission to carry dispatches to General Gomez in Cuba and returned June 8 from his dangerous mission to Puerto Rico.

Leaving Newport News, Virginia, for Puerto Rico with the 2nd, 3rd and 4th Pennsylvania Volunteers.

-269-

Volunteer infantry of the Puerto Rican invasion force pose for a photo before embarking at Newport News, Virginia. They are carrying the horseshoe roll, made popular during the Civil War. They have their standard issue canteens, tin cups and .45-.70 Springfield rifles.

Some of the reporters off of Ponce. Stephen Crane and Richard Harding Davis were very prominent in reporting the military action and vied with each other for the first "scoop." They even proceeded the American army into several towns, much to the annoyance of the commanding officers. LC-USZ62-101309

General Miles goes ashore at Guánica on the morning of July 25 to lead the invasion of Puerto Rico. LC-USZ62-65489

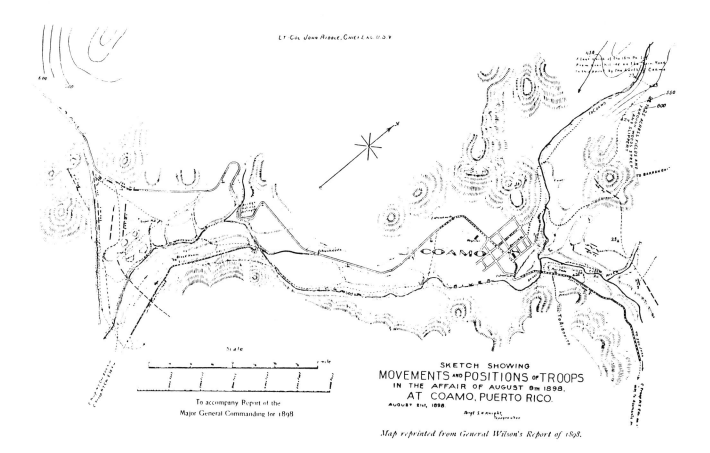

SKETCH SHOWING
MOVEMENTS AND POSITIONS OF TROOPS
IN THE AFFAIR OF AUGUST 8TH 1898,
AT COAMO, PUERTO RICO.
AUGUST 21st, 1898.

Scale

To accompany Report of the
Major General Commanding for 1898

Map reprinted from General Wilson's Report of 1898.

One of the main engagements in Gen. Nelson Miles' four-pronged advance on San Juan was at the town of Coamo. The town was along the paved highway northeast from Ponce. The Spanish had fortified the area but after putting up a strong defense were driven from their positions. Gen. James Wilson's troops won the battle with one dead and 10 wounded. The Spanish suffered six killed and 35 wounded and lost over 160 taken as prisoners.

The army camped at Ponce. LC-USZ67-53832

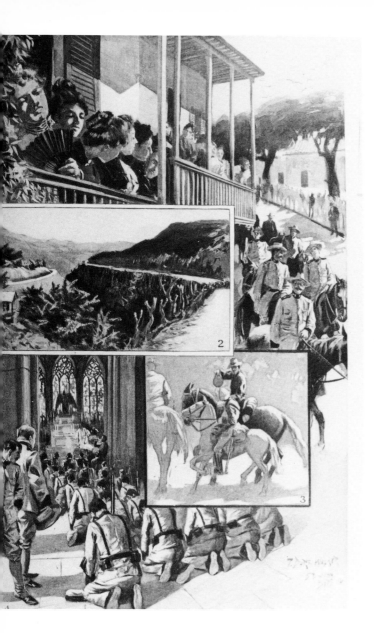

The occupation of Puerto Rico. No. 1, General Brooke and staff entering a village; No. 2, Spanish earthworks (on left) commanding the Military Road; No. 3, A comparison of American and Spanish cavalry; No. 4, Spanish soldiers at Mass with American officers looking on. (FROM *HARPER'S WEEKLY*)

Scenes of the surrender of Spanish forces in Puerto Rico, clockwise from left: Spanish soldiers in the San Cristobal Barracks; Spanish officers in front of San Cristobal Barracks; San Juan Harbor—vessels decorated in honor of the day; United States troops taking possession of the armory of the 1st Spanish Infantry, San Juan, and raising the flag over San Juan, Oct. 18, 1898.

Several dynamite guns, unusual artillery pieces used sparsely in the war, were employed in a small skirmish on the road to San Juan. Several shots were fired at Spanish troops who had ambushed the Americans. Three shots were fired at the enemy who quickly retreated, more from the morale effects of the guns than from their destructive nature.

Medical and Benevolent Activities

The medical condition of the troops, mainly in Cuba, was a major concern in the conduct of the war. Medicine had made enormous strides since the Civil War, but bad food, poor sanitation and continuous rains had led to outbreaks of typhoid fever and dysentary in the army camps. In Cuba due to the same conditions, malaria and yellow fever were added to the list of diseases.

Dr. Nicholas Senn, chief surgeon of the army in Cuba reported: "Those who saw the different regiments leave our State and national camps would find it difficult to recognize and identify the soldiers of the Cuban campaign. The men left in excellent spirits. Most of them return as mere shadows of their former selves. The pale faces, sunken eyes, the staggering gate and the emaciated forms show only too plainly the effects of climate and disease. Many of them are wrecks for life, others are candidates for a premature grave, and hundreds will require the most careful attention and treatment before they regain the vigor they lost in Cuba."

In August, no less then 4,000 of General Shafter's troops were on sick call. It was lucky the war ended so quickly or disease might have done what the Spanish couldn't—defeat the American army.

Several volunteer groups in the United States such as the Auxiliary of the National Army Relief Association for Porto Rico, Army Christian Commission of the YMCA, The Women's Relief Corps of the G.A.R., the Central Cuban Relief Committee of the Red Cross and the American (National) Red Cross offered supplies to the troops at the camps and in the battle zones. The Red Cross recruited about 700 nurses, one-third of the total employed by the Army. In addition, the Red Cross supplied relief to the civilian population of Cuba.

The Army Christian Commission headquarters at Camp Thomas.

Clarissa Harlowe (Clara) Barton was born in 1821 in North Oxford, Massachusetts. She became a teacher and in the1850s, she was hired as a clerk at the Bureau of United States Patents, the first woman ever to work in Washington at a government office. During the Civil War, she gained fame as a battlefield nurse and became known as "the Angel of the Battlefield." After the war she was authorized by the government to trace missing soldiers, a total of more than 22,000. In 1870, she served the wounded in the Franco-Prussian War using the symbol of the International Red Cross. On May 21, 1881, Barton founded the American Red Cross and was elected its first president. In the 1880s, she assisted people in a yellow fever outbreak in Florida, the great flood in Johnstown, Pennsylvania, and hurricane victims in South Carolina. In 1893, she went with a relief ship to Havana and lunched on the battleship *Maine* just two days before it blew up. She stayed on in Cuba to aid victims, both civilians and soldiers. In 1900, she did her last field work in the devasting Galveston, Texas, hurricane. Barton continued to serve as the Red Cross president until 1904. After leaving the Red Cross, she created the National First Aid Society, which assisted accident victims. Clara Barton died of pneumonia on April 23, 1912.

A group of Red Cross nurses, wearing the uniform of their respective school of nursing, on board the *Relief* bound for Cuba. ARC #22328

Clara Barton in a Red Cross boat in Tampa Bay. ARC

This ambulance was used at Camp Thomas and later by Clara Barton at her home in Glen Echo, Maryland. It was acquired by the American Red Cross from private owners and loaned to the Smithsonian Institution's National Museum. ARC 69-150

American Red Cross members waiting at Tampa to board the transport The *State of Texas* for Cuba. ARC

This small boat, named for Gustav Moynier, president of the International Committee of the Red Cross, helped distribute Red Cross supplies in Cuba. ARC

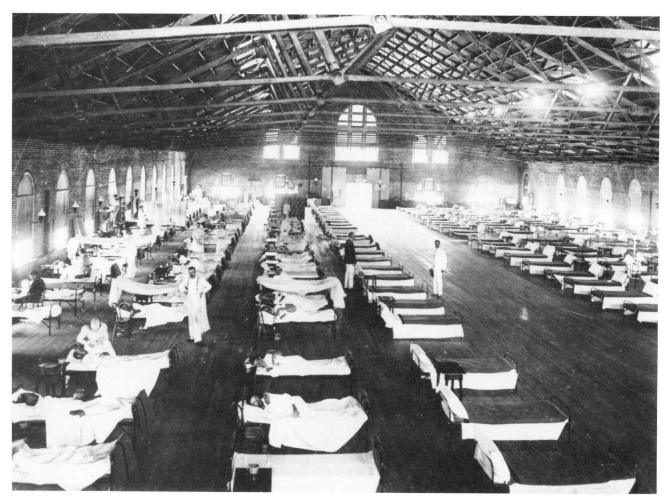

Hospital interior at Fort Meyer, Virginia. At the time of this photo, the hospital was only half full. LC

Miss Annie Wheeler, who the soldiers called "Miss Sunshine," on duty in charge of nurses at the Nautical Club Hospital in Santiago. ARC

Ambulance used in Cuba.

Charles Longden of the
1st Cavalry, 8th Army
Corps, ambulance corps.
USAMHI

This is an unusual view of
a hospital corpsman
posing with his hospital
corps knife. HOC

Wounded soldiers from the Santiago campaign in a U.S. hospital. HOC

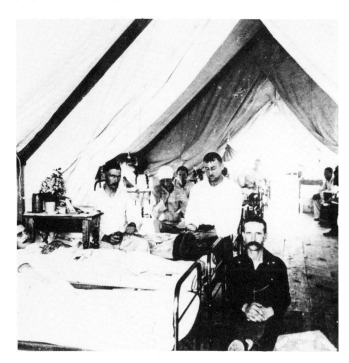

Kentucky's 1898 Ambulance Train

by Charles H. Bogart

While the Spanish American War is often viewed as a triumph of American industrial power over Spain, another side of the war is often overlooked—the failure of the U.S. Army to care for its soldier's health. It has been estimated that over 50 per cent of the deaths suffered by the army during the war were due to cholera. This deadly disease was spread by the army's failure to have kitchen and hospital workers wash their hands, accentuated by an overall failure to enforce hygiene throughout the army. Army officers at the time blamed much of the sickness in the army on malaria and yellow fever. In reality, the Army Medical Corps preferred to call cholera by any but its correct name. To admit to the wide-scale presence of cholera meant that the Medical Corps had to admit it had failed in basic preventive medicine.

As an example of the effect of disease on the army, the 6th Infantry Regiment left Fort Thomas, Kentucky in April 1898 for the battlefield with a strength of 483 men. When the regiment returned in September it had 81 men on its rolls. Of the 402 men who did not return, 135 were killed or wounded in action. The other 267 men were in hospitals due to sickness. Thus, in a six-month period over 50 per cent of the regiment was rendered ineffective due to disease.

In mustering the troops for the war the War Department concentrated them in four main areas—the Presidio of San Francisco, California; the Port of Embarkation at Tampa, Florida; Camp Thomas in Georgia, near Chattanooga, Tennessee; and Camp Alger in Virginia, outside of Washington. These mustering stations soon became cesspools of disease that almost destroyed the U.S. Army. The odds are that if the Spanish in Cuba could have survived the siege of Santiago until September, they would have won the fight. The U.S. Army had so many people sick they could not field a homogenous force for battle.

The Medical Corps, however, in a rare moment of enlightenment, did establish a dedicated hospital train to transport the sick to "hospitals" beyond the camps. These hospitals were in fact no more than empty barracks of a number of forts whose soldiers had departed for the war. The hospitals that the ambulance train was to feed were those at Fort Thomas, Kentucky, across the Ohio River from Cincinnati, Fort Monroe at Newport News, Virginia, Fort Myer at Washington, D.C., and Fort McPearson at Atlanta, Georgia.

The hospital train was placed in service on June 16, 1898. It consisted of 10 Pullman sleepers, a combine car, a private car, and a dining car. It was staffed by a surgeon, an assistant surgeon, two hospital stewards, 20 Hospital Corps privates, and three civilians. The trains's first run was from Washington to Tampa on June 17, 1898. There, on June 19, it loaded patients for Fort McPherson. This first movement of the train turned up a number of problems. The greatest was the lack of ventilation in the Pullmans. They were replaced with tourist sleepers, creating a maximum capacity of 270 patients.

Incomplete records show that the army's ambulance train made three trips to Fort Thomas. They originated at Camp Thomas at Chattanooga. The patients were transported over the Queen & Crescent Route (Cincinnati, New Orleans & Texas Pacific), which hauled them north to Cincinnati. At Cincinnati the cars were turned over to the Chesapeake & Ohio and backed to Newport, Kentucky. At the Newport station the patients were off-loaded onto streetcars of the Cincinnati, Newport & Covington Railway Company and transported the four miles to the fort by streetcar.

During the last week of July 1898, the newspapers of the nation began to fill their pages with horror stories of the conditions of the army's camps. The Medical Corps came under bitter criticism for their failure to provide basic medical service to the soldiers. At Camp Thomas, sick soldiers were found lying on the ground because there were no beds to accommodate them. Soldiers from infantry regiments detailed to work at the hospitals were shirking their duties out of fear of becoming sick themselves. An outcry against the army came from local politicians to bring the boys home where their families could care for them. Kentucky, which had provided from its militia four infantry regiments and two cavalry squadrons, was among the States calling for the return home of their sick soldiers.

The success of the Army's ambulance train led at least four states to develop their own version of an ambulance train—New York, Pennsylvania, Ohio, and Kentucky. Thus, on Sept. 1, 1898, Governor Bradley of Kentucky set in motion the organizing of two ambulance trains. Over 200 Kentucky soldiers were in hospitals at Fort Monroe and Camp Thomas. General Collins, the Adjutant General, was placed in charge of organizing the trains. With no money in his State account and the legislature not in session, the General was forced to ask for donations to hire the trains. As it would take time for the money to be collected, Col. Charles Hoge of the State National Bank in Frankfort personally guaranteed a loan from his bank so the trains could be dispatched immediately. With money in hand, General Collins signed contracts with the Queen & Crescent and Chesapeake & Ohio to transport the sick back to Kentucky. The Q&C would bring back those at Camp Thomas and the C&O those at Fort Monroe.

The C&O train departed Frankfort on Sept. 2 at 7:40 p.m. More correctly, two cars carrying the staff for the ambulance train from Fort Monroe left Frankfort behind the *Washington Express*. The C&O had already taken from Frankfort to Lexington for interchange with the Q&C the coach carrying the medical staff for Fort Thomas. With the Camp Thomas contingent went Governor Bradley and General Collins. The two cars, a sleeper and a baggage car, travelling to Fort Monroe had on board the Assistant Adjutant General, Walter Forrester, Dr. Williams of Frankfort, and 17 nurses. At Lexington, a range provided by Charles Milward was loaded into the baggage car so food could be cooked for the party and the sick.

General Forrester and his party arrived at Fort Monroe at 7:30 p.m. on Sept. 3. Upon arrival, General Forrester proceeded to the hospital, only to find it closed for the night. The next morning, when he returned to the hospital, the commanding officer had a muster list of 91 Kentuckians from the First and Third Kentucky under his care. It was, however, quickly proven that not all of these men could be transported. Some were too sick to move, and others were convalescing under friends or family care outside the hospital. The result was that only 50 men were identified as being present and capable of making the trip back to Kentucky safely. Sadly, even as they were speaking, Pvt. George Hicks, one of the Kentucky sick, died of typhoid.

At 8 p.m. on Sept. 4 the "Kentucky Relief Train," as it was now called, left Fort Monroe for Kentucky. On board were the 50 soldiers considered fit to take the ride back to Kentucky. Left behind were 40 men too sick to travel or convalescing away from the fort. As it was, six of those aboard the train were confined to bed due to their health.

The *Louisville Courier Journal* reported that, "The delicacies donated by the Louisville Board of Trade were a godsend. The delicious soups, beef extract, and other supplies were deftly prepared and generously served in place of medicant" to the soldiers. Regular meals, though, were supplied from the train's dining car.

As the train headed west it began to drop the soldiers off near their homes. First to get off was George Owsley of Farmers, Ohio, who had enlisted in the Third Kentucky. He "was taken off at Clifton Forge, Virginia, early in the day and placed in the C&O hospital, there to await the night train to Cincinnati." The next off were two at Catlettsburg, then one at Ashland, one at Salt Lick, two at Winchester, five at Lexington, one at Midway, one at Frankfort, and one at Shelbyville.

The train was taken to the Tenth Street Station in Louisville instead of the Seventh Street Depot because the majority of men were transferring to the Louisville & Nashville Railroad. It arrived at 1:35 a.m. on Sept. 6 with 35 soldiers still on board. Only one soldier who was from Louisville left the train. The remaining men stayed on board the cars at the station. Part of them left later at 2:55 a.m. on a southbound L&N train. The remaining men, travelling west, caught the L&N morning train or were taken by taxi to an Illinois Central train later in the day.

On the afternoon of the sixth it was first reported that the C&O relief train would return in a few days to Fort Monroe to pick up the other Kentucky soldiers who had been too sick to travel on the first train. This proved unnecessary because the army made sure that no significant number of "cured" Kentuckians were ever present at the hospital. This was accomplished by dispatching a party of Kentuckians discharged from the hospital over the C&O every few days. Thus, no pool of men ever developed at Fort Monroe making it worthwhile to dispatch another train from Kentucky to pick them up.

Peace returned, with the exception of the Philippine Insurrection, and there were no further ambulance trains until World War I.

A hospital tent at Camp
Tampa. USF

A field hospital showing an
apparent amputation.
USAMHI

The walking wounded in
Cuba. USAMHI

Hawaii's Annexation

The annexation of the Hawaiian Islands took place during the Spanish American War period but was only indirectly involved with the war.

In 1842 the United States, Great Britain and France recognized the Kingdom of Hawaii as an independent government. Laborers from many countries poured into Hawaii to work the sugar cane and pineapple fields. In 1887, the United States was given exclusive rights to use Pearl Harbor as a naval station.

King Kalakaua died in 1891, and his sister, Liluokalani became Queen. She was removed in 1893 by a bloodless revolution led by the powerful American planters. They received help from U.S. Marines and sailors who landed to keep the peace.

A Treaty of Annexation to the United States was signed on Feb. 14, 1893, that provided the United States would assume Hawaii's debt, pay an annuity of $20,000 to Queen Liluokalani and grant $150,000 to Princess Kaiulani, the last heir to the throne. Many of the American sugar growers opposed the annexation, however, so President Cleveland recalled the treaty from Congress and a fierce debate ensued.

The provisional government established a republic on July 4, 1894, and Sanford B. Dole, a judge, became the first and only president of the republic.

A short-lived revolution occurred in early 1895 and in May 1897, a crisis developed with Japan over the restriction of Japanese emigration to the islands. It was rumored that Japan wanted to take over the islands which sharpened the annexation issue.

Dole went to Washington, D.C. in January 1898 to plead for annexation. The outbreak of war on April 25 created a furor of expansionist sentiment and influenced American public opinion in favor of annexing Hawaii to the United States. Hawaii's

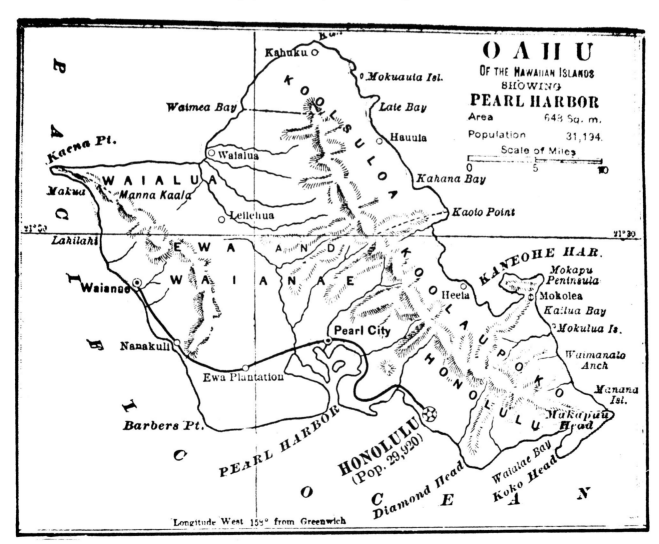

Commercial

Advertiser.

Established July 6, 1856.

VOL. XXVIII, NO. 4571.   HONOLULU, HAWAIIAN ISLANDS, THURSDAY, JULY 14, 1898.   **PRICE FIVE CENTS.**

ANNEXATION!

"HERE TO STAY!"

And the star-spangled banner
In triumph shall wave,
O'er the Isles of Hawaii
And the homes of the brave.

— H. M. WHITNEY.

FIRST NEWS.

HONOLULU, H. I., U. S. A., July 13, 1898, 3:30 p. m.—The Pacific Mail S.S. Coptic signals from off Waikiki that these islands have been annexed to the United States by the passage in the Senate at Washington of the House Joint Resolution.

Flags are being hoisted everywhere.

Thousands flocked to the water front.

There are great crowds on the streets evidencing the very delirium of joy.

At 4:15 a salute of 100 guns was fired.

At 4:20 all the whistles were sounding.

VOTE AT WASHINGTON.

WASHINGTON, July 6.—With a rush, without the change of a word, the resolutions which make Hawaii a part of the United States were passed by the Senate this afternoon. From out of a situation which gave no promise of ending for weeks, perhaps, and at a time when those who have had charge of the filibuster against the measure had been assuring every one that they could not see a vote for a week, there came a demand for a roll call on the first amendment of the list of eight which had to be disposed of before the main question could be considered. Senator White almost surprised himself when he shut off debate, ended the filibuster which has prevented the acceptance of the Hawaiian resolution and gave the majority of the Senate a chance to express its will.

An agreement was reached partly last night and partly this morning, but has been in sight for several days. The Republican leaders had been hard at work for two days in their endeavor to blockade the windward passage of the anti-annexation filibuster. They succeeded when they showed the utter inability of the Democrats to keep up their performance sufficiently long to have any effect whatever. Not more than 22 votes against the resolution could be counted by the most sanguine, while the annexationists' forty-five was still intact.

So it was that, ungraciously enough, the obstructionists stepped out of the way and the will of the people, expressed in the vote of their representatives by 42 to 21, declared that Hawaii must be a part of the Union of States. But one Republican vote was cast against the measure. The venerable Justin Morrill voted no. Spooner and Thurston were paired against the resolution. From the Democratic side came six full round "ayes." Gorman headed the list, and following his lead were Morgan, McLaurin, Pettus and Sullivan. The other men were somewhat split, Pettigrew and Jones of Nevada joining with the Democrats, while the others were on the Republican side.

When the Vice-President announced the vote and the fact that the two-thirds, which would have been necessary to ratify a treaty, was indicated, there was applause from floor and gallery. From staid Senators in their seats and Congressmen collected in numbers about the walls of the chamber occupying vacant seats came cheers which found echo in half-filled galleries above and which, strangely enough, the Vice-President made no effort to check.

It is believed that the President will receive and sign the measure tomorrow and that he will at once transmit the message containing the resolution and setting forth the action which is expected of the Republic of Hawaii to President Dole

and the Congress of the Islands. It is believed that this will be done by a special messenger, probably John W. Foster, former secretary of State, and that the cruiser Philadelphia will carry the messenger to the Islands.

Immediately upon the passage by the Hawaiian Congress of an act which makes effective the Newlands resolution the commissioner will raise the American flag and the Philadelphia will salute it.

It is believed that the commission which will be sent to the islands to frame the laws for their future government will be made up of either W. O. Smith or W. A. Kinney of Honolulu and John Richardson of Maui, M. M. Estee of California, N. W. McIvor, former Consul-General to Japan, now of Cedar Rapids, Ia. The fifth member will come either from Minnesota or Massachusetts. The commission probably will be appointed at once. It is believed the President will appoint all incumbent officers to administer the islands' affairs until new laws are passed.

The laws under which the officials will operate, it is understood, will be those now in force, and nothing will be done to change the routine of procedure in the various departments until the commission reports an entirely new code and form of government.

It is deemed very probable that a regiment of infantry and two batteries of heavy artillery, with such guns as may be available at San Francisco, will be sent to the islands at an early date.

DR. JOHN S. McGREW.
"Father of Annexation."
(Photo by WEDeas.)

treaty which has never been ratified, but is now pending in the Senate of the United States."

The details of the voting was as follows: White offered an amendment striking from the preamble of the Hawaiian resolutions the words "in due form" and inserting the words "by a"

After a statement by Hale in which he said he supported the resolution, but not as a war measure, a vote was taken on White's amendment. It was rejected—46 to 26.

Pettigrew then offered his amendment to repeal the contract labor laws now in force on the Hawaiian Islands. It was rejected—41 to 22.

Bacon of Georgia offered an amendment providing that the annexation resolutions should not be operative until they had been approved by a majority of the electors of Hawaii. Defeated—20 to 42.

Faulkner of West Virginia offered an amendment providing that the duties of the civil, judicial and military powers shall be exercised under authority of existing laws not in conflict with the Constitution and laws of the United States. Rejected—20 to 42.

Allen offered an amendment placing an internal revenue tax of 1 cent a pound on Hawaiian sugar. It was defeated, 57 to 4, the four voting for the amendment being Allen Morrill, McEnery and Pettigrew.

Pettigrew offered an amendment that all native-born male Hawaiians over 21 years of age and all naturalized aliens shall be allowed to vote in the

(Continued on Third Page.)

CERVERA'S FLEET IS ANNIHILATED

Attempted to Run the Blockade at Santiago.
He Is a Prisoner---Heavy Losses.

CERVERA'S FLEET WIPED OUT.

WASHINGTON, JULY 4.—The following bulletin from Commodore Watson was received tonight:

PLAYA DEL ESTE, July 3.—To the Secretary of the Navy:

COMMANDER W. S. SCHLEY.
Commodore Winfield Scott Schley first attracted the attention of the world in 1884, when he was put in command of the expedition sent to the Arctic for the relief of the Greely expedition party. He also had a part in the Chilean trouble in 1892, as commander of the Baltimore.

At 9:30 a. m. today the Spanish squadron, seven in all, including one gunboat, came out of Santiago harbor in columns and was totally destroyed within an hour, excepting the Cristobal Colon, which was chased forty-five miles to the westward by the commander-in-chief, the Brooklyn, the Oregon, and the Texas, surrendering to the Brooklyn, but was beached to prevent sinking.

None of our officers or men were injured except on board the Brooklyn. Chief Yeoman Ellis was killed and one man wounded.

Admiral Cervera, all the commanding officers, excepting of the Oquendo, about 70 other officers and 1600 men are prisoners. About 350 were killed or drowned and 160 wounded. The latter are cared for on the Solace and the Olivette.

WATSON.

HOW IT WAS DONE.

WASHINGTON, July 4.—There seems to be no doubt that the Cristobal Colon, and, perhaps, the other three Spanish armored cruisers, would have escaped had it not been for the prompt action of Commodore Schley. The Brooklyn, his flag-

THE ARMORED CRUISER BROOKLYN.

ship, alone was in a position to attack the Spanish vessels as they left the harbor, and the Commodore steamed directly

(Continued on Page 2.)

strategic importance was realized with thousands of American troops stopping off on their way to the Philippines.

The House of Representatives resolved in favor of annexation on June 15, 1898, by a large majority, 209-91. On July 6, the Senate passed the joint resolution by 42 to 21. President McKinley signed it on July 7 saying, "Annexation is not change; it is consummation." On Aug. 12, 1898, with many sailors from American ships and soldiers on the way to the Philippines in attendance, the formal ceremony of annexation took place at the Iolani Palace in Honolulu.

The islands became a U.S. territory on June 14, 1900, and the 50th state on Aug. 21, 1959.

In front of a large Hawaiian-American flag rosette, and red, white and blue bunting studded with gold stars, Chief Justice Herbert F. Judd administered the oath of allegiance to a bareheaded, white-bearded President of the Hawaiian Republic, Sanford Ballard Dole. The time was shortly before noon on Aug. 12, 1898, at the makai entrance to the former Iolani Palace of the monarchy, and after members of Dole's cabinet had been sworn in and the ceremony concluded, government officials, the National Guard and police adjourned to the parade grounds and took the same oath of allegiance to the United States. In this brief but impressive ceremony at Iolani the sovereignty of the Republic of Hawaii was transferred to the United States. Distinguished participants and guests included the Hon. Lorrin A. Thurston, Samuel Mills Damon, Capt. James A. King, H.E. Cooper, William Owen Smith, Dr. John S. McGrew, P.C. Jones, William R. Castle, Charles L. Carter, Captains Wadleigh and Book from the USS Philadelphia and USS Mohican, Minister Harold M. Sewall, Chief Justice Herbert F. Judd, the Reverend Pearson and President Sanford Ballard Dole. One reporter obviously unsympathetic toward annexation reported: "Mr. Cooper and other notables were stiff and attentive in new bell toppers, apparently purchased to catch the gentle dews from Heaven, and Parson Pearson was inspired with an unconscionably long prayer. Mr. Sewall was making a fervid oration, but accommodations for the press were so execrable that we declined to immortalize his utterances. Nearly every store in town was closed, a few ships dressed, and much powder burned."

1st New York Volunteer Infantry Regiment in the mess line at Camp McKinley. USAMHI #1838

Troops and band at Camp McKinley. USAMHI #0126

Camp McKinley

The first U.S. Army troops to be stationed in Hawaii arrived on Aug. 16, 1898. The 1st New York Volunteer Infantry Regiment and the 3rd Battalion, 2nd Volunteer Engineers established Camp McKinley in what is now Kapiolani Park on the southeast end of the Waikiki area. The first regular army troops to be stationed at the camp were four batteries of the 6th Artillery Regiment in April 1899. Two batteries remained and were redesignated the 66th and 67th companies of the Coast Artillery Corps (1901). Camp McKinley remained as army headquarters for Hawaii until Fort Shafter was opened in June 1907.

Christmas - 1898

So hallowed and so gracious is the time.—*Hamlet*.

"K" 2, U. S. V. ENGRS.

- - - MESS OF - - -

Co. K, 3rd Battalion, 2nd Regiment

.... U. S. VOLUNTEER ENGINEERS ....

Is all our company here?—*Midsummer Night's Dream*.

McKINLEY BARRACKS, HONOLULU, H. I.

We must go... from here.
On the other side... we're overdue.—*Kipling*.

Camp McKinley looking
towards the Waianae
Range. USAMHI #2122

Camp McKinley. HA

THE WEEKLY

News  Muster

Vol. 1]   CAMP McKINLEY, HONOLULU, H. I., SATURDAY, SEPT. 24, 1898.   [No. 1

J. H. Barber
Br. Cmdg.

First Regt. Infty., N. Y. V.

* COURTESY OF THE U.S. ARMY MUSEUM HAWAII

CAMP BLACK.

NUMBER ONE of a Series of Historical Sketches of the First Regiment of N. Y. Volunteers.

On the first day of last May while the separate companies were in their armories eagerly preparing to depart for the mustering field, there was hardly a man in any company who supposed that scarcely twenty-four hours would elapse before he would regret the fact that he had ever volunteered. Yet at nine o'clock at night on the second of May, I dare say there were at least a hundred weary, hungry, rain-soaked fellows who, as they rolled up in their damp blankets and prepared to lie down to sleep on the mud of Hempstead plains, heartily wished themselves back home again. Of course they had expected to encounter some hardships when they enlisted; but the baptism of mud and rain coming so soon, went a little beyond their expectations. The picture of a weary soldier lying down to rest in the mud and gore of a battlefield has a pleasing halo of glory around it; but it is

GUARD DUTY.
A Memory of Camp Black.

altogether different when there is all the mud and none of the glory in the picture. We learned this lesson thoroughly on the first night of our stay in Camp Black.

However, this first night on the camp field was by no means the worst. During our entire stay on Hempstead plains the weather makers seemed to be in league with Spain and tried their best schemes to discourage and drown the patriotism of the unfledged troops. All varieties of the worst possible weather was served to them. It rained most of the time and when there was no water left in the sky for a shower, a cold wind was produced to fill in the interval. Once in a while the sun would show just enough of his face to tantalize us, then he would retire behind a larger shower than ever.

The seventh and eighth days of May was about the severest weather we ever had. Hail, rain and wind were all served in a bunch. Tents were blown over; water stood on the ground on which we had to sleep

in pools six inches deep; fires could not be built the soaked wood, hence food could not be cook hunger was added to our troubles. A chain was kept around the camps. Everybody took and the patriotism was almost frozen out of us.

Under these adverse conditions, it is not at al prising that some of the men were glad to be rej by the physical examinations which took place May tenth to the fourteenth. I presume there we few who even "faked" sickness in order to get a jection was a severe blow; men who had eagerly g ed this first chance to fight for their country, who not at all discouraged by the ills of Camp Black. they all had to return home, willing and unwil together. However, there were thousands of oth waiting to take the places of those who were s home. Five days after, the fourteen or fifteen n from each company who were rejected had returr home, recruits were in their places and every comp was ready to join the United States army.

The mustering in ceremony took place on M twentieth. If our arrival at Camp Black was unpr pitious, our entrance into United States service wa not, a warmer more beautiful day could not have bee selected. The entire regiment was marched out on th parade ground about ten o'clock in the forenoon There we lay and sunned ourselves for four hour waiting for the mustering officers. Some of the fel lows might have starved during this time had not an accommodating pie-man with a well-stocked wago come up to the lines. I think most every man in th regiment got a pie although I am not so sure that the pie-man got his nickle for every pie.

After we were U. S. soldiers our life at Camp Black was merely a case of watching and waiting for orders. This was the starting point for the numerous news bulletins which have flooded camp ever since. Dozens of times we expected to start for the front in a few days; but each time we were disappointed until about the tenth of June when the report came that our regiment was to be reserved as a guard in the forts around New York harbor. This rumor culminated in real orders and thus our first regular service began in a way we had never before dreamed of.

PRIZE CONTEST.

Wishing to secure some views to illustrate our paper the editor offers the following prizes for the best collection of photographs taken by members of the regiment.

I.—A prize of one dollar for the four best views of Camp Black.

II.—A prize of one dollar for the four best views of any garrison in which troops from our regiment have been stationed.

III.—A prize of one dollar for the four best views of our trip across the continent.

IV.—A prize of one dollar for the four best views of our camp and vicinity at San Francisco.

V.—A prize of one dollar for the four best views or our trip across the Pacific.

VI.—A prize of one dollar for the four best views of Honolulu.

The conditions of the contest are as follows: Any member of the First New York may compete. The pictures are to be handed to the editor before the last day of October at which date the prizes will be paid in cash. The pictures may be handed in either mounted or unmounted and the ones taking prizes are to remain in possession of the paper, all the rest to be returned to their owners in as good condition as they were presented.

There are more than a hundred kodaks owned by members of the regiment, so we trust this will be an interesting competition. The pictures will be exhibited at the Y. M. C. A. headquarters building.

THE WEEKLY
News Muster

Vol. I]   CAMP McKINLEY, HONOLULU, H. I., SATURDAY, NOV. 12, 1898.   [No. 8

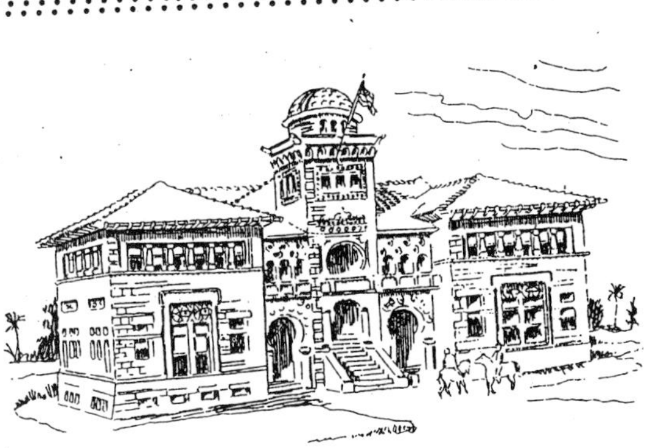

PAUAHI HALL OF OAHU COLLEGE.

A descriptive article of Oahu College was printed in the News Muster last week.

The Weekly News Muster.

HERBERT HUNGERFORD, } Editors.
CHAS. W. FETHEROLF, }

Published Weekly at Camp McKinley, in the interests of the First Regiment of Infantry, New York Volunteers.

Price 5 cents per copy.

BATTALION MANAGERS.

1st Battalion, Corporal E. M. Decker, Co. I.
2nd Battalion, Corporal J. Roy Wilbur, Co. H.
3rd Battalion, Private Charles F. Donnelly, Co. B.
Engineer Battalion, William H. C. Drake, Co. K, 2d, U. S. V., Eng.

HONOLULU AGENTS.

Golden Rule Bazaar, Hawaiian News Co., Wall, Nichols & Co.

THE BLUFFER.

In almost every company of soldiers there is at least one fellow who makes life unendurable to his comrades by his phenomenal gift of "gab." This man always heralds his approach by his loud bluffing voice. He thinks his comrades regard him as manly because he assumes the air of a swager and can be more profane than his fellows. Before the unassuming men of the company; the men who hold the respect of the men, he blows and puffs about and is so silly as to think the quiet fellows believe him a demon.

This bluffer calls his fellows vile names, lays rough hands on them and seems to make a special study of the art of appearing a big rough fellow.

Inwardly he is a coward. Once in a while he will offend one of the quiet fellows who knows when patience ceases to be a virtue. Then the quiet fellow shows some roughness that is not shammed. The faker collapses. In an instant he is a baby. The big puffed balloon of make-believe manhood flattens down and the veriest fool in the company sees the blusterer as he really is,—a big hulk of flesh and bones that never had any manhood to be lost.

Rid us of the camp bluffer, with his vile tongue, his disgusting display of fake manhood and babyish traits. He is the most pusillanimous object in the army. He is never a good soldier and he is an object of pity to everyone.

NOT ENOUGH MILK.

The Hawaiian Islands Can Not Supply Enough Milk for Sick Soldiers at the Hospital.

This is a note of warning to such Americans as, attracted by misleading and false statements made in [???] to allure people to the Hawaiian Islands, may [???] of coming here to live.

The seral score sick men at the hospital are dis-[???]ssed for the want of fresh milk. It appears from [???]tements in the Honolulu papers that the Islands can supply enough milk for the additional demand. In [???] cases of typhoid fever fresh milk is a necessity and hospital is greatly handicapped in efficient treat-[???] of the disease.

[???]at think ye New Yorkers of this? In the accounts [???]ks that are read widely the people are made to [???] that the Hawaiian Islands yield up an opulent [???]sily gained livelihood. The fact of the matter

[???] a Soldier needs, can be [???]ed at the Lowest City Prices at

is that the Islands yield up a scant food supply. S[???] fruit as is imported to New York State and plac[???] within the reach of all, is here dwarfed and not all[???] ing to the palate.

What would the New Yorker think of paying fi[???] cents for a poor orange; ten cents for three rott[???] apples, and corresponding high prices for lemon[???] pears and grapes. None of the fruit just mention[???] grows on these Islands.

If he left his native state for Hawaii he would b[???] in the land of wretched restaurants and imported eat[???] ables. In his home by the Mohawk he reached to th[???] branch above his door for a mellow fall pippin, or [???] saunter about the orchard brought him face to fac[???] with "rustics," pound sweets, etc. Fine luscious grapes, if he had no vineyard of his own, were had for a song. Peaches were delivered to his kitchen for a farthing. At the village grocer's crates of raspberries, blackberries, currants, and what not littered the sidewalk.

All these the veriest pauper might enjoy. The laborers there get $1.25 a day. On these he had buckwheat pancakes, maple syrup, pumpkin pie, bread, butter, milk, and in fact good substantial food in fine variety. On holidays he had his turkey, cranberry sauce, ice cream and the likes of that.

Now here in these beautiful Hawaiian Islands the white laborer is placed in direct competition with hordes of Chinese and Japanese contract laborers, who work for about $10 a month. On this they feed themselves. The white laborers who gets such wages must pay about double the price for food fit to eat than he would be asked in the United States.

To be sure they have a beautiful climate here. The temperature is about the same always. New Yorkers, however, are not used to living on temperature and fine atmosphere, and therefore, we believe, will not take kindly to the Hawaiian Islands.

The First Tennessee Regiment en route to Manila, arrived at Honolulu early this week. Soon after setting foot on the Islands they proved themselves the same blustering cowards that they were at the Presidio. Men who will flock in hundreds to do bodily injury to a single defenseless man, as these Tennesseans did at the Presidio, lack every instinct of manhood. It is men of their stripe who uphold Judge Lynch. Their chief complaint against the New Yorker, against whom they made some babyish demonstrations in California, was that the Empire State men wore white collars, blacked their shoes and kept clean.

The New York soldiers never picked a fight with any other soldiers, but in every instance where they were insulted by the Tennessee soldiers our men upheld our dignity in fine style.

THANKSGIVING IN A FOREIGN LAND.

President McKinley Issues the Proclamation Setting Aside November 24th as the Time for a National Display of Gratitude.

WASHINGTON, Oct. 28.—The President, after the Cabinet meeting today, issued the following Thanksgiving proclamation:

BY THE PRESIDENT OF THE UNITED STATES.
A PROCLAMATION:

The approaching November brings to mind the custom of our ancestors, hallowed by time and rooted in our most sacred traditions of giving thanks to Almighty God for all blessings he has vouchsafed to us during the past year.

Few years in our history have afforded such cause for thanksgiving as this. We have been blessed by abundant harvests, our trade and commerce have been

THE ASSEMBLY.
A Gathering of Condensed News Items.

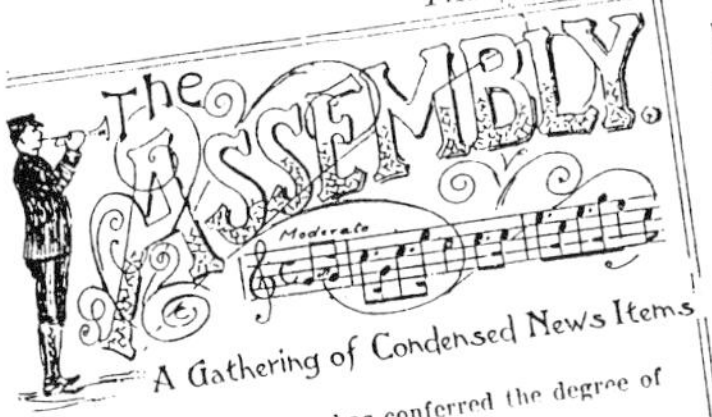

—The Chicago University has conferred the degree of LL.D. upon President McKinley.

—The first detachments of the American Army of occupation for Cuba has probably landed on the island within the past few days.

—Unless there are further complications in the Philippines it is likely that there will be no more military expeditions to those islands from the United States.

—It is generally believed that Spain will not return to hostilities but will abide by the demands of the United States commissioners.

—A war between England and France over Fashoda now seems inevitable.

—Philadelphia has had a big peace jubilee and a peace cross has been unveiled at Washington.

—Advices of October 28 from Paris give a very hopeful account of the progress of the Peace Commission. One of the Parisian papers believed at that date that the commission might conclude its labors within four or five days.

—The Emperor of China is reported critically ill.

—Temporary recruiting stations are being established in the larger cities of the United States and it is hoped by this means to raise the regular army to such strength that there will be regular soldiers to relieve the volunteers doing garrison duty at Honolulu and other places.

—California is to have a good National Guard so far as the physical qualifications of its members is concerned. All applicants for membership must submit to as rigid an examination as do applicants for enlistment in the United States army.

CAMP NOTES.

—It is a dreary, deserted appearance that Camp McKinley has now-a-days. The tents are gone, the pendygrabbing soda water stands and stores that flocked about the camp to rob the soldier of his scant wages by their exhorbitant prices are gone. No one is surprised to hear that the place was not a success as an ostrich farm. It would have taken a tough ostrich indeed that could have lived in such a place.

—The scroping of kukui nuts and the engraving of designs on the polished surfaces continues to be the chief occupation of the men while off duty.

—There is a pronounced superfluity of mongrel canines about the camp of the regiment. These dogs do no particular harm except to make the night hideous once in a while with their nocturnal carnivals.

—The voting for New York State gubernatorial candidates on Tuesday furnished a little diversion. There were disciples of "Teddy" and the upholders of Van Wyck were in evidence. Who has won? That is the question the men are waiting to have answered.

—The other evening while wading on the coral reefs in the sea, hard by the convalescent camp an Engineer was nearly scared to death when a devil fish caught hold of his leg and Private Duren, [???] ject was captured by Sergeant Cary and Private Duren. The hideous looking obfilled with alcohol. "H." Now the devil fish is soaking in a quart fruit can

—Camp Otis is a thing of the past. The troops that

peopled it are now sweltering on the transport Arizona as she ploughs the blue sea toward the Philippines.

—Sergt. "Pete" Powell, "H" has been made acting first sergeant of the rough riders.

—The departure of the Camp Otis troops made about a dozen vacancies among the rough riders. These vacancies have been filled by detail from the First New York regiment.

THE CONVALESCENTS' CAMP.

It is a Great improvement Over Camp McKinley—No Dust—Pure Air—The Men are Much More Contented.

The convalescent's camp at Waialae (the Isenberg plantation) has become the camp of the First New York regiment. Tuesday of this week found all the companies of the regiment excepting "B," "D," "K" and "M" located there. The later two companies left Tuesday for a trip to Hawaii Island. This left the first two companies as headquarters guard. By the time this issue of the Muster is out the headquarters of the regiment may have been removed to the convalescent camp.

Since coming to the convalescent camp there has been an improvement in the health of the men.

This result could not help but follow, for the superiority of the new site over that of Camp McKinley is very pronounced.

The wind which strikes the camp is invariably from the ocean and the air consequently is as pure as can be found anywhere. Then too every sanitary precaution has been taken to protect the health of the men. The sinks are so located that their odors instead of being blown into the camp are wafted away. Again there is practically no dust. In this respect the new camp is a paradise compared with all the camps of the regiment since leaving the East.

As the result of improved conditions there appears to be much less dissatisfaction. The men will look with much more complacency upon a long period of tedious garrison duty in such a camp than they will in such places as Camp McKinley.

There is perhaps one superiority in the location of Camp McKinley—its nearness to bathing facilities. But then the San Souci bathing shanties for the use of which the soldiers paid $500 a month were so wretchly filthy that they were a menace to the health of the men.

VOLUNTEERS FOR REGULARS.

The United States is desirous to Have the Volunteer Soldiers Go Into the Regular Army.

The following are some of the inducements held out for the volunteers to enter the regular army:

Volunteers who enlist in the regular army will be credited with service in the volunteer army and enlistment papers so endorsed. Enlistment in the regular army will be for three years from the date of such enlistment, without condition regarding discharge, and will be preceded by the usual medical examination at the recruiting station. Examination forms and figure cards will be prepared and disposed of, in accordance with the instructions governing other enlistments in the regular army.

Soldiers of the volunteers, ordered to be mustered out, who desire to enlist in the regular army without availing themselves of furloughs, may be subjected to the usual examinations at the recruiting station, and if they meet all requirements, be discharged from the volunteers to enable them to enlist in the regular army, upon application. It is required that applicants shall be unmarried, strong, well proportioned, and between the ages of twenty-one and thirty.

Tents at Camp McKinley,
1898. HA

1st Infantry Hawaii
National Guard, 1898. HA

California National Guard
troops on the 13-knot
steamer, *Australia*, at the
Oceanic Wharf in
Honolulu, June 4, 1898.
They would be the first
American troops to see
action in the Philippines.
The *Australia* was in
convoy with the *City of
Peking, City of Sidney* and
the *USS Charleston*. HA

Camp McKinley Today

Today the Camp McKinley site is partially occupied by the Honolulu Zoo, founded in 1914, and Kapiolani Park at the southeast end of the Waikiki area and at the foot of Diamond Head Crater.

Officers of the Hawaii
National Guard at the
Iolani Palace in Honolulu.
HA

Troops of the 1st Colorado
Regiment lined up in front
with Hawaii National
Guard troops behind them
on the grounds of the
Iolani Palace, June 28,
1898. The Queen's tower
(now the Administration
Building) is in the back-
ground. DPL #10431

Unidentified troops at the
Palace. HA

Sailors and marines from the *USS Philadelphia* at the Honolulu dock assembling for the formal transfer ceremony, Aug. 12, 1898. HA

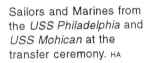

Sailors and Marines from the *USS Philadelphia* and *USS Mohican* at the transfer ceremony. HA

The center flag on the Iolani Palace was 36 feet tall, the largest in use by the U.S. Navy. At noon on Aug. 12, the flag was hoisted to the top of the building. On a signal from Admiral Miller, the band from the *USS Philadelphia* struck up the *Star Spangled Banner* while smaller flags were run up on the corner tower standards. A second double 21-gun salute sounded from shore and harbor batteries. HA

The Hawaiian flag is lowered while the Hawaiian Band plays "Hawaii Ponoi." HA

Officers of the First Montana Regiment being introduced to President Dole and his wife. MHS #358.001.008

President Dole (with white beard) receives a certified copy of the joint resolution ceding the sovereignty of the Republic of Hawaii to the United States from Minister Sewall in front of the Iolani Palace. HA

The Capture of Guam

The First Expedition to the Philippines left San Francisco on May 25, 1898. The three transports *Australia, City of Sidney* and *City of Peking* had 2,544 troop on board. The cruiser *Charleston* had preceded the expedition to Honolulu and would accompany the transport ships to Manila.

On June 15, the ships left Honolulu. Captain Glass of the cruiser opened his sealed orders and signaled Brig. Gen. Thomas M. Anderson on the *Australia*: "My instructions require me to capture the Spanish forts and vessels at the Island of Guam, en route to Manila. The transports will accompany this ship as only two or three days' delay will occur. This may be made public."

Guam is the largest of the dozen Marianas Islands. The capitol of the Islands is Agana. In 1668 the islands were named in honor of Maria Ana of Austria, the widow of Philip IV of Spain. In 1898 the population of the island group was estimated to be 27,000. The harbor of Apra was appropriate for a naval coaling station and Guam was on a direct line between Honolulu and Manila, so it was a desirable piece of territory to secure for the U.S. Navy.

The expedition arrived off Guam on June 20 without any idea of the strength of the Spanish garrison or its fortifications. There were two forts, St. Iago and Santa Cruz, and the ruins of the old fort San Luis.

The *Charleston* left the convoy and proceeded with the attack. She passed St. Iago in silence and stationed herself opposite Santa Cruz. She then lobbed 13 shells against the fort with no response.

The battle lasted four and a half minutes. By this time the Spanish settlement was aroused, and the captain of the port came aboard the *Charleston* and said he had recognized the salute but could not answer as he had no battery, but would try in the future to have one so salutations could be answered.

The Spanish had not heard of the declaration of war. Upon learning of this, they tried to parley for delay but were immediately taken as prisoners of war.

The garrison, if you could call it that, consisted of 108 men, 54 Spanish soldiers and the rest native Chamorros. The Spanish soldiers along with the Spanish governor and his staff were taken aboard the *Charleston* and proceeded to Manila.

The other main islands of the Marianas group were taken over by the German government and again by the Japanese after World War One. Except for a three-year occupation by the Japanese in World War Two, Guam has been a territory of the United States. The rest of the group, the former Japanese mandate, is now an independent country.

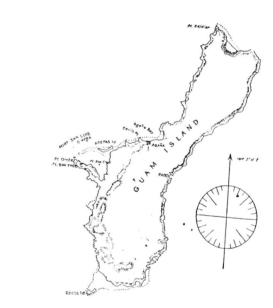

GUAM ISLAND.

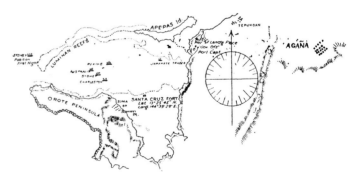

DISPOSITION OF AMERICAN FLEET AT THE SURRENDER OF GUAM.

THE CAPTURE OF GUAM.

THE BELL IN OLD TOWER AT SUMAI.

COLONEL OWEN SUMMERS, SECOND REGIMENT, OREGON VOLUNTEERS, COMMANDING THE REGIMENT FROM WHICH THE LANDING PARTY AT GUAM WAS SELECTED.

CAPTAIN A. L. HEATH, OF THE SECOND OREGON VOLUNTEERS, WHO COMMANDED THE FIRST SECTION OF THE LANDING PARTY AT GUAM.

CAPTAIN AUSTIN F. PRESCOTT, COMPANY D, SECOND OREGON VOLUNTEERS, IN COMMAND OF SECOND SECTION OF LANDING PARTY.

INTERIOR OF FORT SANTA CRUZ AT GUAM.

GUAM, OUR NEW NAVAL STATION IN THE PACIFIC.

THE VALUABLE LITTLE ISLAND WHICH SPAIN CEDES TO THE UNITED STATES UNDER THE NEW TREATY

There had been no provision for the takeover of Guam. Captain Glass selected Don Francisco Portasach, a local American citizen to be interim governor until an official governor arrived. It would take a year to get a permanent governor to the island. The U.S. Navy took responsibility for the island to use it as a coaling station. Capt. Richard P. Leary became the first permanent governor and also commander of the newly established Naval Station on Aug. 7, 1899.

Raising "Old Glory" at Fort Santa Cruz in the Harbor of San Luis d' Apra, Ladrone Islands.

Landing party under Gen. F.V. Greene which hoisted the American flag on Wake Island on July 4, 1898. On the way to the Philippines, the steamship *China*, of the Second Philippine Expedition, stopped at the remote island of Wake, approximately halfway between Midway Island and Guam, to reclaim it for the United States. It had first been claimed by Commodore Charles Wilkes in 1840. In 1935 Pan American Airways established a base on Wake Island (one of the three islands of the atoll) for their China Clipper planes and in December 1941 the Japanese captured the island after a fierce 16-day battle.

USS Charleston

The second ship named *Charleston* (C-2), a protected cruiser, was launched in 1888 by Union Iron Works in San Francisco and commissioned in 1889.

In 1890 she joined the Pacific Squadron as its flagship. She carried the remains of King Kalakaua of Hawaii to Honolulu after his death abroad. She operated in the Pacific until 1892 then sailed in the Atlantic and along the east coast of South America. She returned to the Pacific in 1894 and was placed out of commission on July 27, 1896.

Upon the outbreak of the Spanish American War she was quickly made ready for service and recommissioned on May 5, 1898. She sailed for Honolulu and then captured the island of Guam while protecting army transports on the way to the Philippines.

She arrived in Manila on June 30, 1898, to reinforce Dewey's fleet and joined in the final bombardment on Aug. 13 which brought about the surrender of Manila. She remained in the Philippines through 1898 and 1899, bombarding insurgent positions to aid Army forces advancing ashore. She took part in the naval expedition in September 1899 to capture Subic Bay.

On Nov. 2, 1899, the *Charleston* grounded on an uncharted reef near Camiguin Island, north of Luzon. Wrecked beyond salvage, she was abandoned by her crew, who made camp on a nearby island. The crew later moved to Camiguin while the ship's sailing launch was sent for help. On Nov. 12, the *Helena* arrived to rescue the remaining crewmen.

Capt. Henry Glass of the *USS Charleston*. MNG

The "Charleston" at Sea.

Welcome Home

Camp Wikoff

The fighting in Cuba was over but a new enemy soon emerged—sickness in the form of yellow fever, or Yellow Jack, and malaria. What the Spanish bullets couldn't do the sickness could—debilitate the army.

On July 31, Roosevelt spoke to a friend: "At present I am ardently longing to be out of here before fever knocks us out. I would rather go to Porto [sic] Rico; if not that, then to the north."

The situation was getting desperate with over 3,000 cases of fever in the army by late July. General Shafter petitioned Washington to return his army to the United States but some authorities were reluctant to bring a diseased army home and others thought the army should stay to protect the defeated Spaniards from the Cubans. Meanwhile Roosevelt, with the knowledge of Shafter, wrote a letter to the general stating that the army was facing a disaster and must leave Cuba as soon as possible. The letter was purposely leaked to the press and appeared in American newspapers just as the U.S. government was negotiating a peace with Spain. The War Department finally had no choice but to bring the army home.

A site at the tip of Long Island, 125 miles east of New York City at Montauk Point was selected. It was an isolated site but on the railroad to the city, a perfect place to quarantine an army. It was named Camp Wikoff for Col. Charles A. Wikoff of the 22nd Infantry, who was killed in the Santiago campaign.

> Charles Wikoff was born and raised in Easton, Pennsylvania. He enlisted as a private in Co. H, 1st Pennsylvania Infantry during the Civil War, became a lieutenant and then in 1864, was promoted to captain. He fought at Shiloh, Chickamauga and Missionary Ridge. Joining the 14th Infantry he became a major in 1886 and lieutenant colonel of the 19th in 1891. He was made colonel of the 22nd in 1897. Colonel Wikoff lost an eye in the Civil War.

Two camps were set up. A small camp for new arrivals to spend a five-day detention and a large general camp. Maj. Gen. S.B.M. Young was in command of the camp before Gen. Joe Wheeler was put in charge. Camp Wikoff eventually housed about 22,000 troops. Of this number about 250 died during the detention period.

The camp was apparently closed in the Fall of 1898 and all the troops were sent home or to other hospitals.

Dock and railroad facilities at Camp Wikoff. USAMHI

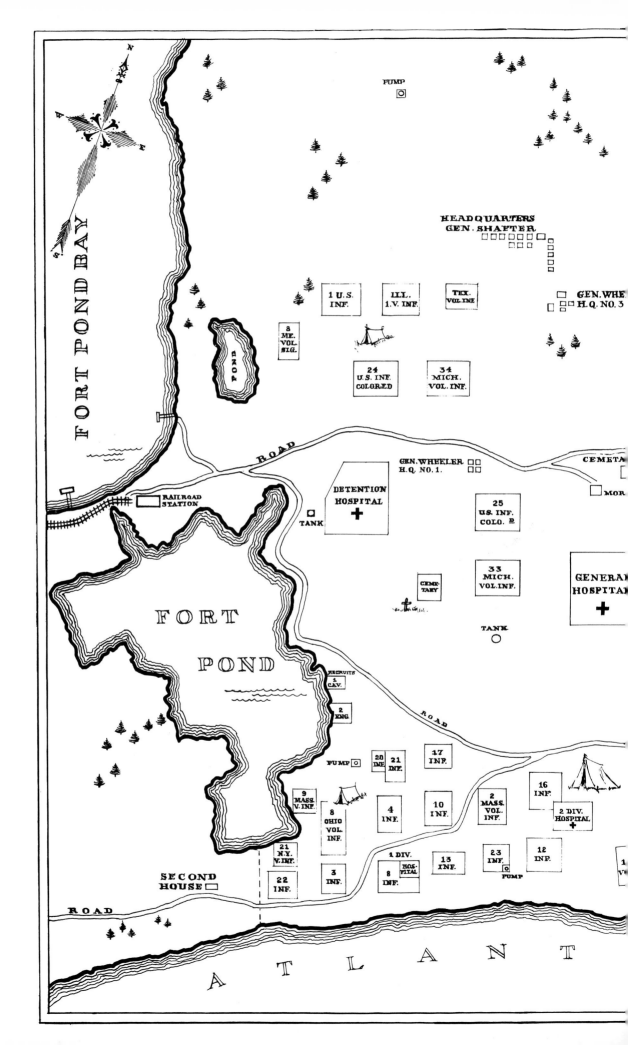

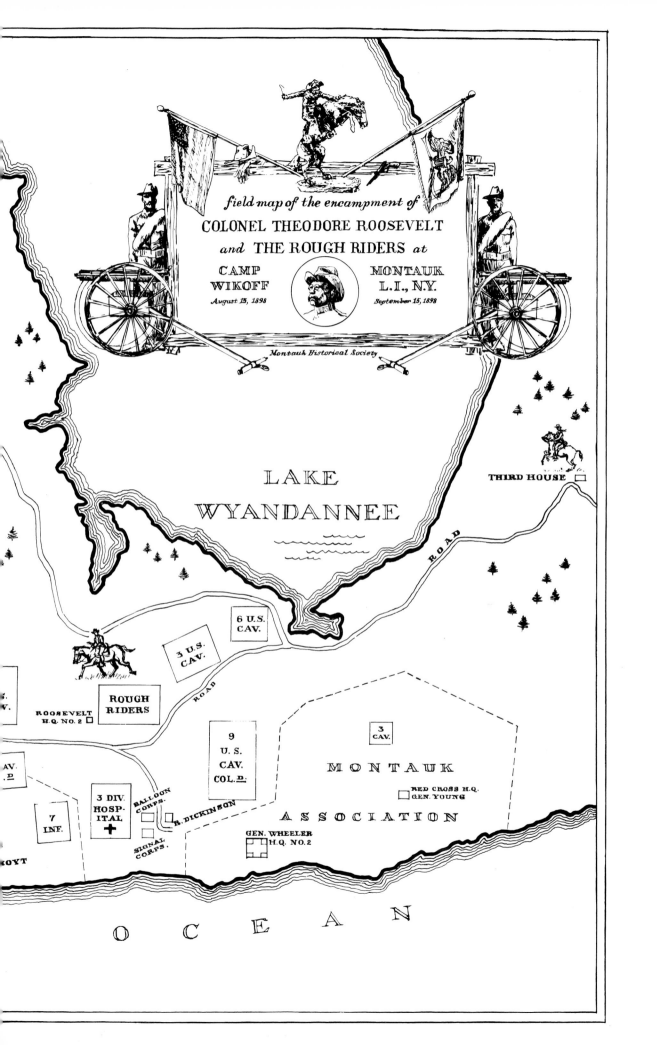

field map of the encampment of

COLONEL THEODORE ROOSEVELT

and **THE ROUGH RIDERS** *at*

CAMP WIKOFF
August 15, 1898

MONTAUK L.I., N.Y.
September 15, 1898

Montauk Historical Society

LAKE WYANDANNEE

THIRD HOUSE

ROAD

6 U.S. CAV.

3 U.S. CAV.

ROAD

ROUGH RIDERS

ROOSEVELT H.Q. NO. 2

9 U.S. CAV. COL. D.

3 CAV.

MONTAUK

RED CROSS H.Q. GEN. YOUNG

ASSOCIATION

3 DIV. HOSPITAL

BALLOON CORPS.

R. DICKINSON

GEN. WHEELER H.Q. NO. 2

7 INF.

SIGNAL CORPS.

HOYT

OCEAN

Top left: Welcome home sign on the home of W.F. Lewis of the 13th Minnesota in St. Paul, Minnesota, October 1899. MNHS #7273-A

Top right: Decoration on the front porch of the Chester Wilson home at 623 South Broadway, Stillwater, Minnesota. Wilson was in Company K, First Minnesota Volunteers. He later served on the Mexican border and in World War One. MNHS #30861G

President McKinley and Vice-President Hobart escorted by General Wheeler through the general hospitals at Camp Wikoff.

SECRETARY ALGER ON A TOUR OF INSPECTION.

HELPING A SICK COMRADE INTO CAMP.

3D AND 20TH REGULARS LANDING AT QUARANTINE CAMP.

CARRYING A SICK SOLDIER TO THE HOSPITAL.

CONVALESCENTS WAITING TO BE TAKEN TO THE HOSPITAL.

HOSPITAL SCENES AT CAMP WIKOFF

PHOTOGRAPHS TAKEN ESPECIALLY FOR "HARPER'S WEEKLY."

GENERAL WHEELER AND COLONEL ROOSEVELT RIDING INTO CAMP.   MAJOR-GENERAL YOUNG, COMMANDING CAMP WIKOFF.
General Wheeler on Right.

THE 3D CAVALRY MARCHING TO THE DETENTION CAMP.

THE 9TH CAVALRY ON GUARD AT THE QUARANTINE LINE.   CAPTAIN HIGGINS OF THE 16TH (PENN.) SIGNAL CORPS.

ON THE WAY TO CAMP.   A SCENE IN CAMP—WATERING MULES WHILE DRAWING SUPPLY-WAGONS.

SCENES AT CAMP WIKOFF, MONTAUK POINT, LONG ISLAND.

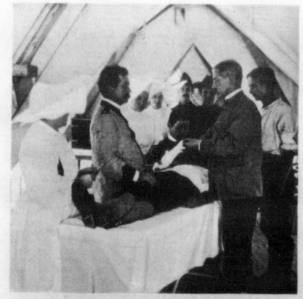

OPERATING TABLE, FIELD SURGICAL WARD, GENERAL HOSPITAL.

HELPING COMRADES ON THE WAY TO BOSTON HOSPITALS.

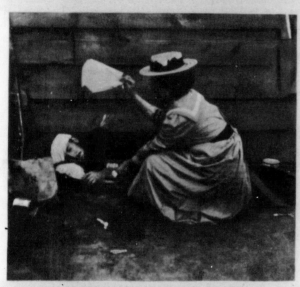

RED CROSS NURSE HELPING A SICK SOLDIER AT RAILROAD STATION.

MISS WHEELER, DAUGHTER OF GENERAL WHEELER, A NURSE IN THE
GENERAL HOSPITAL.

GENERAL WHEELER AND SURGEON-GENERAL STERNBERG GOING TO INSPECT THE
HOSPITAL.

SISTERS OF CHARITY ON THEIR WAY TO CAMP TO ACT AS NURSES

SCENES AT CAMP WIKOFF.
Photographs taken especially for "Harper's Weekly"

Top left: The Peace
Jubilee in Chicago, Oct.
18, 1898. Top right: Peace
Jubilee in Philadelphia,
November 1898.
Lieutenant Hobson and
the crew of the *Merrimac*
passing through the Court
of Honor.

Chicago had a peace
jubilee from Oct. 16 to 21,
1898. It included a
parade, ball, banquet and
several receptions.
President McKinley
attended and was given a
Doctor of Laws degree by
the University of Chicago.

Front page of the *Butte Miner*
welcoming home the Montana
Volunteers from the Philippines. MNG

Banners or arches, such as this in an Idaho town, were put up in cities throughout the country to welcome home the soldiers and sailors from the Caribbean and the Philippines in 1898 and '99. ISHS #72-193.29

Homecoming arch in Salt Lake City, Utah. USHS #973.89

Utah veterans returning to the Presidio of San Francisco, date unknown. NPS

Welcoming home the 13th
Minnesota Infantry from
the Philippines on Oct. 12,
1899, at the Minneapolis
Bridge Square. MNHS 54-BG

The First Idaho Volunteers
returning to San Francisco
on Aug. 29, 1899. ISHS

LIEUT.-COL. BARNETT AND STAFF PASSING
THE REVIEWING STAND.

Return of the 10th Pennsylvania
Volunteers from Manila marching
through the streets of Pittsburgh.

Troops marching down a street in
New York after their victorious
campaign in Cuba. BA

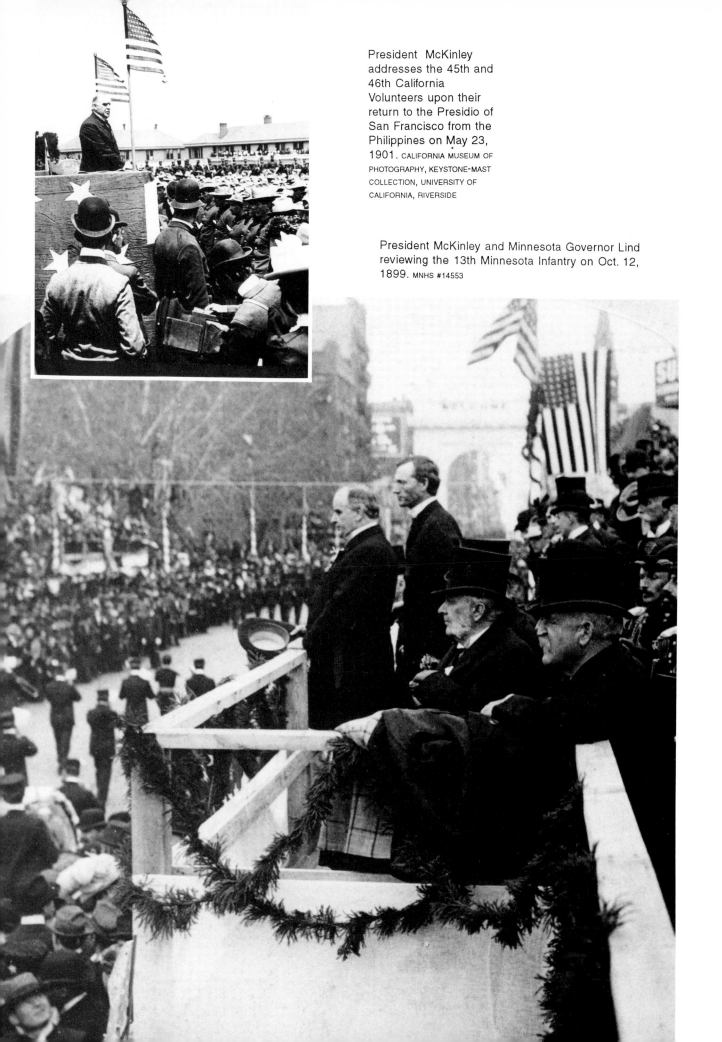

President McKinley addresses the 45th and 46th California Volunteers upon their return to the Presidio of San Francisco from the Philippines on May 23, 1901. CALIFORNIA MUSEUM OF PHOTOGRAPHY, KEYSTONE-MAST COLLECTION, UNIVERSITY OF CALIFORNIA, RIVERSIDE

President McKinley and Minnesota Governor Lind reviewing the 13th Minnesota Infantry on Oct. 12, 1899. MNHS #14553

The 9th Pennsylvania
Volunteers march in the
Philadelphia Peace Jubilee
in the fall of 1898. KE

Washington State troops
return to Seattle on Nov.
9, 1899, from duty in the
Philippines. WSHS

This welcome home arch was
erected at the intersection of
Granite and Main streets in
Butte, Montana, in October
1899 to welcome the Montana
National Guard troops home
from the Philippines. Each
arch stretched 90 feet, and in
the center of the street the
height to the top was 48 feet. It
was made of lumber and
covered with white muslin, with
black and white drawings in
imitation of relief. The contour
of the arch was shown at night
by 800 red, white and blue
electric lights. MHS

The *USS Indiana* (BB-01) during the New York fleet review with her crew lined up for the ceremony. USN NH63503

The *USS New York*, Admiral Sampson's flagship, led the way down the Hudson River.

THE "NEW YORK," ADMIRAL SAMPSON'S FLAG-SHIP, LEADS THE WAY—COMING DOWN THE HUDSON RIVER

The *USS Brooklyn*, Admiral Schley's flagship, off the Statue of Liberty.

THE "BROOKLYN," ADMIRAL SCHLEY'S FLAG-SHIP, IN THE HARBOR, OFF THE STATUE OF LIBERTY.

The *USS Texas* (BB-000), Commodore Philip's command.

THE "TEXAS," COMMODORE PHILIP'S REFORMED HOODOO.

The *USS Oregon* (BB-03) commanded by Captain Clark.

THE "OREGON," CAPTAIN CLARK'S "BATTLE-SHIP CRUISER."
THE HOME-COMING OF THE FLEET—THE NAVAL PARADE, NEW YORK, AUGUST 20, 1898.
PHOTOGRAPHS BY HART

The Sept. 8, 1898, issue of *Leslie's Weekly* lead article was on the grand review.

The fleet is welcomed to the New York harbor on Aug. 20, 1898, for a grand review.

Troops marching down a
street in San Francisco
pass the famous Victorian-
style townhouses after
returning from the
Philippines. CSL #19,980

This memorial arch was
built in Chicago spanning
the corner of Washington
and LaSalle streets. The
war scenes decorating the
arch were painted after
H.C. Christy's war
illustrations in *Leslie's
Weekly*.

The Dewey Reception in New York City

Between Sept. 27 and 30, 1899, over three million people welcomed Admiral Dewey and his fleet on water and land in New York City. Dewey had promised that his flagship, the *Olympia*, would arrive in New York on Sept. 28, but he actually arrived at daybreak on the 26th.

On the 27th, the *Olympia* left her anchorage near the New Jersey Highlands and steamed up the bay to the naval rendezvous off of Staten Island. The coastal batteries at Forts Wadsworth and Hamilton opened fire with 17 guns in salute.

Two days later the New York harbor witnessed the greatest naval display to that time. Hundreds of yachts, tugs, fireboats and steamers were decked-out in bunting to welcome the *Olympia, New York, Indiana, Massachusetts, Texas, Brooklyn, Chicago* and other naval vessels in a naval parade. One hundred and fifty thousand people were on board the flotilla. Thousands more lined the shores from Grants' Tomb to the dispersing point off West 23rd Street.

On Saturday, Sept. 30, a massive parade to honor Admiral Dewey and the soldiers and sailors who defeated the Spanish was held in the city. It started at 122nd Street and proceeded for seven miles down Riverside Drive to 72nd Street, then to 8th Avenue, or Central Park West, to the Columbus statue in Central Park at 59th Street, then down 5th Avenue to the Washington Centennial Arch in Washington Square.

Governor Theodore Roosevelt, himself a war hero, was in attendance as were thousands of soldiers, sailors, John Philip Sousa's 130-piece band as well as 16 state governors. At the end of the procession, 12 veterans of the Santiago campaign carried, like a blanket, the first American flag to be hoisted on Morro Castle.

It would be another 20 years, at the end of World War One, before New Yorkers would witness such a spectacle of patriotism.

The Brooklyn Bridge, over the East River, as it appeared during the nights of Sept. 28 to 30, 1899. The electric light sign was 30 feet high.

The Dewey Arch
in Madison Square, New York City

The Quadriga, surmounting the arch and representing Victory on the Sea, as sculpted by John Q.A. Ward.

Views of the arch.

Opposite page: The Dewey Arch on the Madison Square Plaza was placed at 24th Street and 5th Avenue with the addition of a colonnade, starting at 23rd Street and ending at 25th Street. The arch resembled the Arc de Triumph of Paris and stood 80 feet high with the figures of the quadriga, which crowned it, bringing the height to 100 feet. The space inside the arch was 30 feet from pier to pier and the full width was 70 feet. The material cost was $35,000 with another $350,000 worth of donated sculptors' labor. It was constructed of a material known as "white stuff," closely resembling marble, but was not to be a permanent fixture at the site. Many famous sculptors were involved in the multitude of patriotic statues on the arch and colonnades. NEW YORK HISTORICAL SOCIETY

The gold loving cup on the right was presented to Admiral Dewey in New York City. USN NH50583

Admiral Dewey and Mayor Van Wyck leave New York's city hall after presentation of the gold loving cup.

Presentation of New York City's loving cup to Admiral Dewey by Mayor Van Wyck and Governor Roosevelt on Sept. 30, 1899.

Top left: The *Olympia* arriving at New York on Sept. 26, 1899. Top right: The *Olympia* crew in the Sept. 30 parade in New York City.

President McKinley, Cardinal Gibbons and Admiral Dewey at the United States Capitol in September 1899. Dewey was presented with a sword voted to him by Congress.

Dewey Day, Montpelier, Vermont, October 12, 1898

A celebration took place in Admiral Dewey's hometown of Montpelier, Vermont, on Oct. 12, 1898. Dewey was still in the Pacific. The State Capitol was decorated for the event (top) as was the schoolhouse where Dewey went to school in the 1850s. VHS #2893 AND #14231

Peace Negotiations

On Dec. 10, 1898, a peace treaty was negotiated in Paris between the United States and Spain.

In the agreement, Spain ceded the islands of Cuba, Puerto Rico and Guam to the United States. She also ceded the Philippine Islands but the United States agreed to a payment of $20 million as compensation to the Spanish government. Prisoners of war of each side were to be sent home and all political prisoners held by Spain were to be released. The United States and Spain mutually relinquished all claims for indemnity, national and individual, of every kind, of either government or its citizens against the other government, including the cost of the war, since the beginning of the Cuban Insurrection up to the signing of the peace treaty.

There was strong opposition to the treaty in the U.S. Senate. Sen. Henry Cabot Lodge, a strong advocate of military action against Spain, fought hard for passage. Speaker of the House, Thomas Brackett Reed, strongly opposed paying for the Philippines.*

A two-thirds majority was needed for ratification. William Jennings Bryan, who had recently left the army, advocated for the treaty, although it was for his own personal political reasons. It took 56 votes to pass and on Feb. 8, 1899, 57 senators voted for the treaty.**

The House voted the $20 million payment and it was a done deal.

* Fifty-eight-year-old Reed was from Maine. He was against upgrading the navy and was a bitter loser to McKinley for the 1896 Republican presidential nomination. Strongly against the war, he was unable to stop the war fever in Congress. He was the most powerful congressional leader of his time but quit Congress over the payment of the money to Spain for the Philippines. Reed died in 1902.

** The Philippine Insurrection under Aguinaldo began just as Congress was deliberating over the Paris Treaty. This action pushed some senators to vote for the treaty.

The New Territories

Cuba: The island was occupied in 1898 and the first municipal elections were held in 1900. On May 20, 1902, military rule ended and the government was turned over to the new president, Tomás Estrada Palma. In 1906, the U.S. Government had to send troops back to Cuba because of the collapse of the Cuban government. A civilian provisional government came to an end in 1909 and Cuba was ruled by a series of dictators up until the present time. The United States broke off diplomatic relations with the new government under Fidel Castro on Jan. 3, 1961.

Philippines: American governors administered the islands from 1900 to 1942 when the Japanese occupied the country. The Philippines attained commonwealth status in 1934 and in 1935, Manuel Quezon defeated Aguinaldo to become the first president of the commonwealth. On July 4, 1946, the Republic of the Philippines was established after being liberated by United States troops in 1945. Subic Bay was a U.S. Naval base from 1899 to 1992.

Puerto Rico: The island was ruled by a military governor until May 1900, when civilian government was established. In 1917 the island became a territory of the United States. The governor was appointed by the president of the United States until 1947 when popular elections began. Since 1952, the island has been a self-governing commonwealth.

Guam: After the United States captured the island, it was placed under the administration of the U.S. Navy. The Japanese occupied the island from Dec. 10, 1941, to Aug. 15, 1944. The United States declared Guam a territory in 1950 and transferred its supervision to the Department of the Interior. The inhabitants became U.S. citizens and in 1970 the popular vote was instituted. Commonwealth status is now being avocated.

Hawaii: The United States annexed Hawaii on Aug. 12, 1898, and established the Territory of Hawaii on June 14, 1900, with all inhabitants becoming United States citizens. It was admitted to the Union as the 50th state on Aug. 21, 1959.

GENERAL R. CERERO.

MR. J. DE GARNICA.

MR. EUG. MONTERO RIOS, PRESIDENT.

MR. W. Z. DE VI LAURRUTIA.

THE SPANISH PEACE COMMISSIONERS.

MR. BUENAVENTURA ABARZUZA

Hon. Whitelaw Reid, Editor of the New York *Tribune*. Mr. Moore, Secretary. Senator William P. Frye, of Maine.
Senator George Gray, of Delaware. Ex-Secretary William R. Day, of Ohio. Senator Cushman K. Davis, of Minnesota.

THE PEACE COMMISSION IN SESSION AT PARIS.

The Providence Daily Journal.

VOL. LXX. NO. 192. PROVIDENCE, R. I., FRIDAY, AUGUST 12, 1898. TEN PAGES. PRICE TWO CENTS

PEACE PROTOCOL WILL BE SIGNED TO-DAY.

The French Ambassador Has Received Full Authority from Spanish Government.

HOSTILITIES TO CEASE.

The Spanish Cabinet Approved the Terms of the Protocol, and the Minister of Foreign Affairs Announced That Negotiations for a Peace Treaty Will Take Place in Paris.—Secretary Day and Ambassador Cambon to Meet This Morning and Affix Their Signatures to the Peace Protocol.—As Soon as Possible Thereafter Proclamations Declaring an Armistice Will be Issued by Both Governments. President McKinley and Officials of the Administration Gratified by the Termination of the War.

A SHARP FIGHT

With Spaniards Near Mayaguez.

TWO KILLED, 14 WOUNDED

ENEMY DRIVEN FROM POSITION

One of the American peace negotiators, Whitelaw Reid had a varied career throughout his life. He was born in Xenia, Ohio, in 1837 and during the Civil War worked as a correspondent for the *Cincinnati Gazette*. In 1872, he purchased the *New York Tribune*, and 20 years later, became the Republican nominee for vice-president of the United States. In 1905 he was appointed the U.S. ambassador to Great Britain where he remained until his death in 1912.

M. Jules Cambon, French ambassador to the United States, signing the Peace Protocol on behalf of Spain. From left: Lieutenant Colonel Montgomery, President McKinley, Secretary of State Day, Assistant Secretary of State Moore, Secretary of the French Embassy M. Thiebaut, Ambassador Cambon, Assistant Secretary of State Pruden, Assistant to the President Cortelyon, Assistant Secretary of State Cridler and door-keeper Charles Loeffler.

The War in Films

Rough Riders

Tom Berenger stars as Theodore Roosevelt in the [Tu]rner Network Television (TNT) Original miniseries [Ro]ugh Riders, the story of the cavalry soldiers Roosevelt [le]d in a legendary charge on San Juan Hill during the [Sp]anish American War. Gary Busey also stars, with Brad [Jo]hnson, Illeana Douglas, Chris Noth, George Hamilton, [Br]ian Keith and Sam Elliott. John Milius directs the four-[ho]ur epic, which was shot on location in Texas for pre-[mi]ere on TNT in 1997.

Executive-producing *Rough Riders* are Berenger, [La]rry Levinson, Robert Katz and Moctesuma Esparza. [Bi]ll Macdonald and Allan Apone are the film's producers. [M]ilius also contributed his writing talents to the film. The [pr]oject began as a collaboration between Hugh Wilson, [w]ho originally scripted the epic; Berenger's production [co]mpany, 1st Corps Endeavors; and Esparza/Katz [Pr]oductions.

Tom Berenger as Lt. Col. Theodore Roosevelt.
ALL PHOTOS COURTESY TURNER NETWORK TELEVISION

[C]ompare this photo to the one on page 128.

Galaxy of Stars to Playing "The Rough Riders," Story of Theodore Roosevelt's Part in War of '98.

Notables of the Hollywood film colony will arrive in San Antonio Thursday to begin filming Paramount's enthralling story of Theodore Roosevelt's indomitable regiment, "The Rough Riders."

Among the popular players who will make this city their home for the next month or more are Noah Beery, George Bancroft, Mary Astor, Charles Farrell and Frank Hopper, whose photographs are reproduced in the order named. Below is Hermann Hagedorn, biographer of Roosevelt, and author of the story, "The Rough Riders."

In addition to these the company will include Victor Fleming, director of the production; Henry Hathaway, assistant director; Charles Emmett Mack, featured player, and cast and staff members totalling in excess of a hundred.

The motion picture organization will be hosts at a dinner and dance at the St. Anthony Hotel Saturday evening at which members of the military, civic officials, press and prominent citizens will be guests.

Preparations for an enthusiastic welcome of the screen players Thursday afternoon have been made by Mayor Tobin, Porter Whaley, William Furlong and Fred Herndon, representing the San Antonio Chamber of Commerce, and military officers. A military band will be on hand when the Southern Pacific special train pulls in.

Actual filming of the colorful story of Roosevelt's hard-riding, fast-shooting outfit in the Cuban fray is scheduled to begin Monday, although preparations have been perfected to such an extent that an earlier start may be made.

Frank Hopper played Roosevelt in the movie "The Rough Riders." This would be his only starring role.

-324-

Scenes from the movie, "The Rough Riders."

The Earliest Movies

Motion pictures have been in existence since 1895 so they were available for the 1898 war. In May 1898, the American Vitograph Company under the direction of J. Stuart Blackton and Albert E. Smith, shot a short subject entitled "The Battle of Manila Bay." It was shot on the rooftop of Vitograph's headquarters in New York City.

Albert Smith remembered the making of the short movie: "At this time street vendors in New York City were selling sturdy photographs of ships of the American and Spanish fleets. We bought a set of each and we cut out the battleships. On a table, topside down, we placed on the artist Blackton's large canvas-covered frames and filled it with water an inch deep. In order to stand the cutouts in the water, we nailed them to lengths of wood about an inch square. In this way a little "shelf" was provided behind each ship and on this shelf we placed pinches of gunpowder—three pinches for each ship—not too many, we felt, for a major sea engagement of this sort." (from Albert E. Smith with Phil A. Koury, *Two Reels and a Crank*, Doubleday, Garden City, New York, 1952.)

On May 16, 1898, William Selig, a filmmaker from Chicago, went to Camp Tanner in Springfield, Illinois. According to the May 17th issue of *Chicago Inter-Ocean*, "A feature which caught the crowds was the presentation of a series of cinematograph pictures representing scenes of camp life at Camp Tanner. They showed the Illinois volunteers at the various camp avocations: drilling, parading, on review and at their sports. All the pictures are good and they were cheered to the echo. They will remain a feature during the entire week."

The American Vitograph Company produced another short film clip on the raising of the flag over Morro Castle in Havana. It was again shot at their New York City studio and presented on Feb. 4, 1899.

In 1909 Selig Polyscope Co. produced a movie of unknown length called, *Up San Juan Hill.*

The Real Glory

This Samuel Goldwyn production came out in 1939. Directed by Henry Hathaway, it starred Gary Cooper, David Niven, Andrea Leeds, Reginald Owen, Kay Johnson, Broderick Crawford, Vladimir Sokoloff and Henry Kolker. While the plot takes place in the Philippines in 1906, it is a direct result of the American occupation of the country. Moro tribesmen menace the Filipino people protected by the U.S. Army. Cooper is a doctor who almost single-handedly saves the village where he is stationed.

THE ROUGH RIDERS   F2.4710

Paramount Famous Lasky Corp. 15 Mar 1927 [New York premiere; released 1 Oct; c1 Oct 1927; LP24469]. Si; b&w. 35mm. 13 reels, 12,071 ft. [Release version: 10 reels, 9,443 ft.]

Pres by Adolph Zukor, Jesse L. Lasky. *Assoc Prod* B. P. Schulberg. *Dir* Victor Fleming. *Screenplay* Robert N. Lee, Keene Thompson. *Titl* George Marion, Jr. *Adapt* John F. Goodrich. *Story* Hermann Hagedorn. *Photog* James Howe.

Cast: Noah Beery (*Hell's Bells*), Charles Farrell (*Stewart Van Brunt*), George Bancroft (*Happy Joe*), Charles Emmett Mack (*Bert Henley*), Mary Astor (*Dolly*), Frank Hopper (*Theodore Roosevelt*), Col. Fred Lindsay (*Leonard Wood*), Fred Kohler (*Sergeant Stanton*).

Historical melodrama. In 1898, following the destruction of the *Maine* in Cuba, war is declared against Spain by the United States; and Theodore Roosevelt, Assistant Secretary of the Navy, along with Leonard Wood of the Army Medical Corps, are offered the eagles in the first volunteer regiments; but they decline and together assemble the Rough Riders, a motley assortment of volunteers, on the Exposition Grounds at San Antonio. Amidst the regiment are Happy Joe, who skips jail to enlist; his pursuer, a sheriff known as Hell's Bells; Bert Henley, a local boy; Van, a handsome New Yorker; and Dolly, who is the object of Bert's and Van's affections. When the regiment sees action in Cuba, the boys' intense rivalry turns into friendship; and when Bert is wounded, Van carries him back to base in San Juan, where he dies a hero. At the end of the war, Van carries the news to Dolly; later, with the inauguration of Roosevelt as President, Van and Dolly come to the reception with their two children. *War heroes. Friendship. United States—History—War of 1898. Cuba. San Antonio. Theodore Roosevelt. Leonard Wood. United States Army—Cavalry. Rough Riders.*

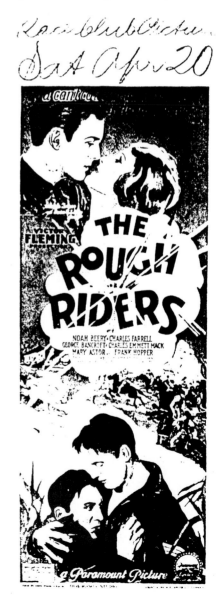

A Wartime Feud

The bloody Scott-Colson gun battle between two eastern Kentucky Republicans grew out of a grudge over a breach of military protocol during the Spanish American War.

In 1898 Ethelbert D. Scott, a Somerset attorney, reported for duty as a newly commissioned subaltern with the 4th Kentucky Volunteers, then stationed in Anniston, Alabama. On his arrival in camp he asked for Col. D.G. Colson the commanding officer and a former congressman, to present a letter of introduction. When Colonel Colson came into the room where Scott was seated reading a newspaper, the lieutenant failed to arise and salute. Angered by this affront, Colson left the room. In many other incidents Scott proved a recalcitrant soldier and was recommended for dismissal from the army but used political influence to stay in place. Such bad blood developed between the two men that after the 4th Kentucky was retired from service and Colson and Scott later met accidentally in an Anniston restaurant, they engaged in gunfire and Colson was wounded in the groin.

On Jan. 16, 1900, Scott and Colson had a second chance meeting, this time in the lobby of the Capitol Hotel in Frankfort. Both were armed, Colson with a .44 service revolver and Scott with a .38 caliber pistol. Coming face-to-face, the two men fired simultaneously. Eighteen shots were fired. Scott, wounded three times, was attempting to escape when Colson shot him dead. The gunfire also killed four bystanders and wounded at least two other men. Colson was arrested, jailed, tried, and cleared. In fact, the court returned his pistols to him. His life, however, was afterward made miserable by ill health and, it was said, by alcohol.

The first pension check of the war was paid to Elsie A. Monfort of Council Bluffs, Iowa, whose son was lost on the *Maine*. It was made out for $14.40 in June 1898.

United Spanish War Veterans

This veterans organization was founded in 1898 by Gen. Irving Hale of Colorado and others to unite veterans of the just concluded Spanish American War. In the 1950s, the USWV still had over 3,000 members in 600 local chapters throughout the United States.

The USWV is still in existence although no veterans of the conflict are living. The 97th annual convention was held at Fort Worth, Texas, in September 1995. Its national headquarters is at 810 Vermont Avenue NW, Washington, D.C., 20013-1915.

Adjutant	Commander	Quartermaster
ORIN P. BAILEY	CHARLES P. APPICH	JOHN F. FARRELL
4936 Butterworth Pl., N.W.	5214 Twelfth St. North	126 Sixth Street, N.E.
Washington 16, D. C.	Arlington, Virginia	Washington 2, D. C.
WOodley 5510	GLebe 6244	

HEADQUARTERS

DEPARTMENT OF THE DISTRICT OF COLUMBIA

United Spanish War Veterans

SOLDIERS' AND SAILORS' TEMPORARY HOME BUILDING

921 PENNSYLVANIA AVENUE, S. E.

WASHINGTON, D. C.

GENERAL ORDERS No. 1   August 20, 1946.
Series 1946–1947

AMERICANISM

Americanism is the unfailing love of Country; loyalty to its institutions and ideals; eagerness to defend it against all enemies; undivided allegiance to the Flag, and a desire to secure the blessings of liberty to ourselves and posterity.

(To be repeated in unison at all meetings.)

COMMAND ASSUMED

1. Having been duly elected and installed as Department Commander of the Department of the District of Columbia, United Spanish War Veterans, at the 47th Annual Encampment, command is hereby assumed.

HEADQUARTERS

2. Department headquarters, for and during the ensuing administrative term, is established at 921 Pennsylvania Ave., S.E., Washington, D. C.

3. The following officers were elected and installed at the 47th Annual Encampment:

Commander, CHARLES H. APPICH (Harden Camp) 5214 12th Street North, Arlington, Virginia. Phone GLebe 6244.

Senior Vice Commander, VINCENT A. OSTERMAN (Miles Camp) 4912 Annapolis Road, Decatur Heights, Maryland. Phone WArfield 2479.

Junior Vice Commander, VALENTINE T. MAYER (Urell Camp) 128 Sixth Street, S.E., Washington 3, D. C. Phone TRinidad 2827.

Inspector, CHARLES COHEN (Pettit Camp) 2827 Seventh Street, N.E., Washington 17, D. C. Phone MIchigan 5809.

Judge Advocate, JOHN LEWIS SMITH (Miles Camp) 2424 Tracy Place, N.W., Washington 8, D. C. Phone DUpont 0567.

Surgeon, VICTOR E. WATKINS (Harden Camp) 4000 Cathedral Avenue, N.W., Washington 16, D. C. Phone WOodley 6149.

Chaplain, (acting) CHARLES C. LEWIS (Miles Camp) 1604 Potomac Avenue, S.E., Washington 3, D. C. Phone TRinidad 7863.

Marshal, CHARLES J. HARLOW (Harden Camp) 2933 Ordway Street, N.W., Washington 8, D. C. Phone WOodley 4668.

The Last Survivors of the Spanish American War and Philippine Insurrection

1. Julian H. Speed, Dallas, Texas, Co. K, (Independent) Texas Infantry, died Oct. 14, 1983, 106 years old.
2. William Amberson, Waynesboro, Pa., Co. M, 5th Pennsylvania Infantry, died Nov. 3, 1983, 106 years old.
3. John F. Riggall, Preble, NY, died Nov. 14, 1983, 102 years old.
4. Peter O. Pederson, Fargo, ND, Co. A, 34th U.S. Infantry, died Nov. 16, 1983, 106 years old.
5. George W. Lewis, Shenandoah, Iowa, Co. K, 1st U.S. Infantry, died Nov. 20, 1983, 104 years old.
6. Joseph I. McNamara, Brookline, Mass., died Nov. 25, 1983, 99 years old.
7. Clarence A. Will, Jacksonville, Fla., died Dec. 4, 1983, 99 years old.
8. Frank Lechleidner, Medford, Ore., Troop I, 8th U.S. Cavalry, died Jan. 20, 1984, 101 years old.
9. Walter E. Neubauer, Brandon, Fla., Naval Reserve, died Jan. 21, 1984, 97 years old.
10. Will Cook, Retsil, Wash., Co. C, 2nd Wisconsin Infantry, died Feb. 12, 1984.
11. George M. McPherson, Payo, Ga., *USS Kentucky*, died Feb. 21, 1984, 101 years old.
12. Joe T. Montgomery, Miles City, Mont., Co. E, 52nd Iowa Infantry, died Feb. 26, 1984, 107 years old.
13. Harry Embree, Independence, Kans., U.S. Army, died March 14, 1986, 105 years old.
14. Wilson L. Dawson, West Palm Beach, Fla., U.S. Navy, died July 14, 1986, 100 years old.
15. Hickory E. Grace Sr., Middleboro, Ky., 7th U.S. Infantry, died Aug. 22, 1986, 103 years old.
16. Walter (?) Sharts, Dayton, Ohio, Co. C, 1st Ohio Volunteer Infantry, died Jan. 27, 1987, 111 years old.
17. Ralph Waldo Taylor, Pompano Beach, Fla., Co. K, 71st New York Infantry, died May 15, 1987, 105 years old.
18. John T. Fitzgerald, Barnegat, NJ, *USS Illinois*, died Jan. 18, 1988, 103 years old.
19. Samuel Leroy Mendel, Galva, Ill., died July 13, 1988, 104 years old.
20. Nathan Edward "Northeast" Cook, U.S. Navy, died Sept. 10, 1992, 106 years old.
21. Jones Morgan, Richmond, Va., 9th U.S. Cavalry, died Aug. 29, 1993, 110 years old. Last survivor of the Spanish American War and last surviving "Buffalo Soldier."

The Last Veterans

The last surviving Spanish American War veteran was a black man named Jones Morgan. He was born on Oct. 23, 1882, and died on Aug. 29, 1993, at 110 years, 10 months and six days old. Morgan was a cook and horse wrangler in the 10th U.S. Cavalry Regiment and tended horses for the Rough Riders. He joined the army in 1896 and left the service in 1900 after serving in Cuba.

On Sept. 10, 1992, Nathan Edward "Northeast" Cook died. It was reported nationally that he was the last Spanish American War veteran but he actually joined the navy as a cabin boy in 1901 and served for 44 years, a remarkable feat in itself, in the Philippine Insurrection, the Boxer Rebellion, the Mexican border crisis, World War One and World War Two. During the first war, Cook commanded a sub chaser that sank two German U-boats. In World War Two, he commanded a seagoing tug stationed in Haiti and a submarine tender in Panama. He died at 106 in Phoenix, Arizona.

In the mid-1980s there were still 32 Spanish American War veterans alive. While none of the approximately 325,000 men who served in uniform during the 1898-1902 period are alive today, the United Spanish War Veterans Organization is still in existence.

Survivor's information courtesy Professor Jay Hoar, Temple, Maine.

Veterans of a USWV camp at the Oriental Park Race Track in Havana, Cuba, October 1928. USAMHI

Monument erected by members of Co. M, 2nd Oregon Volunteer Regiment at the former Camp Merritt in San Francisco, California, May 30, 1902. USAMHI

The Kentucky delegation to the 31st National Encampment USWV at Denver, Colorado, Sept. 11, 1929. USAMHI

USWV veterans at a reunion in Petaluma, California, sponsored by the Lawton Camp #1, April 22, 1948. USAMHI

Arthur McArthur Camp No. 16, Department of Minnesota flag, 1923. MNHS #8085-AG

Spanish American War veterans at members graves on Memorial Day 1911 in Fort Liscum, Valdez, Alaska. CANDY WAUGAMAN COLLECTION

Monument erected at the California camp site of the First California Volunteer Infantry, 1958. USAMHI

Clyde Willse of the Fifth Ohio Volunteer Infantry (left) in 1940. USAMHI

Veterans attending the 35th National Encampment of the United Spanish War Veterans in Los Angeles, June 20, 1933. Left to right: Sam Duganne, Henry Hollister, Wilson Wedney and George Finley hitting the "Barbershop Chorus." BA

This monument in Dunwoody Park at Fort Monmouth, N.J., was erected in 1950 to the officers and men of the Regular and Volunteer Signal Corps, U.S. Army, who established and maintained communications throughout the Spanish American War, The Philippine Insurrection and the China Relief Expedition. USAMHI

A TRIBUTE TO THE HEROIC REGULARS AT SAN JUAN.

Gen. H. W. Lawton Camp

The next regular meeting of Camp will be Wednesday evening, April 4th, 1917, when all arrangements for the Department Encampment, which is to be held in Worcester, Mass., April 18-19, will be made.

The Encampment this year will excel anything previous—in fact you will find it to be the best in the history of the order. In connection with it, on April 19th, the monument for Spanish War Veterans will be dedicated. The celebration is to be preceded by a monster parade. Evening of April 18 a Grand Campfire and Reunion, in which all Spanish War Veterans of this State will take part, and Snake Parade.

Make it a point to attend this meeting. Please sign and return the attached card as early as possible.

Official: By Order,

    J. J. SHEA, *Adjutant*.   L. B. CLARK, *Commander*.

A GROUP of Spanish War Veterans have formed an
association for the purpose of erecting a memorial to
our former President, Theodore Roosevelt, and those who
served in the Spanish-American War.

This memorial will be erected in Buffalo where Colonel
Roosevelt took the oath of office as President of the United
States after the assassination of President McKinley at the
Pan-American Exposition. Colonel Roosevelt was one of
the most outstanding heroes of the Spanish-American War
and was the only Spanish War veteran to become President.

Our aim is to raise at least three million dollars by popular subscription throughout the entire country, and if everyone will give something, regardless of the amount, the result
will be one of the outstanding memorials in the country,—
something which the American people can point to with
pride and satisfaction, knowing that it shows the appreciation and high esteem in which they have held the most
beloved Statesman, Soldier and Author since our great mar-
tyred President, Abraham Lincoln.

Theodore Roosevelt spent practically all of his life in
public service and the record he left behind is too well known
to all of us to elaborate upon here. His fearlessness, character, and love of country were beyond question; his love of
children and home life were manifest. Beginning when he
was first elected to public office in 1881, until he was called
to his eternal rest, his best efforts were always spent for the
welfare of his fellowmen.

The American people will never forget its heroes and
defenders, for every memorial erected and dedicated to the
service rendered in behalf of country is an added assurance
of the perpetuity of American institutions

WE earnestly solicit your cooperation in making this
memorial possible. We are not asking for any specific
amount, even a penny or a postage stamp will help. Give
according to your means, but give something! Be sure to
send in your name and address with your contribution. We
will want it to appear on the list of donors which will be
forever preserved in the memorial. Any donation will be
gratefully appreciated.

It is our ambition and we will do everything in our
power to carry out the idea of building a memorial which
will perpetuate for all time the memory of Colonel Roosevelt
and every branch of service during the Spanish-American
War.

"Better in one ecstatic epic day
To strike a blow for Glory and for Truth,
With ardent singing heart to toss away
In Freedom's holy cause my eager youth,
Than bear as weary years pass one by one
The knowledge of a sacred task undone."

We need the help of every Patriotic, Fraternal, Business,
Social, Political, Labor and Educational Oragnization to make
this the success it merits. We ask that these various bodies
come forward with any assistance and help they can give us.

WE ARE DEPENDING ON YOU!

The workers in this campaign are giving their time and
efforts gratis. We sincerely thank you for any courtesy and
consideration shown them. We wish to express our thanks
to every man, woman and child who in any way may contribute, materially or otherwise, towards the ultimate success
of this undertaking, which will be attained only through your
patriotic spirit and cooperation.

Additional folders may be had on request.

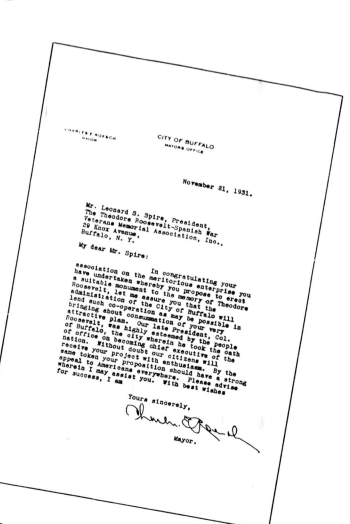
-332-

CAPTAIN CHAS. FRENCH CAMP NO. 4
UNITED SPANISH WAR VETERANS
Cordially Invites Yourself and Friends to Attend the

Thirty-second Anniversary

of the

Sinking of the United States
Battleship "Maine"

IN HAVANA HARBOR, CUBA, FEB. 15, 1898

GREAT FALLS, MONTANA,   FRIDAY, FEB'Y 14, 1930
Palm Room, Hotel Rainbow, at 8 P. M.
No Admission

Fiftieth Anniversary of
SPANISH AMERICAN WAR

Annual Encampment

of

UNITED SPANISH WAR VETERANS, 47th Encampment
AUXILIARY OF UNITED SPANISH WAR VETERANS
29th Encampment

WOMEN'S RELIEF CORPS, Grand Army of the Republic
55th Encampment

LADIES OF GRAND ARMY OF THE REPUBLIC
39th Encampment

and

JOINT REUNION

of

GRIGSBY'S ROUGH RIDERS, Third U. S. Volunteer Cavalry

and

FIRST MONTANA VOLUNTEER INFANTRY

June 13th to 16th, 1948

HELENA, MONTANA

Registration Desk, Placer Hotel Lobby

THE AMERICAN ORDER OF NOBILITY

The "United Spanish War Veterans" is a unique organization. No child can be born into ti; no proclamation of President, edict of King or Czar can command admission; no university or institution of learning can issue a diploma authorizing its holder to enter; no act of Congress or Parliament secures recognition; the wealth of a Rockefeller or a Ford cannot purchase the position; its doors swing open only upon presentation of the bit of paper, torn, worn, begrimed though it may be, which certifies to an honorable discharge from the armies and navies of the nation during the Spanish-American War, the Philippine Insurrection, or the China Relief Expedition. And, unlike other associations, no "new blood" can come in; there are no growing ranks from which recruits can be drawn into the United Spanish War Veterans. With the consummation of peace through victory, its rolls were closed forever. Its lines are steadily growing thinner, and the tramp of its column is with ever-lessening tread; the gaps of the picket line grow wider; day by day details are made from the reserve, summoned into the shadowy regions to return to touch elbows no more, until, by and by, only a solitary sentinel shall stand guard, waiting until the bugle call from beyond shall muster out the last comrade of the United Spanish War Veterans.

"REMEMBER THE MAINE"

Twenty-third Annual Encampment
Department of Oregon
AND

Twelfth Annual Convocation
Grand Lair of Oregon
MILITARY ORDER OF THE SERPENT

SOUVENIR
PROGRAM

LA GRANDE
July 19-22, 1931

Fifteenth Annual Convention
Department of Oregon Auxiliary

United Spanish War Veterans

USWV Auxillary 51 at Franklin, Massachusetts, 1932. USAMHI

A group of former nurses from the war taken at Fort Sam Houston, San Antonio, Texas, in 1954. USAMHI

Charles Barefoot, past National Commander of the USWV said in 1952, "Let me say to you, it was no tin-foil war we were fighting back then."

USAMHI

Artifacts

U.S.S. OREGON

Silver service of the *USS Oregon* (BB-03) on display at the Oregon Historical Society in Portland, Oregon. OREGON HISTORICAL SOCIETY #47202

Display of the *USS Oregon* (BB-03) at the Columbia River Maritime Museum, Astoria, Oregon. A one-pound gun from the ship is also on display. COLUMBIA RIVER MARITIME MUSEUM

Mast of the *USS Oregon* (BB-03) located on Front Avenue at the foot of Southwest Pine Street. Red brick building in the background is the 1872 Smith Block, headquarters of the Oregon Maritime Center and Museum in Portland, Oregon. DR. EVERETT JONES PHOTO

River-end of the Liberty Ship Memorial Park in Portland, Oregon. The stacks are from the *USS Oregon* (BB-03) GENE HARROWER PHOTO

Model of *USS Oregon* (BB-03), owned by Dan and Louis' Oyster Bar in Portland, on loan to the Oregon Maritime Center and Museum. GENE HARROWER PHOTO

Bell and silver service of the *USS Texas (BB-000)* located at the Battleship *Texas* (BB-35) display at LaPorte, Texas. The punch bowl has the Texas star, The Alamo and a steer portrayed on it. WILL MICHELS, TEXAS PARKS & WILDLIFE DEPT. PHOTO

Model of the *USS Charleston* on display at the Patriots Point Naval & Maritime Museum, Mt. Pleasant, SC.

Artifacts of the *USS Olympia* on display at the Bremerton Naval Museum, Bremerton, Washington

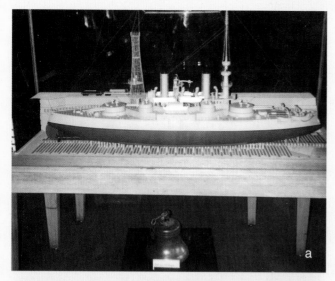

a) Model of the ship.
b) Plate taken from the starboard side of the ship showing a bullet hole.
c) Sofa from Admiral Dewey's cabin.
d) Desk chair from the ship.

Spanish American War artifacts on display at the Virginia Maritime Museum, Norfolk, Virginia.

BT

Opposite page, bottom: The *Maine* painted by Edith Caperton in 1898. It was painted on a piece of oilcloth table covering. The artist lived in rural Oklahoma, and had never seen the ocean. She painted it brown, the same color as the Oklahoma creeks. This was her only painting. COLLECTION OF THOMAS J. CAPERTON, SANTA FE, NM. PHOTO BY CHARLES BENNETT

The mast of the *Maine* in the Arlington National Cemetery, Arlington, Virginia, where it remains today. KE

Capstan from the *USS Maine* presented to Silver Bow County, Montana, in 1914 by Henry W. Lawton, Camp #1 USWV in Butte, Montana. The capstan is on display in the courthouse. KE

Spanish American War display at the Virginia Military Institute Museum in Lexington, Virginia. The Spanish flag was captured at Arroyo, Puerto Rico. One of VMI's graduates was on the converted yacht, Gloucester.

Crest of the Spanish vessel, *Reina Mercedes,* captured after the Battle of Santiago. The crest contains the Spanish coat of arms. The ship was converted into a station ship and served at the U.S. Naval Academy from 1912 until it was scrapped in 1957.On display at the U.S. Naval Museum, Washington Navy Yard, Washington D.C. BT

A plaque to the First Montana Volunteers in the rotunda of the Montana State Capitol in Helena. MHS

Monument in the Crown Hill Cemetery in Denver, Colorado, circa 1930s. DPL

A model of the protected cruiser *Baltimore* on display at the U.S. Naval Museum, Washington Navy Yard, Washington, D.C.. BT

Hawser reel, used to wind in ship's lines.

Hundreds of these tablets were made from metal recovered from the *Maine* and can be found in various locations around the country. KANAWHA COIN SHOP, CHARLESTON, WV

This spare propeller blade was carried on board the *Maine* . In contrast to most modern propellers which are cast in one piece, many at the turn of the century were made with detachable blades and spares were always kept available.

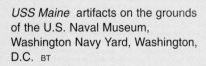

Six-inch .30 caliber gun.

USS Maine artifacts on the grounds of the U.S. Naval Museum, Washington Navy Yard, Washington, D.C. BT

VENTILATOR COWL FROM U. S. S. MAINE
WOBURN, MASS.

The *Maine* monument on Columbus Circle at the southwest corner of New York's Central Park. President Taft, Charles Sigsbee and William Randolph Hearst Sr. along with 10,000 people unveiled it in 1913. BT

Anchor at U.S.S. Maine.
Arlington National Cemetery, Arlington.

Anchor of the *Maine* at Arlington National Cemetery.

Trophy Cannon,
from the wreck of the Spanish Cruiser "Castilla", sunk by the American Squadron under Admiral George Dewey, in the battle of Manila Bay, May 1st, 1898. Presented to the city of Rochester by Hon. Oscar F. Williams, of Rochester, at that time consul at Manila. Dedicated to the City, June 14 th, 1902. Erected by L. Boardman Smith, Command No. 53, Spanish War Veterans.

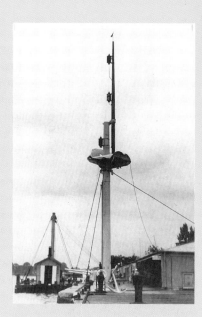

Foremast of the *Maine* on display at the U.S. Naval Academy, Annapolis, Md.

The massive Dewey Monument in Union Square, San Francisco, was erected in 1901.

Spanish American War monument in Union County, Arkansas. AHS 1955

Monument on the grounds of the South Carolina State Capitol building in Columbia. This plaque on the side reads:

South Carolina Troops
In The Spanish American War
First South Carolina Volunteer Infantry
Second South Carolina Volunteer Infantry
Anderson's Battery Heavy Artillery
South Carolina Naval Militia

South Carolinians Who Volunteered For
The Yellow Fever Test in Cuba
Were Honored By The United States Congress
With A Special Gold Medal And
A Lifetime Pension
Tech. Sgt. Levi E. Folk, Newberg
Pvt. James L. Hanneberry, Orangebury
Pvt. Charles G. Sontag, Columbia

Monument to war veterans on the grounds of the California State Capitol building in Sacramento.

Sample of an emblem placed on the graves of Spanish American War veterans.

Hotchkiss 37-millimeter revolving cannon, a Gatlinglike rapid-firing gun with five barrels. It was manufactured in France for the Spanish Navy.

The Spanish used mines, such as this one captured at Havana, to help protect their major ports. They effectively barred enemy ships from entering the harbors. At Manila, Dewey was able to run past them because they had been improperly laid in the deep channel.

Displays at the U.S. Naval Museum, Washington Navy Yard, Washington D.C. BT

Admiral Dewey's artifacts.

Spanish cannon captured at Manila on May 1, 1898. Presented to the city of Towson, Maryland, on May 1, 1903. The inscription on the base reads: "You may fire when ready, Gridley." BT

This gun, set up by the Filipino Insurgents at Olongapo Subic Bay, Philippines, on Sept. 7, 1899, was destroyed by the *USS Charleston.* This was the last action in which the ship was engaged as she was lost on Nov. 2, 1899, after hitting an uncharted reef of Camiguin Island off the north coast of Luzon. This gun was secured from the U.S. Government and brought to San Francisco through the efforts of William Randolph Hearst Sr., and erected in 1908. The plaque was placed on the gun in 1954 by USWV of the Dept. of California. It is now on the lawn of the Museum at the Presidio of San Francisco.

V.F.W. Memorial featuring a deck plate from the *USS Indiana* (BB-01) which was pierced in action at Santiago on July 4, 1898. Siege mortars flank the plate on each side. It is located at the Edinburg Cemetery, Edinburg, Indiana.
USN NH 52657

USS *Olympia*

PHOTOS COURTESY MAX NEWHART,
NEW HOPE, PENNSYLVANIA

8-inch; 35-caliber breech-loading aft gun turrets (reproductions).

Admiral Dewey's footsteps on the *Olympia* where he uttered his famous command, "You may fire when ready, Gridley." BT

8-inch forward gun turrets (reproductions).

CAP RIBBONS OF SPANISH SHIPS SUNK AT MANILA BAY

REINA CRISTINA
CASTILLA
D. JUAN DE AUSTRIA
ISLA DE CUBA
ISLA DE MINDANAO
ISLA DE LUZON
MARQUES DEL DUERO
ARGOS COM ᴰᴺ HIDᴳᴬ
MANILA
D. ANTONIO DE ULLOA
Gᴿᴬᴸ LEZO
VELASCO

Cap ribbons of Spanish ships sunk at Manila Bay, on display on the *Olympia*. BT

Topsides, starboard side.

Starboard side showing two of the 5-inch, 40-caliber rapid-fire guns. A 6-pounder is just above.

Looking forward over the 8-inch turrets.

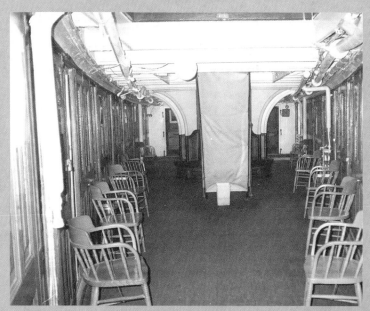

Engine room.

Officer country looking aft.

Original bell.

Senior officers wardroom.

·SPANISH·BLOCKHOVSE·
·PLAYA·CVBA·

·J.H.J·
·DEC.21.1898·

Original paintings done by Joseph Hadland Josephson, a member of Co. L, 2nd Illinois Volunteer Infantry.
His album, with many other paintings, is now in the possession of his granddaughter, Mrs. Paul Miller,
Missoula, Montana.

·WRECK·of·"MAINE"·
·HAVANA·HARBOR·

·J.H.J·
·DEC.15.1898·

HENRY B. PLANT MUSEUM

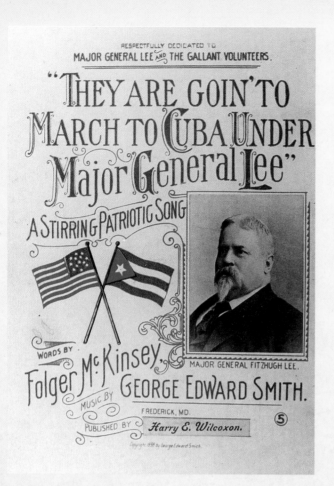

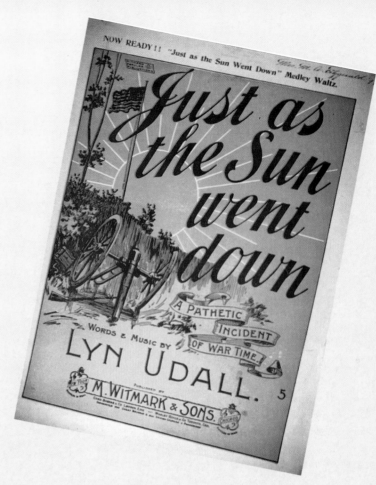

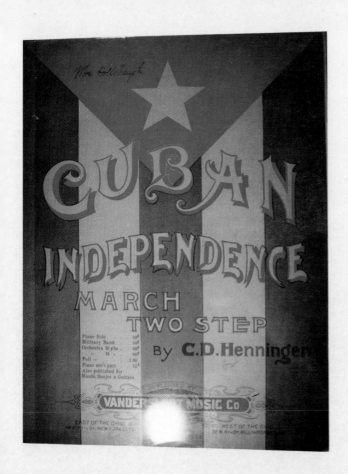

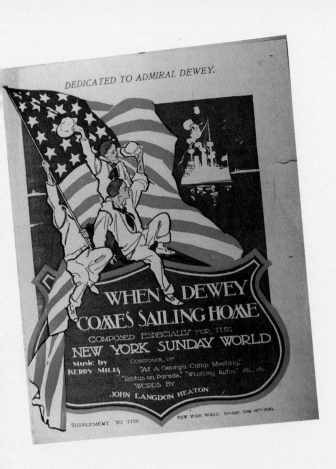

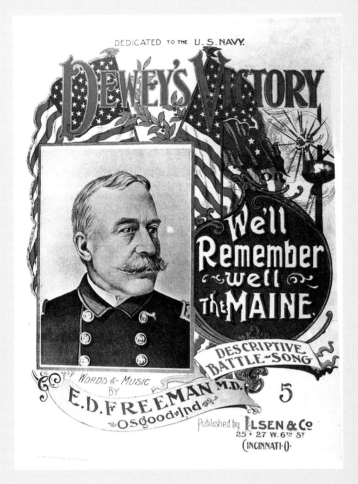

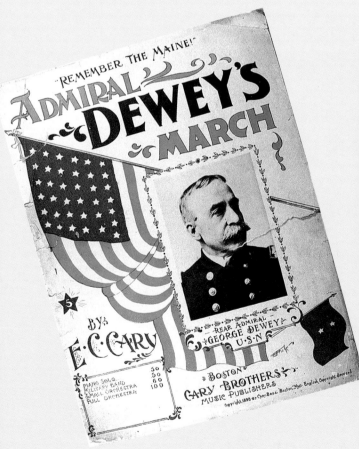

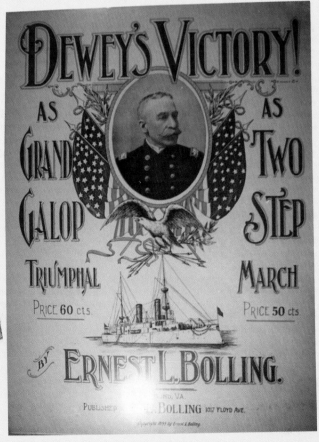

The *Philippine Campaign Medal*–awarded to all officers and men who served during the Philippine Insurrections from Feb. 4, 1899 to July 4, 1902. It was extended for service in the southern islands until the end of 1904, and was also authorized for service in the Moro Campaign in Jolo and Mundanao in 1905, the engagement on Mt. Bub-Dajo in 1906 and in the Bagsok Campaign in Jolo in 1913.

The *Spanish Campaign Medal*–awarded to all officers and men who saw active service during the war in Cuba prior to July 17, 1898, in Puerto Rico prior to Aug. 13, 1898, and the Philippines prior to Aug. 16, 1898.

The *Cuban Pacification Medal*–established in commemoration of the military occupation of Cuba between 1906-1909.

The *Medal For Naval Engagements In The West Indies*, 1898 awarded to all officers and men of the Navy and Marine Corps who participated in the naval engagements in the West Indies between May 6 and Aug. 14, 1898.

Medal presented by congress to Admiral Dewey and the officers and men of his fleet in honor of the great naval victory at Manila. MADE BY TIFFANY AND CO., NEW YORK.

The *Spanish American War Service Medal*–authorized for service in the war and issued to all officers and men who served 90 days, other than in the theater of operations. who were not eligible to receive the Spanish Campaign Medal.

The *Spanish War Service Medal*–established in commemoration of the war and issued to all officers and men of the Navy and Marine Corps who served afloat in the theater of actual naval operations, or in Cuba, Puerto Rico, Philippines and Guam, between May 1 and Aug. 16, 1898.

The *Cuban Occupational Medal*–established in commemoration of Cuba after the surrender of Santiago, and issued to all officers and men who served in the Army of Occupation until May 20, 1902, when control was turned over to the newly established Cuban Government.

The *Philippine Congressional Medal*–established by special act of Congress in 1906, and awarded to all officers and men who had volunteered for the War with Spain and served in the Philippine Islands, but who voluntarily remained in the service after the Treaty of Peace was ratified, in order to suppress the native insurrection.

This was the flag of the Rough Riders dressing station and was presented to Henry Herbert Throp MD, action sergeon of K Troop. On display at Samuel Colt Heritage Museum of Fine Firearms, Gettysburg, PA.

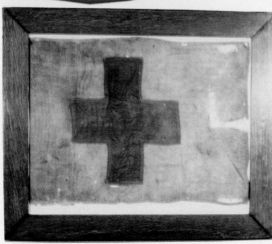

Hardtack.

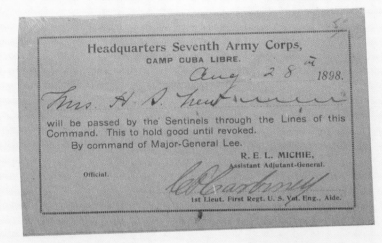

Headquarters Seventh Army Corps,
CAMP CUBA LIBRE.
Aug 28ᵗʰ 1898.

Mrs. H. S. _____

will be passed by the Sentinels through the Lines of this Command. This to hold good until revoked.
By command of Major-General Lee.
R. E. L. MICHIE,
Assistant Adjutant-General.
Official.
_____
1st Lieut. First Regt. U. S. Vol. Eng., Aide.

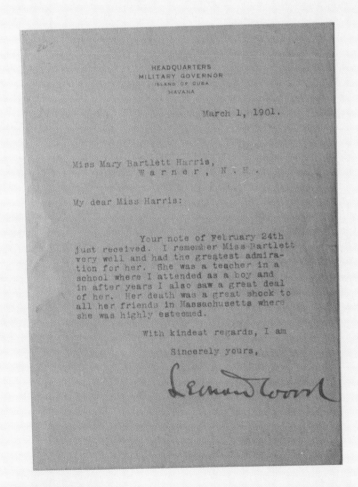

HEADQUARTERS
MILITARY GOVERNOR
ISLAND OF CUBA
HAVANA

March 1, 1901.

Miss Mary Bartlett Harris,
Warner, N. H.

My dear Miss Harris:

Your note of February 24th just received. I remember Miss Bartlett very well and had the greatest admiration for her. She was a teacher in a school where I attended as a boy and in after years I also saw a great deal of her. Her death was a great shock to all her friends in Massachusetts where she was highly esteemed.

With kindest regards, I am

Sincerely yours,

Leonard Wood

ALL ARTIFACTS FROM THE COLLECTION OF THE NEW MARKET BATTLEFIELD MILITARY MUSEUM.

MIRACLE OF AMERICA MUSEUM, POLSON, MONTANA

A cravat supposedly worn by the notorious Skagway, Alaska con man, "Soapy Smith" with the American and Cuban flags sewed on it. On display at the Skagway Trail of '98 Museum. SKAGWAY, ALASKA

RELATIVES BADGE

SOUVENIR
OF RETURN
1ST CAL. REGIMENT
FROM THE PHILIPPINES
AUGUST, 1899

WELCOME
ADMIRAL EVANS

COMPANY
E
FIRST MONTANA
U.S.V.
DILLON-MANILA
1898-9

Reception
To
Montana
Volunteers

Ladies
Committee
ON
Refreshments

Butte
Oct. 23
1899

1898-1899
3RD
NEB.VOL.INF.

U S
J. F. HAUN,
ROCKVILLE, CONN.
CO. C. 1ST
CONN. V.I.

SOUVENIR

RETURN OF 1ST
MONT. VOL.
INF.
FROM
PHILIPINE ISLANDS

ROUGH RIDERS
1898   1948
3¢ U.S. POSTAGE

THEODORE ROOSEVELT
6¢
U.S. POSTAGE

U.S. CRUISER
"MONTGOMERY."

ADMIRAL
DEWEY.   THE
OLYMPIA.

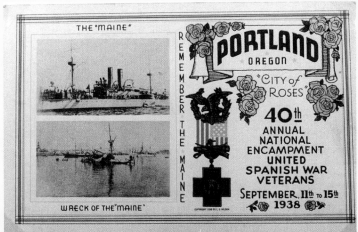

All Mail-Reservations or Information Headquarters 5090-5092 Plankinton Arcade Bldg.

34TH NATIONAL ENCAMPMENT UNITED SPANISH WAR VETERANS MILWAUKEE PLAN NOW TO BE THERE

AUGUST 21 to 25 1932

THE "MAINE"

WRECK OF THE "MAINE"

REMEMBER THE MAINE

PORTLAND OREGON "CITY OF ROSES"

40th ANNUAL NATIONAL ENCAMPMENT UNITED SPANISH WAR VETERANS

September, 11th to 15th 1938

Uncle Sam's High Grade, ROASTED COFFEE

FROM HIS OWN POSSESSIONS,

PORTO RICO, HAWAII, MANILA.

THOMAS WOOD & CO.

IMPORTERS AND ROASTERS.   BOSTON.

UNITED SPANISH WAR VETERANS NEW JERSEY

MADE FROM PROPELLER OF ADMIRAL DEWEY'S FLAGSHIP WHICH SERVED IN THE BATTLE OF MANILA BAY MAY 1, 1898

THE "MAINE" QUESTION.

This piece of tissue paper, when lit, would explode when the flame reached the *Maine.* KE

ALL MAIL 5090-5092 PLANKINTON ARCADE

COME AND GET IT

"PLAN NOW TO BE THERE"

UNITED SPANISH WAR VETERANS 34TH NATIONAL ENCAMPMENT AUG. 21 to 25 1932 MILWAUKEE

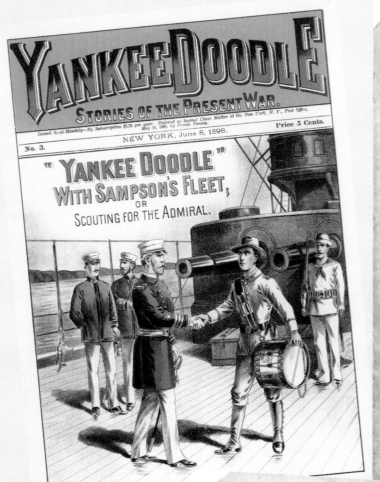

The gun-boat returned with the drummer [...]
flag-ship where he met Admiral Sam[...]
shook his hand. "That's w[...]

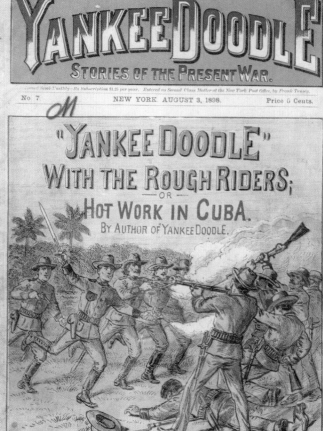

[...] Yankee Doodle to Joe and the two cowboys, as he darted after Pedro, and in a
[...] man had already cut down two, when the
[...]r in each hand, sailed in.

A young girl of fifteen, his only sister, gave a cry and darted toward him at the head of the line.
He leaned over toward her and kissed her—but the drum sticks never ceased to send
out the music that stirred the hearts of the tramping men behind him.

Magazines courtesy the University
of South Florida Archives, Tampa.

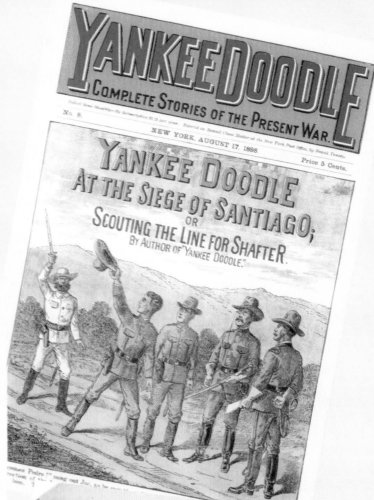

On the deck of the ship stood Young Glory, ready for the fight, with his eyes on the Spanish cruiser.

"Now is our time, senorita!" exclaimed Yankee Doodle, springing up out of the boat and leaping ashore with her, drawing the boat as far up on the beach as he could. Then, seizing her hand, he added: "Quick! Let's get away before the light catches us again!"

There is enough wear and tear on the soldier in the field without the discomforts that come from having to use a strong laundry soap. Common brown soaps, when constantly used for washing the person, are extremely irritating.

Ivory Soap is the ideal soap for the camp, suitable for all purposes, for the kitchen utensils, for washing clothes, and for the bath.

Ivory Soap is not easily lost, for it floats.

Copyright, 1898, by The Procter & Gamble Co., Cincinnati.

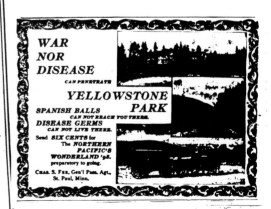

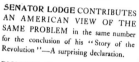

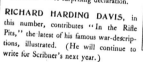

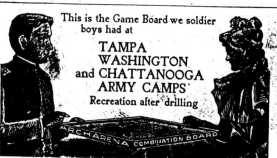

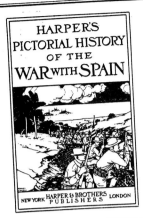

Interesting ads that were
tied to the just-concluded
war.

• Even though the war was of short duration, some shortages and inconveniences to American citizens occurred. This notice was printed in an 1898 book about the Alaska (Klondike) gold rush.

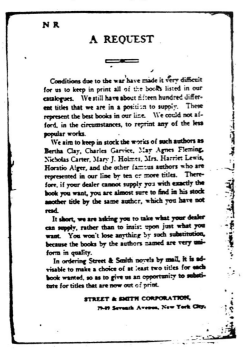

N R

A REQUEST

Conditions due to the war have made it very difficult for us to keep in print all of the books listed in our catalogues. We still have about fifteen hundred different titles that we are in a position to supply. These represent the best books in our line. We could not afford, in the circumstances, to reprint any of the less popular works.

We aim to keep in stock the works of such authors as Bertha Clay, Charles Garvice, May Agnes Fleming, Nicholas Carter, Mary J. Holmes, Mrs. Harriet Lewis, Horatio Alger, and the other famous authors who are represented in our line by ten or more titles. Therefore, if your dealer cannot supply you with exactly the book you want, you are almost sure to find in his stock another title by the same author, which you have not read.

It short, we are asking you to take what your dealer can supply, rather than to insist upon just what you want. You won't lose anything by such substitution, because the books by the authors named are very uniform in quality.

In ordering Street & Smith novels by mail, it is advisable to make a choice of at least two titles for each book wanted, so as to give us an opportunity to substitute for titles that are now out of print.

STREET & SMITH CORPORATION,
79-89 Seventh Avenue, New York City.

• The Civilian Marksmanship Program, a program that costs the U.S. government $2.5 million a year, was created after the Spanish American War alerted the military to the fact that many recruits drawn from an increasingly urbanized society were lousy shots. Its mandate is to encourage shooting clubs and marksmanship competitions through the gift of millions of rounds of ammunition and other supplies. In the 1990s it was proposed in Congress to do away with this archaic program.

• Robert Burns Wilson (1850-1910) was a Kentucky artist whose poem "Remember the Maine" became the nation's battle song during the war.

• Ben Lear Jr. was born in Ontario in 1879. At 19 he joined the Colorado National Guard and saw service in the Philippines. At the 1912 Olympics in Stockholm, Sweden, he won a bronze medal in the Three Day Equestrian Event. He later became a Lieutenant-General in the U.S. Army and died in Memphis, Tennessee, in 1966. He is the only Olympian to have served in the Spanish American War.

• The present Veterans of Foreign Wars (VFW) was formed in 1898 by the 1st United Spanish War Veterans (U.S.W.V.). The tradition of floating a wreath out to sea on Memorial Day was started by a mother of one of the war's soldiers buried at sea.

• The son of Union Gen. John A. Logan, founder of the Grand Army of the Republic, was in the army in Cuba.

• Annie Wheeler, the daughter of Gen. Joseph Wheeler served in Cuba as an army nurse. His son, Thomas was a naval cadet who served aboard the cruiser, *Columbia,* off Cuba. He died in a swimming accident on Sept. 7, 1898, at Camp Wikoff, the day that his father issued his farewell to the Cavalry Division.

• Millionaire John Jacob Astor IV was on board a transport on the way to Cuba as a lieutenant colonel on General Shafter's staff. He would lose his life at sea in the 1912 *Titanic* disaster.

• John J. "Black Jack" Pershing, the leader of the American Expeditionary Force to France in 1917, was a young 1st Lieutenant of the 10th Cavalry (Colored) at the fight before Santiago.

• Winston S. Churchill, a 21-year-old recent graduate of Sandhurst went to Cuba in 1895 to see a war. He went there as a reporter for the *London Daily Graphic* and as an observer for the British army. He saw some action, the first of his career, and returned to England with a taste for Cuban cigars, a habit that would be his lifelong trademark.

• Legendary army scout, range detective and reputed assassin-for-hire, Tom Horn joined the army as a packer during the war. He was accused of killing a 14-year-old boy in 1901 and convicted and hanged for the crime in 1903.

• War fever affected the famous as well as the ordinary citizen. William F. (Buffalo Bill) Cody, the Wild West showman, offered to raise a company of cavalry scouts. General Miles wanted him in the Army but legal hassles stopped Cody from signing up. Two champion heavyweight boxers, James J. Corbett and Bob Fitzsimmons also volunteered to fight. Even Frank James, Jesse's brother, was suggested to raise a company as well as warriors of the fierce Sioux tribe.

• Edgar Rice Burroughs, creator of *Tarzan*, was a 23-year-old cowboy in Pocatello, Idaho, when he tried to join the Rough Riders, but Roosevelt felt he was too far away from San Antonio so he rejected him.

• Famous Civil War Gen. William Tecumseh Sherman's son was a chaplain with the Fourth Missouri Volunteers.

Equipment

Some of the principal arms carried by Regular Army infantry and cavalry units. Krag-Jorgenson .30-.40 infantry rifles, from top: Model 1894 (converted), Model 1896, Model 1896, Model 1898 carbine. At bottom: Model 1894 Colt .38 DA revolver. Also pictured are cartridges, loose and in boxes.

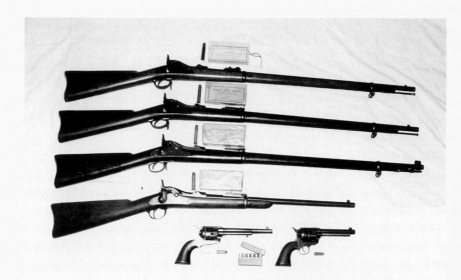

The principal arms carried by most National Guard units, .45 Springfield rifles, top to bottom: Model 1879, Model 1884, Model 1888 and a Model 1884 .45 carbine. Two Colt .45 Army single-action revolvers for cavalry and artillery. Also pictured are cartridges, loose and in boxes.

Johnson & Johnson triangular bandages were imprinted with graphic instructions for their use by medics and individual soldiers in the field.

Spanish mauser rifles captured in Cuba were taken back to the United States, cleaned, repaired and packed in wooden chests by the Springfield Armory.

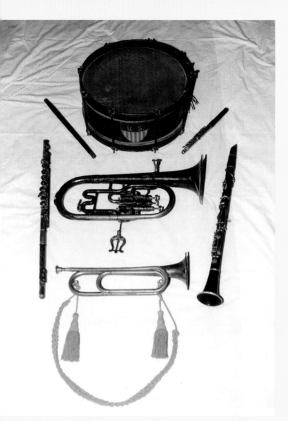

Some of the primary musical instruments of the period for field and band musicians.

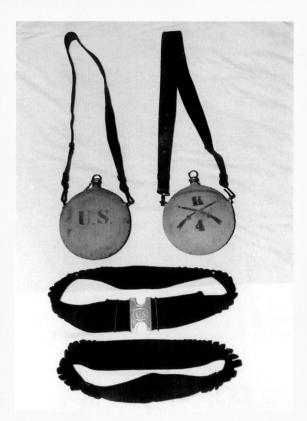

Canteens and their leather slings. Blue woven texture loop cartridge belts, .45 caliber, top, .30-.40 caliber, double-row, bottom.

Noncommissioned officers chevrons and brassard worn on uniform coat sleeves.

Haversack, drinking cup, utensils, condiment bags and clothing bag.

Spanish cavalry bugle, made in Madrid. Captured by an Army veterinarian in Cuba and wrapped with regulation U.S. Cavalry cords, waffles and tassels.

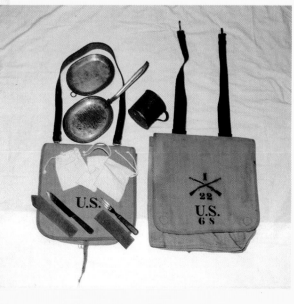

Mess kit (known as a meat can).

Civil War canteen retrofitted to the 1890s period.

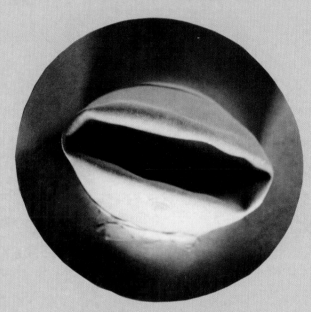

Model 1893 campaign hat usually given to regular army troops.

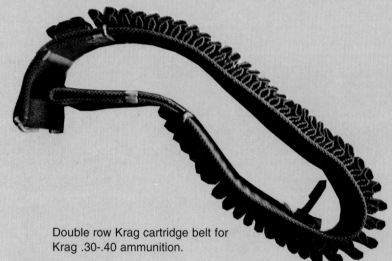

Double row Krag cartridge belt for Krag .30-.40 ammunition.

1895 Garrison cap for a hospital steward.

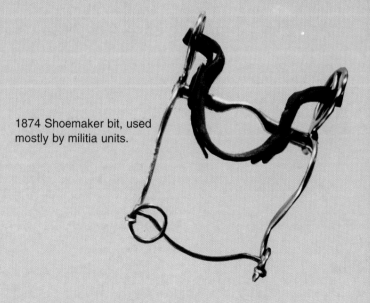

1874 Shoemaker bit, used mostly by militia units.

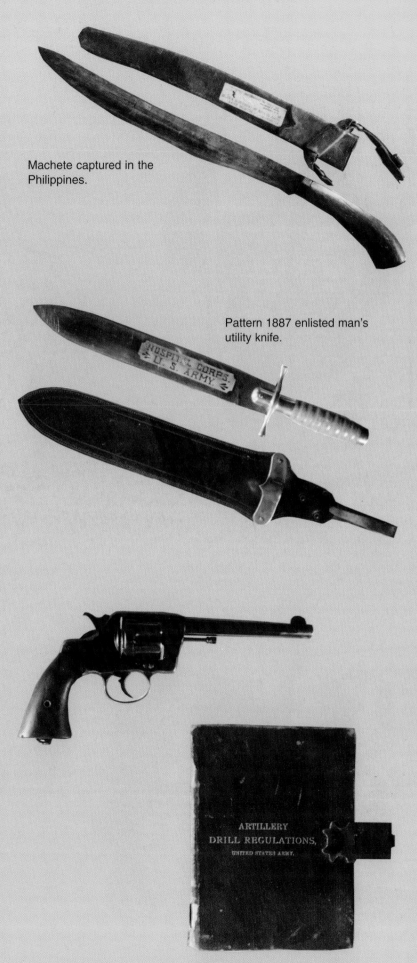

Machete captured in the Philippines.

Pattern 1887 enlisted man's utility knife.

Barracks shoes.

All items from the Hayes Otoupalik Collection Missoula, Montana.

Political Cartoons of the Period

Would make an excellent addition to our museum.—Philadelphia Inquirer.

No Spanish governor-general of Cuba was ever so thoroughly hated and detested as Weyler. The above picture, representing him as an ape, is probably the most expressive form in which public contempt for him could have been shown.

Edited by General Blanco.—Minneapolis Tribune.

The bulletins issued by Captain-General Blanco, of Cuba, relating to battles in the island, always claimed great victories for the Spanish troops.

UNCLE SAM—"I'll just frame this."—Denver Post.

The look of admiration on the face of Uncle Sam as he gazes at a picture of Dewey, represents the national admiration for the hero of Manila when the people heard of his victory.

IN TIME OF PEACE PREPARE FOR WAR.

Uncle Sam's next duty.—Minneapolis Tribune.

The long trip of the *Oregon* around the horn would have been shortened thousands of miles if the proposed Nicaragua canal had been constructed. The cartoon shows that Uncle Sam could easily cut the canal and suggests that it is his duty to do so.

VERY KIND OF HIM.

PRESIDENT DOLE—"Accept a little gift from me—you might need it in your business."
—Minneapolis Tribune.

"Uncle Sam, he pays the freight."—New York Herald.

When the Spanish troops evacuated Cuba and Puerto Rico, they were shipped back to Spain in transports hired and paid for by the United States. The above cartoon shows Uncle Sam making a consignment of Spanish soldiers to Sagasta.

If the war brings nothing else, for this we are thankful.
—New York Herald.

One result of the war was to completely reunite the North and South and reveal the sympathy and friendship between Great Britain and the United States.

Immediately after the declaration of war the Republic of Hawaii, through President Dole, officially offered itself to the United States government. The offer was ultimately accepted.

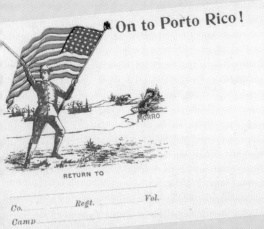

On to Porto Rico!

RETURN TO

Co. _____ Regt. _____ Vol. _____
Camp _____

THE FLOWER OF THE AMERICAN ARMY.

U.S. VOLUNTEER ARMY

CAMP _____

THE FLOWER OF AMERICAN MANHOOD

Sent from Camp Thomas, located at Chickamauga National Park in Georgia.

CUBA LIBRE—ON TO HAVANA!

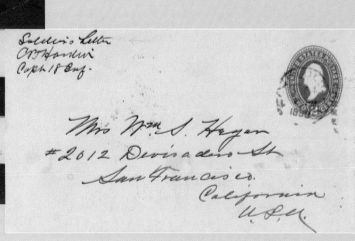

Letter from a soldier in the 18th Infantry on duty in Hawaii, October 1898.

THE CAPTURE OF SAN JUAN HILL.

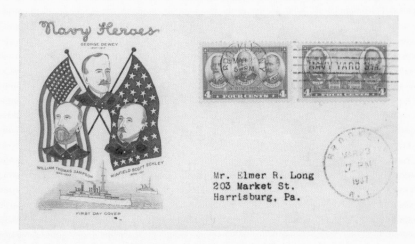

Navy Heroes

GEORGE DEWEY

WILLIAM THOMAS SAMPSON   WINFIELD SCOTT SCHLEY

FIRST DAY COVER

Mr. Elmer R. Long
203 Market St.
Harrisburg, Pa.

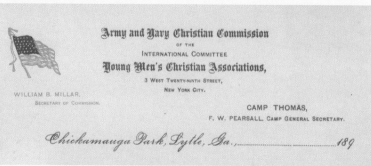

Army and Navy Christian Commission
OF THE
INTERNATIONAL COMMITTEE
Young Men's Christian Associations,
3 WEST TWENTY-NINTH STREET,
NEW YORK CITY.

WILLIAM B. MILLAR,
SECRETARY OF COMMISSION.

CAMP THOMAS,
F. W. PEARSALL, CAMP GENERAL SECRETARY.

Chickamauga Park, Lytle, Ga.,_____189_

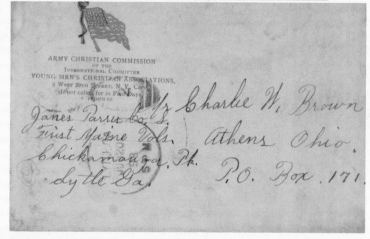

ARMY CHRISTIAN COMMISSION
OF THE
INTERNATIONAL COMMITTEE
YOUNG MEN'S CHRISTIAN ASSOCIATIONS,
3 West 29th Street, N. Y. City.
If not called for in Five Days,
return to

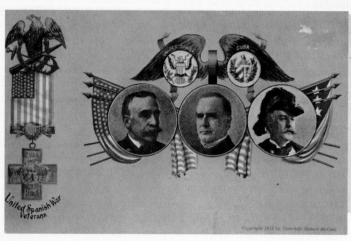

United Spanish War
Veterans

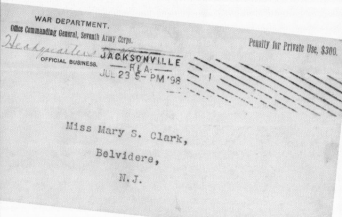

WAR DEPARTMENT.
Office Commanding General, Seventh Army Corps.
Headquarters
OFFICIAL BUSINESS.

JACKSONVILLE
FLA.
JUL 23 5-PM '98

Penalty for Private Use, $300.

Miss Mary S. Clark,
Belvidere,
N. J.

Chas. C. Diers

Belle Plaine, Minn.   Co. "F," 1st Washington Infantry, U. S. V.

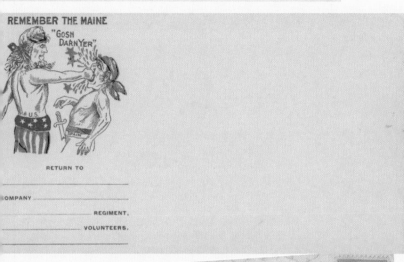

REMEMBER THE MAINE

"GOSH DARN YER"

RETURN TO

COMPANY

REGIMENT,

VOLUNTEERS.

IF YOU DON'T
CATCH HIM
IN 10 DAYS.

JACKSONVILLE
FLA.
AUG 21 9- AM '98

CUBA

RETURN TO

C. H. McGahan
Co. E, 2d Regt., Ill   Vols.
Camp Cuba Libre,
JACKSONVILLE, FLA.

Mr John Ahure
#316 Meeu Block
Chicago
Ill
34 State

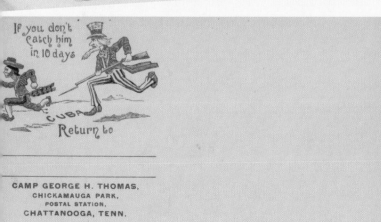

If you don't
catch him
in 10 days

CUBA

Return to

CAMP GEORGE H. THOMAS,
CHICKAMAUGA PARK,
POSTAL STATION,
CHATTANOOGA, TENN.

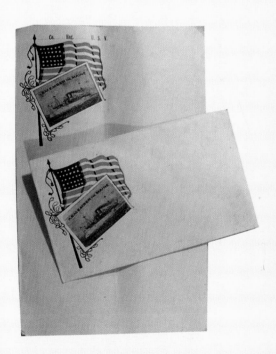

Stationery for soldiers with
"Remember the *Maine*"
slogan.

Medal of Honor Recipients

Number of medals: 109

Army: 30   Marines: 15   Navy: 64

Army

Baker, Sgt. Maj. Edward L., Jr. (Santiago, Cuba)
Bell, Pvt. Dennis (Tayabacoa, Cuba)
Berg, Pvt. George (El Caney, Cuba)
Brookin, Pvt. Oscar (El Caney, Cuba)
Buzzard, Cpl. Ulysses G. (El Caney, Cuba)
Cantrell, Pvt. Charles P. (Santiago, Cuba)
Church, Asst. Surgeon James R. (Las Guasimas, Cuba)
Cummins, Sgt. Andrew J. (Santiago, Cuba)
De Swan, Pvt. John F. (Santiago, Cuba)
Doherty, Cpt. Thomas M. (Santiago, Cuba)
Fournia, Pvt. Frank O. (Santiago, Cuba)
Graves, Pvt. Thomas J. (El Caney, Cuba)
Hardaway, 1st Lt. Benjamin F. (El Caney, Cuba)
Heard, 1st Lt. John W. (Manimani River, Cuba)
Keller, Pvt. William (Santiago, Cuba)
Kelly, Pvt. Thomas (Santiago, Cuba)
Lee, Pvt. Fitz (Tayabacoa, Cuba)
Mills, Capt. & Asst. Adj. Gen. Albert L. (Santiago, Cuba)
Nash, Pvt. James J. (Santiago, Cuba)
Nee, Pvt. George H. (Santiago, Cuba)
Pfisterer, Musician Herman (Santiago, Cuba)
Polond, Pvt. Alfred (Santiago, Cuba)
Quinn, Sgt. Alexander M. (Santiago, Cuba)
Ressler, Cpl. Norman W. (El Caney, Cuba)
Roberts, 2nd Lt. Charles D. (El Caney, Cuba)
Shepherd, Cpl. Warren J. (El Caney, Cuba)
Thompkins, Pvt. William H. (Tayabacoa, Cuba)
Wanton, Pvt. George H. (Tayabacoa, Cuba)
Welborn, 2nd Lt. Ira C. (Santiago, Cuba)
Wende, Pvt. Bruno (El Caney, Cuba)

Marines

Campbell, Pvt. Daniel (Cienfuegos, Cuba)
Field, Pvt. Oscar W. (Cienfuegos, Cuba)
Fitzgerald, Pvt. John (Cuzco, Cuba)
Franklin, Pvt. Joseph J. (Cienfuegos, Cuba)
Gaughan, Sgt. Philip (Cienfuegos, Cuba)
Hill, Pvt. Frank (Cienfuegos, Cuba)
Kearney, Pvt. Michael (Cienfuegos, Cuba)
Kuchneister, Pvt. Hermann W. (Cienfuegos, Cuba)
MacNeal, Pvt. Harry L. (Santiago, Cuba)
Meredith, Pvt. James (Cienfuegos, Cuba)
Parker, Pvt. Pomeroy (Cienfuegos, Cuba)
Quick, Sgt. John H. (Cuzco, Cuba)
Scott, Pvt. Joseph F. (Cienfuegos, Cuba)
Sullivan, Pvt. Edward (Cienfuegos, Cuba)
West, Pvt. Walter S. (Cienfuegos, Cuba)

Navy

Baker, Coxswain Benjamin F. (Cienfuegos, Cuba)
Barrow, Sman David D. (Cienfuegos, Cuba)
Bennett, Chief BM James H. (Cienfuegos, Cuba)
Beyer, Coxswain Albert (Cienfuegos, Cuba)
Blume, Sman Robert (Cienfuegos, Cuba)
Brady, Chief GM George F. (Cardenas, Cuba)
Bright, Coal Passer George W. (Cienfuegos, Cuba)
Carter, Blacksmith Joseph E. (Cienfuegos, Cuba)
Chadwick, Apprentice 1st Class Leonard (Cienfuegos, Cuba)
Charette, GM 1st Class George (Santiago, Cuba)
Clausen, Coxswain Claus K. (Santiago, Cuba)
Cooney, Chief Machinist Thomas C. (Cardenas, Cuba)
Crouse, Watertender William A. (Cavite, Philippines)
Davis, GM 3rd Class John (Cienfuegos, Cuba)
Deignan, Coxswain Osborn (Santiago, Cuba)
Doran, BM 2nd Class John J. (Cienfuegos, Cuba)
Durney, Blacksmith Austin J. (Cienfuegos, Cuba)
Eglit, Sman John (Cienfuegos, Cuba)
Ehle, Fireman 1st Class John W. (Cavite, Philippines)
Erickson, Coxswain Nick (Cienfuegos, Cuba)
Foss, Sman Herbert L. (Cienfuegos, Cuba)
Gibbons, Oiler Michael (Cienfuegos, Cuba)
Gill, GM 1st Class Freeman (Cienfuegos, Cuba)
Hart, Machinist 1st Class William (Cienfuegos, Cuba)
Hendrickson, Sman Henry (Cienfuegos, Cuba)
Hoban, Coxswain Thomas (Cienfuegos, Cuba)
Hobson, Lt. Richmond P. (Santiago, Cuba)
Hull, Fireman 1st Class James L. (Cavite, Philippines)
Itrich, Chief Carpenter's Mate Franz A. (Manila, Philippines)
Johanson, Sman John P. (Cienfuegos, Cuba)
Johansson, Ord. Sman Johan J. (Cienfuegos, Cuba)
Johnsen, Chief Machinist Hans (Cardenas, Cuba)
Johnson, Fireman 1st Class Peter (NOR)
Keefer, Coppersmith Philip B. (Santiago, Cuba)
Kelly, Watertender Francis (Santiago, Cuba)
Kramer, Sman Franz (Cienfuegos, Cuba)
Krause, Coxswain Ernest (Cienfuegos, Cuba)
Levery, Apprentice 1st Class William (Cienfuegos, Cuba)
Mager, Apprentice 1st Class, George F. (Cienfuegos, Cuba)
Mahoney, Fireman 1st Class George (NOR)
Maxwell, Fireman 2nd Class John (Cienfuegos, Cuba)
Meyer, Carpenter's Mate 3rd Class William (Cienfuegos, Cuba)
Miller, Sman Harry H. (Cienfuegos, Cuba)
Miller, Sman Willard (Cienfuegos, Cuba)
Montague, Chief Master-at-Arms Daniel (Santiago, Cuba)
Morin, BM 2nd Class William H. (Caimanera, Cuba)
Muller, Mate Frederick (Mazanillo, Cuba)
Murphy, Coxswain John E. (Santiago, Cuba)
Nelson, Sailmaker's Mate Lauritz (Cienfuegos, Cuba)
Oakley, GM 2nd Class William (Cienfuegos, Cuba)
Olsen, Ord. Sman Anton (Cienfuegos, Cuba)
Penn, Fireman 1st Class Robert (Santiago, Cuba)
Phillips, Machinist 1st Class George F. (Santiago, Cuba)
Rilley, Lman John P. (Cienfuegos, Cuba)
Russell, Lman Henry P. (Cienfuegos, Cuba)
Spicer, GM 1st Class William (Caimanera, Cuba)
Sundquist, Chief Carpenter's Mate Axel (Caimanera, Cuba)
Sundquist, Ord. Sman Gustave A. (Cienfuegos, Cuba)
Triplett, Ord. Sman Samuel (Caimanera, Cuba)
Vadas, Sman Albert (Cienfuegos, Cuba)
Van Etten, Sman Hudson (Cienfuegos, Cuba)
Volz, Sman Robert (Cienfuegos, Cuba)
Wilke, BM 1st Class Julius A.R. (Cienfuegos, Cuba)
Williams, Sman Frank (Cienfuegos, Cuba)

The Spanish War 1898

small group of dedicated reenactors in alifornia formed this group in 1993 to portray e history of the war through the wearing of eriod uniforms and using period equipment. Mock battles are held on occasion. For information on this group contact Mike Lewis, 111 West Central Ave., Tracy, California. 95376, 209-836-753.

The *USS Maine* monument on the Havana waterfront in 1930, the Plaza Del Maine. This monument has apparently been removed. LC

Ceremonies at the *USS Maine* monument. In the foreground are surviving firemen who carried *Maine*'s dead to the cemetery in 1898. Cuban sailors are standing guard. Note inscription, from the U.S. Congressional Resolution on the Independence of Cuba, April 19, 1898. USN NH 100510

Shrine to the Cuban martyrs of their War of Independence. USN NH 100507

Surrender Tree — Arbol de la Paz

No. 42.
Obelisco — Obelisk.

San Juan Hill, Early 1900s

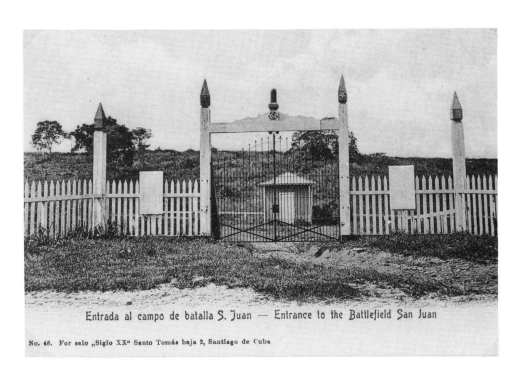

Entrada al campo de batalla S. Juan — Entrance to the Battlefield San Juan

No. 46. For salo „Siglo XX" Santo Tomás baja 2, Santiago de Cuba

The top photo shows the tree under which the Spanish surrendered the city of Santiago on July 17, 1898. The bottom photo shows a monument erected to the memory of the Cuban troops who fought in the battle for Santiago, circa 1928. These sites are now gone. MNG & BA

Photos on next three pages were taken in 1996 by Charles Bennett of the Palace of the Governors, Santa Fe, New Mexico.

Havana Harbor. The large freighter (with the red and black hull) is in the general area where the Battleship *Maine* mysteriously exploded on Feb. 15, 1898, with a loss of 268 officers and men

El Morro Castle at the entrance to Havana Harbor.

Mural in the Museum of the Revolution in Havana (former palace of Cuban dictator Fulgencio Batista y Zaldivar) depicting U.S. troops charging up San Juan Hill on July 1, 1898.

San Juan Hill Battlefield, Santiago. Features include a representation of the Spanish blockhouse which stood on the hill at the time of the assault; several pieces of ordnance, and a number of monuments.

San Juan Hill Battlefield, Santiago.

San Juan Hill Battlefield, Santiago. Ferris wheel in the background is in a nearby amusement park.

Battlefield Monument Inscription, San Juan Hill Battlefield, Santiago, commemorating the action of the "Cuban Army of Liberation: and U.S. Army during the Spanish American War.

El Morro Castle at the entrance to Santiago Harbor. Along this stretch of coast the Spanish fleet, under Adm. Pascual Cervera y Topeta, four cruisers and two destroyers, were destroyed in two hours by the U.S. Navy on July 3, 1898.

San Juan Hill Battlefield, Santiago. Photo taken in the direction of the assault by U.S. troops. The Sierra Maestra Mountains are in the background.

Index

Bold numbers denote photo captions.

Bibliography

Blow, Michael, *A Ship to Remember, The Maine and The Spanish American War*. William Morrow and Co., Inc., New York, 1992.

Brands, H.W., *The Reckless Decade, America in the 1890s*. St. Martin's Press, New York, 1995.

Farrell, Don A., *The Pictorial History of Guam: The Americanization 1898-1918,* (Second Edition). Micronesian Productions, Tamuning, Guam, 1986.

Freidel, Frank, *The Splendid Little War.* Bramhall House, New York, 1958.

Herner, Charles, *The Arizona Rough Riders*. The University of Arizona Press, Tucson, Arizona, 1970.

Jeffers, H. Paul, *Colonel Roosevelt, Theodore Roosevelt Goes to War, 1897-1898*. John Wiley & Sons, Inc., New York, 1996.

Jones, Virgil Corrington, *Roosevelt's Rough Riders*. Doubleday & Co., Inc., Garden City, New York, 1971.

Newhart, Max, *American Battleships, A Pictorial History of BB-1 to BB-71, with Prototypes Maine & Texas*. Pictorial Histories Publishing Co., Inc., Missoula, Montana, 1995.

Nofi, Albert A., *The Spanish-American War, 1898*. Combined Books, Conshohocken, Pennsylvania, 1996.

O'Toole, G.J.A., *The Spanish War, An American Epic, 1898*. W.W. Norton & Co., New York, 1984.

Reynolds, Clark, *Famous American Admirals*. Van Nostrand Reinhold Co., New York, 1978.

Roosevelt, Theodore, *The Rough Riders*. The New American Library, New York, 1961.

_____, *The Rough Riders*, edited by Richard Bak. Taylor Publishing Co., Dallas, Texas, 1997.

Sternlicht, Sanford, *McKinley's Bulldog, The Battleship Oregon*. Nelson-Hall Inc., Chicago, Illinois, 1977.

plus dozens of contemporary books, magazines and newspapers.

About the Author

Stan Cohen is a native of West Virginia and a graduate geologist from West Virginia University. After years as a consulting geologist, owning a ski shop and director of an historical park, he founded Pictorial Histories Publishing Co., in Missoula, Montana, in 1976. Since then, he has authored or co-authored 58 books and published 200, mostly dealing with history subjects with emphasis on the Civil War and World War II.